The Russian Novel
from Pushkin to Pasternak

NOTES ON CONTRIBUTORS

John Garrard is Professor of Russian Literature and Director of the Center for Russian and East European Studies at the University of Virginia.

Donald Fanger is Professor of Slavic and Comparative Literature at Harvard University.

Edward Wasiolek is Distinguished Service Professor of Slavic, Comparative Literature, and English at the University of Chicago.

Kathryn'Feuer is Professor of Russian Literature at the University of Virginia.

Patricia Carden is Professor of Russian Literature at Cornell University.

Robin Feuer Miller is Assistant Professor in the University Studies Program at Brandeis University.

Carol Anschuetz, who lives in Düsseldorf, West Germany, has taught at the University of Texas, Yale University, and Stanford University.

Victor Erlich is Bensinger Professor of Russian Literature at Yale University.

Jurij Striedter is Professor of Slavic Languages and Literatures at Harvard University.

George Gibian is Goldwin Smith Professor of Russian Literature at Cornell University.

Michel Aucouturier is Professor of Russian Literature at the Sorbonne.

René Wellek is Sterling Professor Emeritus of Comparative Literature at Yale University.

EDITED BY JOHN GARRARD

THE RUSSIAN NOVEL FROM PUSHKIN TO PASTERNAK

YALE UNIVERSITY PRESS
NEW HAVEN AND LONDON

Designed by James J. Johnson
and set in Zapf Book Light Roman.
Printed in the United States of America by
Vail-Ballou Press, Binghamton, N.Y.

Library of Congress Cataloging in Publication Data
Main entry under title:

The Russian novel from Pushkin to Pasternak.

  Bibliography: p.
  Includes index.
  1. Russian fiction—19th century—History and
criticism—Addresses, essays, lectures. 2. Russian
fiction—20th century—History and criticism—Addresses, essays, lectures. I. Garrard, John Gordon.
PG3098.3.R87 1983   891.73'009   83–1070
ISBN 0–300–02935–7

10   9   8   7   6   5   4   3   2   1

Contents

Preface

The dozen essays in this book survey the history, practice, and theory of the Russian novel, one of the great achievements of world literature. Following the editor's introduction, which surveys the prehistory of the genre in Russia, the essays are grouped into four sections.

Part I, "The Novel in Russia," consists of two chapters identifying the special features in the Russian novel that differentiate it from the novel elsewhere. Donald Fanger argues that the distinctiveness lies not so much in its "messages and effects" as in what he describes as its "radical *formal* freedom." Edward Wasiolek, on the other hand, sees the Russian novel as the reflection of a "national imperative in literature and in thought to conceive of the universe as coherent and purposive and to insist that a submission to this coherent and purposive universe brings one to harmony, freedom, and beauty." The two scholars agree that the novel in Russia became a uniquely important vehicle for the transmission of spiritual, philosophical, and sociopolitical ideas.

Part II, "High Noon," treats the three major Russian novelists of the nineteenth century. Kathryn Feuer gives a new reading of Turgenev's *Fathers and Sons* that opens out into a discussion of one of the central conflicts in Russian literature: that between the major novelists and the so-called radical critics, most notably Chernyshevsky. Patricia Carden analyzes the role of memory in *War and Peace*, concluding that Platonism provided Tolstoy with an "ideational grid that governs his many choices as novelist." Robin Feuer Miller examines Dostoevsky's use of the Gothic tradition, demonstrating that he "forges a metaphysical system out of a language that in the hands of lesser novelists remains merely a style." All three chapters move by induction from specific texts to reach general conclusions about the works of each writer.

Part III, "Decline and Renewal," focuses on the revival of the novel in the twentieth century that followed the Symbolist period, or so-called Silver Age of Russian poetry. Carol Anschuetz reconstructs a Nietzschean thesis which, she suggests, motivates Bely's parody of the Russian realist novel in *Petersburg*. Victor Erlich uses the works of Konstantin Fedin and Boris Pilnyak to illustrate the crisis that existed in both the novel genre and Soviet society during the twenties. Jurij Striedter provides a theoretical basis for analyzing three works of utopian fiction by Yevgeni Zamyatin, Aleksei Tolstoy, and Andrei Platonov. George Gibian shows how Boris Pasternak's hidden dialogue with his father in *Doctor Zhivago* distills the essence of the Russian character that endured the October Revolution, the civil war, and the long, dark night of Stalinism.

Part IV, "Critics and Criticism," surveys the work of theorists and the reception of the Russian novel in the West. Michel Aucouturier examines the convergences and divergences in the writings of Georg Lukács and Mikhail Bakhtin during the 1930s. René Wellek reviews in detail English and American criticism of the nineteenth-century Russian novel.

The book concludes with two appendixes: a chronology of Russian novels and novelists and a list of recommended translations.

The chronology, though necessarily selective, is designed to give a representative list of novels that possess artistic and historical importance. In certain cases novels that lack artistic value—for example, Chernyshevsky's *What Is to Be Done?* (*Chto delat?*) and Ostrovsky's *How the Steel Was Tempered* (*Kak zakalyalas stal*)—have been included because of their undeniable historical significance.

The chronology demonstrates clearly the fortunes of the genre in Russia over the past century and a half: in particular, the concentration of great novels during the reign of Alexander II (1855–81), the decline of the novel over the next generation, its revival during the 1920s, and again during the sixties and seventies with the relaxation of Stalinist mass terror and of the enforced application of Socialist Realism. Apart from such widely known works as Mikhail Bulgakov's *The Master and Margarita* (*Master i Margarita*) and Alexander Solzhenitsyn's *The First Circle* (*V kruge pervom*) and *Cancer Ward* (*Rakovy korpus*), which appeared in the 1960s, modern Russian literature has produced an impressive range of novels that attempt, often with considerable success, to uphold the great traditions of the past by examining honestly the moral and social issues of Soviet experience. Some of these works have been published in the Soviet Union, others have circulated within the country only in typescript form (*samizdat*, "self-published"), to appear later in the West (*tamizdat*, "published there"). Among the most respected contemporary prose writers are the late Yuri Trifonov, Valentin Rasputin, Vasili Aksyonov, Viktor Nekrasov, and Vladimir Voinovich (the last three are now living in the West). Their works hold out the promise that the best traditions of Russian literature have not been lost forever.

The second appendix offers a short list of English translations of major Russian novels, chiefly translations used or mentioned by the contributors in their essays. I have added translations of novels not specifically treated in the book, for example, Goncharov's *Oblomov* and Saltykov-Shchedrin's *The Golovlyov Family* (*Golovlyovy*).

ACKNOWLEDGMENTS

It is my pleasure to thank the many people and organizations that had a hand in making this book possible—first and foremost my wife, Carol, who provided essential advice and encouragement during the whole course of the enterprise, often at the cost of setting aside her own work.

The idea for this volume first came to me while I was directing a Summer Seminar for College Teachers on the subject, "The Russian Novel in European Perspective," which was sponsored by the National Endowment for the Humanities in 1976 and again in 1977. I am most grateful to the endowment for its support and to the seminar participants for their suggestions.

At a critical stage in the project the Research and Development Committee of the American Association for the Advancement of Slavic Studies provided a grant that enabled contributors to hold a planning conference hosted by the Kennan Institute for Advanced Russian Studies in Washington, D.C. Our sincere thanks go to S. Frederick Starr, at that time executive secretary of the Kennan Institute, and also to James H. Billington, director of the Woodrow Wilson International Center for Scholars.

The Rockefeller Foundation graciously allowed us to hold an International Symposium on the Russian Novel at the Villa Serbelloni in Bellagio, Italy. I am delighted to have this opportunity to express the gratitude of my colleagues and myself to the foundation and to the hospitable staff at the villa.

My personal thanks go to JoAnne Garrison, administrative assistant of the Center for Russian and East European Studies at the University of Virginia, for typing a difficult manuscript with her customary speed and precision, and to my research assistant, Dr. Madhu Malik, for her expert assistance in compiling both appendixes and the index. I also want to express my gratitude to the capable staff at Yale University Press, particularly to Ellen Graham and Lawrence Kenney, who edited the manuscript for publication.

A NOTE ON TRANSLITERATION

The system of transliteration used in this book is designed to be both readable and consistent. Since Russian specialists should have no problem reconstituting the original Cyrillic of a name or phrase, I have concentrated on making things as easy and convenient as possible for the English-speaking reader. In quotes from published sources the original transliteration is retained.

А–A	П–P
Б–B	Р–R
В–V	С–S
Г–G	Т–T
Д–D	У–U
Е–E (YE in initial position or after another E)	Ф–F
Ё–YO (O after Ж, Ч, Ш, Щ)	Х–KH
Ж–ZH	Ц–TS
З–Z	Ч–CH
И–I	Ш–SH
Й–I[1]	Щ–SHCH
К–K	Ъ–omit
Л–L	Ы–Y
М–M	Ь–omit (I before vowels
Н–N	other than I)
О–O	Э–E
	Ю–YU
	Я–YA[2]

[1] In final position - ИЙ and - ЫЙ → Y. In first names final - ИЙ → I (e.g., Yuri).
[2] The combinations ЬЯ and ИЯ → IA (e.g., Tatiana).
In deference to popular usage I have used Leo Tolstoy (not Lev Tolstoi) and Alexander (not Aleksandr).

JOHN GARRARD

Introduction: The Rise of the Novel in Russia

The great age of the Russian novel—and arguably of the novel anywhere—occurred during a twenty-five-year period that coincided exactly with the reign of Tsar Alexander II (1855–81). In the space of a single generation the celebrated Russian novelists Dostoevsky, Tolstoy, Turgenev, and their compatriots Goncharov, Leskov, and Saltykov-Shchedrin, who are less well known in the West, created a series of remarkable works that bear comparison with those produced in other periods of extraordinary cultural genius: Athens in classical antiquity, Renaissance Italy, and Elizabethan England.[1] The great age of the Russian novel began with Turgenev's *Rudin* and ended with Dostoevsky's *The Brothers Karamazov* (*Bratia Karamazovy*). Dostoevsky died in 1881 and Turgenev in 1883; Tolstoy lived on until 1910 but a spiritual crisis in 1879–80 led him to reject his earlier fiction.

The overall Russian achievement during the nineteenth century becomes even more impressive when we recall that the novels of Turgenev, Tolstoy, and Dostoevsky were preceded in the 1820s and 1830s by intensive literary activity of an equally high order in poetry and the shorter prose forms. The so-called Golden Age of Russian poetry produced the lyrics and narrative poems of Pushkin and Lermontov. Both men also wrote important works of prose fiction which, together with those of Gogol, laid the groundwork for the great novels that followed. Russians themselves regard Pushkin's poetry as the centerpiece of their literature, but for most Western readers, and certainly for those who do not know Russian, the novel represents the paramount Russian contribution to world literature.[2]

As will soon become clear, I am not interested in exploring theoretical issues or the problem of defining the term *novel* except as an historical phenomenon, a type of prose fiction that chronologically superseded the romance and the picaresque. The novel cannot be pigeonholed since it gobbles up everything in its path and takes any form or content that it wishes.[3] However, I do attempt in what follows to suggest some of the reasons why the Russian novel evolved as it did.

The sudden appearance of the Russian novel, and at such a high level of quality and universal appeal, naturally raises a number of major questions, none of which is easy to answer. How did this flowering come about? Why did the Russians embrace the genre with such enthusiasm? What factors or personalities helped to determine the form and content of the novel in the Russian context? The answers to these complex questions must be sought in the cultural and sociopolitical traditions of the Russian people. The Russian novel, like any cultural object, is the product of both intrinsic and extrinsic factors. At the same time, one cannot hope to gain a true understanding of the Russian novel, or indeed Russian literature as a whole, without taking into account its subtle relationship to the major literatures of Western Europe.

Russia has presented to the West a distorting mirror in which Europeans sometimes recognize their own ideas and institutions, but more often than not are astonished to see the radically different forms they have acquired in this familiar, yet alien context. In their turn, the Russians have looked at Europe (and in more recent times at the United States) with a mixture of admiration, envy, and disdain. During the nineteenth century they often adopted a tough, no-nonsense attitude toward Western Europe, determined to establish their own independence, while constantly measuring their achievements against standards borrowed from Europe.[4] Thus, they wrote novels that belong recognizably to the European tradition, yet argued that their works could not be called novels at all. Both to themselves and to their Western neighbors, the Russians have sometimes appeared to be part of Europe and at others a peculiar, separate entity.

How did this uneasy, yet productive relationship come about? The first fundamental break occurred at the dawn of Russian history. The Eastern Slavs, ancestors of the Russians, were never colonized by the Roman Empire. They therefore lost an early opportunity to learn Latin, the language of classical learning, the wellspring of Western civilization and culture. In 988–89 Grand Prince Vladimir of Kiev accepted Christianity from Byzantium instead of Rome. He thus denied his subjects, or rather the churchmen, a second opportunity to learn the lingua franca of Europe. The significance of this decision for Russian history and the history of Europe cannot be exaggerated.

Under normal circumstances, acceptance of Christianity from Byzantium would have brought with it the Greek language. However, this did not happen because in the previous century a Slavic liturgy had been created by Saints Cyril and Methodius for use in what is now Czechoslovakia. The Kievan state was granted the dubious privilege of using this liturgical language instead of Greek. Known as Old Church Slavic, it was based on South Slavic dialects, rather than on the Eastern Slavic dialects which provided the foundation for the Russian vernacular. Old Church Slavic, the written language, became less and less intelligible as the Russian spoken language evolved.[5]

Living in a major center of Orthodoxy, *the* center after the fall of Byzantium to the Ottoman Turks in 1453, the Muscovites rejected everything European as tainted by the "Latin heresy." In fact, at precisely the moment when the Renaissance was beginning in Italy, the Kievan Russian state was destroyed by a Mongol invasion (1237–40). Its inhabitants were forced to pay tribute to the khans for 250 years and endure the "Tartar yoke" until the rise of a new Russian state centered in Moscow. By the end of the fifteenth century the Italian Renaissance had spread throughout Western Europe. The Russians thus missed a third opportunity to partake of the heritage of classical antiquity. Never colonized by Imperial Rome, having chosen Christianity from Byzantium, but with a Slavic instead of a Greek liturgy, they failed (in part through no fault of their own) to join the rest of Europe in being "born again" during the Renaissance.

The Russians not only missed the Renaissance, they also failed to participate in the Reformation. The history of Russian Orthodoxy certainly contains its share of disputes. However, these have generally involved a rejection of the established church's wealth and power in favor of an ascetic, .mendicant path to salvation. The parallel in Western Catholicism might be the order established by St. Francis of Assisi.

The Western church has at its core an intellectual tradition, established from the beginning by St. Paul. The tradition of the *disputatio*, carried on by scholars and theologians from the Middle Ages on, ensured that the Roman faith had a rich and vivid theological history. In a *disputatio*, where the Scholastic could debate one side of a question and then switch sides to debate the other, the discussion of church questions could be carried out within the confines of the church herself. It was a monk, Martin Luther, who began the Reformation by declaring that he wished to debate ninety-five theses that he nailed to the church door at Wittenberg.

Russian Orthodoxy, on the other hand, is based on the "kenotic" ideal, in which the believer is called to a personal imitation of the life of

Jesus of Nazareth. In the words of G. P. Fedotov, "In the kenotic religion, which takes its pattern in the humility of Christ, man humiliates himself not only before God but also before the lowest members of society."[6] One could argue that kenosis, Christ's emptying of His Godhead to assume man's dress, is closer to the message of Jesus of Nazareth than all the theological disputations that have taken place in the Western church. But the practical result for Russian society has been that the Orthodox church did not create an intellectual tradition that could have provided a forum for the discussion of ideas, theological or otherwise.

The traditional attitude of the Russian church—"Render unto Caesar that which is Caesar's"—has encouraged blind obedience to authority, whether it be to one's family, to the community, or to the state. The first Russian saints were two brothers who allowed themselves to be killed rather than dispute the authority of their elder brother. To quote Fedotov again, "The non-resistance of Boris and Gleb remains forever the summit of Russian kenotic Christianity."[7] This narrowly focused otherworldliness, lying at the core of Russian Orthodoxy, did not encourage the development of a public discussion of social and ethical problems beyond the severe restrictions imposed by the state. Indeed, the state authorities have always maintained strict control of the church and used it as a valuable ally to further their own aims. Any attempts at reform have been summarily crushed. The only discernible movement in the history of the Orthodox church is toward an ever closer identification with the aims of the government, whether tsarist or Soviet. During the nineteenth century this identification culminated in the promulgation of the tsarist trinity: "Autocracy, Orthodoxy, Nationalism." As an atheist state the Soviet Union keeps the church at arm's length, but has not hesitated to call upon its undoubted appeal whenever appropriate, most notably during World War II.

Vladimir's introduction of Christianity into Kievan Rus constituted the first of three radical transformations that have reshaped Russian history. The second was the modernization, or Europeanization, of medieval, semi-Asiatic Muscovy by Peter the Great (d. 1725), and the third was the destruction of tsarist Russia by Lenin, Trotsky, and their fellow Marxists following the Bolshevik coup in November 1917. Each transformation was not only radical but imposed forcibly at great human cost upon an unwilling population and justified by cultural and ideological arguments imported from abroad.

But all the changes, however sweeping and profound, left one constant untouched: a dictatorial political system. Indeed, each succeeding

regime became far more repressive and autocratic than the one it replaced. The descendants of Peter the Great, just like the Kremlin leaders
of today, sought to borrow Western technological knowhow while excluding supposedly alien and subversive notions of participatory democracy and individual freedom.

The Russians have never enjoyed true cultural or political freedom,
with the result that Russian literature has matured in spite of, and often
in opposition to, the existing authorities. Censorship of written materials
has been exercised, with ever increasing severity, since the Muscovite
state was established. Church censorship continued to exist together
with the state censorship during the tsarist period. Since 1917, the two
have been combined into an ideologically oriented censorship that is far
more restrictive and severe than anything previously experienced.

In brief: three extraliterary factors, the lack of a classical tradition,
the special quality of Russian Orthodoxy, and the repressive nature of the
Russian state, have not only served to differentiate Russia from the West,
but have set the context in which Russian literature would develop.

The lack of a classical tradition meant that the Russians found it very
difficult to create viable examples of those genres closely associated with
the literature of antiquity, namely, the national epic and verse drama. The
modern novel, however, does not depend upon an acquaintance with
classical mythology or Aristotelian poetics. In embracing the novel the
Russians were no longer at a disadvantage as latecomers on the European cultural scene. They entered as equals, and indeed rapidly made
the genre their own.

Paradoxically, it is in the novel that the Russians explore some of the
themes, ideas, and styles found in classical antiquity. For example, many
critics have noted the use of the Homeric epic by Gogol in *Dead Souls*
(*Myortvye dushi*) and Tolstoy in *War and Peace* (*Voina i mir*). However, the
echoes of the classical tradition reverberate at a deeper, more general
level. The novels of Dostoevsky and Tolstoy explore metaphysical and
moral dilemmas that the Western reader is more likely to associate with
classical tragedy or the *Dialogues* of Plato. But it is precisely in the novel
the Russians found their vehicle for the discussion of ideas.

There exists another cultural paradox that has had important results
for Russian literature: the Russian novel has taken over from the Orthodox church the function of engaging in theological debate. Hence, Russian literature is concerned with questions that in the West are viewed as
the prerogative of theologians. Almost all the novels of Dostoevsky and
Tolstoy, as well as those of many other Russian novelists, take the form of

spiritual quests which are not so much described as conducted by the protagonists. Here perhaps we see the impact of a genre that held central importance in the Russian medieval period, the "saint's life" (*zhitie*). At the same time, the Russian fascination with spiritual autobiography and introspection clearly draws upon the Romantic tradition that itself derives from Jean Jacques Rousseau.

Russian literature is, in fact, the most "religious" of all modern literatures. This holds true even in the Soviet period, in which many of the best-known novels continue to use Christian imagery and symbols as a backdrop against which the affairs of man are judged. One thinks of *We* (*My*), written by Zamyatin in 1920, Mikhail Bulgakov's brilliant novel *The Master and Margarita* (*Master i Margarita*), completed in 1940, and Pasternak's *Doctor Zhivago* (*Doktor Zhivago*), completed in 1956. If in the nineteenth century the story and example of Christ provided the Russian writer with an ethic, during the Soviet period they function more directly as a "mythology"—a system of symbols, allusions, characters, and events that are readily recognizable to the reader.[8]

Russian writers have discovered another mythology within literature itself. In almost any Russian work one finds constant allusions to the works of earlier writers. Not only does the author himself compare and contrast his work to that of his predecessors in Western and Russian literature, but he also has his characters quote poetry and prose. Once again, this is a tradition which continues to flourish in the Soviet period. Solzhenitsyn's *The First Circle* (*V kruge pervom*) takes its title and underlying symbol from Dante's *Inferno*. Another of Solzhenitsyn's novels, *Cancer Ward* (*Rakovy korpus*), employs in a similar way a short story by Tolstoy, "What Do Men Live By?" ("Chem lyudi zhivy?"). Toward the end of the novel a disillusioned Bolshevik, Shulubin, tries to enlighten the protagonist Kostoglotov as to the true nature of the Soviet regime by drawing upon Sir Francis Bacon's discussion of deceptive ideas (which he called "idols") in the *Novum Organum* (1620). A more recent example of a novel that employs the classics of nineteenth-century Russian literature as a backdrop to, even as a critique of, contemporary Soviet society is Andrei Bitov's *Pushkin House* (*Pushkinsky Dom*). This work has been published complete only in the West.

The determining factors of Russian history, reviewed above, not only serve as guideposts to the prehistory of the Russian novel, they also set in proper perspective the primitive state of Russian culture, and in particular literature, during the first half of the eighteenth century. At that time, when the citizens of most European countries could look back at long and distinguished literary traditions, the Russians did not as yet possess even a standard literary language, let alone a literature. They were still struggling to find their feet after the draconian Europeanization of their country by Tsar Peter the Great. Peter reset the course of Russian history, turning his country permanently toward Europe.

From Peter's death in 1725 until the end of the century, Russian literature presents an extraordinary hodgepodge of haphazard borrowings from West European, chiefly French, models.[9] One can discern no principle in their selection; it was indiscriminate imitation, not based on needs and concerns that flowed organically from the Russian cultural context.

The Russians were backward, and backward in their borrowings: they devoured everything, old and new, to create a peculiar blend of baroque, neoclassicism, and sentimentalism. This bewildering mishmash of styles and genres, together with a grotesque lexical mosaic, produced bizarre combinations that recall those of early Elizabethan drama: "tragedy, comedy, history, pastoral, pastoral-comical, historical-pastoral, tragical-historical, tragical-comical-historical-pastoral, scene individable, or poem unlimited" (*Hamlet*, II, ii).

During the reign of Catherine the Great (1762–96) literature received official encouragement: the empress considered herself a connoisseur of the arts and dabbled extensively in belles lettres. She published a satirical journal based upon the journals of Addison and Steele, which had enjoyed great popularity throughout Europe for decades. Several of Catherine's subjects, most notably Nikolai Novikov, accepted her veiled invitation to do likewise. Novikov's journals, until they were closed down by the apprehensive empress, published many examples of social satire written in a lively, colloquial style. His example was followed by Denis Fonvizin, whose two prose plays *The Brigadier* (*Brigadir*) and *The Minor* (*Nedorosl*) advanced Russian literature beyond mere imitation to the creation of recognizably Russian social types. Fonvizin's major targets, the ignorant gallomania of landowners and their callous treatment of the enslaved peasantry, found echoes in the extremely popular comic operas of the time and indeed remained a staple of Russian literature well into the nineteenth century. One is reminded of the social satire in Beaumarchais' *The Barber of Seville*.

These developments in other genres, important as they were, did not fertilize and enrich contemporary attempts at prose fiction, which lagged behind drama, nonfictional prose, and particularly verse genres. The fact is that literature had not yet become an institution; almost no one could make a career writing verse, let alone prose fiction, which was regarded with disdain by the cognoscenti. Writing occasional verses became one way of attracting the attention of the rich and powerful, but it could serve only as a potentially rewarding pastime, not a career. Russian literature had yet to emerge from the diamond-studded, gold snuffbox era of court patronage.

Such an atmosphere did not prove conducive to the rise of prose fiction, but we must remember that by the middle of the eighteenth century the Russians remained what one might call second-generation Europeans: they still had a lot to learn. In fact, they made spectacular progress. The prehistory of the Russian novel lasts for less than one hundred years. It may be divided into three periods: first, the eighteenth-century pioneers; second, the Karamzin period from 1790 to 1820; and third, the transitional period following the Golden Age of poetry to the early short fiction of Dostoevsky, Turgenev, and Tolstoy in the 1840s and 1850s. By the end of this time span Russian fiction has gained equality with its counterparts in Western Europe.

Of the pioneers in Russian fiction the two most interesting are Fyodor Emin (d. 1770) and Mikhail Chulkov (1743–92). Their works appeared in a brief flurry of activity during the 1760s.[10] Emin, who was probably born in the Ukraine, had traveled widely, knew several languages, and tried to make a career by translating and adapting Western romances, interminable tales of idealized characters and exotic travels known in French as *romans d'aventure*. Emin's most interesting work is his *Letters of Ernest and Doravra (Pisma Ernesta i Doravry)*, an epistolary novel with distant echoes of Rousseau's *La nouvelle Héloïse*.

Chulkov's range and talent were somewhat more broadly based. His brief literary career presents in microcosm the rise of prose fiction in Western Europe. He telescoped into the space of five years the prehistory of the European novel that had lasted a century or more in England and France: that is, the movement from collections of framed tales through multivolume romances and picaresque antiromances to a combination of the two styles to form a new type of fiction called the novel. Unlike Emin, Chulkov attempted to blend the romance and picaresque, or antiromance, traditions of European fiction. He produced a collection of tales called *The Mocker (Peresmeshnik)*, which recalls the framed narratives of much earlier European fiction, such as the *Gesta Romanorum*, Boccaccio's *Decameron*, and the *Cent nouvelles nouvelles*. In *The Mocker* Chulkov included tales written in the style of both romance and antiromance, set in an imaginary proto-Slavic past. While following the example of Emin in producing romances, by debunking them in the same work

Chulkov took on the role that Paul Scarron had played a century earlier in France.[11]

Chulkov made his most sophisticated attempt to blend the romance and antiromance traditions of prose fiction in his short novel *The Comely Cook* (*Prigozhaya povarikha*), which was published in 1770. This first-person narrative by a pícara bears a striking resemblance to Daniel Defoe's *Moll Flanders*, which had appeared a half-century earlier in 1722. However, it seems unlikely that Chulkov knew Defoe's work. Here, as so often in Russian literature, the inspiration was almost certainly French: *La Vie de Marianne* by Marivaux, published between 1731 and 1741. One of the particularly interesting aspects of this protonovel is that Chulkov sets it in the recent Russian past and makes his heroine the widow of a soldier killed in Peter's wars. This move from a Slavicized never-never land to a Russian setting is significant, even though Chulkov does little with it. He himself abandoned literature to devote his full attention to a career in government service.

But there is another reason why Chulkov's brief foray into prose fiction proved to be little more than an interesting experiment that had no impact on high literature. While prose tales were eagerly read (*The Mocker* appeared in three editions during Chulkov's lifetime, the last in 1789), the audience for this escapist material consisted chiefly of members of the lower gentry, government clerks, the numerous offspring of the clergy, and members of the emerging merchant class. Few of these people could read a foreign language and none had sophisticated literary tastes.[12] They read the equivalent of today's monthly magazine pulp fiction and supermarket paperbacks. The popularity of this type of fiction at the end of the eighteenth and the beginning of the nineteenth centuries is shown by the large numbers of West European novels and tales translated into Russian.

Russian writers were not able to match the popularity of these translated works of fiction; indeed they made little effort to do so, with one notable exception: Nikolai Karamzin (1766–1826). Karamzin was the major transitional figure between the eighteenth century and the beginnings of Russian literature proper in the early decades of the nineteenth century.[13] He, more than anyone else, must be credited with closing the cultural gap between Russia and Western Europe. Karamzin standardized and elevated the language of prose fiction, thus expanding its potential audience to more educated classes. He wrote some verse but is now remembered for his prose: fictional tales, literary criticism, and a lengthy, unfinished *History of the Russian State* (*Istoria Gosudarstva Rossiiskogo*), in which, according to Pushkin, Karamzin discovered Russia just as Columbus had discovered America. So extensive was Karamzin's impact on a whole generation of writers and readers at the turn of the century that the years 1790 to 1820 are known as the "Karamzin period."

In 1789–90 Karamzin undertook his own version of the continental grand tour, visiting Germany, Switzerland, France, and England. His travel notes, written in the conventional form of letters to his friends, opened up a new era in Russian prose while at the same time bringing the sights and sounds of the major European capitals, and their leading writers and intellectuals, into Russian drawing rooms. Karamzin could be said to have "discovered" Europe for his contemporaries, just as he later revealed to them their own history.

It is hard to say which incidents and observations in the *Letters of a Russian Traveller* (*Pisma russkogo puteshestvennika*) actually occurred and which are fictional. Karamzin's declared fiction consists of a dozen tales written over a dozen years prior to 1803, when he accepted the post of imperial historiographer and abandoned belles lettres. His sentimental tales, the most famous of which is "Poor Liza" ("Bednaya Liza"), recall Ossian, Goethe's *The Sorrows of Young Werther*, Thomas Gray's "Elegy in a Country Churchyard" (for the atmosphere of languid regret), and Laurence Sterne. The antecedents in French literature are Rousseau, as well as long-forgotten figures such as Marmontel and Mme de Genlis. In two late tales, "A Confession" ("Ispoved") and "A Knight of Our Time" ("Rytsar nashego vremeni"), Karamzin dropped the sentimental tone to write witty, sharply focused first-person narratives that look forward to Lermontov and Dostoevsky.

Had Karamzin not decided (like Chulkov before him) to enter government service, he might have advanced from the short form to the novel. As it happened, his works in prose gave rise only to second-rate imitations by epigones who caused him some embarrassment by concentrating on the more lachrymose aspects of his early tales. Karamzin's major disciples were poets: Vasili Zhukovsky, Konstantin Batyushkov, and Alexander Pushkin. With their appearance, Russian literature takes its rightful place in European literary history, but with works in verse, not prose fiction.

In theory, at least, the Russians might have followed their own course, abandoning the European pattern whereby the rise of prose fiction is preceded by the development of verse genres. In practice, as we have already seen, they did not leapfrog or reverse sequential patterns familiar in English or French literary history, but simply compressed them into very short periods of time. So, for example, Russia enjoyed its Golden Age of poetry during the 1820s and 1830s before the great age of the novel a generation later. The rise of Russian prose fiction thus reflects in broad outline the pattern familiar to us from the prehistory of the novel in England and France.

It must be understood that we are dealing now with two reading publics, divided roughly along lines dictated by class and social standing. One read almost exclusively Russian prose fiction of a generally low level or more likely Western prose fiction translated into Russian. Another reading public, more sophisticated and better educated, turned its attention to poetry in Russian, frequently of the highest quality since this was poetry's golden age. But this same audience also read widely in French, for both poetry and prose. The aristocracy, as well as the upper levels of the landed gentry, also made extensive use of French in society and for their correspondence.[14]

The two reading publics were addressed by two groups of writers, also divided according to social or class origins. As we have seen, most prose fiction read by Russians consisted of translations, since only a few epigones attempted to follow the lead of Karamzin. The state of Russian prose fiction, and of the novel in particular, may be judged from the fact that Vasili Narezhny, a Ukrainian, published in 1814 the first three parts of a work entitled *A Russian Gil Blas* (*Rossiisky Zhilblaz*), almost exactly one hundred years after Le Sage's novel had begun to appear in France. Primitive as Narezhny's effort is, it should be noted that the use of the picaresque betokened a healthy, if delayed, reaction against the idealistic, sentimental fiction of the time, both domestic and foreign, and the novel's focus on Russian life in the provinces indicated a line that another Ukrainian, Nikolai Gogol, was to follow a generation later in his own inimitable manner.

The vast majority of aspiring authors at this time wrote verse, not prose. In society, one's hostess was bound to present her album to a guest at some time during the evening for a witty quatrain or two. The atmosphere of the period recalls that of Elizabethan England, when every self-respecting man of consequence was expected to be able to turn a decent line of poetry. The reading public for poetry in Russian included the poets themselves, who often addressed their works to one another as much as to readers outside their circle: verse epistles became an especially popular form. The relationship between writer and reader was close, even intimate. It is no accident that the best Russian prose of the time was the poets' correspondence with one another; to those outside their circle they would tend to write in French. Often the relationship between writer and reader would be more accurately described as one between speaker and listener, since readings of poetry, less frequently of prose, constituted one of the major events of soirées and literary circles. Equally suggestive is the popularity of comic operas and the theater at this time.

The poet conducted a dialogue with his reader as a friend, or at least a social and cultural equal. The chatty, sometimes bantering tone was quite appropriate in such a cultural setting, but romantic irony appeared merely precious and died out during the following generation when the relationship between the writer of prose fiction and his audience changed. The narrative problems involved in writing novels necessitated a different authorial point of view and a new attitude toward the reader.

As in England and France, it took quite a long time for prose fiction to become respectable. Social distinctions paralleled the hierarchy of literary genres that had to be observed. Significantly, neither Chulkov nor Emin had belonged to the aristocracy or the landed gentry. In France the development of the novel had suffered because of the suspect connotations of the word *roman*, which had to serve for both "romance" and "novel": Diderot once complained that the word had pejorative associations and could not begin to do justice to the new fiction of Samuel Richardson. The Russians borrowed the word *roman* by imprint and thus have the same problem of distinguishing between the two types of fiction, with similar results for the rise of the novel as a respectable genre.

Well into the nineteenth century we find instances of Russian writers apologizing for presenting their readers with a *roman*, denying that they are writing a *roman*, or parodying the style and characters of a *roman*. However, the term gradually gained acceptance in the meaning of "novel" as a new type of fiction. In popular usage it lost the meaning of "romance" except in the sense of love affair.[15]

It is a good illustration of the instability of the term *roman* and of prose fiction at this time that Pushkin's narrative poem *Eugene Onegin* (*Yevgeni Onegin*), written between 1823 and 1831, is often regarded as the first novel in Russian literature. Pushkin subtitled the poem "A Novel in Verse" ("Roman v stikhakh"), chiefly to exasperate latter-day neoclassical critics who protested the work's deliberate jumbling of styles, genres, and tones. However, the subtitle does faithfully reflect an essential characteristic of the work: it is a narrative, it tells a story. Here we see Pushkin following the lead of Lord Byron, who showed all Europe how to update the traditional narrative epic by drawing upon both serious and mock epic (or burlesque) styles in order to produce a lively tale in verse (the Byronic poem) about a few fictional characters in a contemporary, if often exotic, setting. This must be regarded as one of Byron's major achievements: certainly his impact on Pushkin and therefore on the evolution of Russian prose fiction was considerable.

Byron's works were known in Russia before 1820 through the French prose versions of Amédée Pichot. At first, during his exile to the Black Sea region, Pushkin imitated Byron's romantic style and settings in his four "southern poems" (1820–24). But already in 1823, when he started *Eugene Onegin*, Pushkin began to conflate elements of the English poet's arch-Romantic style, found in such poems as *Childe Harold's Pilgrimage*, with the bantering tone for which *Don Juan* has become famous. Furthermore, he switched the setting from the mysterious Orient to St. Petersburg, Moscow, and the Russian countryside. This introduction of contemporary Russian social reality into high literature marked an important step in the prehistory of the novel, as did Pushkin's creation of influential character types: the "superfluous man" and the more genuine, emotionally mature heroine who loves him.

By 1830, writers had become aware of important changes taking place in Russian culture and society. Increasing numbers of literate citizens were starting to get a taste for prose and prose fiction written in their own language. It must be emphasized that literacy itself did not increase significantly from the beginning of the century to the reign of Tsar Alexander II, or even later.[16] But the potential audience for literature expanded and began to make its interests felt. With the decline of the aristocratic hegemony over the written word, the nature and mode of communication between author and audience underwent a significant alteration. In part it was a change from an oral to a written culture; from poetry readings, verse epistles, and almanacs to the so-called thick journals (*tolstye zhurnaly*) and the publication of large editions of collected works for a "mass" reading public. Symptomatic of these developments was the activity of the remarkable entrepreneur Alexander Smirdin (1795–1857). He inherited in 1825 the Plavilshchikov bookstore, library, and printing press. He made such a success of the whole enterprise that the 1830s are often referred to as the Smirdin decade.

The situation of the writer himself was also changing as commercialism began to play an ever-increasing role. Here once again Pushkin led the way. He was the first professional writer in Russia. He made every effort not to rely on patronage and in fact did succeed in making a reasonable living from his works. Writing late in 1836 to Baron de Barante, the French ambassador to St. Petersburg, Pushkin placed the transition from an aristocratic to a commercial culture somewhat earlier than most literary historians would today: "Literature in this country only became a substantial industry about twenty years ago. Until that time it was regarded as no more than an elegant, aristocratic pastime. Mme de Staël said in 1811 that 'in Russia a few gentlemen have taken an interest in literature.'" [17]

Beginning around 1830 we see the gradual melding of the two reading publics referred to above into a single, more homogeneous audience, whose interests switched from poetry to prose. Pushkin was quick to sense the emergence of this new reading public and did not hesitate to cater to it as best he could. In his narrative poem *Eugene Onegin*, which we have already noted was subtitled "A Novel in Verse," Pushkin spoke of his intention to "descend to modest prose." Public demand for prose fiction was shouldering aside poetic genres that had dominated the stage only a few years earlier. A decade later in 1840 Lermontov began his last narrative poem, which remained unfinished and has been given the title "A Fairytale for Children" ("Skazka dlya detei"), with the frank admission:

> The age of epic poems has long since passed,
> And tales in verse have fallen into decline.

Another sign of the increasing importance of prose fiction, even during an age in which verse forms continued to dominate high literature, was the poets' use of terms normally associated with prose fiction to describe their poems. Lermontov in the couplet quoted above uses the phrase "tales in verse" ("povesti v stikhakh"). One other example will suffice to make the point: Pushkin's famous narrative poem *The Bronze Horseman* (*Medny vsadnik*), written in 1833, is subtitled "A Petersburg Tale" ("Peterburgskaya povest").

A second, related change in literary taste that took place at about this time resulted from the decline in the knowledge and use of French. Nourished for a generation or more on translated novels, readers now looked for novels that would have some more direct contact with Russian themes and characters. Such a desire is perfectly understandable; its chief sources were probably the upsurge of national feeling following the defeat of Napoleon's Grande Armée (1812–13) and the enormous popularity of Karamzin's history, which began to appear in 1818. In addition, the impact of the Romantic movement should not be neglected. For the Russians Romanticism meant a rejection of neoclassicism, an escape from French hegemony, and an encouragement to search for their own cultural roots and national destiny.

The first native efforts at fiction were mostly historical romances, heavily indebted to Sir Walter Scott, whose works had a profound influence throughout Europe and the United States. Mikhail Zagoskin's extremely popular *Yuri Miloslavsky, or the Russians in 1612* (*Yuri Miloslavsky, ili Russkie v 1612 godu*) began this trend in 1829. It was quickly followed by many other works in a similar vein. Even though Pushkin disliked most of the historical romances of the time because they were poorly written, superficial, and lacked true historical sensitivity, he joined the movement with his short novel set in the time of the Pugachov Rebellion, *The Captain's Daughter* (*Kapitanskaya dochka*), published in 1836.[18]

These historical romances are no longer read, except by specialists and writers of dissertations. They were entertaining enough and to a certain extent met the demand for Russian material, but not for narratives about contemporary social reality. To some extent other types of fiction, all in the short form, met the latter objection: the so-called high society tale and the travel adventure tale or military tale set in the Caucasus. This type of story was simply transposed into prose from the narrative poems of Pushkin, Lermontov, and many other poets. Lermontov himself used these popular forms in order to assemble the tales that make up his novel *A Hero of Our Time* (*Geroi nashego vremeni*), published in 1840.

A type of fiction that originated in the French "physiologie" movement proved to have special importance in the prehistory of the Russian novel. It gave rise to the "physiological sketch" (*fiziologichesky ocherk*), which aimed to produce what has been felicitously described as "a daguerreotype of reality."[19] While the physiological sketch demonstrated a healthy interest in the social environment that both writer and reader shared, it remained a transitional form that could only point the way to the novel. The sketch lacked character development, psychological interest, and plot. Most important, it lacked an interpretation, an angle of vision on the naked realia it portrayed.

The state of Russian prose fiction in the 1830s and 1840s has been well described as "a fertile chaos."[20] Major problems of both form and content needed resolution before the major novels could appear. First, Russian writers had to establish an effective point of view, a satisfactory way of narrating their fictions. Second, they had to decide on the role or roles that their novels should play in Russia's social, intellectual, and ethical life.

Given the cultural and spiritual traditions of Russia it was unthinkable that the novel would become merely a source of entertainment; Russians have always been much too conscious of the symbolic value of the word for that to have happened.[21] But it was the literary critic Vissarion Belinsky who played the role of catalyst in guiding the novel on its course. His ideas were borrowed from German philosophy, but what he lacked in originality he made up for by his enthusiasm and sound literary judgment of individual texts. Belinsky appeared on the scene at exactly the right moment in the early thirties, just as new trends were beginning to make themselves felt. Until his death in 1848 he encouraged all the major new writers of the time, even though on occasion they proved unwilling to march to Belinsky's tune. He advocated social responsibility, a concern with burning issues of the time. Belinsky's disciples in later generations cheapened his message, which has developed into an ominous threat during the Soviet period. However, few major writers would reject his call for civic responsibility, providing they are allowed the freedom to express that sense of responsibility in their own way.[22]

Belinsky was but one of many Russians of his time who embraced the world of ideas with a passionate commitment that is less common in the West. Denied an opportunity to engage in public debate and to address social and political issues directly, these young people often turned to philosophical questions and literary criticism as a means of expressing their ideas. Several groups, or "circles," were formed in Moscow and St. Petersburg. Government spies routinely attended these meetings and periodic arrests were made, particularly after the revolutionary uprisings in Europe in 1848. The most famous victim was Dostoevsky, whisked away to Siberia for ten years in 1849.

One of the central issues discussed was the validity of the Petrine reforms, which had Europeanized the dress, manners, architecture, and institutions of Muscovy. Supporters (Westernizers) and opponents (Slavophiles) felt they were debating nothing less than the nature of Russian culture and its relationship to that of Europe, as well as the future direction that Russia should take in order to fulfill its destiny.

The formal (narrational and structural) problems that needed to be resolved are best examined in the context of the fiction written by Pushkin, Gogol, and Lermontov. The transitional nature of the period is demonstrated by the fact that Pushkin and Lermontov spent most of their careers writing poetry, then later turned to prose fiction. Gogol's first published work was in fact a narrative poem, but he quickly realized that he had no talent as a poet and promptly switched to prose fiction after burning all the copies of his poem that he could find.

What is surprising about their works is that they repeat the telescoped development from short to long form that had already taken place in the eighteenth century: it is as though nothing had happened since Karamzin and the process had to be started all over again. This is made clear by the parody Pushkin wrote of Karamzin's famous story "Poor Liza" in his tale "The Stationmaster" ("Stantsionny smotritel"). As the early structuralist Yuri Tynyanov pointed out, with specific reference to Gogol and Dostoevsky, parody can have a dynamic, creative function in the evolution of styles and genres. Pushkin must have felt the need to clear the decks by closing down the sentimental tale associated with the name of Karamzin (using as his target a story published nearly forty years previously!) before proceeding to the creation of a more serious type of fiction.

All three Russian writers in the thirties began by writing short stories, often grouping them in collections framed through the use of stylized narrators. Such collections seemed to be as close as they could get to a long work in prose at this still quite primitive stage in the development of Russian prose fiction. The use of frames to give an epic context to the collections derives from the felt need to demonstrate that the stories, though presented as fiction, actually did take place: this attitude recalls a similar stage that had taken place a century earlier in England and France.

During the 1830s no major author was producing framed collections of tales in Western Europe, but in Russia we find the three most important writers of the day doing precisely that. Pushkin's "The Stationmaster" was one of five stories in a collection called The Tales of Belkin (Povesti Belkina) and published in 1831 (note use of term povest). Gogol began his career with a series of similar collections, among them: Evenings on a Farm near Dikanka (Vechera na khutore bliz Dikanki) and Mirgorod. Mikhail Lermontov made an abortive attempt to write a historical novel, set during the time of Pugachov, and then failed to complete a prose work set in contemporary St. Petersburg. His first published prose fiction were three short stories, which he later grouped with two others to form his novel A Hero of Our Time.

Some years after Pushkin's death in 1836 Gogol claimed he had sought to emulate the great poet as an artist; he also claimed, without any corroborating evidence, that Pushkin had provided him with the plots of his major works and had taken a special interest in his career. The very few comments Pushkin made about Gogol suggest rather that he thought of Gogol as simply a promising young writer of funny stories. Gogol's admiration for Pushkin was genuine enough and it is undeniably true that he gave his novel Dead Souls, published in 1842, the subtitle

Poema, that is, narrative poem or epic, in an obvious attempt at a reverse echo of Pushkin's subtitle "A Novel in Verse."

Henry Fielding's definition of the novel as a "comic epic in prose" in the preface to *Joseph Andrews* is suggestive as a description of *Dead Souls*. At the same time Gogol's work also recalls the picaresque by the episodic nature of its plot and its roguish hero, bent on making a fortune in some rascally enterprise. But any attempt to define the novel in terms of familiar types or styles is doomed to failure; it remains a product of Gogol's extraordinary imagination, an amalgam of disparate entities mediated through a totally unique style. Although a work of genius, it had little influence on the great Russian novels that followed; Gogol's impact on Dostoevsky, for example, stems from his short stories rather than from *Dead Souls*.

The essential differences between Fielding and Gogol help to set in relief the Russian writer's approach and style. They differ in narrative technique and in their view of what art can and should be. Fielding keeps his choric prefaces apart from the main text of *Tom Jones*, which is narrated in omniscient third person. Gogol intrudes frequently in the action of his novel with both comic asides and serious, even lyrical digressions, in a manner clearly modeled on that of Pushkin's *Eugene Onegin*. This narrative approach also flows logically from Gogol's lofty view of the role of the writer, which differs from that of Fielding, not in its moral base but in its much more metaphysical, quintessentially Romantic fervor.

Unfortunately for Gogol, his negative examples did not have the moral impact he intended on the reader, who was inclined to follow Belinsky's lead in considering the book a satire directed at Russian social conditions rather than a clarion call to spiritual regeneration. Gogol planned to make *Dead Souls* the first part of a trilogy, the "Inferno" of a grand design based on Dante's *Divine Comedy*. Gogol's last years remain something of a puzzle, but it seems clear that the Messianic urge in Gogol grew so pronounced that he became dissatisfied with his repeated efforts to reform his recalcitrant hero Chichikov. In trying to write works that did not suit his talents, Gogol eventually destroyed himself as an artist: he berated himself for his own lack of commitment and failure to make proper use of his God-given gifts.

Pushkin and Gogol are often said to have initiated two major lines in the development of the novel: the first, through Turgenev and Tolstoy, and the second, through Dostoevsky and later writers such as Sologub and Bely. There is much truth to this argument, but it has the one disadvantage that it obscures the valuable contribution made by Lermontov. *A*

Hero of Our Time is not only the first novel to be published in Russian literature (that is, in high literature). It offers a perfect illustration of the technical problems that the Russians were trying to solve in order to establish the novel as a viable genre. At the same time Lermontov's work anticipates three of the most important characteristics of the novels produced in the great age that was to follow. These are psychological analysis, concern with ethical and metaphysical ideas, and sociopolitical awareness. Though none of these features is the exclusive property of the novel in Russia, the intensity with which they are engaged does help define the Russian novel and differentiate it from the novel elsewhere.[23]

We can see how far Lermontov has moved the novel along by comparing his treatment of Pechorin to Pushkin's handling of Onegin. As Rufus Mathewson correctly noted, Onegin and Pechorin "established a pedigree for the literary protagonist in the early decades of the nineteenth century which persisted to the point of becoming a stereotype."[24] However, there are important differences between the two heroes: while Onegin is a passive figure, Pechorin is much more dynamic and aggressive. Further, Onegin is "flat" and Pechorin is "round." Pushkin stays outside Onegin, so that we have little insight into his psyche. In contrast, Lermontov gives us what Wayne Booth, in his *Rhetoric of Fiction*, calls the "inside view" of his hero. Pechorin's conflicting emotions, his puzzlement over his motivations, his attempts to understand himself in his "Journal"—all make him a much more complex and enigmatic character than Onegin. Finally, the relationship between Pechorin and Grushnitsky, although apparently inspired by that between Onegin and the young poet Lensky, is handled with great psychological finesse, and anticipates Dostoevsky's use of the doppelganger in ways that are merely adumbrated in Pushkin's narrative poem.

My point here is not to denigrate Pushkin's achievement, but to establish that the prose novel presents the writer with many more opportunities for exploration of motivation and psychological analysis than the narrative poem, even if it is "a novel in verse." The differences between the two works stem essentially from the fact that they belong to two different genres. One can only call *Eugene Onegin* a novel at the risk of ignoring the simple, yet decisive fact that it is written in verse.

Its philosophizing about the human condition, or what the Russians call the "accursed questions" (*proklyatye voprosy*), is the second feature of *A Hero of Our Time* that links it to the mainstream of Russian fiction. The novel's final section, entitled "The Fatalist," articulates the central theme, which is the debate Pechorin holds with himself between free will and predestination. His real quarrel is not with social conventions and the "enemies" he stalks so coldly, but with God's world. Pechorin validates his existence by testing his will in a variety of circumstances, all involving the domination and destruction—either physical or emotional—of other people. As a typical Romantic and Byronic hero, he adopts the attitude that everything is fated and therefore it makes no difference whether one does good or evil. As Albert Camus put it, this type of rebel "feels impelled to do evil by his nostalgia for an unrealizable good." [25] Writing in 1911 Dmitri Merezhkovsky remarked that Lermontov "was the first in Russian literature to raise the religious question of evil." [26]

Here Lermontov has again bequeathed to the Russian novel an enduring concern, although free will and fate also lie at the basis of Pushkin's narrative poem *The Gypsies* (*Tsygany*), written in 1824. Explorations of the dialectic between predestination and freedom are found in Turgenev, Tolstoy, and most particularly Dostoevsky, as well as in several twentieth-century novelists, such as Yevgeni Zamyatin and Mikhail Bulgakov.

The third major feature of the Russian novel, its social criticism of contemporary reality, is made explicit in Lermontov's preface to the second edition of his novel. He states that his hero is a portrait composed "of all the vices of our generation in the fullness of their development." [27] His purpose has been to apply "bitter medicine, some caustic truths." But he refuses to be pushed into overt didacticism: "However, do not think after this that the author of this book ever had the proud dream of becoming the reformer of mankind's vices. . . . Suffice it that the disease has been pointed out; goodness knows how to cure it."

Generally speaking, Lermontov's attitude has been shared by all major Russian writers. The so-called radical critics of the 1860s and of course all orthodox Soviet critics have attempted to force Russian authors to do more than point out the disease. Consequently, Russian writers have been obliged to assume a heavy burden of responsibility. As explained at the outset, the Orthodox church has not played the role of keeper of the national conscience in the public sphere. Nor has there been any other institution or forum for public discussion of ethical and social issues.

Although Lermontov may have helped contour the future Russian novel thematically, he did not leave a model of how to tell the story. *A Hero of Our Time* consists of a series of first-person narratives which recall at times the *récits parasites* of the early French romances or the journals, the diaries, the letters, and the forgotten manuscripts of eighteenth-century English and French novels. The convention that every story told had to have really happened forced authors to pretend to be editing materials written by others. Marivaux goes so far as to claim that he found the manuscript of *La Vie de Marianne* in the closet of a newly acquired house.

While first-person narration offers an author many possibilities, it seems obvious that a more sophisticated and flexible narrative method would be required for the mature Russian novels of the following generation, given their complex psychological, philosophical, and social concerns. The method chosen, not surprisingly, proved to be omniscient third-person narration with embedded first-person narrative where needed—the standard way of story-telling in the modern novel.

This narrative method is so familiar to us now that it comes as a shock to realize how long it took the great Russian novelists of the nineteenth century to adopt it. In fact, Dostoevsky, Turgenev, and Tolstoy all began their careers with first-person narratives and the short form, rather than the full-fledged novels upon which their reputations now rest. Turgenev, after a brief flirtation with poetry, began with a series of tales told in the first person, which he collected and published in 1852 as *A Sportsman's Sketches* (*Zapiski okhotnika*). Dostoevsky's first work was his epistolary novella *Poor Folk* (*Bednye lyudi*), published in 1846. He did not write a novel until returning from Siberian exile in 1859. Tolstoy began with a fictionalized autobiography (in three volumes), and then published his collection of stories *Sebastopol Sketches* (*Sevastopolskie skazki*), in which he continued to experiment with different methods of narration: the first tale is actually told in the second person ("You will see. . . ," etc.), the second is told in the first person.

It is astonishing now to read Dostoevsky's private notes as he struggles to find the appropriate narrative method for *Crime and Punishment* (*Prestuplenie i nakazanie*), which appeared in 1866 when Dostoevsky had already reached the age of forty-five. He originally planned the work as a first-person narration, with Raskolnikov making a confession or writing a journal. He had in fact written substantial portions of the novel before he came to understand that he needed a more flexible narrative method to do justice to his theme. He ponders the limits of first-person narration: "At some points a confession will be immodest and it will be difficult to imagine for what person it was written." Then he contemplates "ANOTHER PLAN"—the use of a third-person narrator: "Tell the story from the point of view of an author, an invisible but omniscient being, but without leaving him [Raskolnikov] for a moment." He returns to this idea:

"One must suppose that the author is an *omniscient* and *infallible* being, who is presenting for everyone to see a member of the new generation."[28] Lermontov had presented for everyone to see a member of his own generation, but in the first person. Dostoevsky finally realized that he needed to use a more complex narrative method.

How can we explain this delay? Why did the Russian novel not appear a little sooner? The first point to make is that the three earlier writers (Pushkin, Lermontov, Gogol) all died young; they had a chance only to lay the groundwork for the appearance of the novel, but could not resolve all the narrative problems. Nor did they have the time to do more than sketch in outline the themes and character types that are given such body and richness in the novels of the following generation.

A second point, which must remain only a hypothesis, is that Dostoevsky, Turgenev, and Tolstoy, who were perfectly well aware of the novels already produced in England and France (Dostoevsky's first publication was in fact a translation of Balzac's *Eugénie Grandet*), still found it necessary to follow in the footsteps of the earlier trio of Russian writers, to come to terms with their creation, to overcome it, before they could advance from the short to the long form and produce the great novels for which Russian literature is celebrated.

What of extraliterary factors? The importance of commercialism and the growth of Russian literature as a social institution are undeniable facts. They might seem to lend support to the views of Marxist critics such as Lucien Goldmann, as well as of Q. D. Leavis, Ian Watt, and Harry Levin, who follow Hegel in arguing that the novel as "a bourgeois epic" emerges from a necessary ideational and socioeconomic nexus. But the Russian case is complex. Although Dostoevsky reminds us of Balzac in his frantic struggles to meet printers' deadlines, Lermontov rarely accepted money for his works, and both Turgenev and Tolstoy were wealthy aristocrats; Goncharov was a full-time civil servant all his life.

The Russian novelists themselves were not members of a bourgeoisie and they did not write about a bourgeois or middle class, which in fact did not yet exist in Russia. The appearance of the Russian novel would have been much delayed if it had waited for the appropriate socioeconomic base, as required by literary historians and theorists. It is true, however, that readers of novels in Russia shared to some degree the tastes and interests of their counterparts in Western Europe and that by the middle of the nineteenth century the narrow, aristocratic domination of Russian culture had come to an end. Here, as so often, one can find rough parallels between developments in Western Europe and in Russia, but one presses such comparisons at the risk of denigrating the specificity of the Russian experience.

As we have seen, the rise of the Russian novel followed a sequential pattern that had run its course in England and France about a century earlier. However, Russian developments were so telescoped and rapid that by the reign of Alexander II the Russian novel had achieved equality with novels produced by much older traditions. What gives the Russian novel its unique flavor is the special role it has played within the society. The novel has taken on functions that are served in the West by other institutions: the church, political parties, the media, even open and free discussion. Thus it has become both vessel and catalyst in Russian culture.

NOTES

1. D. S. Mirsky spoke of an "Age of Realism" which dominated Russian literature for sixty years from about 1845 until 1905. This Age of Realism, which includes shorter prose forms as well as the novel, would begin with Dostoevsky and end with the death of Chekhov. See D. S. Mirsky, *A History of Russian Literature: From Its Beginnings to 1900*, ed. Francis J. Whitfield (New York: Vintage Books, 1958), p. 177. While one may well wish to differ from Mirsky on specific issues and opinions, his book remains the best introduction to Russian literature in any language. Prince Mirsky wrote his studies of Russian literature in English. After spending the 1920s teaching at the University of London he returned to the Soviet Union in the early thirties and soon disappeared in the purges.

2. As an aid to the reader without Russian I have cited wherever possible works in English or in English translation.

3. Mikhail Bakhtin has written persuasively on this issue. See the recent translation of his *Voprosy literatury i estetiki: The Dialogic Imagination: Four Essays by M. M. Bakhtin*, ed. Michael Holquist, trans. Caryl Emerson and Michael Holquist (Austin and London: University of Texas Press, 1981).

4. Many Russians became convinced that European civilization was on the decline. Some said good riddance and laid plans to replace it with a new, more vigorous culture of their own; others wanted to save Europe and felt that Russia had a special mission to do so. Russians of all persuasions in the nineteenth century drew many of their ideas from German philosophy, notably Schelling and Hegel; later from Marx. A good introduction is the Polish scholar Andrzej Walicki's *A History of Russian Thought from the Enlightenment to Marxism* (Stanford: Stanford University Press, 1979).

5. A great deal of OCS lexicon did enter the Russian written language that was put together in the eighteenth century. In fact, OCS remains a productive source of neologisms even today; it has played a role similar to that of Latin and Greek in relation to the English language.

6. G. P. Fedotov, *The Russian Religious Mind* (New York: Harper, 1960), p. 391. This book was originally published in 1946 by Harvard University Press.

7. Ibid., p. 395.

8. Not surprisingly, given their Christian symbolism, each of these novels has had an unusual publication history. Neither Zamyatin's *We* nor Pasternak's *Dr. Zhivago* has ever

been published in the Soviet Union. Bulgakov's *The Master and Margarita* was not published in the Soviet Union until 1966–67, at first only in a censored version.

9. See further on this topic my introduction "The Emergence of Russian Literature and Thought" in *The Eighteenth Century in Russia*, ed. J. G. Garrard (Oxford: The Clarendon Press, 1973).

10. For English translations of selected prose fiction by Emin and Chulkov see vol. 2 of the useful anthology edited by Harold B. Segel, *The Literature of Eighteenth-Century Russia* (New York: E. P. Dutton, 1967).

11. Further on Chulkov and the romance and antiromance traditions in Russian eighteenth-century fiction see J. G. Garrard, *Mixail Čulkov: An Introduction to His Prose and Verse* (The Hague and Paris: Mouton, 1970).

12. Those with more education and elevated tastes had available to them in Russian the moralizing, "Masonic" romances of the neoclassical writer Mikhail Kheraskov, whose chief model was the dated *Télémaque* by Fénelon. Kheraskov had a full-time career as a bureaucrat: he would never have thought of trying to make a living from his prose and verse.

13. The best book on Karamzin, with much useful comment on his role as a writer of prose fiction, is Hans Rothe, *N. M. Karamzins europäische Reise: Der Beginn des russischen Romans* (Berlin: Verlag Gehlen, 1968). For a good short introduction in English see Natalya Kochetkova, *Nikolay Karamzin* (Boston: G. K. Hall, 1975).

14. Russian writers faithfully reflect the mores of the time. Tatiana, the "provincial" heroine of *Eugene Onegin*, addresses her famous love letter to Onegin in French. In another of Pushkin's works, the short story "The Queen of Spades" ("Pikovaya dama"), the old countess expresses amazement at the news that novels in Russian actually exist. In the first edition of *War and Peace*, set during the Napoleonic era, Tolstoy included reams of French dialogue. Only later did he decide that this was carrying historical accuracy too far: by the 1860s far fewer of his readers could read French fluently.

15. The Russians use the following terms to indicate fictional works of increasing length: *rasskaz* (short story), *ocherk* (sometimes used for a fictional sketch, usually with some documentary intent), *povest* (tale, novella), and *roman* (novel). For a discussion of these terms and their usage see Peter Brang, *Studien zu Theorie und Praxis der russischen Erzählung 1770–1811* (Wiesbaden, 1960), pp. 36–52; also Vadim Kozhinov, *Proiskhozhdenie romana: teoretiko-istorichesky ocherk* (Moscow, 1963), pp. 58ff.

16. I am indebted for this point to my colleague Kathryn Feuer.

17. *Polnoe sobranie sochineny v desyati tomakh*, 3d ed., vol. 10, (Moscow, 1966), p. 607. The original is in French; the translation is mine. Mme de Staël's memoirs, *Dix années d'exil*, appeared in 1821, and she visited Russia in 1812 (not 1811), trying to take a roundabout route to escape Napoleon. Further on Mme de Staël's role in Russian literature see my article "Karamzin, Mme de Staël, and the Russian Romantics," in *American Contributions to the Seventh International Congress of Slavists* (The Hague and Paris: Mouton, 1974), pp. 221–46. Elsewhere in his correspondence Pushkin tells Prince Vyazemsky that he regards himself as a craftsman who writes poetry for money, not for ladies' smiles (Ibid., pp. 57 and 83): "Aristocratic prejudices may worry you, but not me. I regard a poem I have finished as a cobbler would a pair of boots he's made: a way to make a profit." Original in Russian; the translation is mine. Pushkin's letters, which are well worth reading, have been translated by J. Thomas Shaw, 3 vols. in one (Madison: University of Wisconsin Press, 1967).

18. Most would agree with Mirsky, *History of Russian Literature* (p. 119), that Ivan Lazhechnikov is the "best of the Russian Scottists."

19. A. G. Tseitlin, *Stanovlenie realizma v russkoi literature: Russky fiziologichesky ocherk* (Moscow, 1965), p. 105. Quoted in an unpublished paper by Jan Meijer.

20. Mirsky, *History of Russian Literature*, p. 147. Mirsky's suggestive phrase is perhaps a submerged quote from Milton's *Paradise Lost*.

21. It is interesting to note the types of Western novels that have *not* been attempted by Russian writers, or at least have played little or no role in the Russian novel; e.g., the bourgeois success novel, the erotic novel, the "pure" adventure novel.

22. See Mirsky, *History of Russian Literature*, pp. 172–6 for a judicious evaluation of Belinsky; such a balanced appraisal is rare.

23. It is instructive to compare two famous novels of adultery: Flaubert's *Madame Bovary* and Tolstoy's *Anna Karenina*. Setting aside questions of aesthetic value, we see clearly that Tolstoy's novel is not only well structured but that it contains a whole forest of ideas and moral dilemmas that are not directly related to Anna. Indeed, Anna dies at the end of book 7, and there is a book 8 that pursues other characters and themes.

24. Rufus W. Mathewson, Jr., *The Positive Hero in Russian Literature*, 2d ed. (Stanford: Stanford University Press, 1975), p. 14.

25. Albert Camus, *L'Homme révolté* (Paris: Gallimard, 1951), p. 68.

26. Dmitri Merezhkovsky, *Lermontov: Poet sverkhchelovechestva* (St. Petersburg: Prosveshchenie, 1911), p. 36. See also John Garrard, *Mikhail Lermontov* (Boston: G. K. Hall, 1982).

27. Quotations are taken from the Nabokov translation (New York: Doubleday Anchor, 1958).

28. F. M. Dostoevsky, *Prestuplenie i nakazanie*, ed. L. D. Opulskaya and G. F. Kogan (Moscow: "Nauka," 1970), pp. 538, 539, 541. The notebooks (from an earlier Russian edition) have been translated into English: Edward Wasiolek, ed. and trans., *The Notebooks for Crime and Punishment* (Chicago: University of Chicago Press, 1967).

I

The Novel in Russia

DONALD FANGER

Influence and Tradition in the Russian Novel

Most critics—Western as well as Russian—who have tried to account for the distinctiveness of the Russian novel in the last century have either tended to sidestep the issue by speculating on origins (the "Slavic soul," Russian social conditions) or sought to address it in terms of its messages and effects. Seldom have they paused to consider that the distinctiveness in question might be sought first of all in literary terms, in the *means* by which those messages are conveyed and those effects created. Yet that, broadly speaking, is where Tolstoy located it when he drafted a preface to prepare readers for the novelty of *War and Peace* (*Voina i mir*). Denying that his work was to be approached as a novel, an epic, or a historical chronicle, he defined it simply as "what the author wanted to and managed to express, in the form in which it got expressed." And he claimed a sanction for that form in "the history of Russian literature from the time of Pushkin on"—which, he says, not only offers many such examples of deviation from "European form," but hardly provides a single major example of the contrary.[1]

The statement is doubly noteworthy. It shows the nineteenth-century Russian writer's characteristic consciousness of participating in a tradition of recent origin—in a literal handing-on of certain key ways of rendering experience—and it suggests that what defines the tradition may be independent of the nature of the experience rendered, a matter, rather, of radical *formal* freedom.

It is my purpose to sketch one central line of that tradition, from its origin in Pushkin's "free novel," *Eugene Onegin* (*Yevgeni Onegin*), through Gogol's "poema," *Dead Souls* (*Myortvye dushi*), to the poetics of the late Dostoevsky. The first connection has been remarked but not investigated;

the second has scarcely been suspected to exist. All the same, taken together they may help us construe more precisely the three key terms in this paper's title.

Pushkin's demonstratively subtitled "novel in verse," *Eugene Onegin*, was hailed by Belinsky as the first such "national" work, filling a void at once qualitative and quantitative. Not only, as Belinsky claims, had there been "not a single decent [Russian] novel in prose"; one Soviet scholar has reckoned that with the exception of Narezhny's neglected fictions, not a single Russian novel of *any* kind had appeared between 1802 and 1823![2] Hence Belinsky's interest in playing down the hybrid nature of *Onegin* and viewing it as primarily narrative. It was, in his view, at once a study in contemporary character, an affecting story, and an encyclopedia of Russian life. As for the poetic form, he and most of his followers in the nineteenth century tended to treat that as no more than an effective, if eccentric, means—ignoring the fact, as Eikhenbaum later put it, that an *Onegin* in prose would require "much more complex motivation, a far greater number of events and characters, and would have excluded the possibility of introducing into the narration a whole volume of lyrics."[3]

It remained for the twentieth century to explore what many readers must have sensed: that this radically "free novel," as its author called it, achieves its freedom by consistently playing off the conventions of prose against those of poetry.[4] For present purposes, the nature of this freedom may be located in three key features: the nature of character, the handling of plot, and the role of the narrative persona. All raise conventional expectations in the reader, only to baffle them.

In the traditional novel, as Ian Watt has suggested, either plot or character may be dominant, but always at the expense of the other term.[5] A complex plot (as in a mystery story) requires a certain *disponibilité* of character; the complex patterning of episodes demands a particular consistency from the principal characters, who must in no case be problematic enough to rival the situational problematics in which they are involved. Conversely, novels whose main purpose is to explore the complexities of character must simplify and reduce the patterns of event, since their logic arises from the characters and relationships in question. *Onegin* would seem, if only from its title, to belong to the latter category. And in fact, as Lotman has observed, it is their relations with *him* (and not with each other) that provide a rationale for the presence of virtually all the significant characters in the novel—with the partial exception of Tatiana, who threatens increasingly to usurp Onegin's centrality, because her suggestive presence depends equally on a series of juxtapositions with others.

In both cases, those others are presented sketchily (if in varying degree), as familiar *givens*: Lensky takes such form as he has from the motif of mistiness (misty Germany, cloudy romanticism), Olga from the stereotyped novels of the day; and Tatiana's husband—whose appearance in the final chapter would call for a great deal more description and explanation in a prose novel—amounts as presented to no more than "a personified circumstance," not mainly of plot, as Lotman claims, but of the central *theme* (which, as I shall try to show, might be identified as biography).

For Pushkin demonstrably mocks plot by making it minimal and schematic. Slonimsky has noted that its central line—the Onegin–Tatiana love story—rests before the denouement in chapter 8 on three meetings, at each of which one partner speaks while the other is silent.[6] Gukovsky confines it more strictly to two mechanically symmetrical situations:

FIRST PART

1. They meet.
2. At first glance, she falls in love with him.
3. She writes him a letter.
4. There is no reply. She suffers.
5. They meet tête-à-tête; no one is around. She trembles and is silent. He makes a didactic and unfair speech, though one marked by honesty and warmth. At this point the line breaks off.

SECOND PART

1. They meet.
2. At first glance, he falls in love with her.
3. He writes her a letter.
4. There is no reply. He suffers.
5. They meet; no one is around. He trembles and is silent. She makes a speech, of the kind he had made earlier. Here the line breaks off: the novel is over.[7]

The novel, however, is not over; plot is merely abandoned in favor of what has been the main thing all along. Here are the concluding four stanzas (the translation is Nabokov's):

XLVIII

She has gone. Eugene stands
as if by thunder struck.

In what a tempest of sensations
his heart is now immersed!   4
But there resounds a sudden clink of spurs,
and there appears Tatiana's husband,
and here my hero,
at an unfortunate minute for him,   8
reader, we now shall leave
for long . . . forever . . . After him
sufficiently along one path
we've roamed the world. Let us congratulate   12
each other on attaining land. Hurrah!
It long (is it not true?) was time.

XLIX

Whoever, O my reader,
you be—friend, foe—I wish to part
with you at present as a pal.
Farewell. Whatever in these careless strophes   4
you might have looked for as you followed me—
tumultuous recollections,
relief from labors,
live images or witticisms,   8
or faults of grammar—
God grant that in this book, for recreation,
for dreaming, for the heart,
for jousts in journals,   12
you find at least a crumb.
Upon which, let us part, farewell!

L

You, too, farewell, my strange traveling
companion, and you, my true ideal,
and you, my live and constant,
though small, work. I have known with you   4
all that a poet covets:
obliviousness of life in the world's tempests,
the sweet discourse of friends.
Rushed by have many, many days   8
since young Tatiana, and with her
Onegin, in a blurry dream
appeared to me for the first time—
and the far stretch of a free novel   12

I through a magic crystal
still did not make out clearly.

LI

But those to whom at amicable meetings
its first strophes I read—
"Some are no more, others are distant,"
as erstwhiles Sadi said.   4
Without them was Onegin's picture finished.
And she from whom was fashioned
the dear ideal of "Tatiana" . . .
Ah, much, much has fate snatched away!   8
Blest who left life's feast early,
not having to the bottom drained
the goblet full of wine;
who never read life's novel to the end   12
and all at once could part with it
as I with my Onegin.

What these lines demonstrate is the way the elements of a novel are, in *Onegin*, embedded in a kind of poetic discourse that uses them for larger, non-novelistic purposes, and from which they take their sense. The narrative persona presents, evaluates, and dismisses his characters; his concerns in the passages usually labeled digressions dovetail with the novelistic elements but finally subsume them through his insistence on having created the narrative in the first place. There is thus a dual emphasis—on presentation and on creation: *Eugene Onegin* must be read at the same time as a fiction and as a meditation on the writing of fiction, its expressive possibilities and its limits. But even the second element bifurcates: all the attention to literary stereotypes and conventions (which led Leon Stilman to claim that *Onegin*, which Varnhagen von Enze called an encyclopedia of Russian life, should rather be regarded as a *literary* encyclopedia) makes it a disquisition about writing, its means and ends—and about its reciprocal relations with active experience ("life's novel").[8]

The constant literary discussions and demonstrations in *Onegin* have a strategic function which, as Lotman shrewdly observes, is to overcome not particular forms of literariness—that is, identifiable styles or conventions—but "literariness as such," by devising an artistic structure (something organized) that would imitate nonartistic (unorganized) reality: "to create a structure that would be apprehended as the *absence* of

structure."[9] This is essentially a variation on the principle of the *Quixote*,
with the difference that here the creator participates openly as such. The
ending of chapter 6, no less than the ending of chapter 8 just quoted,
shows this with a complexity too rich to do justice to here:

> In due time I shall give you an account
> in detail about everything.

XLIII

> But not now. Though with all my heart
> I love my hero;
> though I'll return to him, of course;
> but now I am not in the mood for him.   4
> The years to austere prose incline,
> the years chase pranksome rhyme away,
> and I—with a sigh I confess—
> more indolently dangle after her.   8
> My pen has not its ancient disposition
> to mar with scribblings fleeting leaves;
> other chill dreams,
> other stern cares,   12
> both in the social hum and in the still
> disturb my soul's sleep.

XLIV

> I have learned the voice of other desires.
> I've come to know new sadness.
> I have no expectations for the first,
> and the old sadness I regret.   4
> Dreams, dreams! Where is your dulcitude?
> Where is its stock rhyme juventude?
> Can it be really true
> that withered, withered is at last its garland?   8
> Can it be true that really and indeed,
> without elegiac conceits,
> the springtime of my days is fled
> as I in jest kept saying hitherto,   12
> and has it truly no return?
> Can it be true that I'll be thirty soon?

XLV

> So! My noontide is come, and this
> I must, I see, admit.

But anyway, as friends let's part,
O my light youth!   4
My thanks for the delights,
the melancholy, the dear torments,
the hum, the storms, the feasts,
for all, for all your gifts   8
my thanks to you. In you
amidst turmoils and in the stillness
I have delighted . . . and in full.
Enough! With a clear soul   12
I now set out on a new course
to rest from my old life.

XLVI

Let me glance back. Farewell now, coverts
where in the backwoods flowed my days,
fulfilled with passions and with indolence
and with the dreamings of a pensive soul.   4
And you, young inspiration,
stir my imagination,
the slumber of the heart enliven,
into my nook more often fly,   8
let not a poet's soul grow cold,
callous, crust-dry,
and finally be turned to stone
in the World's deadening intoxication   12
in that slough where with you
I bathe, dear friends!

Here, too, one notes the dropping of the narrative thread in favor of a meditation on the seasons of life ("Can it be true that I'll be thirty soon?") and on the corresponding stages of *poetic* life ("The years to austere prose incline"). These are the reciprocating themes that unify the work; and they come together in the notion of biography—the picture of life, which subsumes the biographies of the characters in the meditations of a creator-narrator who keeps them company; that is, treats them as instruments of self-expression and at the same time as independent beings. The lyrical burden of *Onegin* is carried only in part by the story; much of it arises from the poetic discourse (asides and personal references) that subsumes the story. Both emphasize the work of time, the passing of youth and passionate illusion, and the overt insistence on art adds a transcendence even as it registers their limitation in a real world that offers no other transcendence.* So one might say that the ultimate "hero" of *Onegin* is Youth, whose fate is to become the constitutive factor of adult biography.

This is the implication of the ending (a non-ending in terms of plot)—and a rationale for abandoning Onegin at a critical point in his fortunes. Eugene's baffled love, like Tatiana's faithful love, is dropped (along with the theme of love itself) in favor of a closing emphasis on the larger themes of creation, youth, time—with specific stress on the fact that this text was written and published over a period of eight years, in the course of which the author, the reader, and the very age changed.[10] The work itself embodies these changes, in its evolution from an improvisational exercise in the free generation of a text to the glorification of a verbal medium—which, without ever ceasing to proclaim itself as such, at length takes on a moral value alongside the aesthetic, the narrative, the cognitive.

Eugene Onegin, in other words, is not only major fiction but a poetic meditation on the creation and the sense of fictions. Thus Pushkin terms it a "free novel"—a designation no less apt for Nikolai Gogol's sole novel, that other "free" fiction that prepared the way for Russian realism, not least by taking poetic ambition as one of its own central themes. The ambition in question is already signaled in Gogol's demonstrative subtitle, *poema* (narrative poem), with its paradoxical epic associations; and *Dead Souls* similarly combines the elements of prose with those of a transcendent "poetry," though the dominance is different and the transcendence more enigmatic. More than forty years ago, Chizhevsky observed in passing that *Onegin* was "a work of great significance for Gogol, though up to now scarcely recognized as such"; both parts of the assertion remain true today.[11]

There is, to be sure, a considerable literature on the Pushkin–Gogol relationship, but it continues to center perversely on the biographical connection. It weighs Gogol's many statements on the subject, tries to assess their veracity—and neglects the main point, which is that, early and late,

---

*Compare Keats's "Ode on a Grecian Urn":

Fair youth, beneath the trees, thou canst not leave
Thy song, nor ever can those trees be bare;
Bold Lover, never, never canst thou kiss,
Though winning near the goal—yet do not grieve;
She cannot fade, though thou hast not thy bliss,
For ever wilt thou love, and she be fair!

Pushkin represented for his younger colleague a *qualitative* ideal. The young Gogol's essay on *Boris Godunov* contains this climactic effusion (whose motifs recur strikingly in *Dead Souls*):

> Great one! over this, thy immortal creation, I make my vow! . . . I am yet pure; not one contemptible feeling of greed, obsequiousness or petty self-love has yet sunk into my soul. If the deadening cold of the lifeless world sacrilegiously ravishes from my soul even a part of what belongs to it; if this ardent heart should turn flinty; if despicable, insignificant sloth should fetter me; if·I should bare the marvelous moments of my soul to the marketplace of popular praises; if I should sully in myself the sounds wrenched out by thee . . . [The sentence expires in dots at the very thought.] O! then may that heart be drenched in incessant [*sic*] poison . . . [etc.] [12]

Rhetoric aside, what this amounts to is a clear proclamation of affinity with Pushkin's genius, and that is the strategy of his better-known article, "A Few Words About Pushkin" (from *Arabesques*, 1835), where Gogol praises in Pushkin precisely what he sought to achieve in his own subsequent work: the poetry of "Russian nature, the Russian soul, Russian character, Russian language" as seen through the depiction of the most apparently unremarkable phenomena. When the news of Pushkin's death reached Gogol early in 1837, he declared, "Whatever of mine is good I owe entirely to him," and claimed that he had "never written a single line without imagining him before me." [13] The implication is plain: Pushkin was the personification of the highest demands he could make on himself as an artist.

Indeed, the very formulation of those demands is credited to Pushkin: "He cited to me the example of Cervantes, who, though he had written several very good and remarkable stories, would never have gained the place he now occupies among writers if he had not undertaken *Don Quixote*—and, in conclusion, he gave me a subject of his own, from which he had intended to make something in the nature of a narrative poem (*poema*) . . . This was the subject of *Dead Souls*." [14] The story is familiar, and might not be worth citing again if its logic had not been so consistently ignored: given the crucial importance to Gogol of the Pushkinian subject and auspices for the project that was to dominate the rest of his life, it should hardly be surprising to find him looking to Pushkin's work for a *model* as well, something he might adapt to the very different nature of his genius and his medium. This, I submit, is what he did. Before *Dead Souls*, his frequent borrowings from other writers took motifs, situations, details, only to incorporate them into a radically original system; for his major work, by contrast, he takes key elements of a system (the "free novel") to organize afresh his characteristic motifs, situations, details.

Before *Dead Souls*, Gogol had elaborated a manner in his best work that challenged current fictional conventions, baffling the reader's assumption that character and story should carry some clearly decipherable significance. The most pointed example comes in the closing lines of "The Nose," where the narrator disconcertingly acknowledges a few of the absurdities he has been retailing, and comments: "But what is strangest and most incomprehensible of all is how authors can take up such subjects." "And yet," he concludes, "all the same, when you think it over, there really is something in all this. Whatever people say, such events do happen in the world—rarely, but they do happen." "Such events," the context makes clear, are not the alleged adventures of Major Kovalyov and his nose, but certain kinds of stories—literary performances—which register apparently meaningless data to insist that existence and value are separate matters, and that the latter must be *conferred* on the former (in life and in art). The orchestration of attitudes (some of them mutually exclusive) toward a given aspect of existence is the heart of "Gogolian" narration; thus Vinogradov speaks of the latter as "an orchestra of voices." Gogol poses his riddles (ontological, aesthetic, ultimately moral) through a language that is, in his own words, "often more precious" than what it designates—which is to say that the linguistic is the one unambiguous value in his writing and at the same time an earnest of potentiality, an instrument of further possible values. His most original prose art was thus self-referential and self-glorifying, one whose greatness lay not in reflecting the great questions of life but in aspiring to appear, ultimately, as one of them.

All this he had already worked out in shorter narrative forms, where the complex problematics of major art appear not in the experience rendered but in the reader's experience of the text, where the aesthetic center of gravity is not in plot but in a patently verbal dynamic and the peripeties are stylistic, so that the medium itself threatens constantly to assume a thematic centrality.* The long form could accommodate this

---

*Lest the point appear a critical sophistication, it may be well to recall Ivan Aksakov's reply to a letter in which his father had written of Gogol's reading from the continuation of *Dead Souls*: "You ask me whether you should tell me the contents [of the chapter Gogol read]. . . . The anecdotal interest in Gogol's works, for me as for you, is not important. You would have to tell either nothing or else too much, i.e., cite his own phrases, from which it is difficult to drop a single word: to such an extent does each note depend on its function in the general chord!" (Quoted in Nikolai Barsukov, *Zhizn i trudy M. P. Pogodina*, 22 vols. [St. Petersburg, 1888–1910] 11:135.)

tendency without difficulty; so Sinyavsky, analyzing *Dead Souls*, can speak of narration for the sake of narration and find the work exhibiting "the lofty aimlessness of a narrative speech that knows no limits or prohibitions and has no greater care than its own flow."[15] This is, of course, a defining feature of Pushkin's manner in *Onegin*. Is there a third Russian work in the nineteenth century that might be said to show it?

All the same, once Pushkin had urged the challenge and offered the idea of a long work, problems of adaptation did appear which Gogol solved by directly assimilating key strategies of his mentor's novel in verse. These begin with the external. *Onegin* was written and published over a period of nearly eight years; its author was twenty-four at the beginning of his work, thirty-two at the end. Gogol wrote the first volume of *Dead Souls* over a period of some seven years; he was twenty-six when he began and thirty-three when the book appeared. What makes the parallel worth remarking is the way the process is encoded in the works themselves. Both began as improvisations. The narrator of *Onegin* congratulates himself at the end of chapter 1 on having named his hero and determined a plan; in the last lines of the final chapter he recalls the time when he first "dimly descried" the outlines of his "free novel." As for Gogol, he reports in "An Author's Confession" how he "started to write without working out a plan and without a clear conception of what the hero himself should be. I simply thought that the funny project on which Chichikov was engaged would, of itself, lead me to a variety of characters and that my own desire to laugh would, of itself, create a plethora of comic happenings, which I intended to interlard with affecting ones." But as he neared the completion of volume 1 he saw a "colossal" work in prospect and wondered at "the powerful thoughts and profound phenomena to which an insignificant subject can lead."

The thoughts and phenomena in question are the result of a dynamic which has even less to do with the unfolding of story and character than does the poetic message of *Onegin*, for the episodes of *Dead Souls* have no necessary order, and the characters therefore cannot be called personified circumstances of plot. They are, along with the inanimate matter of the book, examples of "all the trivia with which our earthly path swarms," and they manifest a disconcerting and primary *thereness* that seems anterior to their description and is (with the exception of Plyushkin) undetermined biographically. Deprived of a past and a future that might confer meaning, they remain static in spite of all their dynamism, condemned like the inhabitants of Dante's *Inferno* to reenact endlessly the routines that define them.

The evolution registered within Gogol's text as a result is—like Pushkin's in *Onegin*—that of the author and his project: elements of a creative autobiography inform a "free novel" which, so far as the poetic message is concerned, is largely "about" its author and its own writing. Chapter 6 opens (as Pushkin's chapter 6 closes) with the author's lament for the passing of his youthful qualities; there he contrasts at length his former curiosity about new places, and the way his imagination would work on them, with the state to which time has brought him: "What would in previous years have awakened liveliness in my face, laughter, and endless talk, now glides past, and my motionless lips preserve an apathetic silence. O, my youth! O, my freshness!" A comparable change takes place in the project itself. The unrelieved presence of the comic is interrupted in chapter 3 with a meditation on its instability ("the gay can in an instant turn into the grave if you stand contemplating it too long") and defended as a value at the opening of chapter 7, where the author justifies his concentration on trivia by urging the parity of "lofty, rapturous laughter" and "lofty lyricism."

Such passages, traditionally referred to as "lyrical digressions," are—like their counterparts in *Onegin*—not digressions at all but, in Vasili Gippius's phrase, "necessary links in the epic whole." One might say rather that they constitute the epic medium, supplying through tone and announced intention the absences so conspicuous in the narration proper—and hinting an answer to the question (implicit, as before, in the narration) of "why authors write such things." Through their recurrence Gogol, too, manages to include "a whole volume of lyrics" alongside his narrative and to strengthen on the level of creation his own version of *Onegin*'s chief lyric theme, the passage of time, seen here (in Chichikov's biography, Plyushkin's decline, and the death of the public prosecutor) in moral rather than ontological terms.

The passages in question are by turns open confessions and defiant manifestos; even when they are self-justifying, self-encouraging, or self-pitying, they have in view only the authorial self who creates, and their work is to emphasize the dignity, the uniqueness, and the difficulty of the creation in progress. They lack almost entirely the irony that permeates the narrative part of the text (where digressive embellishment is, among other things, a way of emphasizing how weak a gravitational field the trivia being reported possess)—which is to say that they are all direct addresses to the reader, designed to redirect his expectations of a literary text. Throughout, the author anticipates and rebuts objections: to the "low" language he introduces, to having taken "a scoundrel" as hero, to his exclusion of love interest, and so on. These amount to an attack on the conventional fiction of Gogol's time; their function (like that of Pushkin's play with alternative styles in *Onegin*) is to emphasize the generic novelty of the work at hand and to make an overtly literary product tend to transcend literariness, not only by insisting on its difference from familiar texts, but by enhancing its direct connection with life: on the one hand through the miscellaneousness of reported detail, on the other through the concentricity of Chichikov's enterprise with the author's (who speaks of traveling "hand in hand with my strange heroes")*—and ultimately with the reader's, since the moral metaphor of the road includes him, too.

Like *Onegin*, then, *Dead Souls* treats a series of themes on several levels—contemporary Russian mores, seen both descriptively and in terms of cultural allegory; literary forms and conventions; poetic autobiography; time as moral trajectory—all in a shifting mixture which, given the unresolved nature of the plot, makes it impossible to call any of them clearly primary. As a result, in Bely's phrase, the very notion of prose was reborn in Russia—thanks precisely to its incorporation of the functions of poetry:

> Gogol introduced into prose the whole sweep of lyricism, conveyed through rhythms from which Pushkin consciously abstains in his prose; he makes his lines, stretched taut like strings, vibrate with the sounds of assonances and alliterations. . . . The victory he won . . . all but constitutes a revolution in our literature.[16]

The last-mentioned fact was sensed by all the major writers who followed; all of them responded willy-nilly to the centrality of Gogol in the evolution of Russian fiction, though most appeared to react against his manner—pursuing instead the kind of literature he aspired to produce after *Dead Souls* but could not: one marked by "that fidelity and simplicity which mine has not shown," one that would "lead the reader to a greater knowledge of what a Russian is," whose images and characters would serve forever as a lesson to people, though no one would call them ideal, feeling rather that they have been taken from our own body, from our own Russian nature;" one that would speak to "precisely those questions that present-day society is revolving around."[17]

The realist tradition that began to take form in the decade after *Dead Souls* reflects its influence in two major areas: aspiration and poetics.**

---

*Compare Pushkin's reference to Onegin as "my strange travelling-companion" (*moi sputnik stranny*; 8, 50).
**The traditional notion of influence deals with simple creative mimicry: with outright imitation of style or with elements of structure that suggest more than an accidental resemblance. These are found most often in minor writers (or in the early works of major ones), a

The aspiration, broadly speaking, is to transcend the "Gogolian," to move from a negative and ironical to a positive concern with the question of how to live. It arose from the very logic of Gogol's novel and found explicit form in the book that grew out of the authorial digressions, *Selected Passages from Correspondence with Friends* (*Vybrannye mesta iz perepiski s druziami*). This is a matter not only of fictional realism; it involves also a model of the Russian writer, whose social and moral duty finds expression in and beyond his art—a model which, purged of its Gogolian eccentricities, can be seen in Dostoevsky, Turgenev, and Tolstoy. (In our own century it survives distorted in Gorky, restored by the late Pasternak, and explicitly renewed by Solzhenitsyn.)

Deserving of more study than it has received, this subject, alas, is too tangential to pursue here. But we might note parenthetically the ways in which Tolstoy carries forward the program of his predecessor—to such an extent, indeed, that Annensky, in an essay entitled "The Aesthetics of *Dead Souls* and Its Legacy," could find Tolstoy representing "the quintessence of Gogol," "Gogol stripped of his romanticism."[18] The qualification is large enough (and vague enough) to give one pause, but if we think only of Gogol as writer, leaving aside the peculiarities of temperament, the statement is defensible. More fully than Turgenev or any other Russian writer, Tolstoy achieves the unrealized aspirations of the late Gogol. This can be seen first of all in his lifelong reliance on soul-to-soul communication between author and reader, which was the late Gogol's definition of poetry.[19] The drafts for his first publication, *Childhood* (*Detstvo*), contain a definition of his ideal reader, among whose qualities must be an unabashed readiness "to shed tears over an imagined personage [he has] taken to heart" and to find "an echo in his own [soul] to every sound in mine."[20] Here already is the germ of his treatise *What Is Art?* (*Chto takoe iskusstvo?*) with its famous notion of infection through feeling, and nearly half a century later he continues to ring variations on this essentially Gogolian view: "The chief aim of art," he writes in 1896, "if there is such a thing as art and if it has an aim, is to manifest and express the truth about

---

case in point being the relation of the so-called Natural School to Gogol. Bulgarin, who believed that no one had more muddied the purity of Russian writing than Gogol, coined the term to brand his putative followers, and Belinsky promptly gave it a positive sense by using it to label the best young prose writers of the late forties. It was never a school. Indeed, it is doubtful just what (if any) kind of entity lies behind the phrase, though it became so quickly established that the ingenuity of scholars continues to be taxed by efforts to explain it. What *is* clear is that Gogol himself was a school through which the beginning writers of the forties and early fifties had, inevitably, to pass, and that if his influence, conventionally construed, was most pervasive in this period, it was also least lastingly significant.

the human soul, to express such secrets as cannot be expressed by a simple word. . . . Art is a microscope which the artist trains on the secrets of
his own soul so that he may display to people these secrets which are
common to all." [21] There is more than coincidence here; Tolstoy explicitly
corroborates Gogol's views. Rereading *Selected Passages* forty years after
its first appearance, he finds himself "discovering the America discovered
by Gogol thirty-five years ago with respect to the meaning of true art. The
significance of the writer in general is defined there . . . in a way that cannot be bettered." Gogol has "said, and said excellently, what literature
should be." In 1909 he adds new grounds for sympathy: "How glad I am
that I am rereading Gogol! I am now reading *Selected Passages*. What
deep religious truths there are alongside the vulgarities." [22]

   This sympathetic endorsement of the late Gogol, achievements and
aspirations alike, points to an affinity that is almost an identification.
Tolstoy, who defends Gogol's renunciation of his early "frivolities," had
done the same thing himself (albeit with less finality). Both writers were
centrally preoccupied with the question of what art should be, and both
based their views (as they had their art) on a deep personal crisis which
moved them toward religion—a crisis they felt impelled to share with
their readers by means of a direct public "Confession." That each should
openly take his experience as exemplary is what sets them apart from
the other major nineteenth-century Russians. It explains their common
insistence that authentic social change could come only through the
moral regeneration of each individual, as well as their common ideal of
the writer's role in Russia. The affinity is determined, moreover, by a tendency that predates all programmatic statements and underlies the fiction of both from the beginning. Gogol pointed to it when he claimed that
his works constituted simply "the history of my own soul," Tolstoy when
he wrote that his life consisted only "in saying what I have come to understand through the errors and sufferings of a whole lifetime." [23] "Errors"
may be a hindsight term, but the total text as symbolic autobiography has
the same value in both—for all the differences in temperament, situation,
and artistic method. And it is precisely this shared feature that made
them two of the most radically original, restlessly improvisatory writers
of the century.

The same cannot be said of Gogol and Dostoevsky, whose relation is the
closest of all, for while Dostoevsky's radical originality can hardly be over-
stated, it develops with a clear logic and a minimum of experimentation.
In that development the example of Gogol plays a crucial role, one that

shows influence at work in the largest and deepest sense—as a licensing and enabling factor in the self-discovery of genius. Only a part of that influence has so far been recognized.

That Dostoevsky began by *using* Gogol—ringing polemical variations on Gogolian situations and motifs—is by now well known.[24] Even contemporary readers could hardly miss the presence, though many missed its point, taking as helpless imitation what was in fact principled attack. When the protagonists of Dostoevsky's first book, *Poor Folk* (*Bednye lyudi*), read and discuss "The Overcoat," they not only express critical viewpoints toward it but *embody* them. Comparable signals in *The Double* (*Dvoinik*) evoke "The Nose" ("Nos") and "Diary of a Madman" ("Zapiski sumasshedshego"), and for the same purpose of critical amplification; where the young writer had earlier replaced Gogol's eroticized overcoat with a living female character to justify a more consistent and complex pathos, he here replaces the Nose with Golyadkin Junior to make clear the psychological significance of the usurpation. Gogol and the early Dostoevsky are linked, in Sergei Bocharov's phrase, as question and answer; and if Dostoevsky entered literature as "another Gogol," it was not as an imitator but as a contender for the succession.[25]

The relationship is generally taken to end with Dostoevsky's first period—in 1849 with his arrest or in 1859 after his return to St. Petersburg followed by the parodic attack on Gogol in *A Friend of the Family* (*Selo Stepanchikovo*)—in any case before *Notes from Underground* (*Zapiski iz podpolia*) gives evidence of his mature autonomy. To be sure, Gogolian references persist throughout the major novels; in the last of them Ivan Karamazov's devil is described as "a Khlestakov gone gray" and actually cites Khlestakov's creator. But in this period they are no longer privileged and take their place alongside other items constituting a broad subtext of strategic literary allusion. Nonetheless, the influence may be seen to persist, more subtly and more centrally, to the point where one can claim that the new novelistic structure fashioned by Dostoevsky represents his adaptation of tendencies that lie at the very heart of Gogol's fictional genius.

It is clear that Dostoevsky's effort in the first period was to humanize what seemed to him inhuman in Gogol: the detached stance of the narrator, whom he likened to a puppetmaster.[26] This meant accepting Gogol's themes while rejecting his techniques, chief among them the use of a mediating narrative persona which arrogated to itself a freedom that should properly have been bestowed on the characters. Thus Dostoevsky begins by transposing the surface problematics of Gogol's narrations to the level of psychological–situational problematics, shifting the balance of significance from the exhibition itself to what is being exhibited. This achievement prepares the transition to the major period, whose hallmark—the dramatic orchestration of ideas—is usually traced to biographical factors; indeed, the specific thematics of the late Dostoevsky are not largely related to anything we find in Gogol. (Though they may be at their most general: I have in mind the concern that enters Dostoevsky's work with *Notes from Underground*—the concern with "living life" [*zhivaya zhizn*], which so plainly extends Gogol's attacks on "dead souls" and the state he imaged as death-in-life into the area of the positive. This quest for a spiritual authenticity, dramatized in all the major novels and linked to a notion of essential Russianness, would in fact seem to represent a continuing sign of the Gogolian legacy.)

Still, it is precisely Dostoevsky's major period that shows him appropriating and transposing key aspects of Gogol's artistry. If at first he had developed Gogolian situations while rejecting Gogolian techniques, in the second period, having discovered his own themes, he actualizes them by a bold adaptation of Gogolian techniques *on the level of strategy*. Consider this recent description of Dostoevsky's fictional world:

> In [it] there are no facts that stand on their own feet. They all prop each other up; heaped one on top of another, each depends on the others. All the phenomena are, as it were, uncompleted [*nezaversheny*]: the ideas are uncompleted . . . the tale is uncompleted; the information which the storyteller has collected about events is contradictory; details are unclear and so is the whole. Everything, as it were, is still in the stage of coming to light, of being "under investigation." Everything is still taking shape, hence undetermined, and far from static. Characters frequently act contrary to expectation, in defiance of ordinary psychology, for people in Dostoevsky are subordinated to their own particular metapsychology. The phenomena of life project out of some obscurity, some Rembrandt-like play of darkness and penumbras. . . .
>
> Dostoevsky's is a style that clearly aspires to an incompleteness that will stimulate the reader's thought.[27]

The key terms here are all applicable to *Dead Souls* (as well as to "The Overcoat" ["Shinel"] and "The Nose")—expressions of Gogol's highest artistry which, Dostoevsky found, "overwhelm the mind with questions whose profundity makes them all but intractable and [which] evoke in the Russian mind the most disturbing thoughts."[28]

Dostoevsky, in other words, saw the elusiveness and indeterminacy of Gogol's writing as a provocation to the reader, as indications of a subtly encoded meaning. This, it should be noted, is one of the features that makes Gogol seem so "modern" today—and it is one which similarly gives Dostoevsky's own major novels their twentieth-century flavor. In them he, too, shows a fondness for indefinite qualifiers and lays deliberate emphasis on the strange, the uncanny, the indefinable and inexpressible. His major characters, too, "overwhelm the mind," teasing it with the most profound questions. The fact that they, in contrast to Gogol's, do not simply represent but *articulate* those questions makes them seem incommensurable, but their function is (in Dostoevsky's own view) the same; only the degree of explicitness is different.

Considered in this light, *Notes from Underground*, the work which is generally taken to constitute the "prologue" to the great novels, is as clearly linked to "The Overcoat" as is *Poor Folk*. Where earlier the link was thematic, here it is strategic. Both works have engendered widely differing interpretations because of the crucial and ambiguous association of a defective character with the most serious questions (moral, social, metaphysical), leaving open the possibility that we are meant to entertain the questions seriously in spite of the unworthy vehicle; at the same time, the unworthy vehicle may be there to question the questions. What persists is a puzzle to which the author offers no final key.

In speaking of Gogol's "profundity," Dostoevsky emphasized his "artistic types," and it is in character that he roots his own discovery. The Underground Man flaunts his hyperbolic departure from the normal, taunting the reader with the claim that "I have only carried to an extreme what you have not dared to carry even half way, and what is more, you take your cowardice for prudence, so that I may even be more alive than you!" Gogol's characters depart no less sharply from the norm, though in a different direction: where Gogol simplifies, Dostoevsky intensifies. Having begun by more fully imaging Gogol's characters and situations, and so bringing them into the range of the normal, he now does the same thing with respect to their extremity, taking care to preserve it as such—by making it a matter of experience rather than assertion. "Character," in fact, is as misleading a word to apply to the personages of the one as of the other, suggesting as it does that they may *have* character in the usual sense. For this, Gogol's are too primitive, Dostoevsky's too fluid—a fact which implies the possibility of "normalization" in the future for both, since both are to a marked degree undetermined by past experience. (One of Dostoevsky's explicit concerns in the major period, spiritual rebirth, is a buried theme, implicit not only in *Dead Souls* but in the bulk of Gogol's writing after he abandons the Ukrainian setting.)

The Gogolian character, however, like a bas-relief, is inseparable from the narrative presentation in which he is embedded. What Dostoevsky does is to emancipate him, parceling out the contradictory "voices" of that narration to his characters, so that what had been a one-man band in his predecessor becomes in his own work a genuine orchestra. Each voice, as Bakhtin observes, represents a world of its own—but these worlds overlap, whereas the solipsisms of Gogol's work can only intersect and only be personalized by the defining external perceptions of the voice that presents them. When Bakhtin identifies the chief pathos of Dostoevsky's works as "the struggle with the reification of the individual,"[29] he points to a tendency that began as a struggle against Gogol and, I submit, remained that, even as Dostoevsky's terms became more complex and Gogol's presence as subtext diminished.

I cite Bakhtin because his definition of Dostoevsky's mature creation, the "polyphonic novel," shows such a striking Gogolian provenience when considered as dynamic structure. The central adaptation, to repeat, consists in distributing to characters the absolute freedom which Gogol had arrogated to himself alone as narrator. It is the latter who in "The Nose," "The Overcoat," and *Dead Souls* resists any possibility of definition; in the late Dostoevsky it is the protagonist, the axiom in both cases being that "so long as a man is alive, he lives by virtue of being uncompleted and of not yet having spoken his final word."[30] From this follow the peculiar verbal forms which the polyphonic novel entails: "the word with a sideward glance," "the word with a loophole"—both prime Gogolian categories as well on the level of narration.

This is not the place to explore the connection in detail. My purpose is only to argue its legitimacy—and its importance as an example of influence in the deepest sense, where the achievement of one writer suggests to another the possibility of an enterprise so original as to obscure the very suggestive link. If Gogol's significance for the young Dostoevsky is a matter of record, the later record is no less indicative. The word *poema*—the badge of Gogol's maximal artistic aspiration, whose application to prose marks the beginning of a tradition—begins to appear in a Dostoevskian context precisely in the 1860s, coincidentally with the first of his major works. The subtitle "A Petersburg *poema*" is added to *The Double* on its republication in 1866. Later its author reports that his projected "Life of a Great Sinner" will be "a real *poema*," applying the same word to his penultimate novel, as indeed he might have done with respect to any of them from *Crime and Punishment* on. One of the last note-books refers to a "fantastic *poema*-novel" that would deal with "the so-ciety of the future, the commune, the uprising in Paris."

One can hardly doubt the source of this term or the peculiar signifi-cance of the fact that Gogol's successor—not the author of *Poor Folk*, but of *Crime and Punishment, The Idiot, The Possessed, The Brothers Ka-ramazov*—chose consistently to identify himself as a poet rather than a novelist.[31]

To summarize and conclude: Influence at its most significant—the influ-ence of one major writer on another—has nothing to do with imitation and cannot be recognized by searching out parallel passages. Rather, it is what creates the crucial links in a tradition: suggestive, liberating exam-ple. What Gogol appropriates for *Dead Souls* is the amplitude of poetic purview in *Eugene Onegin*, vertical as well as horizontal, and he does so essentially by adopting and adapting Pushkin's enabling device of roman-tic irony. D. C. Muecke summarizes the heart of the concept when he re-fers to texts where the artist contrives to "stand apart from his work and at the same time incorporate [his] awareness of his ironic position into the work itself," thus creating "something which will, if a novel, not sim-ply be a story but rather the telling of a story complete with the author and the narrating, the reader and the reading, the style and the choosing of the style, the fiction and its distance from fact, so that we shall regard it as being ambivalently both art and life." [32] In the cases at least of Pushkin's novel in verse and Gogol's prose *poema*, this is a maximalist strategy, and it produces what Boris Bursov has termed "supernovels" [33]—works based on a freedom of formal experiment which the times made both legitimate and necessary, since the institution of Russian literature in the 1820s and 1830s had not yet developed to the point where a code of accepted con-ventions defined and united its constituent entities: writer, reader, and fiction.

By the time of Dostoevsky and Tolstoy, the crystallization of literature as an institution, coinciding with the triumph of realism, rules out ro-mantic irony as a method. The fictional text may no longer be openly self-referential; hence different means must be employed to transcend "liter-ariness." The maximalism of the fictional enterprise, however, persists as the mark of a tradition being consciously extended.[34] Indeed, even Che-khov, who ends that tradition at the close of the century, is paradoxically faithful to it through his principled renunciations, the provocative brevity of his form, and the unprecedented narrative poetry its "incompleteness" produced. Even he produced his effects by defying conventional expectations, and no less radically than had the novelists against whose work he defined his originality.

NOTES

1. L. N. Tolstoy, "Neskolko slov po povodu knigi *Voina i mir*," in his *Polnoe sobranie sochineny* (Jubilee edition), vol. 16 (Moscow, 1955), p. 7.

2. V. G. Belinsky, "Stati o Pushkine," Statia vosmaya, in his *Polnoe sobranie sochineny*, vol. 7 (Moscow: Izd-vo Akademii Nauk SSSR, 1955), p. 440. The Soviet scholar is A. G. Tseitlin; see his essay, "Iz istorii russkogo obshchestvenno-psikhologicheskogo romana," in his book *Masterstvo Turgeneva-romanista* (Moscow, 1958), p. 7.

3. Boris M. Eikhenbaum, *Lermontov: Opyt istoriko-literaturnoi otsenki* (Leningrad, 1924; repr. Wilhelm Fink Verlag: Munich, 1967), p. 127.

4. See, in this regard, Yuri Tynyanov, "O kompozitsii Yevgeniia Onegina," in his *Poetika. Istoria literatury. Kino* (Moscow, 1977). The remarks that follow draw on this article and on the monograph by Yuri Lotman, *Roman v stikhakh Pushkina, "Yevgeni Onegin"* (Tartu, 1975).

5. *The Rise of the Novel* (London: Chatto and Windus, 1957), p. 279.

6. A. Slonimsky, *Masterstvo Pushkina* (Moscow, 1959), pp. 318–19.

7. G. A. Gukovsky, *Pushkin i problemy realisticheskogo stilya* (Moscow, 1957), pp. 271–72.

8. "Problemy literaturnykh zhanrov i traditsii v *Yevgenii Onegine* Pushkina," in *American Contributions to the Fourth International Congress of Slavists* (The Hague: Mouton, 1958), pp. 321–68.

9. Lotman, *Roman v stikhakh Pushkina*, p. 45.

10. The final observation is made by Lotman, ibid., p. 8.

11. "The Composition of Gogol's 'Overcoat,'" *Russian Literature Triquarterly* 14 (1977): 389.

12. N. V. Gogol, *Polnoe sobranie sochineny*, 14 vols. (Moscow, 1937–52), vol. 8, p. 152.

13. Ibid., vol. 11, pp. 89, 91.

14. Ibid., vol. 8, pp. 439–40.

15. Abram Tertz (pseud.), *V teni Gogolya* (London, 1975), p. 467.

16. Andrei Bely, *Masterstvo Gogolya* (Moscow-Leningrad, 1934), p. 5.

17. Gogol, *Polnoe sobranie sochineny*, vol. 13, p. 262; vol. 14, p. 40; vol. 13, p. 370; vol. 13, p. 293.

18. Innokenti Annensky, "The Aesthetics of Gogol's *Dead Souls* and Its Legacy," in *Twentieth-Century Russian Literary Criticism*, ed. Victor Erlich (New Haven and London: Yale University Press, 1975), p. 58.

19. Gogol, *Polnoe sobranie sochineny*, vol. 8, p. 429. See also Donald Fanger, *The Creation of Nikolai Gogol* (Cambridge, Mass.: Harvard University Press, 1979), pp. 172, 220, 224, and passim.

20. *Polnoe sobranie sochineny*, vol. 1, p. 208. Aylmer Maude sets this text ("To My Readers") as preface to his translation of *Childhood, Boyhood and Youth* (London: Oxford University Press, 1947).

21. *Polnoe sobranie sochineny*, vol. 53, p. 94.

22. Ibid., vol. 26, p. 874; vol. 38, p. 499.

23. Ibid., vol. 63, p. 93.

24. See Donald Fanger, *Dostoevsky and Romantic Realism* (Cambridge, Mass.: Harvard

University Press, 1965), pp. 152–66. See also S. G. Bocharov, "Perekhod ot Gogolya k Dostoevskomu," in *Smena literaturnykh stilei* (Moscow: Akademia Nauk SSSR, Institut mirovoi literatury im. A. M. Gorkogo, 1974), pp. 17–57.

25. Bocharov's phrase, "Perekhod ot Gogolya k Dostoevskomu," p. 42. See also his superlative "O stile Gogolya," in *Teoria literaturnykh stilei; Tipologia stilevogo razvitia novogo vremeni* (Moscow: Akademia Nauk SSSR, Institut mirovoi literatury im. A. M. Gorkogo, 1976), where (p. 415) Dostoevsky is shown to have deliberately connected his work with Gogol's, just as Gogol had connected his with Pushkin's. Thus Bocharov concludes that "the connection Pushkin-Gogol-Dostoevsky is the deepest [such] connection in Russian literature, one of its main lines," and emphasizes the importance of its having been "consciously and actively proclaimed by the last of these authors already in his first work."

26. See his "Peterburgskie snovidenia v stikhakh i proze," in F. M. Dostoevsky, *Polnoe sobranie sochineny v tridtsati tomakh*, vol. 19 (Leningrad, 1979), p. 71.

27. D. S. Likhachov, "'Nebrezhenie slovom' u Dostoevskogo," in Akademia Nauk SSSR, Institut russkoi literatury, *Dostoevsky, Materialy i issledovania*, vol. 2 (Leningrad, 1976), pp. 30, 35.

28. *Dnevnik pisatelya*, April 1876, I, ii.

29. M. Bakhtin, *Problemy poetiki Dostoevskogo* (Moscow, 1963), p. 84.

30. Ibid., p. 78.

31. See Leonid Grossman, "Dostoevsky—Khudozhnik," in *Tvorchestvo F. M. Dostoevskogo*, ed. N. L. Stepanov (Moscow, 1959), pp. 336ff.

32. D. C. Muecke, *Irony* (London: Methuen, 1970), p. 20.

33. See B. Bursov, *Natsionalnoe svoeobrazie russkoi literatury* (Leningrad, 1967), p. 356.

34. See Donald Fanger, "On the Russianness of the Nineteenth-Century Russian Novel," in *Art and Culture in Nineteenth-Century Russia*, ed. Theofanis G. Stavrou (Bloomington: Indiana University Press, 1983).

EDWARD WASIOLEK

Design in the Russian Novel

The nineteenth-century Russian novel is a literature of sloth, idlers, parasites, swindlers, cripples, crooks, phrase mongers, charlatans, rapists, tramps, and con men, but always of beautiful dreamers. A veritable cauldron of speculation, dreams, and mental energy pours out of those lying in bed, guzzling champagne, slobbering at dinner parties, and vegetating in provincial towns, as if the Russians did not inhabit the world their feet were stuck in.

The nineteenth-century critic Dobrolyubov said that if the Russian hero is stuck in the swamp of reality, he climbs a tree to look at the stars. Manilov in Gogol's *Dead Souls* (*Myortvye dushi*) looks over a green, scummy pond and imagines it to be traversed by a beautiful bridge. Devushkin in Dostoevsky's *Poor Folk* (*Bednye lyudi*) lives in a kitchen and chokes on the smell of frying fish while he dreams of writing poetry for his beloved. Olenin in Tolstoy's *The Cossacks* (*Kazaki*) watches Maryanka slopping in the mud, brushing off flies, and herding cattle, and sees a woman as majestic as the distant snowy mountains.

Dostoevsky shows us a world in which men are destined to destroy one another and themselves and dream of a world in which all will forgive all. The peasant for Dostoevsky is a wife-beater, sadist, drunkard, but he is also beautiful and pure and the salvation of Russia. Akaki Akakievich in Gogol's story "The Overcoat" ("Shinel") may be without thoughts, character, identity, a mechanical drudge hunched over his copying, but he has a golden heart. Maksim Gorky describes the dregs of humanity, but they are the best of people. In Dostoevsky's novel *The Idiot* (*Idiot*) Nastasia Filippovna may believe that she is corrupted, but she is really incorruptible and perfect. Russia may appear to be backward, savage, cultureless,

51]

but a different Russia is in the offing—the leader of men, the moral paragon, the unifier of nations, and the guide to a transfigured humanity.

The last point was tirelessly repeated by the thinkers of the nineteenth century, by Westernizer and Slavophile alike and by radical and reactionary. We are better than the West, growled Dostoevsky, whatever their technical achievements; only the Russian nature will save the world. Danilevsky gave a quasi-scientific scaffolding to the same ideas, arguing that radical and national types grow like secret roots flowering at different times in the march of civilization, and the Russian time was about to come. The Slavophile Khomyakov admitted without demur that the Russian past was empty, its present uncertain, but insisted that its future would be full.

There is hardly a Russian thinker or writer who did not hold his candle before the darkness of the future. And there is nothing more insistent in Russian thought and literature than the belief that the future would be good and the golden gates would someday open to the holy city. For the Slavophiles a secret Russia, hitherto unrevealed but also undefiled by the corruptions of the West, lay in glorious offing. For Khomyakov, Solovyov, and Danilevsky, the future beckoned with a transformed and transfigured Russia. The Westernizers, while accepting the premises and accomplishments of the rationalistic West, carried reason toward hope and desire.

The phenomenal popularity of Chernyshevsky's novel *What Is to Be Done?* (*Chto delat?*) lay in its promise of a purified and utopian Russia. The promise lay in the belief that a science of behavior, following on the science of minerals and chemicals, would find a special and perfect adjustment between the temperaments of people and between people and their surroundings. Chernyshevsky was persuaded, as were other utilitarians, that disharmony, stress, and disagreement were not in the order of things, but harmony, beauty, and fulfillment were. Turgenev, to be sure, argued relentlessly against the view of special and unique national development for Russia and insisted that Russia would have to travel the same road to civilization as had Western Europe. But the measure of how tenacious and widespread was the view of Russia as destined to achieve some form of apocalyptic perfection is the castigation that he endured for his unpopular views.

No two men, for example, were further apart on all issues than were Dostoevsky and Chernyshevsky. Yet both men had their visions of the holy city, and if the building blocks of that city differed, the visions did not: for Chernyshevsky the dark night of man against himself, of self-destruction, conflict, moral agonies would pass into memory and history when the laws of matter were discovered in the moral and psychological nature of man. Dostoevsky speaks often of his golden age in the *Diary of a Writer* (*Dnevnik pisatelya*), and in all his works he dreams that all will be reconciled to all. Dmitri Karamazov cannot understand why the faces of the babies suckling their mothers' dried-out breasts are not happy, and why everyone is not singing and feeling joy. Alyosha rises from the tears of resentment at the dream of Cana of Galilee to realize that the gift that Christ offers the world is joy and happiness.

The dream is there in this greatest of Russian writers, but the nightmare is also there. One of the important distinctions between his work and that of Chernyshevsky is the fury with which he reacts against his own dream, against those Schiller-like souls who believe that there is justice somewhere, against those liberals who believe in some future institutional harmony, against the naivety of those who believe that all will embrace and dance together. If he incorporates in his work that national obsession with the transfiguration of the earth, he also embodies the fear and doubt that the transfiguration can be effected or will be effected. The fear that the crystal palace will be a hen house is never far away. He embodies, if you will, the whole axis of thought.

Tolstoy, like Dostoevsky, is as broad as the whole axis. No one railed against the corruptions of this world with the gargantuan wrath that he did, and no one believed as firmly as he in the possibility and actuality of harmony and fulfillment. Wherever he turned his gaze he found corruption, sloth, selfishness, greed, and most of all, deception. Civilization is a series of veils drawn across the face of truth. But the truth was there. His golden city lay in the order of things and was identified with the laws of nature and the movement of history. It was a necessity one reached by leaving behind not only the past of civilization but the past of oneself. It was a new beginning, a fact that Chernyshevsky perceived in his remarkable review of *Childhood* (*Detstvo*) in 1856, when he spoke of the moral purity (*nravstvennaya chistota*) of Tolstoy's psychological processes. What kept one from the holy city was the past, the ossification of emotional and spiritual being by past habits and reflexes. It was the tendency to immobilize one's being by such subjective impulses as grief, regret, and desire that was the negative force that kept one from opening oneself to the free necessity of historical reality.

Everything fits, finally, in the Tolstoyan version of the good experience. Freedom becomes necessity, outer and inner nature become one, self-denial and self-fulfillment become reconciled. Everything fits, and with that phrase we come, I believe, to what animates the Russian flight from the past and its pursuit of the future, its consciousness of a sordid reality and its dream of another reality. There is no fear more poignant, insistent, widespread in Russian thought and literature than that things "do not fit."

Whether it is Westernizer or Slavophile, Chernyshevsky, Dobrolyubov, and Pisarev or Grigoriev, Danilevsky, and Strakhov, there is an unspoken repugnance to a conception of reality that is unhinged from design, subject to unresolvable contradictions, ruptured, fragmented, directionless, where things do not fit, and individuals are autonomous and isolated and isolating. To be sure, some way had to be found to accommodate the empirical or circumstantial reality that often embodied or appeared to embody the very traits that were held in repugnance. Chaadaev's way, at least in the views he expressed in the *Philosophical Letters* (written in French), was not the way and the views were not imitated. Khomyakov's insistence that a new, better, and more coherent and organic Russia, whose spiritual principles had continued to germinate and develop without rupture and corruption, lay under the empirical veneer was more in keeping with the Russian reconciliation of what was with what should be.

The Russian vision, as it is embodied in the novel, oscillates between the conviction that reality is design-haunted and the fear that there is no design, the belief that the world is continuity and the fear that it is rupture, the conviction that there is a place for everything and everyone and a place for nothing and no one. The Russian novel is design-haunted, and when design is lacking in the Russian novel, you get its image of hell. Something of this is found in Gogol, where the normal coherences have come apart, and motion, conversations, logic, and purpose are going nowhere.

Turgenev's novels are the record of heroes looking for somewhere to fit. Rudin follows the cloud of his rhetoric, looking for something that corresponds to what he believes, until by the end of the novel he is wandering over the bleak landscape of Russia without purpose or direction. "We must submit," says Liza, Turgenev's quiet and beautiful heroine in *A Nest of Gentlefolk* (*Dvoryanskoe gnezdo*), and with that statement she touches on what the heroes are searching for: something to submit to when they find harmony and repose. Lavretsky, after a pathetic and shattered life, senses the purpose and direction of life by looking at the silent and harmonious life of the village, where "the sun ran its course across the tranquil blue sky, and the clouds floated silently upon it" and where both knew "why and where they were going." In *On the Eve* (*Nakanune*)

Yelena falls in love with Insarov because he knows where he fits and because he has purpose. She craves purpose and place, as do all Turgenev's
heroes and as do all Russian heroes. They are struck with sterility when
they do not find it and with harmony and fulfillment when they do.

Turgenev was undoctrinaire; he shared neither the dogmatic convictions of Tolstoy nor the gargantuan passion of Dostoevsky, and yet like
them he felt the pressure of national experience. Nevertheless, the turn
of the Russian axis, of the view of purposive history, design, and dream of
necessary happiness is seen nowhere better than in the works of Dostoevsky and Tolstoy, who more than any two figures comprehend the
breadth and spirit of Russian fiction. Both men show us that the road to
harmony and fulfillment lies in the submission of oneself to an inelucta-
ble and incomprehensible force. It is both fascinating and instructive
how worlds so different could have a common ground.

The two men differed at almost every turn. Tolstoy hated nationalism and was a bitter enemy of the established institutions; Dostoevsky
was a fierce nationalist, an upholder of existing institutions, a defender of
the tsar and the status quo. Tolstoy sought for what was common to all
men in all time; Dostoevsky sought for what was exclusive, personal, re-
gional, and particular. Tolstoy came to believe in a religion purged of mysticism, miracles, and even of a personal God and immortality; his religion
was like geometry, a series of moral maxims and axioms. Dostoevsky believed in a religion of mystery and of wrenching personal agony, and he
believed life was meaningless without a personal God and immortality.

The creative works of both show the same sharp differences. The
people in Dostoevsky's world cough blood, their faces have an unhealthy
pallor; they laugh senselessly and hysterically; they beat their children,
usually from love; they wear tattered and dirty clothing; they climb narrow staircases with greasy railings, and they live in small, dark rooms. His
is a world without nature, of constricted space and time, and of people in
perpetual crisis. An epigraphic Dostoevskian scene is probably the one in
Crime and Punishment in which Raskolnikov accompanies the drunken
and repentant Marmeladov back to his apartment and to the room where
Yekaterina waits for the husband who has reduced the family to ruin and
his daughter to prostitution. Yekaterina has red blotches on her face and
a determination to hurt herself as much as he has hurt her. The windows
in the room are shut to the clean air of the outside that might help her
difficult breathing, but the door is open to the smoke from an adjoining room, and the door to the landing is open to the foul smells of
the hallway.

Such a scene is unthinkable in Tolstoy's fictional world, as is the final scene of *Family Happiness* (*Semeinoe schastie*) for Dostoevsky. There, husband and wife talk about their past, their children, and their future. The scene is environed by the sounds of frogs croaking, the smell of flowers, and the scent of rain-washed air. The scene is gentle, calm, natural, and domestic, all of which are absent in Dostoevsky's fictional world and unassimilable to his vision. There is health in Tolstoy's world and disease in Dostoevsky's. People and things are permitted to assume their natural form for Tolstoy, and there is ample space and time to accommodate the range of human wisdom and folly. Everything is a disfigurement of natural form in Dostoevsky: chairs are broken, rooms are crooked, geraniums are ugly, candles are twisted, people enjoy being hurt and are miserable in happiness. People do not eat, work, or love; they do not grow up and regret, reflect, or grieve. They do for the most part only one thing: hurt others and themselves, and there is hardly space or time enough to accommodate their ingenuity in doing so. In Tolstoy's world people eat, love their parents, hug their sisters, ache to grow up, dream of honor and glory, grow up, age, and die. Two plus two is equal to four, as Tolstoy reminded the church authorities who came to persuade him to return to the church at the time of his serious illness in 1902; two plus two as equal to five is a pleasant prospect for Dostoevsky's Underground Man.

Dostoevsky and Tolstoy, however great their differences, shared the Russian passion for a universe that is designed and a reality that is necessary. They find their common ground in a reality that has no gaps, that contains no ruptures and no abstract individualism; they envisage the overcoming of contradictions and reaffirm the national passion for submission to a necessary course of things. It is to be expected that such reaffirmation would be more complex, subtle, oblique, and dense than one would find in the prose of fact on these matters or in the works of other writers and that it would not preempt differences in techniques, themes, and language.

That said, one would seem to make a case for Tolstoy more easily than for Dostoevsky. Tolstoy was the propagator of a view of history that left little or no room for human freedom and contingency, and he dreamed of a moral and psychological world that would operate with the necessities of biological and chemical processes. Freedom as it is ordinarily understood is always rupture and sterility for him.

The case for Dostoevsky is harder to make. Dostoevsky was, after all, the uncompromising enemy of the rational organization of human happiness, of every view that would ensure the well-being of individuals by way of utopian and socialist means, and of any means that constricted the freedom of the individual on grounds of necessary reality. That is, he was the uncompromising enemy of Chernyshevsky and his views. Chernyshevsky was the most extreme representative of the view of reality as governed by design and necessity; and there would seem to be no way in which one could reconcile the conviction of Chernyshevsky that there are "laws of nature" and Dostoevsky's furious rejection of such laws. Dostoevsky's attack on the principles embodied in Chernyshevsky's "The Anthropological Principle in Philosophy" and in *What Is to Be Done?* may be an indication of how locked in by way of reflex he was to the problem of necessary reality. He surely did not share Chernyshevsky's conviction that there were necessary laws, but he shared his passion and concern for the importance of the problem. Even more, the violence of his opposition to a view of necessary happiness may not in itself betoken an argument against life viewed as submission to an unalterable course of things, but only an argument against a view of "necessary" happiness as conceived by Chernyshevsky. He bases his opposition to Chernyshevsky's "laws of nature" on the grounds that a belief in such laws is destructive of the dignity and freedom of man, but the freedom put forth in *Notes from Underground* (*Zapiski iz podpolia*) is itself destructive of those very same values.

It does not follow that, because he opposes the rational organization of human happiness, Dostoevsky champions the capricious freedom of the Underground Man. The Underground Man may mount a rhetorical and flamboyant argument against the crystal palace, but the argument is itself qualified by the attacker, who is portrayed as petty, mean, self-contradictory, and most significant of all, enslaved by his capricious will. Those who follow in his train—the great transgressors and sinners—may be more awesome, aesthetically impressive, but they are everywhere shown to destroy life—others' and their own—and to perish in self-contradiction and sterility. Dostoevsky fulminates against the rationalistic and utopian view of happiness because such views are destructive of freedom and the dignity of man while everywhere demonstrating that the freedom itself is destructive of the dignity of man. What at first appear to be alternatives are shown to be similarities, so that the argument against Chernyshevsky's rational organization of human happiness in the name of man's free will is not in fact an argument against design and a necessary view of reality. It is an argument against a special view of necessary reality, one erected by will and reason, arrogantly put forth as identical with the laws of nature, but in reality arbitrary, manipulative, and coercive of man's nature. That is, the necessities that are proposed are not necessities but arbitrary and subject to the manipulations of the will of the designers, a dialectic that becomes cynically apparent in the relentless logic of Shigalyov in *The Possessed* (*Besy*). Dostoevsky fulminates against the rational organization of happiness and against the various utopian schemes not because they are necessary but because they are not necessary enough.

In this sense Dostoevsky's attack on Chernyshevsky's rational laws of happiness is similar to Apollon Grigoriev's attack on the radical critics' view of necessary history. In both cases and by men of similar philosophical temperament the views of the radical critics were rejected on the grounds that the necessities they put forth were spurious necessities or not necessary enough. Dostoevsky has made his mark on Western freedom, but it was not freedom that he pursued—at least not individual self-willed freedom—but the unqualified and unconditional submission of the individual will to a course of things that could not be understood, manipulated, or altered. The path to truth lay in the humiliation of the will and the prostration of the self before all living things, so that no one and nothing was left out of one's relation to the living universe. It is judgment, separation, and glacial isolation, and the myriad forms of the will that are the obstacles to the truth. One abases oneself before everything and everyone in order to still the impulse to judgment and separation, and one accepts a force and design beyond one's hope, expectation, and understanding. Father Zosima bows down before the would-be murderer to repress the impulse to judge him, and his younger brother begs forgiveness of the birds and all living creatures. One must be worse than everyone and everything because otherwise one is better, and in being better one has left someone or something out. Dostoevsky calls this faith and such faith is built on the brutalization, if not annihilation, of everything that we consider to be subjective and human in men. The promise of such faith is a new freedom, happiness, and fulfillment.

To be sure, Dostoevsky dramatizes not submission but revolt, sickness and not health, disfigurement and not design. He dramatizes what threatens him and what threatens him tells us what attracts him. He feared the hurt one visited upon others and upon oneself, the love of pain, and the fate of men to destroy others and themselves. He feared rupture, isolation, the dissolution of society, the family, and of oneself. The panic he arouses in his readers is the panic before a world that has no ties, no foundations, and no force beyond the individual will. The strength of his fears is a token of the strength of his hopes for the op-

posite. It is because he ached for a true necessity and cohesion that he
reacted so furiously against the facile designs that were substituted for
them. He attacked not only the facile solutions of harmony and beauty of
the radical thinkers, but what he feared were his own facile solutions. It
was the strength of his hopes that drove him to seek out what he feared,
to question every solution he brought forth, to cast a shadow over every
impulse of goodness and beauty.

Nothing was left unquestioned, and those who take his saintly characters—his Sonyas, Myshkins and Alyoshas—as dramatic embodiments
of what was good and holy have missed the final assault. Sonya may, in
intention, be beautiful, good, humble, forgiving, and self-denying, but
in Dostoevsky's world intention and purity are not adequate weapons
against being hurt and hurting. If we can agree that his great transgressors—the Raskolnikovs, Rogozhins, Stravrogins, and Ivan Karamazovs—destroy, we may agree less that those who are meek, gentle, and
beautiful in spirit may also hurt and destroy, whatever the impulse of
their heart and spirit. It may be that not only his "dark angels" but also
his "bright angels" feel the shape and pressure of his hope and his fear:
that everyone is a destroyer, whatever his qualities and whatever his intentions, and that the facile design of creating his bright angels as an answer to his dark angels is another deception. Myshkin in *The Idiot* was
one attempt at such a design, and no one will question his goodness in
being, and perhaps no one will question that he was in part responsible
for the murder of Nastasia Filippovna. Sonya may be all humility, love,
compassion, and selflessness, and yet she is in part responsible for the
suicide of her father. For it is precisely her qualities of acceptance, suffering, and forgiveness that increase his guilt and it is the guilt that moves
him to walk in front of a carriage.

The final test of Dostoevsky's fear that men destroy even when they
love and forgive lies in the confrontation he gives us of the Grand Inquisitor and Christ. The confrontation is at the same time an attempt to deny
the fear and a confirmation of the fear. It is a denial because Christ is his
"brightest" angel and the Grand Inquisitor is his "darkest" angel, and because Christ is the most powerful argument that true goodness, compassion, love, and forgiveness exist. It is a confirmation because in the terrible alternatives he gives us between those two visions of man there is no
alternative. Both Christ and the Grand Inquisitor deliver man from contingency and willfulness, and both find his redemption is a necessity beyond his will. It is true that the necessity of the Grand Inquisitor denies
freedom and the necessity of Christ promises freedom. But the freedom

of Christ is founded on a total, unconditional and unquestioned submission to a force beyond one's reason and will. Dostoevsky's vision and art were vaster and deeper than most of his compatriots, but it was not vaster and deeper than the psyche of his nation. Nor was Tolstoy's.

Dostoevsky's greatest wrath was directed at those social seers and planners who would transform the society of man and make it into a society of disfigured and traduced harmony. Tolstoy's wrath was directed against the institutions that existed and had disfigured and traduced actual life. His wrath was gargantuan and little in civilization and culture escaped it. Governments, education, art; how one married and how one had children; how one prayed and how one blasphemed—all came into the purview of his critical gaze. But this minute, careful, and encyclopedic criticism of human institutions was not an argument for better institutions. There were no better institutions because all institutions were the contrivance of men and the willed interference of one person into the life of another. Good institutions interfered in one's life as much as bad institutions. But the argument against institutions, that is, the collective interference into the lives of individuals, was not an argument against the constriction of individual freedom.

Those collective forms of civilization and society that distort life and against which he thunders in essay and novel are corrupt not because they deny freedom but because they are not the necessary and unalterable forms of life, because they are invention and artifice, and because they are in the final analysis the imposition of one will on another. The principle of coercion and therefore of corruption runs from the crudest punishment to the most subtle operation of the individual psyche. The principle is rooted in the nature of perception and consciousness. Tolstoy proceeds from the assumption that one's being, as part of that design, is inviolate to interference by any other being. One has no right to interfere in the life of another, nor any right to interfere in one's own life. Despite this, such interference was endemic and almost identical with the power and reach of civilization; art, education, religion, as well as conscription, government, taxation were such interferences, that is, attempts to impose the being and models of others on what was unique and inviolate.

What one could do to others, one could also do to oneself, that is, violate the given unique and induplicable nature of one's being, not only by voluntarily accepting as models the beings of others, by generalizing one's being and by imitating others, but also by impulses that would seem to involve no interference in one's life. The tendency to violate one's own being was hidden in such seemingly natural impulses as grieving, sacrificing, regretting, loving, and sentimentalizing, and seems to be implied in every act of consciousness and feeling. To the extent that one identified one's being with the necessities of design (the incomprehensible ends of history and God), one's consciousness was in touch with the richness and reality of that design. To the extent that one "willed" one's life, one interfered with it, separated oneself from the necessities and realities of consciousness. It is a question of real consciousness in the design of the universe or one's own limited arbitrary and subjective consciousness, which by its nature impoverished life and being.

By casting the net of one's thoughts and feelings over life, one restricted its depth and extent to the circle of one's feelings and thinkings. When one regrets, one silently commands the world to be other than it has been; when one sentimentalizes, one deludes oneself that it is better than it is; when one hopes, one commands the world to be as one would like it to be. It is not only the "false" emotions and "false" thoughts that are so afflicted; every emotion, thought, and impulse of the will is so afflicted if it is subjectivized, that is, if it flows from one's own center rather than from the objective and unfathomable currents of life.

There is an attracting and repelling force in the gravity of this world; one is drawn toward the truth or the repelling force keeps one away from it. The repelling force is always—whatever the specific content—the impulse to make the world one's own, and the attracting force is always to let go and accept the necessities of life. One can pursue honor and impoverish life; seek truth and the force of one's seeking will keep one from the truth; sacrifice oneself and the sacrifice may empty one's life or fill it, depending on whether it is a subjective and conscious design or whether it flows from the necessities of one's being. As with Dostoevsky, though not in the same way, the specific content of a feeling, impulse, or thought will not determine its truth and reality, but only a total and absolute submission to an incomprehensible and necessary force will determine what is true, good, real, and beautiful. This is why the less one does the more one accomplishes; the less one knows, the more one knows; the smaller one is, the larger one is. These are not mere paradoxes; they are reinforced by a logical, consistent dialectic of true and false reality.

What is astonishing is that writers so different as Tolstoy and Dostoevsky should have been so constrained by the force of a national imperative as to conceive of the form of truth in such remarkably similar ways. I will not deny for one moment what is so obvious: that the vision, temper, atmosphere of the worlds are different, that the worlds are populated in different ways, that the inhabitants breathe a different literary air and live in different fictional countries. There is no circle of hurting and being hurt; situations do not turn on spite for Tolstoy; men do not imagine delusional worlds; the candles are not bent; the staircases are not greasy; people are not always coming into the capital to redress some wrong done obscurely by vengeful and anonymous persons in a distant province; the children do not tremble in corners, and the pallor of Tolstoyan faces is not covered with red blotches of the final stages of consumption.

But despite different visions, techniques, and psychologies, both were constrained to structure their worlds on a dialectic that turns on the submission of oneself to an unquestioned absolute, an unalterable course of events. They are both overridden, if you will, by the national imperative in literature and in thought to conceive of the universe as coherent and purposive and to insist that a submission to this coherent and purposive universe brings one to harmony, freedom, and beauty.

Dostoevsky envisions the "holy city" by showing its disfigurations, expresses the dream by picturing the nightmare, approaches the whole by showing what has been broken. Tolstoy dramatizes those moments of plenitude, harmony, and insight that flow from objectifying one's nature, by accepting one's place in the scheme of things. There are no scenes— not even the confrontation of Christ and the Grand Inquisitor—in Dostoevsky in which what is holy, good, beautiful, and harmonious is not environed with doubt and anxiety, no bright light without its shadow, no certitudes without incertitude. Dostoevsky shows us how nothing fits; Tolstoy how everything fits. Dostoevsky shows us the agony of separation from truth; Tolstoy shows us for the most part the experience of truth. Olenin in the stag's lair in *The Cossacks*, Natasha at the ball in *War and Peace* (*Voina i mir*), Lyovin at the mowing scene in *Anna Karenina*, and others give us glimpses of what it means to empty oneself and to become oneself.

To the extent that Tolstoy turns away from the dream to the nightmare, his vision begins to resemble Dostoevsky's, as in his later works. In *Anna Karenina* the love torn from natural necessities and moved by will and passion has something of the mordant, punishing, delusional, and impenetrable character of human motives that is so prevalent in Dostoevsky. The differences in style remain, of course, and the later works are more schematic, judgmental, and formulaic than anything Dostoevsky could have written. But the differences turn on an axis of similarity.

Whether it is the harmony of self and others, of sense and intellect, the inside of a person and the outside, that is, Tolstoy's vision of the golden experience, or the metaphysical holy city of Dostoevsky in which all will become one in the acknowledgment of their vileness, the axis that bends differences to likenesses is the fear and the consequent aspiration that everything will fit, that there will be a place for everything and everyone, that nothing will be left over, and that the pattern will be complete.

What is demonic is what does not fit. It is the rationalism and individualism of the West and above all, self will, or the illusion and self-deception of stepping out of the necessities of reality, that characterizes the negative pole of the axis. Tolstoy decries the folly of believing that you can step out of history and judge it, and his denigration of Napoleon is an obvious example of this view. But the same view permeates his most subtle insights into character and psychological processes. What keeps his characters from happiness and fulfillment are the isolating and subjective impulses of the mind. As in everything, Dostoevsky raises this fear to its mythic and universal level, projecting a national psychosis into universal proportions, for there is in his world the fear that nothing fits and the hope that everything fits, that all are against all, or all for everyone, that all is permitted and all are responsible for all.

The question must arise as to why writers as different as Tolstoy and Dostoevsky have been constrained to structure their works on an axis of self-willed freedom and necessity and why they should see the demonic element in individuality and the sacramental element in the submission of one's will to some absolute and necessary power. It is a disturbing fact that individuals and nations take their ideals from what they experience, and if that experience is painful and brutal, they will take their ideals from what brutalizes them. The long history of autocracy and absolute submission of self to a force beyond oneself may have contributed to the special character of the Russian psyche and consequently something to the axis on which Russian fiction turns.

II

High Noon

KATHRYN FEUER

Fathers and Sons: Fathers and Children

That *Fathers and Sons* (*Ottsy i deti*) is a novel about the conflict between Russia's liberal, idealistic "men of the 1840s" and the radical, materialist "men of the 1860s" hardly needs demonstration. Most impressive in this respect is the delicacy and subtlety with which Turgenev has introduced many of the key signata of that debate into his fiction: the Pushkin–Gogol quarrel is there because Kirsanov senior loves to read Pushkin; Büchner's *Kraft und Stoff* is there as a "popularization" which Bazarov recommends for the elder Kirsanov's first step toward enlightenment (though nothing that we hear from Bazarov suggests that his own scientific sophistication extends beyond Büchner); even the seminarists are there—Bazarov's grandfather, we learn in a side remark, was a sexton, while Pavel Kirsanov refers to Bazarov as a "dirty seminarist." Many more instances could be cited of beautifully integrated specific references to Russian intellectual life in the late 1850s and anticipatory of the early sixties. As D. S. Mirsky has observed, "*Fathers and Sons* is Turgenev's only novel where the social problem is distilled without residue into art. . . ."[1] It is even prophetic, in its clash between the force of nihilistic destruction (Bazarov) and reverence for created beauty (Nikolai and Pavel Kirsanov), of three great future novels of revolution: Dostoevsky's *The Possessed* (*Besy*), Joseph Conrad's *Under Western Eyes*, and Henry James's *The Princess Casamassima*. Perhaps the most decisive argument for the novel's topicality, if any is needed, can be derived from the characters not included in its cast. In *Fathers and Sons* there are no reactionaries, not even any conservatives (except Nikolai Kirsanov's coachman, "who didn't share the latest views");[2] in a novel set in 1859, on the eve of the emancipation of the serfs, there is not one landowner who regrets, let alone op-

67]

poses, this measure which, as Tolstoy wrote at the time, "deprived them of half their property." Here then is no panorama or even slice of Russian country gentry life but rather a selective representation of one small part.

The social-political interpretation of *Fathers and Sons* has been widespread. It was most recently articulated by Isaiah Berlin in his Romanes Lectures, published as *Fathers and Children*, where he calls the "central topic of the novel . . . the confrontation of the old and the young, of liberals and radicals, traditional civilization and the new, harsh positivism which has no use for anything except what is needed by a rational man."[3] Ralph Matlaw, in his preface to the valuable Norton Critical Edition, explains that he has chosen the widely used English title "Fathers and Sons" rather than the literal "Fathers and Children" because " 'Sons' in English better implies the notions of spiritual and intellectual generations conveyed by the Russian *deti*." Matlaw, with the majority of non-Soviet critics, sees Turgenev as having drawn on the specific details and data of the debate between Russian liberals and radicals for the portrayal of a not merely political but universal theme, the eternal conflict of generations.

Yet can our interpretation of the novel stop here? Only, I believe, at the cost of ignoring its deepest layer of meaning and thus missing its consummate achievement. The most perceptive discussion of *Fathers and Sons* that I have read is also, regrettably, very brief, an "introduction" to the novel by René Wellek. Wellek begins by explaining and paying tribute to the admirable "concrete social picture" of an era and its disputes which Turgenev presents. Calling "the eternal conflict between the old and the young . . . one of the main themes of the book," nevertheless, he asserts, *Fathers and Sons* "goes beyond the temporal issues and enacts a far greater drama: man's deliverance to fate and chance, the defeat of man's calculating reason by the greater powers of love, honor, and death."[4] "Man's deliverance to fate and chance" is indeed, I would submit, one central theme of the novel, but to see this clearly we must go a step further in the rejection of traditional interpretations. We must dispense with the notion that the novel portrays the conflict of generations and recognize that instead it portrays love between generations, the triumph of love over tension and conflict; that its essential core is the intertwining of two great themes, affectionate continuity from parent to child and child to parent and "man's deliverance to fate and chance," that is, man's knowledge of his own mortality. It is to this novel that Turgenev gave the title *Fathers and Children*, which is, moreover, a novel far more profound in its political implications than we have heretofore realized.[5]

This reading of the book can best be elucidated by beginning at its conclusion, at the almost unbearable closing picture of Bazarov's aged parents kneeling and weeping at his grave. Waste, futility, and anguish are overwhelming, but then comes a dramatic reversal, and the novel ends with a declaration of hope:

> Can it be that their prayers, their tears, will be fruitless? Can it be that love, sacred, dedicated love will not be all-powerful? Oh no! However passionate, guilty, rebellious the heart concealed in the grave, the flowers growing over it gaze at us serenely with their innocent eyes: not only of eternal peace do they speak to us, of that great peace of "indifferent" nature; they speak also of eternal reconciliation and of life without end. . . .   [chap. 28]

This passage is remarkable, almost incomprehensible as a conclusion to all that has gone before it in the novel; the incongruity has been described best by Wellek: "Turgenev puts here 'indifferent nature' in quotation marks, but as early as in *A Sportsman's Sketches* (*Zapiski okhotnika*) he had said: 'From the depths of the age-old forests, from the everlasting bosom of waters the same voice is heard: "You are no concern of mine," says Nature to Man.'" And he adds, with reference to *Fathers and Sons*: "There is no personal immortality, no God who cares for man; nature is even a disease beyond reason—this seems the message Turgenev wants to convey."[6] The contradictory quality of the last sentence of the novel has been noted by many readers, yet Wellek alone has commented on the particular peculiarity of Turgenev's having written "'indifferent' nature" with the adjective in quotation marks, seeming to imply rejection of the idea of nature's indifference, an implication almost insulting to the reader, so opposite is it to the text of *Fathers and Sons* and to the major body of Turgenev's writings over the preceding quarter of a century.

The quotation marks can be read another way, however, as meaning not "so called" or "not really" but denoting—literally—a quotation, in this case a quotation from Pushkin, from the last lines of one of his best-known poems, "Whether I wander along noisy streets" ("Brozhu li Ya vdol ulits shumnykh"):

> And let indifferent nature
> Shine in her eternal beauty.

That Turgenev could have had the poem in mind is not difficult to suppose. For most writers there are other writers whose lines, paragraphs, works, exist as part of their consciousness, touchstones which may only occasionally be specified but whose presence is constant. For Turgenev, Pushkin was such a writer. The last stanza of the poem, indeed, is a major passage in the conclusion of one of Turgenev's most important

early works, "Diary of a Superfluous Man" ("Dnevnik lishnego cheloveka").
Moreover, Pushkin's poetry is an important presence in *Fathers and Sons*:
as a thematic element, as an emotional vector, as an emblem for the existence of beauty.

The significance for the novel of the proposed allusion to "Whether I
wander . . ." emerges only from the entire poem:

Whether I wander along noisy streets,
Or go into a crowded temple,
Or sit among carefree young men,
I give myself up to revery.   4

I say: the years will pass,
And though so many of us are here today,
We shall all reassemble beneath the
Eternal vaults—And for some one   8
Of us the hour is already near.

If I gaze at a solitary oak tree
I think: this patriarch of the forest
Will outlive my transitory age,   12
As it has outlived that of my fathers.

As I caress a sweet little child,
Already I think: farewell!
I yield place to you: 16
It's time for me to decay, for you to flower.

Every day, every season
It's become my habit to accompany with the thought
Of the anniversary of my approaching death   20
Trying to guess what day it will be.

And where will fate send death to me?
In battle? On the road? On the sea?
Or will a near-by valley   24
Receive my cold ashes?

And although to my lifeless body
It can make no difference where it will molder,
Still I would wish to rest   28
Close to a dear familiar place.

And at the entrance to my tomb
Let there be young life at play.
And let indifferent nature   32
Shine in her eternal beauty.[7]

Pushkin's poem is about death and about the poet's morbidly haunted awareness of the random uncertainty of the time when it will come and the utter certainty of its coming. What we find in *Fathers and Sons*, I suggest, is the onset of Pushkin's malady in Bazarov, as a direct consequence of his love for Odintsova. Once this love has infected him, he becomes haunted by the knowledge of his own mortality. It has always been recognized that Bazarov's love crippled him, although some readers see Odintsova's rejection as the decisive event. I am proposing here that the effect of love on Bazarov was not some sort of general demoralization coming from a recognition that his nature does not correspond with his ideology, but a specific effect, the one I have called Pushkin's malady: an obsession with the knowledge of his own mortality.[8]

Throughout the first fourteen chapters of the novel Bazarov is a triumphant expression of the life-force, a man exuberantly intelligent and supremely self-confident, caring for no one's good opinion but his own. He is liked by the peasants, works assiduously, takes pride in being Russian, exhibits a zest for life in a variety of ways: his pleasure in Fenichka's "splendid" baby, his eagerness for a visit to town, his appreciation of pretty women. His serious concerns are positive. He scorns upbringing or the "age we live in" as excuses for weakness: "As for our times—why should I depend on that? Let my times depend on me" (chap. 7).

In chapter 15 the crucial transition occurs. When Bazarov and Arkadi first call on Odintsova, Arkadi sees that "contrary to his habit Bazarov was talking a good deal and obviously trying to interest" Odintsova. Then, as they leave, when Odintsova expresses the polite hope that they may visit her estate: "Bazarov only bowed and—a last surprise for Arkadi; he noticed that his friend was blushing." Shortly after, when Arkadi comments on Odintsova's beauty, Bazarov agrees: "A splendid body! Perfect for the dissection table." And three days later, as the friends are driving to Odintsova's estate: "'Congratulate me,' Bazarov suddenly exclaimed, 'today is June 22nd, my guardian angel's day. Well, we'll see how he'll take care of me.'"

What has happened here? Bazarov has called on his "guardian angel"; whether he realizes it or not he is aware for the first time of his vulnerability to death; he is subconsciously asking Pushkin's question: "Is the hour already near?" He will continue to ask the question until he dies, and his preoccupation, usually just below the surface though sometimes bursting forth in bitter outrage, will be expressed in the imagery of disease or death, which first enters his consciousness and conversation in the moment we have witnessed: "A splendid body! Perfect for the dissection table."

In chapter 16 he illustrates a nonmedical argument to Odintsova by an analogy with "the lungs of a consumptive." In chapter 17, when he has acknowledged his passion to himself, this love "tortured and possessed him," for he regarded such feelings "as something like deformity or disease." In chapter 18, when Odintsova asks whether happiness exists, Bazarov can answer only: "You know the proverb: it's always better where we don't exist." A little later, when she tries to question him about his plans and ambitions, he answers ominously: "What's the point of talking or thinking about the future, which for the most part doesn't depend on us?"

Immediately after this exchange come Bazarov's declaration of his love and Odintsova's refusal. Now the images of disease increase: in Bazarov's speech there is a movement from the sense of vulnerability to that of fatality. Moreover, new motifs appear: insecure megalomania supersedes self-confidence, hostility to Arkadi replaces condescending but genuine friendship. In chapter 19 he agrees to Arkadi's accusation of elitism: "'Is it that *you're* a god while I'm just one of the blockheads?' 'Yes,' Bazarov repeated weightily, 'you're still stupid.'" Besides increasing in number, Bazarov's images of disease and death are now applied to himself: "The machine's become unstuck." Then, still in chapter 19, Bazarov articulates the first unequivocal statement of his intimation: "Every man hangs on a thread; the abyss can open up beneath him at any moment. . . ."

Soon after, his preoccupation with his "approaching . . . anniversary" breaks forth more explicitly:

> "I think, here I am, lying under a haystack . . . the tiny, cramped spot I occupy is so minute in comparison with the rest of the universe, where I don't exist and where I don't matter; and the space of time allotted for me to live in is a mere moment in that eternity of time where I was not and will not be. . . . And in this atom, in this mathematical dot, the blood circulates, the brain works, there's even a desire for something. . . . How outrageous it is! How petty!"   [chap. 21]

Bazarov now gives way to impotent fury, vindictiveness, malice:

> "Ha! There's a fine fellow of an ant, dragging off a half-dead fly. Take her, brother, take her. It doesn't matter that she resists, make use of her as you will."

When Bazarov lauds hatred, "How strange!" Arkadi observes, "why I don't hate anyone." "And I hate so many," Bazarov replies:

> "Hatred! Well, for example take yesterday—as we were passing our bailiff, Phillip's cottage—and you said that Russia will attain perfection when every

last muzhik has such a place to live, and that every one of us ought to work
to bring that about. . . . And I felt such a hatred for your every last muzhik.
. . . Yes, he'll be living in a white cottage, while the nettles are growing out of
me. . . ."

"Ah, Arkadi, do me a favor, let's have a fight, a real fight, till we're laid out
in our coffins, till we destroy each other."

This attack on Arkadi has been triggered by his comment on a dead leaf
falling to earth, fluttering like a butterfly: "Gloom and death," he remarks,
"and at the same time gaiety and life!" What seems to enrage Bazarov is
that Arkadi can accept the unity of life and death, can see death as a part
of life rather than as its negation.

Bazarov's bravery during the duel with Pavel Kirsanov only under-
lines the depth and inner intensity of his preoccupation with death. It is
not the concrete incident in which his life is endangered which obsesses
the death-haunted man; it is the subliminal question, when and where,
which accompanies him whether wandering noisy streets or lounging
beneath a haystack.

After his departure from the Kirsanovs Bazarov pays a brief visit to
Odintsova; once again the imagery of death is related to himself. When
Odintsova tells him that he is a "good man," he replies: "That's the same
as laying a wreath of flowers on the head of a corpse" (chap. 26). Is there
also a presentiment of fatality in Bazarov's parting words to her? When
she tells him she is sure they will meet again (as of course they do, at
Bazarov's deathbed), he answers: "In this world, anything may happen!"
Such an interpretation of his words is prepared by the grim pun with
which he has just before informed Arkadi that he is stopping by at Odintsova's on his way home: "Well, so I've set off 'to the fathers.'" As Matlaw
points out, Bazarov here "mockingly (and ominously) recalls the '*ad pa-
tres*' used by Bazarov's father earlier [in chap. 20] as an expression for
death."

Bazarov goes home for six weeks to settle down to work. Are the leth-
argy and melancholy that soon overtake him further evidence of his morbid preoccupation? It hardly matters. Soon, whether by accident or suicide, he *is* dying and, as when he faced death in the duel, his behavior is
calm and courageous. The fear has dissolved, once it has become recognized reality. On one occasion he does rebel: he takes hold of a heavy
table and manages to swing it around: "'Strength, real strength,' he mur-
mured. 'It's all still here, and yet I must die! . . . Well, go and try to refute
death. She'll refute you, and that's that!'" (chap. 27). Bazarov is no longer
haunted by wondering: the question of the date of the "approaching . . .

anniversary" has been answered and we have come to the scene of Bazarov's grave, to the grieving parents, to Turgenev's assertion that the
flowers speak of eternal reconciliation and not just of " 'indifferent' nature," and so back to Pushkin's poem.

The poet is haunted by the question of when death will come and
then proceeds to a corollary question; *where* will it come? But this question is not obsessive; rather it provides a transition to the one consideration which can make the question of "when" bearable, for it allows him to
imagine the grave in which—since there must be one—he would choose
to lie. He has spoken of "moldering" or "decaying," but now he writes of
"the place where I shall rest." It is, he hopes, a nearby valley, radiant with
the beauty of "indifferent nature" but also alive with "young life at play."
Death is bearable because life goes on. Pushkin has prepared this final
statement in stanza 4: "As I caress a sweet little child." He speaks, moreover, of the continuity of generations not only for the future but from the
past; in stanza 3 he writes of the oak tree which will outlive his age as it
has outlived those of his fathers. (The force of the juxtaposition is vitiated
in translation; in the original, "fathers" is the last word of stanza 3 and
"child" is the first word of stanza 4.)

Once again the poem sheds light on *Fathers and Sons*. At Bazarov's
grave are only his aged parents, grieving for the worst thing that can happen to parents, for the most unnatural pain which Nature can inflict, to
outlive one's own child. Despite the birds and flowers and young pine
trees there is no "young life at play;" Bazarov has been denied the single
solace Pushkin offers to the man beset by the knowledge of his own mortality. This solace not only sheds light on the novel's closing scene but
also states its second, inextricably related theme: love and continuity between generations.

Sharp conflict in the novel there is, but it is not between fathers and
sons: it is between two men who dislike each other because they are fundamentally so much alike, Pavel Kirsanov and Bazarov. Were they contemporaries they might find different things to quarrel and duel over, but
quarrel and duel they would. The father–son and son–father relationships are, on the other hand, respectful, affectionate, and deeply loving,
despite the faint note of menace at the very outset, on the ride home after
Arkadi's father has met him and Bazarov at the station. Arkadi and his
father, riding together in the carriage, are renewing their acquaintance
with affectionate sympathy when Bazarov, from the other coach, interrupts to give Arkadi a cigar. Arkadi lights the cigar, and it emits "such a
strong and sour smell of stale tobacco that Nikolai Petrovich . . . could not

avoid averting his face, though he did so stealthily so as not to offend his son" (chap. 3). But the threat of estrangement dissipates; it is never more substantial than cigar smoke in the breeze.

Arkadi's father defers to him on occasion after occasion and tries hard to adopt his attitudes and opinions. When he cannot, it is himself he considers inferior, as, when musing in the garden, he reflects:

> "My brother says that we are right, and putting aside any element of vanity, it does seem to me that they are farther from the truth than we are, but at the same time I feel that behind them there is something that we don't possess, a kind of superiority over us. . . . Is it youth? No, it's not just youth. That's not the source of their superiority; isn't it that in them there are fewer traces of the slave owner than in us?" [chap. 11]

At the end of this remarkable scene Kirsanov is called by Fenichka, and he answers her more offhandedly than he would a woman of his own class: "I'm coming—run along!" And yet throughout the novel, although she is the housekeeper's daughter, both Nikolai and his brother treat her with perfect courtesy: Pavel Kirsanov, for example, always addresses her formally. It is only Bazarov who, having no right to do so, uses the familiar form of her name. And it is only Bazarov who flirts with her as with a servant girl, who behaves as he does not and would not behave with Odintsova. It is only Bazarov, in fact, who displays "the slave owner's mentality."

Bazarov's mother beatifically adores him, while his father does not merely defer to his son's views, he suppresses some of his own deepest feelings. The love of the fathers for the sons, however, hardly needs demonstration; instances can be found in every scene in which they appear together. The interpretation of the novel as a depiction of the conflict of generations rests rather on the attitudes of the sons toward the fathers. Where are these conflicts to be found? In a few moments of condescension or irritation or even unkindness by the sons, in Nikolai Kirsanov's hour of melancholy in the garden, in the disappointment of Bazarov's parents that his visit is so short. One can apply the term *conflict* to such moments only under the assumption that gentle condescension, slight irritation, unkindness, sorrow, and disappointment are not normal components of all human relations, under the assumption that we are living on the planet of Dostoevsky's Ridiculous Man before he visited it.

From the outset Arkadi is glad to be hugged and kissed by his father and hugs and kisses him in return, calling him "daddy" (*papasha*); even Bazarov's presence is only faintly inhibiting. The one feeling Arkadi has toward his father that could be called critical is that of condescension; it occurs on three occasions. First, when Arkadi, smiling "affectionately," tells him that his shame at his relationship with Fenichka is "nonsense" . . . "and his heart was filled with a feeling of condescending tenderness toward his good and soft-hearted father, combined with a sense of a certain secret superiority" (chap. 3). Second, when he displays conscious magnanimity in paying a formal call on Fenichka. Third, when Arkadi agrees to give his father *Kraft und Stoff* to read, approving this choice because it is a "popularization" (chap. 10). Not only does Arkadi never once manifest hostility or irritation toward his father, there is even no friction between them. On the three occasions when he condescends to him he does so tenderly, with affectionate respect, with embraces, with loving compassion and gentleness.

Perhaps even more significant is Arkadi's behavior to his uncle. Their mutual affection is open, and for a man of Pavel Petrovich's deep reserve, even demonstrative. When Pavel criticizes Bazarov (and on this occasion unjustly) Arkadi's response is the one with which we are acquainted—a silent look of compassion for his uncle's noncomprehension. When Bazarov criticizes Pavel (both wittily and aptly) Arkadi attempts a weak rejoinder, then deflects the attack: "Maybe so, only truly, he's a fine, good person" (chap. 4). Most important is that, despite his imitation of Bazarov's opinions, awe of his powers, and fear of his disapproval, despite, in short, Arkadi's schoolboy crush on Bazarov, he never wavers in his defense of his uncle.

Bazarov can be brusque to his parents but never treats them with the rudeness with which he treats everyone else. He submits to their repeated embraces ("Just let me hug you once more, Yenyushechka"), and he willingly kisses his mother (chap. 20). He is perfectly good-humored about having the priest to dinner, understanding what this means to his mother and father. When he decides to leave—abruptly and even cruelly after a visit home of only three days—part of his motivation is, in fact, love for his parents:

> "While I'm here, my father keeps assuring me: 'My study is all yours; no one will bother you there'; and he can't keep a foot away from me. And it makes me feel guilty to shut myself away from him. And it's the same with mother. I hear through the wall how she's sighing—and so I go out to her—and then I have nothing to say to her."   [chap. 21]

Though he tells himself, "never mind, they will get over it," all the same it takes Bazarov a whole day to bring himself to inform his parents that he is leaving, and having gone: "Bazarov was not altogether satisfied with himself" (chap. 22). At the one place in the novel where he exposes his inner feelings with ruthless honesty, the scene beneath the haystack, there is the following solemn exchange:

"Do you love them, Yevgeni?"
"I love them, Arkadi."

The supreme expression of Bazarov's love for his parents comes with his ultimate sacrifice for their sake. He is willing to receive extreme unction, though "at the sight of the priest in his robes, of the smoking censer and the candles before the icon something like a shudder of horror passed for a moment over the death-stricken face" (chap. 27). This is for him a final negation of all that his life has meant to him.

May it not even be said that Bazarov, who loves his parents and understands their love for him, has intimations not only of his mortality but also of the despair that will surround his grave, where there will be no "young life at play"? Consider his final parting with Arkadi:

"There is, Arkadi, there is something else I want to say, only I won't say it because it's romanticism—and that means soggy sentiments. You get married, as soon as you can, and you build your nest, and you have lots of children. . . ." [chap. 26]

I began with the thesis that *Fathers and Sons* is a novel with two entwined themes: "man's deliverance to fate and chance" and the love between generations, the continuity of generations as man's only consolation for the knowledge of his inevitable mortality. The political details of the debate between the men of the forties and the men of the sixties, I suggested, were only the temporal, particular setting for Turgenev's eternal and universal theme. Yet the implications of this theme are profoundly political, for the good pragmatic reason that it is the continuity of generations which is probably the most counterrevolutionary force in the world. On some level of consciousness, I would suggest, the real import of *Fathers and Sons* was sensed by Chernyshevsky when he set out to reply to Turgenev in his novel *What Is to Be Done? (Chto delat?)*[9] Doubtless there were other contributing factors: his desire to present his social theories in popularized form, his belief that Turgenev had slandered the radicals by portraying Bazarov in an alien environment, his conviction that Bazarov was a deliberate caricature of his recently deceased comrade, Dobrolyubov. Chernyshevsky's novel was indeed a successful manifesto; it recruited countless thousands into the radical movement and led Lenin (who is known to have read it at least five times) to declare, "[it] profoundly transformed me" and "created hundreds of revolutionaries." [10] It played this role not only because of its idyllic prophecies but because of its reply to the affirmation in *Fathers and Sons* of love and continuity between generations.

What, after all, is the usual experience of youthful political idealists? They rebel against their parents and against Society, which they seek to remake, often with a partner. Time passes, children are born to them, and their concern for the future becomes personalized, for it is hard—and abstractly inhuman—to pit one's own child's welfare against humanity's, and these are not always in self-evident accord. Having children of one's own has a further effect, that of placing the young rebels in the role of parents themselves. Other factors enter in: compromises of principle come to be accepted as expansion of experience, as recognition of life's ambiguities; more specifically, those who have created life and come to love what they have created are less willing to contemplate its destruction in the name of some abstract goal.

Chernyshevsky understood this process well; moreover, he knew from his own experience in the radical movement that rebellion against parents (and their surrogate, Society) was in fact a primary factor in many young revolutionaries' act of commitment. Given the widespread phenomenon, in Russia at that time, of youthful departure from parents' homes and ways for progressive activity, it is not difficult to suppose that Chernyshevsky's anger at *Fathers and Sons* was at least partially fueled by Turgenev's portrayal of these relationships as loving and positive. In *What Is to Be Done?* he provides in answer an effective presentation of life which fixes and crystallizes youthful rebellion, a program which substitutes for love between the generations a whole other world of affections and loyalties among peers.

This vision of a future with no bothersome babies or bothersome old folks, of a way of life in which revolutionary commitment can escape transformation into generational continuity reaches its apogee in Vera Pavlovna's "Fourth Dream" in the description of man's life in the Crystal Palace, where all social problems have been rationally solved, where there is prosperity and pleasure for all: "Everywhere there are men and women, old, young, and children all together. *But mostly young people: there are few old men, even fewer old women, there are more children than old men, but still not very many"* [11] (italics added). It is significant, I think, that when Dostoevsky sat down to answer *What Is to Be Done?* in

Notes from Underground (*Zapiski iz podpolia*) (begun as a review of the novel), he ended:

> We even find it a burden to be men—men with *our own* real flesh and blood; we are ashamed of it, we consider it a disgrace and strive to be some sort of imaginary men-in-general. We are still-born and indeed not for many years have we been conceived by living fathers, and this pleases us more and more. . . . Soon we shall contrive somehow to be born of an idea.[12]

We know that Dostoevsky admired *Fathers and Sons*, at least that he wrote to Turgenev about it in terms of appreciation which Turgenev said "made me throw up my hands in amazement—and pleasure."[13] We do not know what Dostoevsky wrote about the novel; we can be sure that he would not have been impressed by the notion of conflict between the men of the forties and the men of the sixties because he argued explicitly, in the first two chapters of *Notes from Underground* and throughout *The Possessed* (*Besy*), that the men of the sixties are not the opponents but the direct descendants, the necessary offspring of the men of the forties.

Many speculations are possible, but it seems to me likely that Dostoevsky, the great poet of the "living life," would surely have responded to Turgenev's portrayal of Bazarov the nihilist as a man doomed by his preoccupation with death. And it seems even more likely that Dostoevsky, author of the magnificent birth scene in *The Possessed* and of the unforgettable burial scene in *The Brothers Karamazov* (*Bratia Karamazovy*), understood Turgenev's affirmation of the reconciliation and continuity of generations, his affirmation of "young life at play" as that which makes bearable the inevitability of the grave.

NOTES

1. D. S. Mirsky, *A History of Russian Literature: From Its Beginnings to 1900*, ed. Francis K. Whitfield (New York: Alfred A. Knopf, 1958), p. 203.

2. Quotations are from I. S. Turgenev, *Polnoe sobranie sochineny i pisem* (*Complete Collected Works and Letters*), 8:193–402. The best English translation, which I have sometimes followed, is by Ralph E. Matlaw (New York: W. W. Norton, 1966). Several studies cited in this essay are included in Matlaw's valuable critical apparatus.

3. Isaiah Berlin, *Fathers and Children* (Oxford: Clarendon, 1972), p. 25.

4. René Wellek, "Realism and Naturalism: Turgenev, *Fathers and Sons*," in *World Masterpieces*, vol. 2, ed. Maynard Mack (New York: W. W. Norton, 1956), p. 502.

5. I consider a literal translation of the Russian title to be significant and to have a bearing on my argument, but I will continue to use the generally accepted translation for convenience.

6. Wellek, "Realism and Naturalism." I think the pronouncement of Potugin, in Turgenev's *Smoke*, best expresses the author's essential message: "Man is weak, woman is strong, chance is all-powerful. . . ." And in Turgenev's writing, all-powerful indifferent chance is represented again and again, through imagery or fact, as nature.

7. Translated from A. S. Pushkin, "Brozhu li Ya vdol ulits shumnykh," *Polnoe sobranie sochineny v desyati tomakh (Complete Collected Works in Ten Volumes)* (Moscow-Leningrad: Akademia Nauk, 1949), 3:133–34. R. D. B. Thomson has pointed out to me that in the notes to the Russian text of *Fathers and Sons*, A. I. Batyuto mentions that, "'indifferent' nature" is a "concealed citation" from this poem of Pushkin. No commentary is, however, offered. I. S. Turgenev, *Polnoe sobranie sochineny*, 8:621, note to p. 402.

8. Hjalmar Boyeson records Turgenev as saying (originally in *The Galaxy* 17 (1874): 456–66): "I was once out for a walk and thinking about death. . . . Immediately there rose before me the picture of a dying man. This was Bazarov. The scene produced a strong impression on me and as a consequence the other characters and the action began to take form in my mind." Quoted from the Russian in "K biografii I. S. Turgeneva," *Minuvshie gody* 8 (1908): 70, in Richard Freeborn, *Turgenev, The Novelist's Novelist* (Glasgow: Oxford University Press, 1960), p. 69.

9. N. G. Chernyshevsky, *Chto delat?* (Leningrad: Khudozhestvennaya literatura, 1967). The English translation by Benjamin R. Tucker is both inaccurate and incomplete.

10. Nikolai Valentinov (N. V. Volsky), *Encounters with Lenin*, trans. Paul Rosta and Brian Pearce (London: Oxford University Press, 1968), p. 73.

11. N. G. Chernyshevsky, "Excerpts from *What Is to Be Done?*," in *Notes from Underground and the Grand Inquisitor*, ed. Ralph E. Matlaw (New York: E. P. Dutton, 1960), p. 169.

12. Ibid., p. 115.

13. Letters to F. M. Dostoevsky, March 18 (30), 1862. The text may be found in Matlaw, *Notes from Underground*, pp. 182–83. Dostoevsky responded warmly to the work of the philosopher N. F. Fyodorov, *The Philosophy of the Common Task*. Konstantin Mochulsky, Dostoevsky's great biographer, says that according to Fyodorov, "All living sons will direct their forces to a single problem—the resurrection of their dead fathers. 'For the present age,' writes Fyodorov, 'father is the most hateful word and son is the most degrading.'" Konstantin Mochulsky, *Dostoevsky, His Life and Work*, trans. Michael A. Minihan (Princeton: Princeton University Press, 1967), pp. 567–69.

PATRICIA CARDEN

The Recuperative Powers of Memory: Tolstoy's *War and Peace*

The first intimation that *War and Peace* (*Voina i mir*) is on the horizon occurs in a letter Tolstoy writes to his sister-in-law in October 1862: "I am drawn now to leisurely work *de longue haleine*—a novel or something of the sort."[1] By October of the next year work on the novel is under way, and Tolstoy writes confidently to his relative Alexandra Tolstoy, "I have never felt my intellectual and even all my moral forces so free and so ready for work. And I have that work. That work is a novel from the period of the 1810s and 20s, which has occupied me entirely since autumn. . . . I am now a writer with all the powers of my soul and I write and think as I never wrote and thought before."[2] In letters to his friends and acquaintances the phrase "a long novel" recurs, for example, to Borisov, "I spend all my time writing a long novel, which I will finish only if I live a long time."[3] A long breath, a long life, a long novel—these become interchangeable in Tolstoy's thinking in 1862 and 1863.

Finding a task that will sustain and extend his powers is a godsend to Tolstoy. Throughout the year in which he conceives and begins work on *War and Peace* he is troubled by fear of dissolution and mortality. "I thought that I had no strong interests or passions (how not have? why not have?)," he writes in his diary. "I thought that I was getting old and I was dying; I thought that it was terrible that I was not in love. I was horrified at myself because my interests were money and vulgar well-being. That was a periodic sleep. It seems to me that I have awakened."[4] But he returns to his condition of torment and doubt and within months is writing in his diary, "I am horribly dissatisfied with myself. I reel and reel under the load of death and barely feel strength in myself to put a stop to it.

81]

But I don't want death, I want and love immortality. There's no point in choosing. The choice was made long ago. Literature, art, pedagogy and the family."[5] This within days of boasting to Alexandra Tolstoy of his intellectual and moral powers. Escaping the burden of mortality becomes intimately tied up with writing the novel. Thus Tolstoy embarks upon his great meditation upon the powers that sustain life and hold death at bay. He is thirty-five years old and the task will occupy the next seven years of his life.

A novel "de longue haleine" "from the epoch of the 1810s and 20s" implies a sustained retrospective movement. It will of necessity be dependent upon the collective operation of memory that forms history. In fact, Tolstoy prepared himself to write the book by gathering up all the histories and memoirs of 1812 that he could lay hands upon. He engaged many people in the task of collecting materials, among them his sister-in-law Elizabeth, whom he instructed to find accounts of the daily life of the epoch.[6] In his use of history and memoirs Tolstoy consistently chose the concrete and anecdotal, preferring memory functioning in its immediacy to the theorizing and organizing faculties of historians.

Memory was also to provide the basic stuff of plot. At the heart of *War and Peace* is the imagined world of the past at Yasnaya Polyana, Tolstoy's family home. He peoples his novel with the members of his family in the two previous generations, beginning with his father and his mother, who figure in the novel under their own names of Maria and Nikolai, and continuing back into the generation of the grandparents. The two principal families of the novel, the Rostovs and the Bolkonskys, transparently recreate the characters and conditions of life of the Tolstoys and Volkonskys, though Tolstoy has preserved his author's license to change much and even to add fictional characters to the families. The two family traditions are swelled out by the girlhood reminiscences of Tolstoy's wife and her sisters and by Tolstoy's own memories of childhood, youth, and military service. Memory, then, operating on many levels, collectively in the retrieved national experience, as family tradition, and in the immediacy of recollected personal experience, was to be the primary instrument for constructing the novel.

Yet memory was more to Tolstoy than the instrument he used to recover his materials. He had steeped himself in the texts of a philosophical tradition from Plato to the German idealists that made memory the keystone to the coherence of reality. At every stage in the constructing of the novel, he turned to a web of assumptions that were the very philosophical ground of his being, as natural to him as breathing. The argument for the primacy of memory, elaborated from Platonic doctrine, may be stated as follows: Memory guarantees the continuity of human experience against the dissolution imposed by temporal flux, which separates our every moment of experience from every other. Through the work of memory we retrieve and make present to ourselves the whole of our experience. Not only is memory capable of binding together that which seems disparate and discontinuous in our earthly lives, not only is it the very basis of our sense of a coherent self, but it provides the most powerful argument for immortality of the soul. Since we seem to hold notions like "immortality of the soul" and "afterlife," where can we have gotten them if not through the operation of memory, for how could we conceive ideas of which we have no previous knowledge? When Western thought has moved toward rationalism, and our sense of a possible immortality has required explanation, memory has been called upon to supply the plausible ground for our expectation that after death we will go on to a higher world. The metaphysical model is based on operations of the mind: if memory can make present to us that which is absent, then cannot we apprehend a higher reality that cannot be made present to the senses? Memory proves to us every day the existence of a reality not evident to the senses.

The doctrine of memory appears explicitly in the text of *War and Peace* in a curious form. Its basic provisions are laid out in a conversation among the young people of the Rostov household during the winter spent in 1811 at Otradnoe, and the exponent is, unlikely as it seems, Natasha.[7] Nikolai, Natasha, and Sonya have gathered casually in the sitting room and begin reminiscing about their shared childhood. Their conversation leads to more abstract, speculative considerations, such as whether we have recollection of past lives and what these past lives might have been. They come at last to discussion of the immortality of the soul.

Natasha begins the colloquy with a question couched in a language strikingly commonplace, wholly devoid of any suggestion of the metaphysical or even the philosophical. "Does it sometimes happen to you . . . that it seems to you that there's nothing more to come—nothing; that everything good has already been? And it's not so much boring, as sad?"[8] Nikolai answers in like manner, confirming that the same feelings have recurred to him (*byvalo*). The confirmation as well as the reiterative form of the verb used by both speakers asserts a norm of human experience. We are alerted to Tolstoy's intention to develop the philosophical point of view directly from shared feeling rather than from abstract argument.

This is the axiomatic ground of the philosophical dialogue that is to follow.[9]

Though the exchange among the young people is at first confined to trivial memories of childhood, when the music master Dimmler approaches them, saying, "How quiet you young people are!" Natasha responds, "Yes, we're philosophizing." Dimmler's appearance on the scene "names" the occasion's tonality. It is "musical," it is "nocturnal" (Mme Rostova asks Dimmler to play a nocturne by Field and as he plays dusk falls, and the silver rays of the moon shine into the sitting room), and, above all, it is "German." It was the Germans who had most exalted music as the expressive language of the soul, in Herder's words "a wonder-music of all the affections, a new magical language of the feelings."[10] The references create a sense of period, reminding Russian readers of the time when their forefathers loved Field, dabbled in German sentimentalism, and read Herder, Schlegel, and Mme de Staël's *De l'Allemagne*. But Tolstoy does not belong to the interior decorator school of novelists, and he means to do more than furnish his scene with the appropriate accessories. Dimmler's appearance ratifies, as it were, the plunge into Platonic thought that the young people's conversation is about to take.

The key ideas of the Platonic doctrine of memory are introduced into the dialogue by Natasha, whose language now becomes more than simple—it is infantile: "You know, I think . . . that when you remember like that, you remember, remember everything, you remember all the way back to what was earlier, before you were on the earth."[11] The essential seriousness of these ideas propounded in a kind of baby talk is made clear by the sudden interest that Dimmler takes in the conversation. "He had approached the young people with a gentle, condescending smile, but now he spoke as quietly and seriously as they." To understand what in Natasha's naive formulation could interest the philosophical Dimmler, we shall have to translate her ideas back into the language of high philosophy, where they have their origins.

That we "remember" things in our current existence because we knew them in past existences is the very soul of Platonic doctrine. In the *Meno*, Socrates points to memory to answer the question, How can we seek for what we are totally ignorant of? As Alexandre Koyré has put it, "Socrates answers the objection by evoking a myth and invoking a fact. The myth of the pre-existence of souls permits us to conceive of knowledge as a reminiscence, and the fact that it is possible to teach a science to someone ignorant of it without actually 'teaching' him, but on the contrary having him discover it for himself, demonstrates that knowledge is actually merely remembering."[12] In other words, "recollection brings back to our minds knowledge that our soul has always possessed in its own right." The doctrine of recollection originates, then, not in the necessity to affirm the immortality of the soul, but as a means for accounting for our ability to know. It figures in the colloquy between Natasha and Nikolai in its extended form, as it was developed by Socrates in the *Phaedo*.[13] As he waits to drink the hemlock, Socrates is concerned to reassure his disciples that his death is not an occasion for mourning. He does so by affirming the continuity of earthly existence with the true reality, the eternal forms. The philosopher of all men should be happiest to die for he has in this earthly existence beheld the Ideas and he can hope to ascend into that realm "where the god resides in order to be divine"— that is, into the realm of pure forms. It is this continuity of the earthly with the divine that Socrates means when he uses the famous phrase, so critical for Tolstoy's own metaphysics, "Death is an awakening."

This body of ideas is the stuff of Natasha's discourse on remembering. The doctrine of recollection is restated in her simple language as, "You remember all the way back to what was earlier, before you were on the earth." Our apprehension of the realm of pure forms through past existence is adumbrated in her childish metaphysics as, "We were angels there some place, and were here, and from that remember everything." And the continuity of the self in immortality is restated as, "Why do I know what I was before? . . . After all the soul is immortal. It must be so if I will always live as I lived in the past, as I lived for a whole eternity."

I mean to argue that the Platonic doctrine of remembering underlies the shape that *War and Peace* took as a novel, but first it would be well to say something about Tolstoy as a thinker. Tolstoy's contemporaries thought him intellectually muddled, though they admired his gifts as an artist. Tolstoy was for the most part a self-taught man, with both the fresh response and the lack of system that that implies. He had a tremendous appetite for ideas and read voraciously in philosophy from Plato to Schopenhauer, yet no one would claim that he is a rigorous thinker. Two of the best critics of Tolstoy's work, Boris Eikhenbaum and Viktor Shklovsky, once quarreled about Tolstoy's merits as a thinker.[14] In his major study *Lev Tolstoy* Eikhenbaum had argued that Tolstoy was considerably influenced by the thought of his day. Shklovsky, in keeping with his predilection for popular culture as the source of new art, argued that Tolstoy had been a man of the middle level of cultural life, not really able to follow the philosophical discussions that had so shaped the intellectual life of the 1860s. Both Eikhenbaum and Shklovsky intuited something fundamental to a full description of Tolstoy as thinker. His reading in philosophy and his immersion in the climate of ideas are among the most important experiences that shape Tolstoy's art. Yet Shklovsky is right to think that there is something peculiar about Tolstoy's relationship to ideas.

Tolstoy as thinker comes into focus only when we understand that he does not belong primarily to the logicians or the analysts among the philosophers. Rather, he belongs to the line of the philosopher-fantasts of whom his idol Rousseau is the prominent example. The philosopher-fantasts are characterized by their resort to revery as well as to logical procedure. Their philosophy is colored by the making of myths and narratives, by the exercise of the literary imagination. Plato was himself a philosopher-fantast and his resort to myths has created a problem for rationalists, who continually find it necessary to reinterpret the Platonic myths into a rationalist framework. The philosopher-fantasts often have an impact more far-reaching and lasting than the philosopher-analysts. Rousseau's work, with its reveries, novel, autobiography, had an impact on the nineteenth century that can hardly be measured. Its influence persists to our day. Tolstoy, like Rousseau, had a generous conception of what philosophy encompassed, and like Rousseau he mingled his philosophizing with fantasizing. Thinking and the creating of narratives were implied in the same gesture of the mind.

Certain interests have made philosophical thinkers find revery a congenial form of mental activity. In particular, problems that have seemed resistant to the application of logic, like the nature of our existence in time, the possibility of immortality, and the content of consciousness, have led naturally to mythmaking. Revery and myth have been the philosophers' instruments for projection of possible better worlds. Perception, time, and memory have been the great questions for the philosopher-fantasts, and it is not surprising that critics are beginning to find Rousseau and Tolstoy close to Proust.[15]

The question remains, Why has Tolstoy chosen to make Natasha the advocate for Platonic doctrine? The answer lies in Tolstoy's acquaintance with several significant deviations from the doctrine incorporated into the tradition in later times. Tolstoy knew the *Phaedo* directly, but Rousseau and the German romantics had reinforced his predisposition to idealism in the Platonic vein.[16] The very passages we are looking at echo a scene in Goethe's *The Sorrows of Young Werther*, a book that Tolstoy had read a number of times in his youth and reacted to ecstatically.[17] Werther, who is falling into despair over his love for Lotte, who is engaged to the estimable Albert, has been invited by the couple to join them in Lotte's garden at sunset. Lotte and Albert come out as the moon rises, and the three friends make their way to a favorite spot, where "the path is darkened by the adjoining shrubbery, until all ends in an enclosure that has a mysterious aura of loneliness." Moved by the beauty of the moonlight, Lotte says, "I never walk in the moonlight, never, without being reminded of my dead. In the moonlight I am always filled with a sense of death and of the hereafter. We live on . . . but, Werther, do we meet again? Shall we recognize each other? What do you feel? What do you believe?" Werther responds, "Lotte, we shall meet again. Here and there . . . we shall meet again." Lotte is drawn to tell the story of her young mother, who on her deathbed entrusted her very young children to her care. Lotte has taken their care as a sacred trust. "'And she had to die in the prime of life,' Lotte continued, 'when her youngest son was not yet six months old. She was not ill for long. She was so calm, so resigned. Only when she saw her children did she feel pain, especially the baby.'"[18] This scene could not have failed to move Tolstoy, whose mother died when he was not yet two. Maria Tolstoy's memory was preserved at Yasnaya Polyana on the same exalted note as Lotte's mother's at Wahlheim. But what concerns us here is the similar constellation of narrative motifs and philosophical questions. In a nocturnal setting a young woman, speaking simply and without reserve, does not hesitate to raise questions about the immortality of the soul that more sophisticated spirits shy away from. (Indeed, Albert gently tries to dissuade her from the topic.) It would seem that Tolstoy, without necessarily consciously imitating Goethe, is drawing upon types that are deeply embedded in his memory.

A more conscious use of his predecessors occurs in Tolstoy's incorporation of Herder's ideas into the colloquy between Natasha and Nikolai. While working on *War and Peace* and reading the periodicals of the early part of the century for background, Tolstoy had come across an exposition of Herder's ideas which renewed his interest in the Platonic doctrine of recollection.[19] The Herderian text penetrates the drafts of *War and Peace* more deeply than it does the final form of the novel, where it figures in three episodes: the one in which Prince Andrei overhears Tushin discussing the immortality of the soul, the scene on the raft in which Pierre attempts to educate Andrei in what Andrei calls his "Herderian ideas," and the scene we are now examining.

In the drafts and in the text of the novel Tolstoy returns repeatedly to Herder's restatement of the idea that memory is the guarantor of immortality and particularly to the phrase reiterated from Plato, "Death is an awakening." But one article of Herder's version struck Tolstoy as comic.

Herder, with his strong biological interests, had tried to give a new turn to the idea of immortality by proposing that we have a specifically biological immortality based on the food chain: each kind devours the beings lower than itself and thereby insures them a continuing immortality in the process of life: "An elephant is the grave of a thousand worms." Though Tolstoy was attracted to the idea of the ladder of beings, in the long run it aroused his scepticism and he finally has his character reject it. The sticking point comes when we try to transfer the neat economy of consumption from those beings lower than us on the ladder to those who might be higher than us: "I don't agree that some kind of higher beings eat us, no."[20] In the exchange between Natasha and Sonya in the music room at Otradnoe, Sonya incorrectly identifies Natasha's belief that one can "remember what happened before one was in the world," as "metempsychosis," and defines it thus: "The Egyptians believed that our souls have lived in animals, and will go back into animals again." Tolstoy is careful to repudiate this deviation and returns to the more purely Platonic doctrine of our continuity with beings higher than ourselves: "'No, I don't believe we ever were in animals," said Natasha, still in a whisper though the music had ceased. "But I am certain that we were angels somewhere *there*, and have been here, and that is why we remember. . . .'"

If Tolstoy rejected the "biological" deviation from Platonic thought, he was more sympathetic to another refinement. Plato had assumed that recollection is a function of the mature man—indeed, it is the function that defines the philosopher. Proclus had changed the locus of our tie with the higher reality by proposing that the child brings into the world visions of an earlier ideal existence which become dimmed by the experiences of earth. Proclus's reinterpretation, filtered into Romantic thought through the Cambridge Platonists, caught writers' imaginations and became a staple of Romantic metaphysics. We are familiar with this doctrine through Wordsworth's "Ode: Intimations of Immortality":

> Our birth is but a sleep and a forgetting:
> The Soul that rises with us, our life's Star,
> Hath had elsewhere its setting,
>   And cometh from afar:
> Not in entire forgetfulness,
> And not in utter nakedness,
> But trailing clouds of glory do we come
> From God, who is our home.[21]

Tolstoy did not have a Coleridge to educate him in Neoplatonic thought, but Karamzin and the *lyubomudry* ("wisdom-lovers") had publicized similar ideas in Russia.²² The doctrine of preexistence had so many conduits through Romantic thought that a writer so susceptible to the rhetoric of sentimentalism as Tolstoy could hardly have escaped knowing it. Proclus's doctrine was ready to hand to bolster the new emphasis on growth and process as the primary principle of being with its attendant emphasis on the child. That philosophical program is everywhere in Tolstoy, determining the shape of his first book, aptly named *Childhood* (*Detstvo*), influencing his theories of pedagogy, and shaping the characters of *War and Peace*.

When Natasha speaks in her infantile language of remembering the world where we were angels before, she represents Proclus's doctrine not only in what she says, but in her person. She is that very child who has come not in entire forgetfulness. The events that she and Nikolai recall from their childhoods have an aura both trivial and fantastical.

> "And do you remember how we rolled hard-boiled eggs in the ballroom and suddenly two old women began spinning round on the carpet? Was that real or not? Do you remember what fun it was?"
>
> "Yes, and do you remember how Papa in his blue overcoat fired a gun in the porch?"

Tolstoy means to affirm that children have a particular power of seizing and remembering the plastic reality of the moment and that the capacity for remembering is a sign of the expressive capacity of the self. Flat Sonya cannot recall much and what she does recall does not awake the poetic feeling experienced by Nikolai and Natasha. The poetry of youthful memories is what Tolstoy means to evoke: "So they went through their memories, smiling with pleasure: not the sad memories of old age, but poetic, youthful ones—those impressions of one's most distant past in which dreams and realities blend—and they laughed with quiet enjoyment." Childhood's poetry naturally carries over into the metaphysical realm, and so, though the rational Dimmler finds eternity hard to comprehend, Natasha explains it with ease: "Why is it difficult to imagine eternity. . . ? It will be now, it will be tomorrow, it will be always, and it was yesterday and the day before yesterday. . . ." Natasha's closeness to the undifferentiated state of nature confers on her the authority to speak about immortality and eternity.

What have we discovered by tracing the roots of Natasha's discourse in the Platonic tradition of thought? If we are merely to name these ideas as Platonic, merely to specify an influence, we have not come very far. Platonism is important for *War and Peace* because it provides Tolstoy with an ideational grid that governs his many choices as novelist in constructing the book. We can see the process at work by turning our attention to the families. Tolstoy conceives not only a wide range of principal characters, each with a carefully delineated core of traits, but also family characters, conceptually unified groups which hold individual characters together within their bounds. Each family has a distinct role to play in the work's moral economy: the Rostovs and Bolkonskys represent alternative versions of the good, the "just" life for Tolstoy, just as the Kuragin–Karagin complex (the near-identity of names is revealing) represents the corrupt life of society.

The key to the Rostovs' place in the novel's scheme lies in the very section we are examining. Volume 2, part 4 of *War and Peace* (book 7 in the Maude translation) is devoted to a picture of Rostov family life at the country estate of Otradnoe. It encompasses the scenes of the wolf hunt, the feasting and dancing in the Russian folk style at the uncle's, and the masking party at Shrovetide with its magical sleighride. As life at Otradnoe unfolds, we are treated to the spectacle of vigorous youth indulging in innocent pleasures, but all within a framework of unity of the generations and of the classes. Old Count Rostov is in harmony with his son Nikolai; the hunting master Daniel is accorded full authority within his own sphere, though he is a serf; the masters and serfs join together in the traditional amusements. This section of the novel is unique in its unity and self-containment (to such an extent that it is the part omitted in "abridged" versions of the novel).

This family idyll is one of the most congenial chords in Tolstoy's imagination. How he dreamed upon the theme of Yasnaya is revealed in a remarkable letter he wrote from the Caucasus in 1852 to his Aunt Tatiana:

> Here is how I imagine the happiness that awaits me in the future. The years pass and I find myself, already no longer young, but not yet old, at Yasnaya. My affairs are in order, I have no worries or problems. You are still living at Yasnaya. You have grown a little older, but you are still active and in good health. Life goes on as before: I work in the morning, but we are together almost all day. After dinner in the evening I read something aloud to you that you won't be bored listening to. Then conversation begins. I tell you about my life in the Caucasus, you recount your recollections of the past, of my father and mother. You tell me the horror tales that we used to listen to with frightened eyes and open mouths. We recall those who were dear to us and are no longer living. You cry and I do, too, but with reconciled tears. We talk of my brothers who come to visit us and of dear Mashenka [Tolstoy's sister], who will visit her beloved Yasnaya with the children for several months every year. We will have no acquaintances. No one will come to bother us

and spread gossip. A beautiful dream, but I allow myself to dream of even more. I am married. My wife is gentle, kind and loving and she loves you as I do. Our children call you "grandmother." You live upstairs in the big house, in that room where grandmother used to live. Everything in the house is the way it was when papa was alive, and we continue to live that life, only changing roles: you will take on the role of grandmother, I the role of papa, though I don't hope ever to deserve it, my wife, that of mama, our children, our role. Mashenka will be in the role of both the aunts, but not unhappy as they were. Even Gasha [Toinette's servant] will be in the place of Praskovia Isaevna [the former housekeeper]. The only thing missing is a person who could replace you in a relationship to the whole family. We won't find such a wonderful loving soul. No, you will not have a replacement. . . . If you made me the Russian emperor, if you offered me Peru, in a word if a fairy god-mother appeared with a magic wand and asked me what I want, I can say in all honesty with hand on heart: Just one thing, to realize my dream.[23]

When he turned to the writing of *War and Peace* and thought to embody the lives of his forefathers in the narrative, the idyll that he had conceived in youth gave him the stylistic key.

Yet the Otradnoe scenes are not entirely idyllic. They are colored by foreboding. The dark and the light are folded into each other like a marble cake, and Tolstoy keeps before us not only the special joys of country life but the impending war, the dissolution of the family's way of life due to the father's mismanagement, the going awry of Natasha's marriage to Andrei, and the mother's despair over her children's choice of mates. The section ends, "In the Rostov home it was not merry."

Natasha's colloquy with Nikolai in the sitting room about memory and immortality has all the beauty of "natural" philosophy arising out of the direct experience of untutored and unspoiled souls. Yet she has fallen into revery as a comfort against the dissatisfaction she feels over Andrei's continued absence and the postponement of their marriage. At the end of the conversation she is asked to sing and does so with feeling, but breaks off in a torrent of unexplained weeping. Nor can the Rostov idyll in the country be long sustained. In the next section the family goes to Moscow, where Natasha will be exposed to the very different amusements of society: shopping for her trousseau, the opera, the reading of Mlle George, and the admiration of Anatoli Kuragin. The two sections clearly compose a counterpoint in the novel's structure.

In the Otradnoe scenes both Tolstoy's analytical and compensatory imaginations are at work. He affirms the value of a self-expression rooted in the moral consciousness and connected to a transcendental reality.

(Indeed, Tolstoy never loses faith in this most basic of his beliefs. In *What Is Art?* (*Chto takoe iskusstvo?*), written toward the end of his life, we find him still struggling to hold self-expression together with moral purpose as natural and reconcilable parts of a true aesthetics.) While his compensatory imagination creates the idyll in which the values can be made manifest, his analytical imagination shows how reality departs from them. Otradnoe is the flawed earthly paradise that nevertheless links us to the true world of innocence and truth, which in Plato's view is retained dimly in our memories and seized again by philosophy, or in the romantic view remains accessible to the innocent consciousness.

Why are the Rostovs the proper inhabitants of the idyllic world of Otradnoe? We shall have to turn once again to the function of memory in the philosophical and literary tradition. When Socrates was confronted with the necessity of showing the continuity between the world of ordinary human perception and the world of the ideal forms, it was to memory that he turned as the guarantor of their joining. But the doctrine of recollection also had implications for the individual self's unity. As the memory reaches backward to recover our knowledge of the higher truth, it also reaches toward the future, toward what we ideally will become. Memory becomes the chief instrument for achieving the unity of consciousness over time, with all the moral resonance that Platonic doctrine gives to that unity. The doctrine of recollection gives a cue to the novelist, whose need for a coherent sense of character, a theory of human action, and a ground of motivation is satisfied by its provisions.

Rousseau was the first of the modern novelists to understand the significance of memory and to test its possibilities. His preoccupation with individual psychology made him acutely aware of the intermittences of character:

> Everything upon earth is in continuous flux. Nothing in it retains a form that is constant and fixed, and our affections, attached to eternal things, necessarily pass and change like the things themselves. Always, ahead of or behind us, they recall the past which no longer exists, or they anticipate a future which often will never come to pass: there is nothing there solid enough for the heart to attach itself to.[24]

The viable self is called into doubt by the flux of experience, raising the question, Is memory powerful enough to withstand the "I's" disparate and contradictory movements? The individual's problem of finding an autonomous self becomes the author's problem. Not only must the author find ways of achieving whole characters in the face of doubt about the unity of the self, he must also overcome the disintegrating effect of the lacunae in the character's experiences which the selectivity of narrative makes inevitable. His task is doubled.

La Nouvelle Héloïse is one of the most complicated novels ever written on the powers of recollection and retrospection.[25] Rousseau realizes the potentiality of the epistolary form to make even experience that is immediately past subject to the organizing and unifying powers of recall. In their letters Julie, St. Preux, and Claire mirror back and forth to each other a finite set of experiences, made infinitely rich by multiple reflection. Not only is recollection the implicit organizing principle of the novel's structure, but Rousseau more directly confronts the problem of memory in the novel's exposition. After the lovers have been separated, Julie affirms to St. Preux the power of memory to overcome the fundamental changes that occur in the self through time: "As long as those pure and delightful moments return to the memory, it is·not possible that thou shouldst cease to love what renders them sweet to thee, that the enchantment of moral beauty shouldst ever be effaced from thy mind." [26] But after Julie has renounced St. Preux to marry the husband chosen by her parents, her faith is called into question. Her wise husband applies what has come to be known as "M. de Wolmar's method" to convince St. Preux that his feeling for Julie is a relic of the past and has no validity in the present.

> It is not Julie de Wolmar with whom he is in love, it is Julie d'Étange. . . . The wife of another is not his mistress; the mother of two children is no longer his former pupil. It is true that she resembles her greatly, and that she often recalls to him the memory of her. He loves her in time past.[27]

M. de Wolmar takes a risky step to test his theory: he invites St. Preux to become the tutor of his children, and he demonstrates his certainty in the outcome by going away and leaving the former lovers tête-à-tête. And indeed his "cure" works. St. Preux acknowledges that the Julie he loved was the Julie of memory and not the "real" Julie of the present. In allowing this outcome, Rousseau establishes the fluid view of character that will dominate romantic literature and persist into realism. Yet if M. de Wolmar successfully proves the power of time over St. Preux's love, he is disproven in the end by Julie's constancy, for Julie confesses on her deathbed that love for St. Preux has persisted in her memory against all attempts to eradicate it. She thus has the power to reconstitute the past in the present and restore the self to wholeness.

Like so much of Rousseau's text, the lesson that memory is the key to the self's wholeness sank deep into Tolstoy's consciousness. Memory not only gives coherence to the characters of Nikolai and Natasha, who are depicted as having a rich shared experience extending far beyond what can actually be conveyed in the novel, it is the key to the Rostovs' unity as a family group. Here Tolstoy returns to his incipient Platonism, envisioning the Rostovs as the novel's link with the remembered past, including, as Natasha's colloquy shows, the past that exists before birth. Nikolai and Natasha's shared memories push us back to the boundary between the earthly life and the realm from which we come (perhaps) trailing clouds of glory. The tie to childhood memory marks the Rostovs' way of being in the world and the life choices they make.

If the Rostovs pick up the thread of life as it flows out of the source, the Bolkonskys are connected to the continuum at its other end, where in death it rejoins eternity. In Prince Nikolai Bolkonsky we see the present disappearing into the maw of history as one generation gives way to another. Upon the approach of death, Prince Nikolai thinks back to his youth at the court of Catherine the Great, recalls his rivalry with the favorite, Potyomkin, and remembers his struggle with Zubov over her coffin about his right to kiss her hand. He occupies himself with composing his memoirs, which are to be given to the emperor upon his death. His recollections lead him to think, "Oh, quicker, quicker! To get back to that time and have done with all the present! Quicker, quicker—and if only they would leave me in peace!"[28] Recollection makes time whole for him, not by joining him to the eternal world of forms, but by reuniting him with the events that gave meaning to his life as a public man. Of all the public men in the novel, only Kutuzov has a claim to greater dignity of person or clearer rectitude in the public sphere. Nevertheless, in Prince Bolkonsky Tolstoy shows us the limitations of even the best public man.

Andrei and Maria, while resembling their father in high-minded devotion to duty, express themselves in modes more characteristic of Tolstoy's Platonism. Andrei comes to be the center of Tolstoy's meditations upon the fluid boundary between life and death. In 1865, when the opening sections of *War and Peace* were just appearing, under the title *1805*, Tolstoy wrote playfully, yet revealingly, to his cousin, who had inquired about Prince Andrei's prototype:

> In the Battle of Austerlitz which is yet to be described, but with which I began the novel, I needed a brilliant young man to die; in the further course of the novel I only needed old Bolkonsky and his daughter; but since it is awkward to write about a character not connected with anything in the novel, I decided to make the brilliant young man the son of old Bolkonsky. Then he

came to interest me, a role was found for him in the further course of the novel, and I took pity on him, only wounding him severely instead of letting him die.[29]

"Brilliant" (*blestyashchy*) is in many ways the key to Andrei's character. In the context of the era it means first of all socially brilliant—belonging to the aristocratic society and acting there with perfect *comme il faut*. Prince Andrei is in fact a persuasive image of aristocratic hauteur and noblesse oblige. He represents the aristocratic ideal in its substantial form in contrast, say, to Hippolyte Kuragin, a fool posing as an arbiter of society, or Boris Drubetskoi, a phoney and an *arriviste*. But Tolstoy does not mean to assert a St. Simonian sense of grandeur: his elevation of Andrei is in the mode of the metaphysical dandy, whose social impeccability becomes the outward sign of his inner spiritual grace. In Russian as in English "brilliant" points finally to the scintillation that makes the hero the "shining one." It prepares us for Andrei's turn to the light.

It is not surprising, then, that Tolstoy's merciful reprieve turns out to be temporary. Perhaps the most critical moment for the development of the novel came late in its writing, when Tolstoy discovered that indeed he was going to let Prince Andrei die. A sizeable portion of the novel had been set in type. Tolstoy was working on the concluding parts within the framework of his original design: all the principal characters would survive. Prince Andrei would be reconciled with Natasha, who would nurse him during his convalescence from the wound incurred at Borodino, but upon learning of Pierre's love for her, he would step aside in favor of his friend. His abdication would prepare the denouement that Tolstoy had intended from the start: Pierre would wed Natasha, Nikolai—Maria. The heroes would be reunited at Kutuzov's farewell to the troops. Indeed, "all's well that ends well," as Tolstoy had it in his projected title.

Still, Andrei's stepping aside was a weak move in the plot, and Tolstoy returned to it to find a more plausible solution. The solution rose to him out of the web of connections already preexisting in his understanding of Andrei as a character: Prince Andrei would die. No scene in *War and Peace* more "stands for" the novel in the reader's consciousness than that of Prince Andrei's delirium in the hut at Mytishchi with its celebrated images of the "hovering fly" and the "edifice of needles" that rises and falls above his face. And yet the manuscript was ready for the printer and no such passages were there. In the first version, Natasha, wearing her nightdress, came to Andrei's bedside to ask his forgiveness. In his softened state he forgave her, as he had forgiven Anatole in the hospital tent. The scene bore the ethical message of Christian love but lacked metaphysical dimension.

The decision to resolve the problem of plot by having Andrei die set in motion a tremulous structure of associations connecting the concept of memory to death and immortality. Since memory is not only the power of recall, but also the link between reality and the higher world, it is the philosopher's instrument in the quest to reach the ideal forms. So thought Plato. Using the Platonic doctrine as his key, Tolstoy now returned to the printer's copy of the manuscript and added the passages describing Andrei's delirium in its margins. He followed through with the scenes at Yaroslavl where Andrei engages in "the last spiritual struggle between life and death, in which death gained the victory." He wrote with such sureness of purpose that the scenes were published in their first versions almost without corrections.[30]

Prince Andrei's visions as he approaches death return the novel decisively to its Platonic core: death is an awakening in which the philosopher's lofty search for truth will be rewarded by his becoming one with the eternal ideas. Seen in this light much in Andrei's character becomes newly intelligible to us. His austerity can be seen as an intimation of that philosophical asceticism that Socrates enjoins upon those who would seek truth. His estrangement from earthly life, which frightened the life-loving Rostovs when Natasha became engaged to him, intensifies in his last days:

> He was conscious of an aloofness from everything earthly and a strange and joyous lightness of existence. Without haste or agitation he awaited what was coming. That inexorable, eternal, distant, and unknown—the presence of which he had felt continually all his life—was now near to him and, by the strange lightness he experienced, almost comprehensible and palpable. . . .[31]

It is significant that childhood memory is almost totally suppressed in the Bolkonskys in spite of their strong family feeling. The one moment of shared memory between Maria and Andrei is mentioned to negate it: "[Maria] smiled, pronouncing the word 'Andryusha.' Clearly, she herself found it strange to think that this severe, handsome man was that same Andryusha, the thin, mischievous boy, the companion of her childhood." The Bolkonskys put childhood behind them to advance toward the reality of the pure forms. Theirs is the forward projection of consciousness—not memory but vision. They turn from watching the shadows on the wall and look into the light.

Socrates has set out with complete clarity the conditions for knowing the pure reality:

> [I]f ever we are going to obtain pure knowledge, we must get away from the body, and with the soul itself see things themselves. And then it would seem, we shall have that which we desire, that which we say we are in love with, wisdom; we shall have it when we are departed, so signifies the argument, and not while we are living; for if it is impossible to have pure knowledge of anything whatsoever with the body present, there are two alternatives. Either we never can attain to knowledge, or we can attain it only after death; for then the soul will be alone and by itself, without the body, and before that it will not. . . . [A]nd thus, pure, emancipated from the unreason of the body, it is probable we shall join with beings of like nature, and through ourselves know all the pure reality.[32]

Andrei's getting of wisdom is unfolded for us on three planes. First, the physical process of his disease leads to the weakening of the body's hold on the mind and frees it to seek the true reality. Then the philosophical process through which the mind reaches into the unknown and retrieves reality is adumbrated in a series of aphoristic passages. The physical and mental processes connect with each other in the delirium of Andrei's fever, which is the body's decay but the mind's freedom. Tolstoy makes his most brilliant narrative move on a third level by finding a metaphor appropriate to the exalted nature of the theme: an objective correlative for the pure reality. Socrates' notion of the other reality seems to be that of a convocation of philosophers. Herder sees it mirroring the biological variety of living things. Tolstoy reaches for a metaphor that will convey the otherness that must be native to a reality separated from our own.[33] "Together with the sound of this whispering music, Prince Andrei felt, that over his face, over its very center, there was rising some kind of strange airy structure of thin needles or splinters."[34] The structure of shining rays (*luchina* means a splinter of wood used for light like a candle) is a pulsating structure of truth, the Platonic Idea itself, as yet undifferentiated into its verbal axioms by the process of analysis. Here we need to be reminded once again that memory in the Platonic tradition is something more than recall of the past; it is the function of mind that connects us to the higher reality. In the Mytishchi scene memory as such does not figure, but the threads leading from the doctrine of recollection bind the scene together and furnish forth the truths Andrei arrives at in the weeks before his death. Vinogradov long ago remarked the aphoristic quality of Andrei's thoughts, exemplified in this characteristic passage:

"Love hinders death. Love is life. All, everything that I understand, I understand only because I love. Everything is united by it alone. Love is God, and to die means that I, a particle of love shall return to the general and eternal source."[35] These are verbal crystallizations of bits of the truth condensed out of the seamless perfection of Truth itself. The phrases' laconism reflects that fragmentation, as it reflects truth's weightiness.

It is undoubtedly no accident that when Tolstoy sought a place in his novel for "a brilliant young man who was to die," he attached him to that narrative core devoted to evoking the sainted memory of his dead mother. Princess Maria provides the key to the Bolkonsky family's definition as "those who will die." Though she does not herself die in the course of the narrative, her early death is predicted in the epilogue. The death of his mother was what was given to Tolstoy as fact. What required invigoration by the powers of imagination was the story of her life. But the life must be one in which the meaning of her death is prefigured. A passage late in the novel directs us to the right understanding.

> As suddenly when the internal light is lit there shows forth on the sides of a carved and painted lantern with unexpectedly striking beauty that intricate, skillful, artistic work that had earlier seemed coarse, dark, and senseless, so Princess Maria's face suddenly was transformed. For the first time all that pure spiritual travail through which she had lived up to now appeared on the surface. All her inward labor, that labor of her own self-dissatisfaction, her suffering, her yearning towards the good, her humility, love and self-sacrifice—all that shone now in these radiant eyes, in the delicate smile, in every feature of her tender face.[36]

The comparison of Maria's face to a magic lantern continues the pattern of metaphysical reference that has been worked out in earlier passages of the novel. The imagery links Maria to Andrei's heroic spiritual travail. Tolstoy had introduced the magic lantern into Prince Andrei's vision on the eve of Borodino: "All life appeared to him like magic-lantern pictures at which he had long been gazing by artificial light through a glass. Now he suddenly saw those sadly daubed pictures in clear daylight and without a glass."[37] For Andrei the lantern is an image of the false world of appearances, akin to the flickering shadows on the wall of Plato's cave, and it prepares the way for the renunciation of earthly reality Andrei will achieve on his deathbed. For Maria the perspective has been turned: instead of looking outward to the false pictures cast by the flickering flame, we look inward to the source of light. Maria is thus included among that elect group of characters—Natasha, Andrei, Pierre—to whom Tolstoy vouchsafes visionary experience. She "sees through" to something beyond the world of appearances and even to another life. But it is Maria's destiny as Tolstoy has created her to represent holiness in the lowly way—through the example of her humility and Christian charity. Hers is the holiness of the ethical life based on piety rather than of the questing mystical spirit.

The doctrine of memory serves, then, the compensatory side of Tolstoy's imagination. He holds in his mind the idyll that reality must be judged by. Once it has been called into question, there is need to discover a new equilibrium on which a just universal moral economy can be founded. That desire to compensate, to find a new just equilibrium in which the essential rightness of life will be confirmed, is a powerful stimulus to the writing of *War and Peace*. Tolstoy originally meant to call the novel *All's Well That Ends Well*, and the epilogue brings us to that happy ending in which the right pairs are joined in fruitful unions leading to the continuation of the best potentialities of life. But a confirmation of life resting on a partial view, one excluding the harsher aspects of reality, would be trivial. Tolstoy includes all the evils which prevent us from attaining the ideal forms in this human life: moral corruption, desires of the flesh, cruelty, war, death. Every kind of degradation, every kind of threat, must be overcome if true equilibrium is to be achieved. If we compare *War and Peace* to *Anna Karenina*, we see at once how strong the compensatory imagination is in the first, where anything, even death, can be transformed into a vehicle of happiness or enlightenment. In *Anna Karenina*, on the contrary, reality has infinite capacity to harm. The doctrine of memory is the foundation of the just equilibrium striven for and achieved in *War and Peace*.

NOTES

1. Letter to Ye. A. Bers of October 1, 1862, *Polnoe sobranie sochineny*, vol. 60 (Moscow: GIKhL, 1949), p. 451. (Tolstoy's work will hereafter be cited in this edition as *PSS*.) Tolstoy employs the phrase "k svobodnoi rabote" ("to free work"), but in the context "leisurely" better suits the sense of unrestrained work.

2. Letter to A. A. Tolstoy of October 17, 1863, *PSS*, vol. 61 (1953), p. 23. As he worked on the novel, Tolstoy's interest shifted back to 1805, and he eventually reached the 1820s only in the epilogue, having devoted the novel to the events leading up to 1812 and to 1812 itself.

3. Letter to I. P. Borisov of December 19, 1863, *PSS*, vol. 61, p. 27.

4. *PSS*, vol. 48 (1952), p. 53.

5. *PSS*, vol. 48, p. 57. It is striking that we find Tolstoy toward the end of his life returning to the same words with which he had embarked upon *War and Peace*: "[An idea for a story having come to mind], I began to think about how I would write it, and then began to think how good it would be to write a novel *de longue haleine*, illuminating it with my present view of things. And I thought that I could unite in it all my literary projects, whose incompletion I regret. And I became so happy, so optimistic" (*PSS*, vol. 52 [1952], p. 5).

6. Boris Eikhenbaum, *Lev Tolstoy*, vol. 2 (Moscow-Leningrad: GIKhL, 1931), p. 227.

7. For convenience the reader may refer to the scene as it appears in the Maude translation (Leo Tolstoy, *War and Peace: The Maude Translation, Backgrounds and Sources, Essays in Criticism* [New York: Norton, 1966], pp. 573–76). I have revised the translation of dialogue to convey the greater ellipsis and more colloquial flavor of the Russian text. Russian readers may refer to the text in *Sobranie sochineny v dvadtsati tomakh*, vol. 5 (Moscow: GIKhL, 1962), pp. 306–09.

8. The passage reads in Russian: "Byvaet s toboi . . . chto tebe kazhetsya, chto nichego ne budet—nichego; chto vsyo, chto khorosheye, to bylo? I ne to chto skuchno, a grustno?"

9. My student David Sherman has made an interesting comparison of the forms of the philosophical dialogue as they occur in Plato and in *War and Peace* ("Philosophical Dialogue and Tolstoy's *War and Peace*," *Slavic and East European Journal* 24, no. 1 [Spring 1980]: 14–24).

10. On the German romantics' elevation of music see M. H. Abrams, *The Mirror and the Lamp* (New York: Oxford, 1953), p. 94.

11. In Russian the repetitions and ellipses reduce the language almost to incoherence: "Znaesh, ya dumayu . . . chto kogda etak vspominaesh, vspominaesh, vsyo vspominaesh, do togo dovspominaeshsya, chto pomnish to, chto bylo yeshcho prezhde, chem ya byla na svete."

12. *Discovering Plato*, trans. Leonora Cohen-Rosenfield, Columbia Studies in Philosophy, 9 (New York, 1945), p. 10.

13. Plato, *On the Trial and Death of Socrates*, ed. Lane Cooper (Ithaca: Cornell University Press, 1967).

14. Shklovsky reports the argument in *Podyonshchina* (Leningrad, 1930). An excerpt is reprinted in *Za sorok let* (Moscow, 1965), pp. 111–13.

15. The strong similarities between Rousseau and Proust were remarked by Marcel Raymond in an influential article in *Annales Jean-Jacques Rousseau* 29 (1941–42): 7–57. More recently, Lidia Ginzburg has juxtaposed Proust and Tolstoy the better to bring into relief their individual approaches to consciousness (*O psikhologicheskoi proze* [Moscow, 1977], pp. 368ff).

16. Tolstoy listed the *Phaedo* (in Cousin's translation) among the works that had a great influence upon him between the years 1848 and 1863. (*PSS*, vol. 66 [1953], p. 68). Sergei Averintsev has recently called attention to Tolstoy's preference for the "Hellenic" side of antiquity, remarking that Tolstoy's dislike of the state and suspicion of artistic embellishment predisposed him against Latin antiquity. See "Tolstoi et le monde antique," in *Tolstoi aujourd'hui: Colloque international Tolstoi* (Paris: Institut d'études slaves, 1980), pp. 71–76.

17. During his first serious involvement with literature in February–March 1851, concurrently with his beginning "work on himself," Tolstoy read *The Sorrows of Young Werther* along with Bernardin de Saint-Pierre, Lamartine, and Sterne (*PSS*, vol. 46, pp. 69–76). In the summer and fall of 1856 he read the novel again and wrote in his diary that it was "ravishing" (*PSS*, vol. 47, p. 93). On June 2, 1863, just as the plans for *War and Peace* were forming in Tolstoy's mind, he noted in his diary, "I am reading Goethe and thoughts swarm." This was at the very time he was writing, "I thought that I was growing old and that I was dying" (*PSS*, vol. 48, p. 54).

18. *The Sorrows of Young Werther and Selected Writings*, trans. Catherine Hutter (New York: Signet, 1962), pp. 67–69.

19. The excerpts from Herder, published by Karamzin in his journal *Vestnik Yevropy* on the occasion of Herder's death, were titled "Man Is Created in Expectation of Immortality." They appeared in no. 16 (1804), pp. 71–90.

20. Tolstoy reworked the scenes with Tushin many times, and some variant of Herder's ideas occurs in almost every version. For the most notable occurrences see *PSS*, vol. 13, pp. 367–68, 389–91, and 408–09. Tolstoy's debt to Herder has been competently surveyed by G. V. Krasnov ("Filosofia Gerdera v tvorchestve Tolstogo," in *L. N. Tolstoy*, vol. 4 [vol. 56 of *Uchonye zapiski Gorkovskogo Gosudarstvennogo Universiteta*] [Gorky, 1961], pp. 157–74.) Krasnov also lays out the variants of the scenes involving Tushin to show the evolution of Tolstoy's attitudes toward Herder. The article first appeared in German ("Herder und Lev Tolstoj," *Zeitschrift für Slawistik*, 1961, vol. 3).

21. William Wordsworth, *Selected Poetry and Prose* (Oxford: Oxford University Press, 1964), p. 181.

22. Karamzin is a significant source for Tolstoy's Platonism, as is made clear in an entry in the diary for 19–20 December 1853:

> Reading Karamzin's philosophical preface to the journal *Morning Light*, which he published in 1777 and in which he says that the goal of the journal will lie in love of wisdom, in development of the human mind, will and feeling, directing them to virtue, I was amazed that we could have so lost the understanding of literature's only goal—the moral, that if one were to speak now of the necessity for moral teaching in literature no one would understand one. . . . In *Morning Light* were published discourses on the immortality of soul, on the significance of mankind, Plato, the life of Socrates and so forth. It may be that it went to extremes, but now we've come to worse (*PSS*, vol. 46, pp. 213–14).

23. Letter to T. A. Yergolskaya of January 12, 1852, *PSS*, vol. 59, p. 160.

24. *Les Rêveries du promeneur solitaire*, ed. Henri Roddier (Paris: Garnier Frères, 1960), p. 70.

25. "M. de Wolmar's theory" has become a principal topic of discussion in Rousseau criticism of the last decades, beginning with Étienne Gilson's seminal article, "La Méthode de M. de Wolmar" (*Les idées et les lettres* [Paris, 1955], pp. 275–98).

26. *Julie, ou la Nouvelle Héloïse* (Paris: Garnier Frères, 1960), p. 201.

27. Ibid., p. 492.

28. *Sobranie sochineny v dvadtsati tomakh*, vol. 6, p. 127. See p. 772 in the Maude translation.

29. Letter to L. I. Volkonskaya of May 3, 1865, *PSS*, vol. 61, p. 80.

30. The sequence of work on these scenes was reconstructed from the manuscripts by E. E. Zaidenshnur (*Voina i mir L. N. Tolstogo: Sozdanie velikoi knigi* [Moscow: "Kniga," 1966], pp. 210–13).

31. *Sobranie sochineny v dvadtsati tomakh*, vol. 7, p. 71. See p. 1087 in the Maude translation.

32. Cooper, ed., *On the Trial of Socrates*, p. 122.

33. Taking up where I leave off here, John Weeks, a graduate student at the University of California, Berkeley, has made a brilliant reading of this passage to show how the physiological, sensual reality becomes transformed into metaphysical reality. The paper was read at the national meeting of the American Association for the Advancement of Slavic Studies, September 1981.

34. *Sobranie sochineny v dvadtsati tomakh*, vol. 6, p. 431. See p. 1023 of Maude translation.

35. *Sobranie sochineny v dvadtsati tomakh*, vol. 7, p. 74. See p. 1089 of the Maude translation. V. V. Vinogradov's remark appears in his article, "O yazyke Tolstogo" in *Literaturnoe nasledstvo*, vol. 35–36 (Moscow: Akademia nauk, 1939), p. 188.

36. Ibid., p. 29. See p. 1054 of Maude translation.

37. *Sobranie sochineny v dvadtsati tomakh*, vol. 6, p. 231. See p. 858 of the Maude translation.

ROBIN FEUER MILLER

Dostoevsky and the Tale of Terror

The bees plunder the flowers here and there, but afterward they make of them honey, which is all theirs; it is no longer thyme or marjoram. Even so with the pieces borrowed from others . . .

—Montaigne, "Of the Education of Children"

In the destructive element immerse.

—Stein, in Conrad's *Lord Jim*

In his essay "A Philosophical Enquiry into the Origin of Our Ideas of the Sublime and Beautiful" (1757) Edmund Burke wrote, "Whatever is fitted in any sort to excite the ideas of pain and danger, that is to say, whatever is in any sort terrible, or is conversant about terrible objects, or operates in a manner analogous to terror, is a source of the sublime." Burke rigorously separated the beautiful from the sublime. One fills us with pleasure, the other with delight; the beautiful induces "in us a sense of affection and tenderness," but the sublime "is productive of the strongest emotion which the mind is capable of feeling."[1] Although the Gothic novelists of the late eighteenth and early nineteenth century (such as Horace Walpole, Ann Radcliffe, Matthew Lewis, Charles Maturin) were profoundly influenced by Burke's understanding of the terrible as a necessary part of the sublime,[2] they were not, however, interested in reproducing Burke's entire aesthetic system: they did not attempt to separate the beautiful from the sublime. Instead, they described a world in which the beautiful and the sublime were tightly entangled.

In his fiction Dostoevsky partakes of this Gothic tradition: his themes, plots, and characters all embody the heady mixture of the awful and the beautiful found in the Gothic novels. But Dostoevsky raises the themes

103]

and techniques of the Gothic novelists to new heights, for he forges a metaphysical system out of a language that in the hands of lesser novelists remains merely a style, an effective fictional point of view. The language of the Gothic novel and its themes offered Dostoevsky a powerful rhetoric for describing modern man's predicament.

Such writers as Sue, Soulié, Hugo, Dumas, Sand, Poe, Hoffmann, Balzac, Scott, and Dickens all influenced Dostoevsky's artistic work. But these writers themselves drew on the tradition of the Gothic novel as it developed in the works of Walpole, Radcliffe, Lewis, and Maturin. Dostoevsky too had a firsthand knowledge of these "tales of terror."

In 1861, Dostoevsky had written to Yakov Petrovich Polonsky, "How many times have I dreamed, since my childhood, of visiting Italy. Ever since I read the novels of Radcliffe, which I had already read by the age of eight, various Alfonsos, Catherines and Lucias have been whirling around in my head. I'm still crazy about Don Pedros and Donna Claras. Then came Shakespeare—Verona, Romeo and Juliet—The devil knows what an enchantment they were to me. To Italy, to Italy! But instead of Italy I found myself in The House of the Dead."[3] It is possible that Dostoevsky, who was notoriously forgetful, meant Alphonso d'Alvarada or Alonzo the Brave in Lewis's *The Monk* or the Donna Clara (Immalee's mother) and the Alonzo in Maturin's *Melmoth the Wanderer*. Indeed, as a student in engineering school, Dostoevsky had read to his friends from the works of Maturin.[4]

In 1863, on the first page of his *Winter Notes on Summer Impressions* (*Zimnie zametki o letnikh vpechatleniakh*), Dostoevsky recalled his childhood love for the fiction of Ann Radcliffe, "when, during the long winter evenings, before I could read, I would listen, agape and rooted to the spot with delight and terror, as my parents read, at bedtime, the novels of Radcliffe; I would then rave deliriously about them in my sleep" (V, 46). Dostoevsky had remembered and expressed his earliest response to the Gothic novel in terms of the sublime—a mixture of terror and delight.

Nevertheless, Dostoevsky's explicit references to Radcliffe in his fiction are slight and always ironic. The uncle, Colonel Rostanev, in *A Friend of the Family* (*Selo Stepanchikovo i yego obitateli*) vaguely remembers the existence of monks in Radcliffe's novels (III [1972], 134). In *The Brothers Karamazov* (*Bratia Karamazovy*) Mitya's defense attorney ridicules the prosecutor's idea that the missing money is hidden at Mokroe by asking, "Why not in the dungeons of the castle of Udolpho, gentlemen?" (XV [1976], 158). But even though Dostoevsky had no real use for debauched monks and mysterious castles—the paraphernalia of the Gothic novel—

he learned much from the "fantastic romanticism" of these novelists. In the next pages I shall attempt to link some of Dostoevsky's techniques and themes directly back to this older genre of the Gothic novel rather than to the intervening traditions of the *roman-feuilleton*, the historical romance, and the novels of romantic realism.

Consider Dmitri Karamazov's passionate exclamation to Alyosha, "Beauty is a terrible and awful thing! It is terrible because it is indefinable; and it is impossible to define, for God has set before us nothing but riddles. Here the shores meet; here all contradictions exist side by side. . . . Beauty! The awful thing is that beauty is not only a terrible thing, it is also mysterious. The devil is fighting there with God, and the battlefield is the heart of man" (XIV [1976], 100). Dostoevsky, like Burke, has gone beyond the familiar notion of beauty as harmony to acknowledge the existence of another kind of beauty composed of inherently contradictory elements. Indeed, Mitya's vocabulary for describing beauty precisely matches Burke's words for describing the sublime—"terrible," "awful," "indefinable," "mysterious." Like the Gothic novelists, he makes almost a routine use of passionate, highly colored language—such phrases and words as "I can't bear it," "heart may be on fire," "secret," "the devil is fighting." Yet he has taken Burke's aesthetic observation and the vocabulary of the Gothic novelists one step further: the result is an extreme Manichean vision of man in whom acute, contradictory perceptions of the beautiful and the terrible battle with each other. Thus, although other parts of this famous passage from *The Brothers Karamazov* have definite roots in Schillerian romantic Sturm und Drang, we should not overlook these direct aesthetic and stylistic links to the earlier Gothic tradition.[5]

As one might expect, in the Gothic novel descriptions of beauty and horror often coalesce in the same image: "By the side of three putrid half-corrupted bodies lay the sleeping beauty. . . . She seemed to smile at the images of death around her."[6] Or, "So he lay . . . in a kind of corpse-like beauty. . . . A St. Bartholomew flayed, with his skin hanging about him in graceful drapery—a St. Laurence, broiled on a gridiron, and exhibiting his finely-formed anatomy on its bars . . . even these were inferior to the form half-veiled, half-disclosed by the moonlight as it lay."[7] The final description of Nastasia Filippovna at the end of *The Idiot* invokes, though to a lesser degree, the same responses from the reader. The sight of Nastasia's white foot protruding from the cover, the buzzing fly, and the moonlight emphasize both her deadness and her loveliness; they merge into one image. As Dostoevsky may have learned from the Gothic novelists, the death of a beautiful woman offered a powerful way of holding the reader's attention. Edgar Allan Poe observed in his *Philosophy of Composition* that the "death of a beautiful woman is, unquestionably, the most poetic topic in the world."[8]

The Gothic novelists portrayed images of beauty surrounded by and merged with horror, while Dostoevsky has taken these same ingredients and given them a moral cast: he creates a "mysterious" religious sublimity out of the mixture of good and evil, the beautiful and the ugly. Grushenka says to Alyosha, ". . . though I am bad, I did give away an onion." A few moments later, Alyosha, though still immersed in his feelings of doubt occasioned by Zosima's death, can say gently to Grushenka, "I only gave you an onion, nothing but one very tiny onion, only that . . ." (XIV, 318; 323). In this exchange Grushenka is the real "onion giver" of the two, for merely by telling the tale of the wicked old woman she has given Alyosha an important clue to the solution of the riddle about the significance of goodness and of good deeds with which he is so preoccupied throughout the novel.

Yet their mutual "onion giving" precipitates Alyosha's subsequent ability to accept—to love—the complete blending of beauty and ugliness that nature inevitably presents. He returns to Zosima's body and realizes that the odor of its decay has increased. The narrator observes, "But even this thought of the putrid smell, which had only recently seemed to him so awful and humiliating, now did not arouse in him his former anguish or his former indignation. . . . There was reigning in his soul something whole, firm, and soothing. . . . Suddenly he began to pray ardently; he so longed to give thanks, to love" (XIV, 325). Indeed, as we know, *The Brothers Karamazov* is largely *about* the miraculous power of single acts of good, single beauties, single seeds, amidst a world stocked with evil, ugliness, and seeming death. If the mixture of good and evil, of ugliness and beauty is an axiom in the geometry of the Gothic novel, then Dostoevsky has both expressed the baffling riddle such an axiom poses and has offered a moral and religious solution to it.

Throughout his work Dostoevsky raised to a metaphysical level this Gothic tendency to mix the beautiful with the terrible. For the Gothic novelists it was sufficient to portray the paradox of this mixture. Dostoevsky sought a resolution to the paradox. In *The Idiot* (*Idiot*), for example, Myshkin's doctrine of "double thoughts," a central theme of the novel, expresses man's capacity for simultaneous impulses of good and evil, for strivings toward beauty and toward corruption. Though he is plagued by his own double thoughts, Myshkin urges acceptance of them in himself and in others; he urges that goodness be recognized even when it is surrounded by evil. In *The Brothers Karamazov* Dostoevsky had again merged images of beauty and horror to make a similar philosophical statement. Although Dmitri lamented the presence of the "mysterious" and the "terrible" in beauty, Alyosha learned to accept this dichotomy in beauty and to find, by virtue of this acceptance, a higher kind of harmony. When the elder Zosima died, everyone had expected "something extraordinary" to happen: least of all had they expected an odor to arise from his holy corpse. Alyosha's eventual acceptance of the fact that Zosima's body did not decompose in the expected way expressed his realization that nature itself is sinless and that man should not read his own moral notions into its processes. Alyosha's full acceptance and perception of nature led him to a miraculous experience of sublimity, a sublimity which was, paradoxically, devoid of the terrible.

At this point in the novel Alyosha, who has been standing by Zosima's body, has just experienced a vision of that "sweet miracle" of Cana of Galilee. He walks out of the monk's cell and into the garden. "The vault of heaven, full of soft, shining stars, stretched vast and fathomless above him. The Milky Way ran in two pale streams from the zenith to the horizon. The fresh, motionless, still night enfolded the earth. The white towers and golden domes of the cathedral gleamed out against the sapphire sky. . . . The silence of earth seemed to melt into the silence of the heavens. The mystery of earth was one with the mystery of the stars. . . . Alyosha stood, gazed, and suddenly threw himself down on the earth. He longed to forgive everyone and for everything and to beg forgiveness. Oh, not for himself, but for all men. . . . 'And others are praying for me too,' echoed again in his soul" (XIV, 328). This passage brings to mind a paragraph from *Melmoth the Wanderer* (1820) in which Monçada has also just left the body of a dead monk (unlike Zosima, an evil monk, whose last expression had been a "glare of malignity").

> I rushed from the infirmary. . . . The garden, with its calm moonlight beauty, its innocence of heaven, its theology of stars, was at once a reproach and a consolation to me. I tried to reflect, to feel,—both efforts failed; and perhaps it is in this silence of the soul . . . that we are most ready to hear the voice of God. My imagination suddenly represented to me the august and ample vault above me as a church,—the images of the saints grew dim in my eyes as I gazed on the stars, and even the altar, over which the crucifixion of the Saviour of the world was represented, turned pale to the eye of the soul, as I gazed on the moon "walking in her brightness" I fell on my knees. I knew not to whom I was about to pray, but I never felt so disposed to pray.
>
> [Maturin, p. 90]

The similarities between these two passages are especially intriguing because, clustered around the paragraph from *Melmoth* are other, shorter
fragments which resemble portions of Dostoevsky's fiction. It is as if one
has stumbled on to an extended passage which engendered a particularly heightened response in Dostoevsky.

The possible fallacy of suggesting such associations is outweighed
by the more sobering prospect of ignoring such resemblances completely. Monçada's autobiographical *Tale of the Spaniard* is fraught with
tones that later reverberate through Dostoevsky's work. The sentence,
"The genius of monasticism seemed to wield a two-edged sword" calls to
mind Dostoevsky's idea of "the knife that cuts both ways" (Maturin, p. 87).
There is in *Melmoth* an extended passage analyzing the ecstasy of an ascetic which closes with a reference to Mahomet (Maturin, p. 88). Myshkin
also thinks about Mahomet when he tries to analyze the significance of
the ecstatic aura preceding his epileptic fits. The dying, evil monk in
Melmoth who rejoices at the "opportunity to discharge the concentrated
malignity of sixty years of suffering and hypocrisy" suggests an inverted
Zosima and his joyful last exhortations (Maturin, p. 88). The monk describes "those who, like me, diminish their misery by dividing it, and like
the spider, feel relieved of the poison that swells, and would burst them,
by instilling a drop of it into every insect that toils, agonizes, and perishes
in their net" (Maturin, p. 90). A nearly identical image of the spider recurs
throughout Dostoevsky's work—for example, in *Notes from Underground*
(*Zapiski iz podpolia*), *The Idiot*, and *The Possessed* (*Besy*). Monçada, in
his delirium, alternately imagines that he is responsible for the murder of
his brother and that his dead brother is at his bedside, arranging his pillows for him (Maturin, p. 95). The two phases of Monçada's delirium—
his imagining that he is responsible for the murder of a close relative and
his vision of a completely lifelike apparition—resemble Ivan's delirium
near the end of *The Brothers Karamazov*. (Although it is Mitya who mys-
teriously has pillows arranged under his head just before his visionary
dream of the Babe.)⁹ All of these passages from *Melmoth*, a novel of over
four hundred pages, occur within an eight-page span. This physical fact
seems, in the end, to offer the best argument for establishing the possibility
of influence. Moreover, there are several other sections of *Melmoth* which
yield up similar closely bundled sheaves of Dostoevskian association.

The rise of the Gothic novel or tale of terror paralleled the new value
placed on sensibility—the capacity for refined emotion, the readiness to
feel compassion for suffering and to be moved by the pathetic in literature, art, and life. The heroines of these novels often grew up in relative

isolation and had an unhealthy predilection for things supernatural and sublime. Prince Myshkin partakes of this usually feminine tradition. He, too, like many Gothic heroines, grows up in isolation, and his personality has been shaped by his sensibility, by his immense capacity to respond to art and to life. Dostoevsky planned a similar childhood for the hero of his unfinished novel, *The Life of a Great Sinner* (*Zhitie velikogo greshnika*). (Dostoevsky's plans for the structure of this unfinished novel resemble the structure of *Melmoth*, which is composed of six separate but interlocking tales. These tales are united by the same idea: in each, Melmoth tries to persuade someone who is profoundly miserable to trade his misery for Melmoth's date of damnation. Dostoevsky had planned for his work to be broken into three—later, five—separate tales. Each would deal with the same question—the existence of God.) [10]

Gothic novels all contain, as a main theme, the depiction of an anxiety with no possibility of escape.[11] This hopeless anxiety is expressed by a breaking down of categories, and movement in these novels tends toward a union of opposites very likely distantly related to the seventeenth- and eighteenth-century love of the oxymoron. The pages of these novels are filled with hero-villains, corrupted beauties, the intertwining of the natural and the supernatural, the tragic and the comic, and the breaking of taboos—incest, cannibalism, unnatural marriages. Most have at their center a proposed unnatural marriage: the attempt to force unsuitable unions between characters results in much of the action in these novels. The Gothic novels also railed against the practices of the Catholic church during the Inquisition and against the Jesuits in general; they called for a return to a more primitive, natural Christianity. Notions of an ideal education figure in most of the Gothic novels, either through the depiction of a character whose education misled him or by the depiction of one whose natural sensibility ultimately saved him. Of course, many novelists, from Cervantes to Jane Austen to Dickens, have depicted characters who had to unlearn their educations in order to discover their true moral sensibilities, but the Gothic novelists allow their characters to suffer unspeakable, fantastic misfortunes along the way.

Dostoevsky transposes all these themes into his novels. For example, Valkovsky, Svidrigailov, Rogozhin, and Stavrogin are hero-villains; Nastasia Filippovna and Grushenka are corrupted beauties. The intertwining of the natural and the supernatural occurs in such works as "The Landlady" ("Khozyaika"), "The Dream of a Ridiculous Man" ("Son smeshnogo cheloveka"), "Bobok," and *The Brothers Karamazov*. The mixture of tragedy and comedy, so prevalent in the Gothic novel, pervades all of Dostoevsky's fiction; attempts to force unnatural marriages and the breaking of taboos through relationships tinged with overtones of incest both occur frequently in Dostoevsky's works—witness the relationships between Netochka Nezvanova and her stepfather (in *Netochka Nezvanova*), Varvara and Bykov (in *Poor Folk* [*Bednye lyudi*]), Dunya and Svidrigailov (in *Crime and Punishment* [*Prestuplenie i nakazanie*]), Nastasia and Totsky (in *The Idiot*), Maria Lebyadkina and Stavrogin (in *The Possessed*), or Grushenka and Samsonov or Fyodor Karamazov (in *The Brothers Karamazov*), to name only a few.

The Gothic novelists consciously rejected the neoclassical literature of the eighteenth century and turned back to Shakespeare; they admired the mixture of tragedy and comedy found in the Elizabethan drama in which events appeared differently to princes and to common people. Horace Walpole, in his second preface to *The Castle of Otranto*, the first of the Gothic novels, deliberately chose Shakespeare for his model. "Let me ask if his tragedies . . . would not lose a considerable share of their spirit and wonderful beauties, if the humor of the gravediggers, the fooleries of Polonius, and the clumsy jests of the Roman citizens, were omitted, or vested in heroics?"[12] Lewis's *The Monk* (which is full of Shakespearean allusions and quotations) and Maturin's *Melmoth the Wanderer* contain remarkable contrasts of tragedy and comedy, of a style of heightened terror combined with extreme, even vulgar, comic realism.

In fact, the stereotype of the Gothic novel as a repository of underground labyrinths and craggy castles is undermined for any reader once he actually reads either Lewis or Maturin. Instead, the reader comes away from these works having received a description of a universe in which the real and the supernatural are in a state of competing balance. Earthy comedy and verbal wit can occur side by side with mysterious horrors. One would not readily identify the following passages as coming from Gothic novels, yet they are typical of this form after the early experiments by Walpole and Radcliffe. "For my part, I never saw her [Elvira] do amiss, except on the Friday before her death. To be sure, I was then much scandalized by seeing her eat the wing of a chicken . . ." (Lewis, p. 314). Or, "His conscience, like a state coach horse, had hitherto only been brought out on solemn and pompous occasions, and then paced heavily along a smooth and well-prepared course, under the gorgeous trappings of ceremony;—now it resembled the same animal suddenly bestrid by a fierce and vigorous rider, and urged by a lash and spur along a new and rugged road" (Maturin, p. 334).

Dostoevsky's borrowings from the Gothic novel partook of this comic, realistic aspect as well as of its supernatural, terrifying side. Indeed it is precisely the mixture of the two that is significant. Dostoevsky transferred the blend intact to the world of his novels. Of course, the works of other writers, such as Gogol or Dickens, could have provided Dostoevsky with a model for this mixture of comedy and realism with the supernatural and the terrifying, but the influence of the Gothic novel must be considered along with these other more thoroughly examined sources.

The Gothic novels also consciously hark back to Milton as much as to Shakespeare; Milton's Satan becomes a prototype for the Gothic hero-villain. Edmund Burke had helped to repopularize Milton's Satan by his assertion that nowhere else can one meet "a more sublime description than this justly celebrated one of Milton wherein he gives the portrait of Satan with a dignity so suitable to the subject." [13] The dying Melmoth likens himself to Milton's Satan: "Mine was the great angelic sin—pride and intellectual glorying! It was the first mortal sin—a boundless aspiration after forbidden knowledge" (Maturin, p. 380). The Frankenstein monster exclaims, "Everywhere I see bliss, from which I alone am irrevocably excluded. I was benevolent and good; misery made me a fiend. Make me happy and I shall again be virtuous." [14] These Satanic (Faustian) images find an echo in many of Dostoevsky's hero-villains. Such characters as Ivan and Stavrogin share Satan's tragic grandeur. Ironically, even Myshkin stems partly from this tradition. He too, like Satan (or his Gothic progeny), feels an overwhelming sense of exclusion from the beauty of the universe. His feelings about this exclusion are ambivalent; like Satan he would like to participate in the beautiful festival of the universe; like Christ in the garden at Gethsemane, he would withdraw if possible.

Mario Praz links the Miltonic hero-villain type with another type who frequented the Gothic novel, the fatal hero. "What Manfred said of Astarte ('I loved her and destroy'd her') . . . was to become the motto of the 'fatal' heroes of Romantic literature." This could be Valkovsky's, Rogozhin's, or Stavrogin's motto as well. Melmoth, who qualifies as both hero-villain and fatal hero (types which usually coalesce), remotely foreshadows Rogozhin: Melmoth interrupts a wedding feast, and the terrible effect of his stare ultimately causes the death of the bride and the insanity of the groom. This complex of ideas reverberates through *The Idiot*: Rogozhin's stare persistently haunts Myshkin; his presence on the wedding day of Myshkin and Nastasia Filippovna results in the "bride's" death and the "groom's" madness.

Persecuted maidens and fatal women also inhabit the Gothic novel; Praz even links Nastasia Filippovna to this latter type: "It is a type . . .

which . . . ends by modelling itself on the women of Dostoevsky, among whom Nastasia Filippovna is the most characteristic example."[15] In fact several female Gothic types converge in Nastasia Filippovna: she is both the fatal woman and the persecuted maiden; she is a representative of an overall image of beauty mixed with horror, or of corrupted beauty. Myshkin seeks to save her from a permanent embodiment in any one of these images. Finally, in her is reflected what Praz calls the fascination of a beautiful woman already dead. He associates this fascination with the influence of the vampire legend, a theme occasionally present in the Gothic novel.[16] The recurring intimations in *The Idiot* of the possibility that Rogozhin will slit Nastasia's throat join him remotely to the vampire legend. Nastasia's beautiful, pale corpse disfigured only by a small wound, stretched out on a bed amidst her discarded finery, suggests the body of the maiden ravaged by the vampire.

In his next novel, *The Possessed*, Dostoevsky links, albeit ironically, Stavrogin to the vampire legend. Liza, responding angrily to Stavrogin's seeming concern for her despair, exclaims, "And this is Stavrogin, 'the vampire Stavrogin,' as you are called by a lady here who is in love with you!" (X [1974], 401). (The narrator-chronicler's first full physical description of Stavrogin suggests the qualities of a vampire: his hair, "a little too black" [*chto-to uzh*]; his complexion, "a little too white"; the redness of his cheeks which was "too bright," his "coral lips," and the fact that there was "something repellent" about his beauty [X, 37].)

An example of an extended passage of typically Gothic narration occurs in *The Idiot*; here one entire chapter (II, v), save the last two paragraphs, echoes the tale of terror in its mood of heightened terror and in the extreme use of the technique of arbitrary disclosure by the narrator. Fears merely intimated provoke a greater effect than ones which are fully described. The narrative of this chapter borrows from the more stereotyped half of the Gothic novel: there are no moments of comic realism in this chapter. Myshkin has left Rogozhin's house and is wandering through St. Petersburg in a state of feverish revery. He finds the shop window with the sixty-kopek item in the window (Rogozhin's knife—not named here). Throughout the chapter Myshkin experiences the sensation of Rogozhin's eyes being fixed upon him. In his revery he imagines that "A strange and terrible demon had finally attached itself to him and would no longer let him go. This demon had whispered to him in the Summer Garden . . ." (VII, 193).

A typical narrator in a Gothic novel seeks to interest the reader by any means whatsoever, whether by rendering things mysterious or by describing events in ghastly detail. Here the narrator seeks to create an air of overbearing, all-encompassing mystery in order to heighten Myshkin's premonitions while clouding his rational faculties. The language is deliberately mysterious. "Something" pursues Myshkin, a "demon" has attached itself to him. Myshkin's forebodings, in Gothic fashion, inexorably come to pass, for the scene climaxes with Rogozhin's attempted murder and with Myshkin's epileptic fit. The narrator vacillates between fantasy and reality, although, like Ann Radcliffe's narrator, he offers at the end a rational explanation of the events.

Moreover, the narrator links his character's mood to the current state of the natural world. Myshkin's sense of foreboding and his oncoming fit parallel the approach and arrival of a thunderstorm. As Myshkin returns to his hotel the storm finally breaks. Myshkin catches sight of Rogozhin: "'Now everything will be decided,' he thought to himself with a strange conviction. . . . Those two eyes, *those very ones*, suddenly met his stare" (VIII, 194–95). Then follow the climactic coinciding moments of Rogozhin's attempted murder and Myshkin's fit. Throughout the chapter the stifling weather and his own troubled, overwrought mental condition have had a strange appeal to the prince. This coincidence of weather, plot, and character is a cliché of the Gothic novel. These novels share a concern with nature in its sublime, grandiose, and most compelling manifestations—mountains, storms, winds, raging waterfalls. In the chapter cited from *The Idiot* a similarly portentous, though urban, landscape prevails. The corridors of the hotel become like the gloomy passages in a Gothic castle.

Another striking instance in Dostoevsky's fiction of the coincidence between the weather and plot occurs near the end of *The Possessed*. At dawn after their night together Liza observes to Stavrogin, "It ought to have been light an hour ago by the calendar, and still it's almost like night" (X, 398). When Liza leaves Stavrogin, full of the premonition of her own death, she wanders off into the fog and rain. The faithful Mavriki Nikolaevich witnesses her flight: "He saw the woman for whom he had such reverent devotion running madly across the field." He exclaims, "You will get your feet wet, you . . . will lose your reason" (X, 410). As they walk together toward the fire in the town and toward the mob that will soon murder Liza, the narrator brings all of nature to bear in the depiction of his climactic scene: "A light rain penetrated the whole country, swallowing up every reflection, every nuance of color, and transforming everything into one smoky leaden, indistinguishable mass. It had long been day, yet it seemed as though dawn had not yet broken" (X, 411).

When Liza is finally killed by the crowd, Dostoevsky reshapes the Gothic convention of mob violence toward a guilty villain. In *The Monk, Melmoth the Wanderer*, and *The Wandering Jew* (Eugène Sue) such scenes of murder by a mob occur, and while they are terrible, they at least conform to some notion of "rough justice"—to use Sholokhov's chilling phrase. But Dostoevsky used this Gothic scenario to illustrate the tragic complexity of all that has transpired. The crowd, though justly horrified by the disaster and murder that have occurred, wreaks vengeance upon an innocent woman. The narrator suddenly becomes an observer: he acts as a kind of ballast to the macabre scene. "Petrified with amazement, I first noticed Liza at a distance from me in the crowd . . ." (X, 413). He later testifies about what he has witnessed in a deliberately low-keyed manner. His perhaps too rapid return to the rational world resembles the voice of the narrator in *The Idiot* after Rogozhin's attempted murder of Myshkin and again at the close of the novel.

Wayne Booth has pointed out that a primary concern of any narrator is to balance his technique of bewildering the reader with his use of dramatic irony. The reader's bewilderment spurs his interest in what he's reading, but if it becomes excessive the reader will lose interest altogether.[17] The Marquis de Sade, in his essay *Idée sur les Romans* (1800), perceived this problem in almost the same way and related it to the narrative mode of the Gothic novel in particular. He writes of the "inconveniences" caused by the style of writing used by Ann Radcliffe and Matthew Lewis: "Either of these two alternatives was unavoidable; either one must unfold all the enchantment, and from then on be interesting no longer, or one must never raise the curtain, and there you are in the most frightful unreality."[18]

A narrator's assumption of a mysterious voice and an arbitrary logic to govern what he will reveal and what he will keep secret produces the intended effect upon the reader's interest only if they are used with moderation. The narrator of *The Idiot* ends the scene of the attempted murder and the epileptic fit with a sudden return to the real world; a hotel employee identifies Myshkin as a recently arrived guest; and "the confusion was finally ended very happily, thanks to a fortunate circumstance" (VIII, 196). The narrator draws the reader out of the fantastic world he has just been inhabiting by concentrating on Myshkin's epileptic fit rather than upon the fact that Rogozhin has just attempted murder. He dismisses Rogozhin with the conjecture that he had run off, overcome by horror at the awful sight of the convulsed, screaming Myshkin. The shadowy corridor becomes part of the real world as the narrator gives its concrete form; Myshkin has fallen down fifteen steps; five minutes later a crowd had gathered; Kolya emerges from the hotel restaurant where he had been drinking tea and listening to the organ; a doctor arrives; and the Gothic mood has vanished.

At least the terrible event we have just witnessed has conformed to a norm, even a frightful one. "It is well known that epileptic fits, the epilepsy itself, comes on instantaneously. At this moment the face is horribly distorted. . . . A terrible, incredible scream, unlike anything imaginable, breaks forth; and with this cry all resemblance to a human being seems suddenly to disappear. . . . It is actually as if someone else were screaming inside the person. At least this is how many people have described their impression" (VIII, 195). The vocabulary here resembles the Gothic mode of heightened terror—"horribly distorted," "terrible, incredible scream," "all resemblance to a human being seems suddenly to disappear." But the effect on the reader is completely the opposite. It returns him to everyday reality. A mysterious vocabulary illuminates reality; descriptions of things terrible and unhuman serve to comfort and reassure. The language of the Gothic novel is transformed by the familiar tone of the chatty narrator. Similarly, in *The Possessed* in the scene where Liza is murdered, the narrator dissipates the mood of terror at the very moment of most heightened drama: as she is being beaten by the mob, the narrator is already deflating the scene.

Critics of the Gothic novel commonly distinguish the novel of "terror," as practiced by Radcliffe, from the novel of "horror," as practiced by Lewis and Maturin. Radcliffe herself initiated this classification scheme when she wrote, "Terror and horror are so far opposite, that the first expands the soul, and wakens the faculties to a high degree of life, the other freezes, and nearly annihilates them. . . . [N]either Shakespeare nor Milton by their fictions, nor Mr. Burke by his reasoning, anywhere looked to positive horror as a source of the sublime, though they all agree that terror is a very high one." [19] However much Dostoevsky assimilated elements of the horror novels of Lewis and Maturin, he seemed, throughout his career, to share Radcliffe's sense that the most sublime, the most moving effect is that which "expands the soul"; this attitude accounts, I think, for the sudden deflation that occurs at the end of some of his most terrifying scenes.

In the Gothic novel the narrator's habit of capricious disclosure often mirrors the notion of an unjust fate. The reader of a Gothic novel is at the mercy of the narrator's whims just as the characters are at the mercy of fate. At moments of terror or excitement the narrative often breaks off at crucial junctures; relations between characters frequently are not clarified until the end. Though these devices serve stylistically to interest and mystify the reader, they also have a thematic function: they reflect an overall concept of a universe in which man must function on faith without having any real answers. Neither we nor the characters in *Otranto*, the *Mysteries of Udolpho*, *The Monk*, or *Melmoth the Wanderer*, or for that matter in *The Idiot* or *The Possessed*—or in any of Dostoevsky's works—ever learn why the innocent must suffer for the deeds of the guilty. In the Gothic novels this mystery was, ultimately, cause for despair, whereas Dostoevsky transformed it into the bedrock of faith. Leonid Grossman, in his excellent essay "Composition in Dostoevsky's Novels," and George Steiner in *Tolstoy or Dostoevsky* have discussed the role of the Gothic novel in Dostoevsky's work to some extent. Grossman has properly emphasized that the Gothic novel, following the tradition of Cervantes, brought numerous untraditional modes of narration into the novel. He asserts that an abundance of episodes was basic to the Gothic novel and to the novelistic genres it helped shape—the *roman-feuilleton*, the historical novel, the adventure novel, and the novel of romantic realism.[20] The Gothic novels also made heavy use of interpolated tales. (We have seen that the structure of *Melmoth the Wanderer* consists of an elaborately interwoven series of such tales.) Dostoevsky's debt to all these ways of broadening the narrative scope of the novel is obvious.

Radcliffe and Maturin enjoyed astonishing popularity from the early nineteenth century on in Russia. Radcliffe's popularity caused the Russian translation of *The Monk* to be attributed to her. Sopikov, a dedicated librarian of the period, noted: "It is well-known that Lewis is the author of this book, but to make it sell better the Russian publisher printed it under the name Radcliffe." For similar economic reasons, De Quincey's *Confessions of an English Opium Eater* came out under Maturin's name.[21] Dostoevsky read all these novels; and he knew de Sade as well (XV, 546). Grossman stresses the special influence of Radcliffe and Maturin upon Dostoevsky; he had read their novels as a child, "And no matter how he related to these primitive depictions of horror subsequently, Ann Radcliffe and Maturin played their role in the development of his artistic taste." Grossman finds that Dostoevsky borrowed from the Gothic novel both typical characters and plots, plots laden with catastrophes, coincidences, and overheard conversations. "It would seem that there is not a single feature of the old adventure novel which Dostoevsky did not use."[22]

Indeed, the Gothic novels were read by most major writers in Russia. Ann Radcliffe's influence, for example, can be detected in Karamzin's tales.[23] Pushkin's admiration for the English Gothic novels (which, according to Nabokov, he read in French) is well known. Certainly *The Queen of Spades* (*Pikovaya dama*) and the tale of *Dubrovsky* display many Gothic qualities. Moreover, according to Praz, Pushkin in his *Egyptian Nights* (*Yegipetskie nochi*) personified the Gothic-adventure type of the algolagnic Fatal Woman in his incarnation of Cleopatra. Such women, writes Praz, stand in the same relation to their males as do "the female spider, the praying mantis."[24] Nabokov's *Commentary* to *Eugene Onegin* traces at length the allusions to and influence of Matthew Lewis and Charles Maturin as well as the works of other Gothic writers upon the poem. Most striking are the similarities between the opening of *Eugene Onegin* and *Melmoth*: in each the young hero travels to the country to attend a dying uncle whose heir the hero will become (although when Eugene arrives his uncle has already died). Nabokov tends to dismiss the various Gothic influences upon Pushkin rather lightly. He says, for example, of *Melmoth*, "The book, although superior to Lewis and Mrs. Radcliffe, is essentially second-rate, and Pushkin's high esteem for it (in the French version) is the echo of a French fashion." Pushkin had in fact called *Melmoth* "a work of genius," whereas Nabokov, in recounting *Melmoth*'s plot, complains that he begins "to nod."[25] Likewise, Nabokov calls *The Monk*, which Pushkin also admired, an "inept concoction," and he berates Ann Radcliffe's Gothic "megrims" and "divagations."[26] (Nevertheless, I might add parenthetically, Nabokov himself shows, both in the course of his *Commentary* and in *Lolita*, that he knows these novels very well.)

Many Gothic novels (for example, *The Castle of Otranto*, *The Mysteries of Udolpho*, *The Monk*, *Frankenstein*, *Melmoth the Wanderer*) contain, as a stock device, a painting, portrait, or wax figure that either comes to life or seems to be alive. The characters' reactions to these works of art can shape vast sections of the plot. These works of art function, moreover, to break down the boundaries between art (the imagined, created object) and the real world. In *Melmoth*, John's attention is riveted by Melmoth's portrait: "There was nothing remarkable in the costume, or in the countenance, *but the eyes*. . . . Had he been acquainted with the poetry of Southey, he might often have exclaimed in his after life, 'Only the eyes had life, they gleamed with demon light.'" John gazes upon it with "stupid horror," and finally "as he turned away, he thought he saw the eyes of the portrait . . . move" (Maturin, pp. 13–14). Gogol's story "The Portrait" ("Portret") bears the imprint of this demonic portrait with living eyes, a portrait which the young artist Chertkov purchases. Gogol, like most other readers and writers of the time, knew Maturin's novel, and Setch-karev finds a "suspicious" parallel between these two portraits.[27]

For Tolstoy, the Gothic novel seems to have been largely irrelevant. During a period of disillusionment in his youth, Nikolai of *Childhood, Boyhood,* and *Youth (Detsvto, Otrochestvo, Yunost)* buries himself for a summer in the novels of Sue, Dumas, and Paul de Kock. The effects of his reading are to make him believe, although temporarily, in a reality that does not exist and to make him discover in himself "all the passions described in every novel" (*Youth,* chap. 30). The older narrator Nikolai dismisses his earlier reading with an analogy to the nervous man reading a medical book who detects in himself every possible symptom of disease.

But upon Russia's other great realist, Turgenev, the philosophical anxiety, the presence of the supernatural, and the notion of a hostile, at times malevolent, nature—all prevalent in the Gothic novels—may have exerted an influence. Certainly the influence of these novels upon the English, German, and French writers Turgenev admired can be proven. As a child, Turgenev's family library contained some English works in French, including some of Ann Radcliffe's novels. As an adult, Turgenev wrote to Botkin and Gertsen about his admiration for De Quincey's *Confessions of an English Opium Eater,* and this work may have had a direct influence on his story *Phantoms.*[28] Moreover, Turgenev's brother was nicknamed Rochester after the hero in Charlotte Brontë's Gothic masterpiece, *Jane Eyre.* But the single direct reference to a Gothic novel in Turgenev's work is, as such references tend to be in Dostoevsky's work as well, ironic and unimportant. In *Fathers and Sons (Ottsy i deti)* just after their duel, Bazarov and Pavel notice a peasant watching them. Pavel wonders what "that man thinks of us now." "Who knows?" answers Bazarov. "It is quite likely he thinks nothing. The Russian peasant is that mysterious stranger about whom Mrs. Radcliffe used to talk so much. Who is to understand him! He doesn't understand himself!" (chap. 24).

The Gothic novelists, whether they were depicting the quest for the numinous, the presence of all-pervading evil, an atmosphere fraught with appalling tension, or a virtuous maiden in distress, never lost sight of the specific response they were trying to provoke in their readers. The Gothic novel may be "the leaf-mould" in which "more exquisite and stronger plants were rooted" or it may have provided "Romanticism with its first full set of swaddling clothes," but its authors were undisputed masters at holding their readers' attention.[29] More than any other Russian novelist Dostoevsky transmitted this "electric" power into his own novels.

Coleridge wrote in his review of *The Mysteries of Udolpho* that "curiosity is a kind of appetite, and hurries headlong on, impatient for its complete gratification." Scott observed, in his review of the same novel, that "it is not until the last page is read . . . that we feel ourselves disposed to censure that which has so keenly interested us."[30] Dostoevsky first learned these literary axioms in his role of avid reader; he later transferred them to his fiction.

In any novel by Dostoevsky the careful reader can go back and outline the number of months, days, and hours that have passed, but these demarcations blur under the competing intensity of heightened dramatic moments following one after another in exhaustingly rapid succession. Thus the reader has a sense of a narrator, whether in the role of journalist or novelist or narrator-chronicler—and the boundaries between these roles are not fixed—struggling to organize something inherently uncontrollable. The real world of the narrator competes with the more fantastic world of the "author" Dostoevsky. The reader draws on the sensations he derives from experiencing both these worlds. The Gothic sensibility as it manifested itself both in language and in theme offered Dostoevsky a model for a real world and a fantastic one locked in perpetual struggle with each other. Dostoevsky transformed the thematic and scenic commonplaces of the Gothic novel into the metaphysical riddles which permeate his fiction: evil penetrates good; ugliness resides in beauty; guilt colors innocence; and indifference unceasingly battles with responsibility.

NOTES

1. Edmund Burke, *A Philosophical Enquiry into the Origin of Our Ideas of the Sublime and Beautiful*, ed. James T. Boulton (Notre Dame: University of Notre Dame Press, 1958), pp. 39, 51, 39.

2. The impact of Burke's essay was almost immediate—the phrase "the sublime and the beautiful" quickly entered everyday speech. By the late eighteenth century, even the tourist guides to the English Lake Country presupposed a knowledge of Burke. They were backed with such phrases as "native sublimity," "sublimely terrible," "magnificent objects so stupendously great." In Dostoevsky's *Notes from Underground*, the underground man does battle with countless writers, thinkers, and catchall phrases—among them "the sublime and the beautiful." Although this phrase has been often linked to Schiller as well, the editors of the ongoing Soviet edition of Dostoevsky's work have turned back to Burke and Kant (F. M. Dostoevsky, *Polnoe sobranie sochineny*, vol. 5 [Leningrad: Izdatelstvo "Nauka," 1973], pp. 102, 383). Subsequent references to this edition will appear in the body of the text.

3. F. M. Dostoevsky, *Pisma*, vol. 1 (Moscow: Gosudarstvennoe izdatelstvo, 1928), p. 32.

4. Leonid Grossman, *Sobranie sochineny*, vol. 2 (Moscow: N. A. Stollyar, 1928), p. 73.

5. The relationship between the Gothic novel in England and its German counterpart is complicated and often bizarre. See Devendra P. Varma, *The Gothic Flame* (London: Arthur Baker, Ltd., 1957), pp. 31–32, 34.

6. Matthew G. Lewis, *The Monk* (New York: Grove Press, Inc., 1952), pp. 363–64.

7. Charles Robert Maturin, *Melmoth the Wanderer: A Tale* (Lincoln: Univ. of Nebraska Press, 1961), p. 322. Subsequent references to this novel will appear in the text.

8. Praz has quoted Poe in *The Romantic Agony*, trans. Angus Davidson, 2d ed. (New York: Oxford University Press, 1970), p. 27.

9. Vsevolod Setchkarev has written about some of these same parallels, as well as numerous others, between Maturin's *Melmoth* and Dostoevsky's fiction in "Ch. R. Maturins Roman 'Melmoth the Wanderer' und Dostojevskij," *Sonderabdruck aus Zeitschrift fur Slavische Philologie*, vol. 30, no. 1 (MSl.), pp. 99–106.

10. Dostoevsky, *Pisma*, vol. 2 (1930), pp. 244–45, 258.

11. Mario Praz, "Introductory Essay," in *Three Gothic Novels: The Castle of Otranto, Vathek, Frankenstein*, ed. Peter Fairclough (Middlesex, England: Penguin Books, 1969), p. 20.

12. Horace Walpole, *The Castle of Otranto* (New York: Collier-Macmillan, Ltd., 1963), p. 20.

13. Burke, *A Philosophical Enquiry*, p. 61.

14. Mary Shelley, *Frankenstein*, in *Three Gothic Novels*, p. 364.

15. Praz, *The Romantic Agony*, p. 209.

16. Ibid., p. 219.

17. Wayne C. Booth, *The Rhetoric of Fiction* (Chicago: University of Chicago Press, 1961), p. 175.

18. De Sade, *Idée sur les Romans* (Bordeaux: Ducros, 1970), p. 53.

19. Posthumous article by Radcliffe in *New Monthly Magazine* 7 (1826); quoted by Robert Hume, "Gothic versus Romantic," *PMLA* 84 (March 1969): 284–85.

20. L. Grossman, "Kompozitsia v romane Dostoevskogo," in *Sobranie sochineny*, vol. 2 (Moscow, 1928), pp. 21–22; George Steiner, *Tolstoy or Dostoevsky: An Essay in the Old Criticism* (New York: Random House, 1959), pp. 192–214 and passim. Setchkarev's essay on Maturin's *Melmoth* and Dostoevsky represents the most complete, specific case study of the correspondences between Maturin and Dostoevsky.

21. Grossman, "Kompozitsia," pp. 24, 32. The popularity of the Gothic novel caused similar economically motivated maneuvers all over Europe. In England there were numerous bogus "translations from the German," and in France, where many "translations" of English Gothics "were written by the alleged translators," the situation was much the same. See Varma, *The Gothic Flame*, pp. 31–34, and Maurice Levy, "English Gothic and the French Imagination," in *The Gothic Imagination: Essays in Dark Romanticism*, ed. G. R. Thompson (Pullman, Wash.: Washington State University Press, 1974), p. 151.

22. Grossman, "Kompozitsia," pp. 32, 51–52. Grossman has equated the terms *Gothic novel* and *adventure novel*; the Gothic novel is a later manifestation of this type of literature, one which Grossman felt was more important to Dostoevsky than earlier adventure literature.

23. N. I. Mordovchenko, *Russkaya kritika pervoi chetverti XIX veka* (Moscow: Akademia Nauk, 1959), pp. 74, 111.

24. Praz, *The Romantic Agony*, p. 215.

25. *Eugene Onegin: A Novel in Verse by Aleksandr Pushkin*, trans., commentary by Vladimir Nabokov, 4 vols. (New York: Pantheon, 1964), 2:353.

26. Ibid., vol. 2, pp. 356–57; vol. 3, p. 219.

27. Setchkarev, *Gogol: His Life and Works*, trans. Robert Kramer (New York: New York University Press, 1965), p. 127.

28. Patrick Waddington, *Turgenev and England* (London: Macmillan Press, Ltd., 1980) pp. 5, 107.

29. Varma, *The Gothic Flame*, p. 3; Barton Levi St. Armand, "The 'Mysteries' of Edgar Poe: The Quest for a Monomyth in Gothic Literature," in *The Gothic Imagination*, p. 65.

30. Varma, *The Gothic Flame*, has quoted Coleridge and Scott, p. 104.

III

Decline and Renewal

CAROL ANSCHUETZ

Bely's *Petersburg* and the End of the Russian Novel

It may be a provocative gesture to proclaim the end of the Russian novel, but *Petersburg* (*Peterburg*) reflects the provocative gestures of its author, Andrei Bely. *Petersburg* is more than a novel about the revolution of 1905; it is an act of provocation like many other such acts committed in the Russian capital. It has justifiably been read as a departure from the Russian nineteenth-century novel with its psychological analysis of ethical problems. To explain the reasons for this departure, let us turn to the provocateur himself. "Dostoevsky's vulgarity can be overcome in two ways," Bely writes in a comparative essay on Ibsen and Dostoevsky.

> The catchwords of these two ways are: 1) forward to Nietzsche and 2) back to Gogol. To Gogol and Pushkin—those two primary sources of Russian litera-ture—we must return if we are to save literature from the seeds of corrup-tion and death sowed by the inquisitor's hand of Dostoevsky. Or else we bear an obligation to clean out, with free and cadent music, the Augeian stables of psychology which the deceased writer left to us as an inheritance.[1]

These are the reasons for Bely's departure from the nineteenth-century novel; the nature of the departure, however, is parodic. Let us define par-ody as a form of imitation in which the similarity between two texts serves chiefly to underscore the difference between them. Once we have defined it so, Bely's move "back to Gogol" implies not one but two strate-gies: imitation or pastiche of Gogol and parody of Dostoevsky. Just as Dos-toevsky first acquired his own style by parodying the romanticism of Gogol, so Bely returns to Gogol's style with its verbal humor by parodying the realism of Dostoevsky.

Petersburg reformulates a problem which the West has come to as-sociate with the novels of Tolstoy and Dostoevsky: to wit, the problem of theodicy, or the justification of a creator whose world contains evil. It reformulates this problem by allusion to *Anna Karenina*, where Russian society and above all the family threaten moral collapse under the pressures of Westernization; and to *The Brothers Karamazov* (*Bratia Karamazovy*), where the total breakup of the Karamazov family leads Ivan to question the validity of all moral values. What makes *Petersburg* a radical departure from the nineteenth-century novel is that, for the ethical solution offered by Dostoevsky, it substitutes the aesthetic solution proposed by Nietzsche: "For only as an aesthetic phenomenon is existence and the world forever justified." This well-known phrase sums up what Bely meant when he urged a move "forward to Nietzsche" from the traditional concerns of his nineteenth-century precursors. So it is that *Petersburg* simultaneously interprets Nietzsche's philosophy in terms of Russian literature and represents Russian literature in terms of Nietzsche's philosophy.

The purpose of this essay is to demonstrate how Bely's representation of Pushkin, Gogol, and Tolstoy prepares the climactic episode of *Petersburg*, in which Nietzsche's mouthpiece Zarathustra appears to Bely's terrorist hero, Dudkin, just as the devil appears to Dostoevsky's atheist hero, Ivan. In demonstrating this, I shall attempt not so much to interpret the novel as to formulate the premises on which an interpretation of it would have to rest. These premises would necessarily be the same as those of Bely, who, like other symbolist poets, believed the origin of poetry to be metaphor. Traditional rhetoric defines metaphor as an analogy by which particular qualities or circumstances of two dissimilar objects are perceived to be similar. On grounds that those particular qualities or circumstances are similar, Bely characteristically reasons that *all* the qualities or circumstances of the two objects must be similar. Hence, when Pushkin's poetry suggests to Bely an analogy between Peter the Great and Prometheus, he will wholly identify Russian history with Greek mythology. This tendency to reason by the logic, or illogic, of analogy helps to explain why symbolist poetry often appears to be preposterous. Interpreters are usually tempted either to rationalize the preposterous by substituting some commonsensical equivalent or to circumvent it entirely by limiting their discussion to a catalogue of intertextual references. The method of this essay will be that of analogy not because the author believes such logic to be valid, but because Bely believed it to be the basis of myth; and because it will enable us to reconstruct the internally systematic, if otherwise preposterous, thesis which underlies *Petersburg*.[2]

The best-known and virtually canonical novels of Tolstoy and Dostoevsky, together with the narrative poetry of Pushkin and the lyric prose of

Gogol, formed the basis of an aesthetic education which all literate Russians had and still do have in common.[3] The genre in which Russian literature first won recognition in Europe was that of the novel, which, by comparison with the heroic lays of medieval Europe, functioned as a Russian national epic. But in the last decades of the nineteenth century the epic genre ceded its ascendancy in Russian literature to shorter prose, and culture in general was felt to have entered a period of decay both in Russia and in the West. Bely's novel alludes to two events which tended to confirm European decadence in the eyes of contemporary observers: Russia's defeat by Japan at Tsushima (the first defeat of a modern European power by an Asian one) followed by the near collapse of the tsarist autocracy in the revolution of 1905. Nietzsche's philosophy supplied Bely's novel with a broad perspective in which Bely thought he viewed these two catastrophic and even tragic events as Homer viewed the fall of Troy or as Plato viewed the flood of Atlantis. This broad perspective turned the history of European culture into an analogue for the history of Russian literature, which both reaches decadence and begins its resurgence in Petersburg.

It is significant that, as one of the earliest writers on European decadence, Friedrich Nietzsche should have been a philologist rather than a philosopher by vocation. He drew upon etymology to show that, whereas Judaeo-Christian religion opposes good to evil, the original value equation merely opposes strong to weak. From this it followed that the Christians, like the Jews before them, must have inverted the original value equation in a passive revolt against their slave masters. Hence their eschatological vision of a world where the first (that is, the strong) shall be last and the last (that is, the Jews and Christians) shall be first. Nietzsche's philosophy attempts to reinvert this inversion and thereby to restore the original, "noble" value equation. For that reason it sometimes ironically couches itself in terms of the same biblical eschatology which it repudiates. Thus, when Nietzsche calls himself the Antichrist of Revelation 13, he means that he is anti-Christian, not that he subscribes to Revelation.

Judaeo-Christian religion views history as a struggle between good and evil in which God must ultimately triumph over the personification of evil. Nietzsche chooses as his mouthpiece the Persian Zarathustra, who founded a religion still more dualistic than Judaeo-Christian religion. He does so because legend has it that, unlike the Hebrew prophets, Zarathustra laughed on the very day of his birth. In his view Zarathustra's devil is the spirit of gravity; yet, to those who fear evil, Zarathustra himself seems to be the devil. Thus one might say that, when Nietzsche chooses Zarathustra as his mouthpiece, Nietzsche laughs at good and evil. Whereas the real Zarathustra preached an ethical relation to life, Nietzsche's Zarathustra, who heralds the "superman" of the future, teaches an aesthetic relation to life. It is he who, with the words "God is dead," diagnoses European decadence as a necessary effect of Christian morals and prescribes pagan self-affirmation as a cure.

Nietzsche often refers to the Russian novel. For example, in *The Genealogy of Morals* where, in indignation at the loss of values in modern historiography, he exclaims, "Here nothing thrives or grows any more or, at most, Petersburg metapolitics and Tolstoyan 'pity.'" By "Petersburg metapolitics" Nietzsche evidently means the "Christian" and therefore decadent psychology of *ressentiment* which he discovers in the characters of Dostoevsky's novels and particularly in the narrator of *Notes from Underground* (*Zapiski iz podpolia*), who singles out Petersburg as "the most abstract and intentional city on the whole globe." Nietzsche equates the loss of values not only in historiography but in all of culture with what he calls nihilism in philosophy, and, by associating nihilism in philosophy with the Russian novel, he gives Bely grounds to equate nihilism in philosophy with realism in literature. After all, do not the novels of the foremost realists, Tolstoy and Dostoevsky, depict the history of Russia as the history of an intrinsically Christian people?

Tolstoy regards the people as Christian because they live in harmony with nature, from which Tolstoy believes Christian morals necessarily spring. Dostoevsky regards them as Christian because they embody the true Israel, who are chosen to enter Jerusalem at the end of time in accord with God's promise to Abraham. There can be no doubt that Bely's antipathy for Dostoevsky comes as a visceral response to Dostoevsky's vision of the Russian people as the true Israel. Nietzsche's philosophy does not give rise to Bely's antipathy for Dostoevsky, but Bely discovers in Nietzsche's philosophy the weapons with which to combat "Petersburg metapolitics" and "Tolstoyan 'pity.'" Those weapons are images of an archaic, pre-Christian, and thoroughly pagan culture to which Bely can oppose the Christian ethos of the realist novel. Bely writes *Petersburg* to restore the original, "noble" value equation to the genre of Tolstoy and Dostoevsky and to imbue it with the myths of Pushkin and Gogol, who are prerealist writers and therefore the true bards of Russian history.

The main dramatis personae of *Petersburg* include Apollon Apollonovich Ableukhov, a onetime philosopher of law now active as a minister of state, and his son, Nikolai Apollonovich, a student of neo-Kantian philosophy who has idly promised a terrorist organization to murder his father. The relations between Apollon Apollonovich and his son duplicate the Oedipal conflict of *The Brothers Karamazov* but, whereas Dostoevsky's hero Ivan suffers, like all his brothers, from guilt, Nikolai Apollonovich suffers only from shame. Ivan's guilt, or something like it, is shifted from the figure of the parricidal son to that of his fellow student, the terrorist Dudkin, who is also a potential murderer of Apollon Apollonovich. Unbeknownst to Dudkin, who has, nevertheless, delivered a bomb to the Ableukhov house, the terrorist leader and double agent Lippanchenko blackmails Nikolai Apollonovich to keep his forgotten promise. In *The Brothers Karamazov* Ivan has a nightmare of the devil after an interview with his illegitimate brother Smerdyakov; in *Petersburg* Dudkin has a nightmare of the Persian Shishnarfne after an interview with the double agent Lippanchenko. In both novels the protagonist's guilt is brought out by a song which he chances to overhear (in Ivan's case, a drunken peasant's song, in Dudkin's case, the worker Styopka's) but, whereas Ivan overhears this song before his vision, Dudkin overhears it afterwards. In both novels the protagonist goes mad but, here again, difference goes hand in hand with similarity. Whereas Ivan, once mad, is unable to take action, Dudkin murders the double agent Lippanchenko. The significance of these parallels will become intelligible only after an analysis of certain works by Pushkin, Gogol, and Tolstoy, and of the imagery to which they give rise.

The title *Petersburg* alludes to what Pushkin calls "Peter's creation" (*Petra tvorenie*) as the locus for the myth of a city founded on a pact with the devil and condemned to destruction by flood. This eschatological myth is recounted by each of the four writers with whom Bely carries on his dialogue about the nature of creativity. The best-known account is Pushkin's *The Bronze Horseman* (*Medny vsadnik*), which Bely reads as a poem about the founder of the Russian secular state by the founder of Russian secular literature. These two secularizers, who, in accord with Nietzsche, might equally be called paganizers, Bely would see as restorers of the original, "noble" value equation and thus as models for his own enterprise. It is significant that both the poetic norms of "The Bronze Horseman" and the architectural forms of the city itself are strongly neoclassical because they suggest to Bely the classical imagery of Nietzsche's first book, *The Birth of Tragedy*.

Here Nietzsche posits that ultimate reality is an abyss to which man's gaze is normally blinded by the principle of individuality. This principle and its destruction are nature's two art impulses, order and chaos, which the Greeks personified as Apollo, god of dream images, and

Dionysus, god of ecstasy. Nietzsche maintains that Hellenic religion views history as a battle not between good and evil but between Apollo and Dionysus. This battle does not, however, culminate in the victory of the one god over the other as analogy would lead one to expect. It generates successive "revolutions" in which both gods undergo victory and defeat at each other's hands. The Apollonian art of sculpture and the nonimagistic, Dionysian art of music reflect such periodic victories and defeats, but tragedy and only tragedy mirrors the brief truces in which the two gods unite. Then the principle of individuality no longer blinds man to ultimate reality; it becomes a veil through which he gazes, with a terror that leads to ecstasy, into what Nietzsche calls the abyss of destruction.

Although this theodicy depends on the equality of Apollo and Dionysus, Nietzsche actually gives Dionysus priority over Apollo when he stresses that the birth of tragedy was inspired by the spirit of music; and once again when, in the last nine chapters of *The Birth of Tragedy*, he anticipates that a rebirth of tragedy will take place in the operas of Wagner. Nietzsche maintains that, by turning the victory of Zeus over those pre-Hellenic barbarians known as Titans into art, the epics of Homer mark the victory of Apollo over what he calls the "titanic-barbaric" nature of Dionysus. Between the epics of Homer and the tragedies of Aeschylus, however, there lapses a period in which the Olympian art of the Doric period gradually becomes petrified in its own sculptural images. Thus, the epics of Homer are merely a prelude to the tragedies of Aeschylus, which, by reintroducing the Homeric myths into poetry, mark the victory of Dionysus over the beautiful but now petrified culture of Apollo. The tragedies of Aeschylus express that delicate but all-important balance between nature's two art impulses which not only raises human culture to its highest point, but also justifies the evil committed and suffered by the hero Prometheus to achieve it. Prometheus was a Titan, and the birth of tragedy from the spirit of music was a rebirth of his myth; it embodied a second revolt of the Titans but this time the god of tragedy, with his "titanic-barbaric" nature, does not surrender to Apollo, the god of epic. He dies tragically in the dramas of Euripides, a poet inspired neither by Dionysus nor by Apollo but by Socrates, the posttragic surrogate for Apollo, who negated all myth in science.

Petersburg represents Russia's defeat at Tsushima and the near collapse of the autocracy as a victory of Dionysus over Socrates, that is, the end of an Apollonian period of order and the onset of a new Dionysian period of chaos. The images in which it does so draw an analogy between the neoclassical Petersburg of *The Bronze Horseman* and the Atlantis of

Plato's late dialogues, *The Timaeus* and *The Critias*. Atlantis was the island city founded by Poseidon's descendant Atlas and later destroyed in an earthquake of such magnitude that it sank into the sea, never to emerge again. The memory of this catastrophe was obliterated everywhere but in Egypt, where centuries later it was transmitted to the Athenian Solon by a priest of Neis. Plato implies that Solon could have made of the priest's tale a poem to rival the epics of Homer, although he never did so. Our analogy is that, just as Atlantis was founded by Poseidon's descendant Atlas, so Petersburg was founded by that intrepid seafarer, Peter the Great, on an island subject, like Atlantis, to floods. This basic analogy between Petersburg and Atlantis is latent in *The Bronze Horseman*, where Pushkin writes that the Russo-Hellenic image of Petropolis emerges from the flood, submerged like Triton to the waist (*I vsplyl Petropol, kak Triton, / Po poyas v vodu pogruzhon*). Bely uses the "bearded caryatid" (technically an "Atlas," pl. "Atlantes") which supports the city's bureaucracy to develop Pushkin's image where he writes that time itself has risen to the caryatid's waist (*Samoe vremya po poyas kariatide*), as though a flood of time were about to engulf the city. However, the analogy between Petersburg and Atlantis will yield broader implications if we substitute Pushkin for Peter the Great. Just as Atlantis was metaphorically founded by Plato, the author of the dialogues, so Petersburg was founded by Pushkin on a basis subject, like that of Atlantis, to doubt. That basis is nothing but myth.

To understand the Petersburg of Bely's novel is to understand myth, and Bely understands myth in direct contradiction to the theories of nineteenth-century positivists. Historically, positivism is more than the *Positive Philosophy* of Auguste Comte: it is a set of rules for the use of the word *knowledge*. Traditional metaphysics such as Plato's posited abstract or occult (that is, hidden) entities which are unobservable by definition. Nineteenth-century positivists objected that, if these entities are unobservable, they are also unknowable and can be said to exist only as names or words. The positivists thereby abolished the "true" world of Western idealism, but Bely, like Nietzsche, goes further than they. He maintains that, if we abolish the "true" world, we must also abolish the apparent world to which it is opposed. Myth or art (which is the same as myth), unlike science, values appearance more highly than reality because in myth there can be no other reality than the one which *appears* (like the city of Petersburg in Bely's prologue). Where appearance begins, error ceases and Nietzsche proclaims, *Incipit Zarathustra* (Zarathustra begins), or, in other words, *Incipit tragoedia* (Tragedy begins). The actual city of

Petersburg may sink, like Atlantis, into the sea, but the mythical city of Bely's novel rises out of the flood. In this mythical city, which can only be a city of words, exist occult entities which positivism relegates to nonexistence—so that Bely can exclaim, in contradiction to the positivists, that "Beyond Petersburg there is nothing!"

There is nothing beyond Petersburg because it was founded *ex nihilo* by Peter the Great as the Westernized capital of an Eastern nation; and because its foundation marked a conscious attempt to obliterate all memory of the landlocked, Mongolian past of that nation. Face to face with this anomaly, Bely undertakes to write an epic about Pushkin's tale of Petersburg just as Solon might have written one about the Egyptian priest's tale of Atlantis. The typical subject matter for epic is the heroic past of a nation, a past which is often prehistorical or, in other words, mythical. Evidence of Bely's intention to write such an epic is that the novel's prologue begins with the question, "What is our Russian Empire?" an echo of the question posed in the Primary Chronicle, "Whence came the Russian land?"; and that the prologue places Petersburg in historical relation to Kiev, described with the words of Oleg the Wise as "the mother of Russian cities" in direct quotation of the Primary Chronicle.

Bely's epic takes the outward form of an eighteenth-century novel, with its characteristic subtitles and rhetorical narrator, but the heroes of this eighteenth-century novel are Mongols, whose genealogy, like that of the Slavs in the Primary Chronicle, is traced back to Noah's flood. To write his epic is, for Bely, to bring up those submerged myths of pre-Petrine Rus whose memory positivism has obliterated and thus to induce the rebirth of tragedy. Modern, Westernized Russians are blinded to the future and to the past by their scientific optimism, but the ancients foresaw, because they remembered, catastrophes like the one which destroyed Atlantis. The terrorist Dudkin foresees a catastrophe like the one which almost destroys Petersburg in *The Bronze Horseman*. However, the catastrophe foreseen by Dudkin is remembered in terms of pre-Petrine Rus:

> Having once reared up on its hind legs and measured the air with its eyes, the brass steed shall not set down its hooves; there shall be a leap across history: great shall be the tumult; the earth shall cleave asunder; the very mountains shall tumble down in a great earthquake; and in that earthquake our native plains shall rise up in humps. On the humps shall appear Nizhny, Vladimir and Uglich.
>
> Yet Petersburg shall sink.

Beneath the imagery of Petersburg and Atlantis lurks the originally Nietzschean idea that the waters which flood both cities evoke the same profound terror that overwhelms man whenever he gazes into the abyss of destruction. The analogy between the two cities implies a further analogy between two heroes, Peter the Great, hero of *The Bronze Horseman*, and the Titan Prometheus, whose role as hero of *Prometheus Bound* is central to Nietzsche's theodicy. Nietzsche observes in section 9 of *The Birth of Tragedy* that from time to time the "high tide of the Dionysian" shoulders the burden of all individuals even as Prometheus's brother, the Titan Atlas, shoulders that of the earth. On this image Nietzsche bases his observation that the titanic impulse to become the Atlas for all individuals, and thus to destroy the principle of individuality, is the essentially tragic feature which the Dionysian and the Promethean have in common. Nietzsche reasons that the catastrophes of human history are justified when we view history as nature's art work; and that the reversals of life are justified when man lives life in accord with tragedy, his highest art form. A hero who, like Prometheus, destroys the moral order of the gods, must suffer for his guilt, but his act of destruction, unlike that of the Judaeo-Christian Satan, is nevertheless justified because it creates a new order on the debris of the old one. The belief that an act of destruction is an act of creation and, conversely, that an act of creation is an act of destruction, enables Greek heroes to suffer fate "cheerfully." Their *amor fati* is a manifestation of the aesthetic relation to life, which Nietzsche expresses in the formula, "All that exists is just and unjust and equally justified in both."

Peter the Great destroyed the moral order of Rus to bring culture to the Russians just as Prometheus destroyed the moral order of the gods to bring fire to the Greeks. When the Old Believers branded him with the name of Antichrist, he had to suffer for his guilt, but he, like Prometheus, could suffer "cheerfully" because his act of destruction created a new order on the debris of the old one. However, on Nietzsche's theodicy Bely constructs an interpretation of *The Bronze Horseman* by which it is not Peter the Great but his victim Yevgeni who threatens to destroy the moral order and must suffer for his guilt. Stunned by the loss of his beloved Parasha in one of the floods of Petersburg, Yevgeni wanders to the Senate Square where, suddenly provoked by Falconet's equestrian statue of Peter the Great, he ventures to shake his fist at the Titan who founded the city. One might say that, with that shake of the fist, he raises the problem of theodicy or the justification of Peter the Great as a creator whose world contains evil. Yet Yevgeni believes, in consequence of his own guilt, that the statue is about to take revenge on him, not he on the statue, and he flees from it in a terror that leads to insanity. However, his terror is still the terror which leads to ecstasy because ecstasy, in its etymological sense, means insanity or the alienation of the mind from the will, and not that withdrawal of the soul from the body with which Hellenic religion later associated it. If, as Nietzsche maintains, the birth of tragedy embodied a second revolt of the Titans, then Peter the Great's victim Yevgeni plays the role of the Titan Prometheus to Peter the Great's Zeus when, in *The Bronze Horseman*, Yevgeni menaces the once new Petrine order with revolt. Thus, by representing not only Peter the Great but also his victim Yevgeni as Prometheus, Bely can extend the tragic experience from the Decembrist revolt, about which Pushkin wrote *The Bronze Horseman*, to the revolution of 1905.

Petersburg fully exploits the dialectical give and take of Nietzsche's theodicy by which every Apollonian period contains the possibility of Dionysian chaos, and every Dionysian period contains the possibility of Apollonian order. The action of the novel begins at a period when the Petrine order has become petrified in the tsarist bureaucracy of the capital, just as the figure of its creator has become petrified in the equestrian statue of Peter the Great. Bely's "new Yevgeni" is the terrorist Dudkin, who initiates Nikolai Apollonovich, parricidal son of the Apollonian old regime, into the Dionysian mysteries of the Social Revolutionary Party. When the equestrian statue of Peter the Great comes to life, as it does in *The Bronze Horseman*, Peter the Great in effect casts off his role as petrified creator of the old regime and becomes its destroyer. The Persian Shishnarfne of Dudkin's vision disappears with the words, "I destroy irrevocably," whereupon the Bronze Horseman appears in his stead, pours his bronze into Dudkin's veins and, as though to fulfill Shishnarfne's mission, destroys him. Although, or even because, this act of destruction terrifies Dudkin into insanity, it turns out to be an act of creation because it inspires Dudkin to murder his oppressor, the double agent Lippanchenko, whose corpse he finally bestrides in the posture of the Bronze Horseman. Thus Dudkin plays the role of Peter the Great, who spurs Russia into an eschatological leap across history, as well as the role of Peter the Great's victim Yevgeni, whom the statue in Pushkin's poem terrifies into insanity. Here the fate of Dudkin recalls that of Nietzsche, whose insanity demonstrated to Bely that, like the superman of his own philosophy, Nietzsche no longer distinguished between the "true" and apparent worlds of Western idealism.[4]

When Bely exclaims, in contradiction to the positivists, that "Beyond Petersburg there is nothing!" he does not reinstate the "true" world which positivism abolished, but rather postulates that both the "true" and the apparent worlds are abolished in the word, which has the force to create both the one and the other. Bely associates idealism in philosophy with romanticism in literature and, insofar as Nietzsche views positivism as symptomatic of what he calls nihilism in philosophy, he gives Bely grounds to associate positivism, like nihilism, with realism in literature. The move "back to Gogol" is not, however, a move back to romanticism because it presupposes a move "forward to Nietzsche," and to the abolition of the "true" and apparent worlds in symbolism. Thus, although Bely's symbolism is not romanticism, it is like romanticism in that it serves as a polemical weapon against the myth-negating norms of realism, just as romanticism once served as a polemical weapon against those of neoclassicism. In the mythical city of Bely's novel, which can only be a city of words, the erroneous distinction between the "true" and the apparent worlds ceases, and, with the appearance of the Persian Shishnarfne, Bely, like Nietzsche, proclaims, "Zarathustra begins—tragedy begins." This mysterious figure derives from that of the Persian in Gogol's story "Nevsky Prospect" ("Nevsky Prospekt"), in which Petersburg, the capital of the apparent world, paradoxically embodies what for romantics like Gogol is the "true" world of art. The Persian in this story sells the artist Piskaryov opium to induce dreams on condition that Piskaryov draw for him a beautiful woman. Such drugs were customarily imported to Russia from Persia, and for that reason Bely, like Gogol, sees his mysterious Persian as a visitor from the dream world of art.

Dudkin's nightmare of Shishnarfne originates in Ivan's nightmare of the devil, hence the parody of *The Brothers Karamazov*; but this parody is also an evocation of "Nevsky Prospect," and of another of Gogol's Petersburg stories entitled "The Portrait" ("Portret"). The portrait in this story constitutes an icon of the Antichrist which, in part 1, tempts the young artist Chertkov to betray his sacred vocation for the wealth and fame which Petersburg offers a fashionable portrait painter; in part 2 we are told how the eyes of the icon acquired their unholy power and how that power was finally exorcised. Bely concerns himself largely with part 1, where Chertkov (who does not recognize the portrait for what it is) surmises that, because art like that of the portrait is excessively naturalistic, it somehow partakes of the supernatural. The desire to create such art leads the artist to transgress the just boundaries set for human imagination into what Chertkov calls a "terrible reality" (*uzhasnaya deistvitelnost*).

Gogol's story is about the nature of art but the art in part 1 is not Chert-kov's art, it is the art of the portrait which tempts him to betray his art. This is to say that, in part 1 of "The Portrait," art is of the devil. Part 2 explains ad hoc that the portrait was painted by a godly artist who left it unfinished but for the eyes when he saw that his subject was possessed, and who later entered a monastery where he made restitution for his error by painting an icon of the Virgin. Here, art is of the Holy Spirit, but in *Petersburg*, as in part 1 of "The Portrait," art is of the devil. This notion Bely combines with Nietzsche's dictum that Zarathustra's devil is the spirit of gravity yet, to those who fear evil, Zarathustra himself seems to be the devil. Not just naturalistic art but all art partakes by its very nature of the supernatural, and the "terrible reality" which it opens up corresponds, for Bely, to the abyss in which the principle of individuality meets with destruction. The mysterious figure who appears to Dudkin is not the Judaeo-Christian "spirit of gravity" who appears to Ivan; he is Zarathustra, whom we shall call the spirit of levity, and with whom Dudkin's tragedy begins. For Bely's evocation of Gogol makes of Shishnarfne a Persian Antichrist, and when this Persian Antichrist appears to Dudkin, Bely's hero becomes not only a "new Yevgeni" but, as it were, a new Chertkov.

It is in chapter 6 of *Petersburg* that Bely makes his move forward to a Nietzschean revision of Ivan's nightmare by moving back, first to the imagery of Gogol's "Portrait," and then to that of Pushkin's *Bronze Horseman*. Dudkin lodges, like Chertkov, in a garret on Vasilievsky Island to which the moon imparts the sounds and colors of another world. Here the Persian Shishnarfne magically appears to Dudkin as the portrait appears to Chertkov and terrifies him with his bizarre conversation. An important circumstance is that the model for Gogol's icon of the Antichrist is a Greek, Armenian, or Moldavian moneylender by the name of Petromi-khali, to whom Gogol refers as "the Asiatic"; and that, in the second redaction of "The Portrait," Gogol more than once describes the Asiatic's swarthy face as "bronze" (*bronzovy*) in color. Thus, Dudkin is visited not only by an Asiatic, the Persian Shishnarfne, but by Pushkin's Bronze Horseman who, as an image of Peter the Great, is no less an Antichrist figure than Gogol's portrait. These two consecutive visitors from the dream world of Gogol and Pushkin terrify Dudkin into insanity just as two art works, a portrait and a statue, terrify the heroes of Gogol and Pushkin, respectively. Bely does not hesitate to acknowledge in *Gogol's Artistry* that Dudkin's nightmare of the Persian Shishnarfne comes from Chertkov's nightmares of the portrait, but he fails to acknowledge that the double agent Lippanchenko tempts Dudkin to betray his cause just as the portrait tempts Chertkov to betray his art. The theme of betrayal links Dudkin's nightmare of Shishnarfne with his nightmares of that other Asiatic, the double agent Lippanchenko, from which the nightmare of Shishnarfne develops. We shall see that, because Smerdyakov tempts Ivan to betray his brother Dmitri, the theme of betrayal also links Bely's imitation of "The Portrait" with his parody of *The Brothers Karamazov*. For now, however, the theme of betrayal points to what *Petersburg* and "The Portrait" basically have in common, to wit, the concept of art as terror, which, in the context of Nietzsche's ideas, explains Dudkin's experience.

By Nietzsche's definition, tragedy, as the highest art form, is creation predicated upon destruction, and the inevitable response to destruction is terror, albeit a terror which leads to redemptive ecstasy. The concept of art as terror gives rise in Bely's imagination to the image of the artist as a terrorist, and from there it is only one step to the image of the terrorist Dudkin as an artist. Dudkin tells Nikolai Apollonovich that, because all revolutionaries come from Nietzsche, nonrevolutionaries like Nikolai Apollonovich are for them like the keyboard on which a pianist's fingers play. Somewhat nonplussed by this allusion to the Dionysian art of music, Nikolai Apollonovich asks, "So you are sportsmen of the revolution?"[5] Dudkin complements his allusion to music with an allusion to the Apollonian art of sculpture. "Why not?" he replies. "Isn't a sportsman an artist? I am a sportsman out of pure love for art: that is why I am an artist. From the unformed clay of society one can mold a remarkable bust for all eternity." Thus in *Petersburg* the concept of art as terror gives rise to a metaphor which renders terror in politics (*terror*) synonymous with terror in aesthetics (*uzhas*).

This metaphor most obviously draws attention to itself through Bely's use of the word *suddenly*: first, in the context of politics, as an adverb and then, in the context of aesthetics, as a noun on which the narrator engages the reader in a page-long excursus. "Reader! 'Suddenlys' are familiar to you. Why, then, do you bury your head like an ostrich at the approach of the fatal and inexorable 'suddenly'?" Bely's use of *suddenly* should in fact be familiar to the reader of "The Portrait" as well as of *Petersburg*, where it implies that we all feel ourselves pursued by the terrible reality which lurks behind every phenomenon of the apparent world. *Suddenly* (*vdrug*), which in Russian sounds as abrupt as the action it modifies, occurs with idiosyncratic frequency in "The Portrait" (as throughout nearly all of Gogol), but in only one sentence from "The Portrait" does

Gogol's word order set up the expectation that the adverb will be used as a noun. This occurs where Gogol describes how, a decade after Chertkov betrays his vocation for wealth and fame, he tries once more to paint a masterpiece and fails because, as the narrator observes, "At thirty years and more it is harder to mount up the tedious ladder of etudes, principles and anatomy, and harder still to attain that *suddenly* which develops slowly and yields itself only in return for long efforts, great travail and profound self-denial." Here the word *suddenly*, be it an adverb or a noun, does not indicate the manner in which great art is created: it designates great art as the veil through which man gazes into the abyss of destruction. Bely would have found confirmation for his interpretation of "The Portrait" in part 2 of Gogol's story, where the portrait actually destroys a member of the painter's family each time he begins to reveal its secret to the parish priest.[6]

Each of the dramatis personae in *Petersburg* is a pursuer who is himself pursued by another, and the effect of this unbroken chain of pursuit is to strike terror in the hearts of one and all. The terrorist Dudkin strikes terror in the heart of the old senator, Apollon Apollonovich, when their eyes happen to meet in Nevsky Prospect; and Dudkin's pursuer, the double agent Lippanchenko, strikes terror in the heart of Dudkin when Lippanchenko approaches him from behind in a cheap pub. The moment of terror is punctuated in both instances by the word *suddenly*, which appears typographically set off from the rest of the paragraph. The narrator observes that, in following Dudkin to the cheap pub where Lippanchenko approaches him, we have begun to pursue Dudkin as Dudkin pursues Apollon Apollonovich. This confirms for the narrator that "our role" as readers of *Petersburg* is to pursue Apollon Apollonovich's pursuer just as an agent of the secret police would do. But there *is* an agent of the secret police, and he, like Lippanchenko, is on the *qui vive*: our role is therefore a "superfluous" role, the artificiality of which stresses its relation to art. Our role as agents who shadow Dudkin and other "shadows" of the underworld is not merely to investigate the back rooms and side-streets of Petersburg; it is also to decipher the literary conundrums posed by the very nature of Bely's novel. Now that the reader follows the action of the narrator's narrative, the agent will follow Dudkin, Dudkin will follow the senator, and the senator will follow the reader wherever he goes, because the novel is the reader's "suddenly."

The interrelations between Bely and Gogol are far vaster and more pervasive than this brief analysis of *Petersburg* and "The Portrait" can suggest, but the concept of terror which underlies Bely's interpretation of

"The Portrait" leads him to write in the spirit of his essay on Ibsen and Dostoevsky: "It may be that Nietzsche and Gogol are the greatest stylists of European art, if by 'stylists' we understand not style alone, but its reflection in the form of the soul's life rhythm."[7] With the death of Gogol, the last of the true bards of Russian history, the tragic age of Russian literature comes to an end, only to be followed by the Socratic age of Tolstoy and Dostoevsky. The theoretical man Socrates is, as we have seen, the posttragic surrogate for Apollo, whose intellect reduces the principle of individuality to mere logical schematism. Socrates is also the originator of the distinction between the "true" and apparent worlds which serves, in Nietzsche's analysis, to justify Christian morals. However, to grasp what it means to speak of a Socratic age in Russian literature, we must refer once more to *The Birth of Tragedy*.

Just as the genre of the tragic age was tragedy, so the genre of the Socratic age was the Platonic dialogue, which, by abolishing the chorus of satyrs and their Dionysian music, undermines the very basis of tragedy. Nevertheless, in the chapter where Nietzsche treats the Platonic dialogue, he holds out the possibility that the birth of a Socrates who practices music may not be altogether a contradiction in terms. Nietzsche finds his Socratic musician in Richard Wagner, whose operas mark the victory of Dionysus over Socrates just as the tragedies of Aeschylus once marked the victory of Dionysus over Apollo. Moreover, they reintroduce German myths into poetry just as the tragedies of Aeschylus reintroduced Homeric myths into poetry at the end of the Doric period. "What power was it that freed Prometheus from his vultures and transformed the myth into a vehicle of Dionysian wisdom?" asks Nietzsche. "It is the Heracleian power of music which, having reached its highest manifestation in tragedy, can interpret myths with a new and most profound significance." This quotation raises the problem of how the power of music at work in Wagner's operas can be said to affect Bely's novel: the solution to that problem is to be found in the reinterpretation of Nietzsche's thesis that the Platonic dialogue is the prototype for the novel. Nietzsche maintains that, in the novel, as in the Aesopian fable, poetry functions as a mere ancilla to philosophy; the novel and the fable are, in Nietzsche's opinion, the only genres comprehensible to a logician like Plato. Thus the novel would seem an unlikely cradle for the rebirth of tragedy, yet, if the birth of a Socratic musician is not altogether a contradiction, then neither, perhaps, is the birth of a truly poetic novel. By a logic which follows Nietzsche's (although it is not his), the Socratic musician or, as it were, the Richard Wagner of Russian culture is not a composer but a novelist,

whose art must transform the genre of the Socratic age of Tolstoy and
Dostoevsky into that of a new tragic age.

That novelist is Andrei Bely, and his novel *Petersburg* is not a philosophical novel, like those of the foremost Russian realists, but rather a
philological novel because, in its fundamental structure, it exemplifies
certain assumptions about metaphor which Bely held in common with
Nietzsche and Alexander Potebnya, a Russian philologist whom Bely
compared with Nietzsche.[8] Those assumptions rest on the idea that cognition is a linguistic illusion which occurs whenever men describe the
world by metaphor; and that the cycles of intellectual history correspond
to cycles of linguistic history, which Bely describes as follows. A word is
first of all a sound, and metaphor begins to evolve when that sound calls
to mind a poetic image. The poetic image gives birth to myth; myth gives
birth to religion; religion gives birth to philosophy and philosophy to the
scientific term, which lacks both sound and image. The scientific term is
no less a product of metaphor than the original poetic word but science
obstructs the transferal of words from their usual contexts to ones in
which they have not been used before. That transferal, which is the principle of truly poetic metaphor, occurs only when art renews the sounds
and images of words, and the cycle of renewal and decay can thus begin
again. Here Nietzsche's thesis that the rebirth of tragedy is a rebirth of
myth leads Bely to infer that the rebirth of myth is a rebirth of metaphor
which must necessarily precede that of tragedy itself. He believes that, by
engaging in the mythopoeic activity of transferring sounds and images
from the context of nineteenth-century literature to that of his own novel,
he stimulates cognition and thereby attains what for romantics like Gogol
is the unattainable "true" world of art. His goal in *Petersburg* is to herald
an era of transition from a period of linguistic decay to a period of renewal when, as in the childhood of mankind, every man would be a
mythopoet. "Such eras," Bely writes in paraphrase of *The Birth of Tragedy*, "are marked by the intrusion of the spirit of music into poetry: the
musical force of sound is resurrected by the word."[9]

The rebirth of metaphor occurs when the word, which is first of all a
sound, calls to mind a poetic image. The key image of *Petersburg*, which
elucidates the metaphor of art as terror, is that of the time bomb delivered by Dudkin to the Ableukhov house. This time bomb explodes anti-
climactically at the end of the novel with a plosive sound that merely terrifies the old senator but symbolizes a revolution in aesthetics. This
revolution in aesthetics takes priority over the revolution in politics
which the novel depicts. It brings with it not only the rebirth of tragedy

but also, by Bely's inference, the rebirth of metaphor, which is the basis of cognition. Bely's opposition of the tragic age of Pushkin and Gogol to the Socratic age of Tolstoy and Dostoevsky finds its correlative in his opposition of the resonant poetic word to the scientific term, which lacks both sound and image.

The poetic word is epitomized for Bely by the spoken word of oral epic and the scientific term by the written word of the realist novel. He aspires to impart the resonance of the spoken word to the written word of *Petersburg* and, in so doing, focuses on Tolstoy's attitude toward words as that of a typical realist. Tolstoy identified words, and above all the written word, not with the "true" world of nature but with the apparent world of society: this established the inner tension of Tolstoy's life which ultimately led to his so-called conversion. Tolstoy wrote novels to unmask the moral delusions to which society is prone, but later repudiated even his own novels as evidence of moral delusion. The delusions of the characters in those novels do not always take the form of the written word but the written word almost invariably signals delusion. *Anna Karenina* in particular is a realist novel in the context of which words are unreal: Bely transfers the images of *Anna Karenina* to the context of his symbolist novel. Here they illustrate the petrification of metaphor at the end of an Apollonian period yet, by virtue of the parodic and fundamentally metaphorical transferal they have undergone, they also testify to the reality of truly poetic words, Tolstoy's included.

Who is the tsarist minister's wife whose adultery plays itself out against the background of official Petersburg, from which the adulteress escapes with her young lover in a vain attempt to begin a new life on the Mediterranean? This scenario links Ableukhov's wife with Karenin's, but, if we observe that Anna Petrovna Ableukhova abandons her son to the mercy of a husband whose manner is as icy-cold as Karenin's, and whose ears are just as large, it will link Ableukhov at once with Tolstoy's characterization of Karenin and with newspaper caricatures of the archreactionary minister Pobedonostsev, who was forced to retire in 1905. Critics usually mention this superimposition of literary and historical images in *Petersburg* but none has explained what they mean in the context of Bely's novel. They mean two things: that Ableukhov, like Karenin, is one of the victims of Russia's domestic tragedy (be it adultery or revolution) and that Bely's highly placed copyclerk is a worthy successor, if not to Peter the Great, then at least to the cuckolded minister in Tolstoy's novel. One might say that *Petersburg* brings up to date the interpretation of *Anna Karenina* as "The Mirror of the Russian Revolution" which V. I. Lenin published in 1908. To Bely, however, revolution means something quite different from what it meant to Lenin; and exactly what it means depends, in part, on Bely's own interpretation of *Anna Karenina*.

The domestic tragedy of Tolstoy's novel is connected with the industrialization of Russia in the 1880s and with the railroad in particular. The potential tragedy of Bely's novel is connected with the revolution of 1905, by which time the dramatis personae of *Anna Karenina* have all grown older. The chief victim of the domestic tragedy is in both novels the adulteress's son, who gradually acquires the very characteristics of his father which drove his mother to adultery. Whereas *Anna Karenina* shows this process in its incipient stages, *Petersburg* shows its results: here Anna Petrovna is already an old woman and Nikolai Apollonovich, her grownup Seryozha, exudes the same lust with which Apollon Apollonovich once raped Anna Petrovna. It is in a fit of thwarted lust that Nikolai Apollonovich promises a terrorist organization to murder his father, and thus in *Petersburg* the parricidal son, not the adulterous wife (an Oedipus, not, as in *Anna Karenina*, a Clytemnestra), forces Bely's superannuated tsarist minister to retire. But inasmuch as the parricidal son does not actually murder his father and the adulterous wife finally makes peace with her husband, the domestic tragedy of *Anna Karenina* rewrites itself in *Petersburg* as a comedy. How, then, is this comedy a mirror of the Russian revolution?

The answer to this question lies in Bely's representation of Tolstoy's two bureaucrats, the cuckolded minister Karenin and his adulterous brother-in-law, Oblonsky, to each of whom Bely's own bureaucrat, Ableukhov, offers a parallel. The action of *Petersburg* begins at Apollon Apollonovich's writing desk (*pismenny stol*), where we overhear the "cook's hat" tell the lackey that a letter (*pismo*) from Anna Petrovna has arrived. Not only is it Apollon Apollonovich's function to do paperwork but his face itself bespeaks his bureaucratic function. It resembles a paperweight in office hours, and papier mâché in hours of leisure. Apollon Apollonovich is the head of an institution, and his head supplies an analogue to the point on the map from which, in the prologue, printed matter and government circulars emanate. These images have their origin in the same two aspects of Tolstoy's Karenin which have already been mentioned: his situation as a tsarist minister whose wife has committed adultery and his attitude, as a highly placed copyclerk, to the written word. However, even in the very first scene of the novel these images of Ableukhov as Karenin have already merged with images of Ableukhov as Oblonsky.

The first scene of *Petersburg*, like the first scene of *Anna Karenina*, describes part of the master's grand levee, which is in each novel presided over by a manservant. In *Anna Karenina* the master is the heroine's brother, Oblonsky, who has been unfaithful to his wife; in *Petersburg* he is the heroine's husband, to whom she, like Anna Karenina, has been unfaithful. The first scene of each novel links the master's grand levee with news of the heroine's arrival to reunite his strife-torn household: in Tolstoy's novel this news takes the form of a telegram sent by the heroine; in Bely's, it takes the form of a letter. In *Anna Karenina* the news serves both to begin the action and to provoke irony in book 4, where Oblonsky's wife Dolly will intercede with Karenin on Anna's behalf, just as Anna is now about to intercede with Dolly on Oblonsky's behalf. In *Anna Karenina* it serves, in short, to further the dual plot, but in *Petersburg*, where there is no dual plot to further, the news of Anna Petrovna's arrival fails to reach Ableukhov because, in his preoccupation with bureaucratic correspondence, he neglects to open her letter. The letter itself has a significance for *Petersburg* above and beyond the news it bears because, in juxtaposition with other themes that emphasize the written word, it comes to stand etymologically for literature (in Russian, *pismo* for *pismennost*). Its arrival refers the reader to *Anna Karenina* and, by referring to *Anna Karenina*, it also alerts him to the parodic nature of *Petersburg* as a work of literature whose similarity to *Anna Karenina* underscores the difference between the symbolist and the realist novel. The difference between *Petersburg* and *Anna Karenina* is that, although both Bely and Tolstoy take a sceptical attitude toward the written word, they do so for different reasons: Bely for reasons of aesthetics, and Tolstoy for reasons of ethics. Nevertheless, this difference between *Petersburg* and *Anna Karenina* serves in turn to underscore a far deeper similarity between Bely and Tolstoy, for Bely's parody of *Anna Karenina* reaffirms the value of Tolstoy's two bureaucrats as images which give rise to myth.

Apollon Apollonovich, the cuckold, takes on two habits of Oblonsky, the adulterer: his tendency to resolve his anxieties in bons mots (which in Apollon Apollonovich's mouth become childish riddles) and his propensity, for quite other reasons than those of a cuckold, to forget his wife (as when Apollon Apollonovich neglects to open her letter). The basic parallel between Ableukhov and Oblonsky remains, however: they are both bureaucrats and each proceeds from his levee to an office where he does paperwork, the nature of which is brought home to Tolstoy's reader by Lyovin when he drops in on Oblonsky at his office in Moscow.

> "I don't understand what you do," said Lyovin, shrugging his shoulders. "How can you do it seriously?"
> "Why?"

"Because there's nothing to do."
"So you may think, but we're flooded with work."
"With paperwork. Ah well, you have a gift for that," added Lyovin.
"So you think that I lack something else?"
"Maybe you do . . ."

The parallel between Ableukhov and Oblonsky, the Moscow bureaucrat, runs side by side with the more important parallel between Ableukhov and Karenin, the Petersburg bureaucrat; and this parallel directs our attention to the scenes in *Anna Karenina* immediately after the heroine confesses to her husband at Tsarskoe Selo. Karenin rides back from Tsarskoe Selo to Petersburg, where he solves, as it were, the problem of her adultery by writing her a letter. His satisfaction with this letter as a solution to the problem of adultery expresses itself in his satisfaction with the writing accessories (*pismennye prinadlezhnosti*) with which he wrote it. These writing accessories lead him to the solution of a very different problem, the issue of the irrigation of the Zaraisk district, which has been raised by a rival ministry against his own. He decides to counter this issue with the issue of the welfare of non-Russian nationalities, and his decision to do so alters the course of his career, which, as the narrator spells out, has hitherto been determined by an attitude toward the written word as sceptical as that of Tolstoy:

> The peculiarity of Aleksei Aleksandrovich as a statesman, that characteristic trait proper to him alone, which every outstanding bureaucrat possesses, the one which, together with stubborn ambition, restraint, honesty and self-confidence, had made his career, consisted in disregard for paper officialdom, reduction of correspondence, and in the most direct possible relation to real issues as well as in economy.

Karenin's official solution to his wife's adultery eventually turns out to be that of divorce, by which, in Tolstoy's words, Karenin translates an affair of life into a paperwork affair (*delo bumazhnoe*). This solution to his wife's adultery proves no more valid than Karenin's solution to the issue of the irrigation of the Zaraisk district, which fails when the report of his commission is ridiculed as nothing but "paper written-over with words" (*ispisannaya bumaga*). Karenin and a party of those who believe that such ridicule expresses a "revolutionary attitude towards paper" (*revolyutsionnoe otnoshenie k bumage*) are then forced to defend the report of the commission with further testimonies.

On his way to gather these testimonies, Karenin stops in Moscow, where Oblonsky drops in on him at his hotel. Karenin announces to his brother-in-law his intention to sue Anna for divorce, yet Oblonsky insists that he come for dinner and, to avoid the subject of his sister, brings up that of his new supervisor, Count Anichkin.

> "Well then, have you seen him?" said Karenin with a venemous grin.
>
> "Of course, he was in our office yesterday. He seems to know his business thoroughly and is very active."
>
> "Yes, but at what is his activity directed?" said Karenin. "At doing his business or at re-doing the business that others have done? The misfortune of our government is its paper administration, of which he is a worthy representative."

When Karenin judges the misfortune of his government to be its paper administration, the possibility of delusion extends itself in the reader's eyes from Anichkin to Karenin, who is now a representative of that administration as well as its judge, and in turn from Karenin to the Russian empire as a whole. Karenin's judgment offers Bely the terms in which to emend Lenin's interpretation of *Anna Karenina* as a mirror of the Russian revolution, and thus to correlate the "paper administration" of his government both with the realist novel and with the tsarist bureaucracy, which the realist novel so often depicts. Thus *Anna Karenina* explains why the career of Bely's tsarist minister, whose first act in the novel is to write down a "deep" thought, comes to an end when he refuses to sign a paper; and why, in the aesthetic revolution which takes place in Bely's novel, not only the tsarist bureaucracy, but that other paperwork institution, the realist novel, also comes to an end.

The aesthetic revolution which takes place in Bely's novel is a paperwork catastrophe which, by replacing the written word of the realist novel with the spoken word of oral epic, ushers in a new tragic age of linguistic history. When Bely parodies the realist novel, he destroys its ethical content but, in destroying it, he also preserves what for him is the poetic value of its aesthetic form. Thus, no sooner has the realist novel, with its Christian nihilism, come to an end than the epic genre begins anew in Bely's symbolist novel. The reasons for this are closely involved with the difference between the two strategies by which Bely moves "back to Gogol." The strategy of imitation expresses an attitude of receptivity toward the past; that of parody expresses one both of receptivity and of hostility, neither of which fully outweighs the other. Herein lies the source of Bely's two-faced attitude toward Tolstoy, whose images illustrate for him the petrification of metaphor at the end of an Apollonian period, yet testify, at the same time, to the fecundity of truly poetic metaphor. *Anna Karenina* may be the purest example of the myth-negating norms of the realist novel, but, for that very reason, Tolstoy's characters symbolize a necessary phase in the tragic process of destruction and creation.

Our analysis of *Anna Karenina* brings us to *The Brothers Karamazov* by way of what may seem to be a digression because, although parody of the romantics is just as characteristic of Tolstoy as of Dostoevsky, Tolstoy did not adopt from them the forms of the grotesque and the fantastic which predominate in "The Portrait" and *The Bronze Horseman*. However, because Dostoevsky did adopt the forms of the grotesque and the fantastic, he opens himself to the sort of reinterpretation which would invest them with an explicitly anti-Christian and therefore un-Dostoevskian content. This is precisely the sort of reinterpretation Bely gives to *The Brothers Karamazov* when he dramatizes Nietzsche's aesthetic solution to the problem of theodicy by bringing to life those two Antichrist figures who are also art works: the portrait of Gogol's story and the Bronze Horseman of Pushkin's poem. Bely's parody of *Anna Karenina* developed the attitude toward the written word which Tolstoy signals intermittently throughout the first half of that novel. His parody of *The Brothers Karamazov* emphasizes an attitude toward the spoken word which Bely discovers in one particular episode, that of the nightmare in which Ivan converses with the devil. It is complicated by the fact that the petty, realistic devil of Ivan's nightmare is in himself a parody of the fiery, romantic Satan of earlier writers; and that Bely restores what he feels to be the original, romantic nature of Ivan's devil by conceiving his parody of *The Brothers Karamazov* in terms of the interpretation of "The Portrait," which we have already analyzed. Thus *Petersburg* superimposes Ivan's nightmare of the devil upon Chertkov's and invests the nightmare, which in Dostoevsky bears a preeminently ethical import, with the aesthetic content proper to Gogol. This move back to the aesthetic content proper to Gogol constitutes, as always, a move forward to Nietzsche, and it is on that basis that, first in Dudkin's nightmare of the Persian Shishnarfne, and then in his encounter with the Bronze Horseman, Bely's own account of the myth of Petersburg brings his dialogue about the nature of creativity to its high point.

At no point does Bely broach theodicy as a problem to be solved by his characters, as Dostoevsky broaches it in the "Pro and Contra" chapter of *The Brothers Karamazov*, but, in using the terms of Nietzsche's philosophy, he tacitly assumes Nietzsche's solution to the problem. He passes over both the philosophical discussion in "Pro and Contra" and the Legend of the Grand Inquisitor which it contains, and seizes, instead, on Ivan's conversation with the devil as an episode far more suitable to his own aesthetic. The most self-consciously literary episode in *The Brothers Karamazov*, it is full of puns and allusions. What is more, it makes the devil, as a kind of ideological double, the plagiarizer of Ivan's cast-off ideas. In short, it could almost have been written by Bely were it not concerned with ethical rather than aesthetic values. It offers Bely a way to circumvent the ins and outs of the problem of theodicy and yet, at the same time, to manipulate the imagery with which Dostoevsky surrounds it. However, the reader of *Petersburg* must have some grasp of the problem of theodicy to understand the plot situation which Bely parodies.

Ivan maintains that, if God is not justified, then there is no God, and if there is no God, then everything is permitted. Although this position undermines the validity of ethics, it is basically an ethical position because it rejects the creator on grounds that his world contains evil and on those grounds alone. Even before the "Pro and Contra" chapter in which Ivan discusses this position with his brother Alyosha, he has already explained it to his illegitimate brother Smerdyakov, who believes that it gives him carte blanche to murder their father. After the murder of their father takes places, Ivan makes three visits to Smerdyakov, which bring him to the recognition that if Smerdyakov, and not his brother Dmitri, murdered their father, then he must be guilty of parricide by collusion with Smerdyakov; and that, moreover, if he does not confess this at Dmitri's trial the next day, he will also be guilty of betrayal. The nightmare of the devil occurs when, just after his third and last visit to Smerdyakov, Ivan breaks his newly made resolution to confess without delay and thereupon lapses into delirium.

It is clear from Ivan's resolution to confess his guilt and from his subsequent lapse into delirium that he is not fully convinced of his position that everything is permitted; and, in fact, he has already taken the opposite position in the Legend of the Grand Inquisitor, where he argues, by a reductio ad absurdum of his own argument, that the world must contain evil if man is to exercise free will. The figure who arises from his delirium ridicules the solution to the problem of theodicy which Ivan offered in the Legend of the Grand Inquisitor; and he also ridicules the ethical implication of that solution, which is that Ivan ought to confess his guilt. By a second reductio ad absurdum he turns Ivan's argument for the justification of God into an argument for the justification of the devil: good is only good if it be opposed to evil, hence the devil must be necessary to save mankind, if not from sin, then, as the devil says, at least from boredom. Whatever the devil says to Ivan is always in jest, and for that reason his tone is both highly Gogolian and highly Zarathustran. So it is that, when he reappears in *Petersburg* as the Persian Shishnarfne, he embodies not the Judaeo-Christian spirit of gravity but the Zarathustran spirit of levity. The turn he gives to Ivan's argument for the justification of God recalls the view of evil which underlies the aesthetic solution to the problem of theodicy: namely, that evil is just as necessary a condition for good as destruction is for creation. This is why Zarathustra, who, to those who fear evil, seems to be the devil, is not only the spirit of levity but the spirit of tragedy as well.

We have seen that, like Ivan's nightmare of the devil, Dudkin's nightmare of the Persian Shishnarfne deals with the guilt of betrayal. Bely particularly alerts us to this guilt in the worker Styopka's song, which ends with the line, "I have betrayed an innocent to be crucified." If we focus on how unconscious guilt becomes conscious in Dostoevsky and Bely, the difference between the two novelists will begin to outweigh the similarities on which Bely's parody is based. Whereas in Dostoevsky the process by which the unconscious becomes conscious entails the faculty of choice, that is, the ethical faculty, in Bely it entails only the faculty of speech which, for him, is the aesthetic faculty. Bely writes in his essay "Word Magic" that "A wizard is he who is wisest in words; who speaks most and thereby conjures."[10] Hence Dudkin, who, of all Bely's characters, speaks most and thereby conjures the Persian Shishnarfne, is himself a wizard (or, as we inferred before, an artist).

Dudkin is trapped in a compulsive syndrome which the narrator diagnoses in the second chapter of *Petersburg*: guilt drives Dudkin to drink, drink drives him to talk, and talk drives him to dream of his guilt, which only drives him back to drink again. In his dreams he sees the yellow faces of Tartars, Japanese, or other Asiatic enemies whom he subdues with a single nonsense word, *enfranshish*. The narrator emphasizes the verbal origin of these dreams: "Sometimes he talked himself to the point where he later experienced real attacks of persecution mania: arising in words, they continued in dreams." It is in the sixth chapter that Dudkin is waylaid on his stairway by the Persian Shishnarfne, whose voice he has just overheard at the dacha of the double agent Lippanchenko. Once Shishnarfne enters Dudkin's room, the contours of his figure progressively disintegrate into a purely "phonic substance." As they disintegrate, Dudkin gradually recognizes that the phonic substance which they seem to produce is in fact his own voice.

Given Bely's idea that cognition is a purely linguistic activity, Dudkin's conversation with Shishnarfne can be understood as a model of the speech act. Bely theorizes that "[Listeners] think that a speaker's words emanate from the speaker and that they are real. If it seems so to them, then word magic is created, and the illusion of cognition begins to take effect. Then it begins to seem that behind the words there is some sense and that cognition is separable from the word; but the whole dream of cognition is created by the word."[11] In *Petersburg* Dudkin dreams a dream that Shishnarfne's words emanate from Shishnarfne but Dudkin's dream of cognition is created by the word *enfranshish*. But before we can explain why this is so, we must return to the "Pro and Contra" chapter of *The Brothers Karamazov*, and the fourth dimension.

Ivan prefaces his rejection of God's world with an explanation of why it is futile to discuss whether or not God exists. He maintains that, if God does exist, he created the world in accord with Euclidian geometry and the human mind with a concept of only three spatial dimensions. Now, Ivan observes, there are philosophers and geometers who question Euclid and even speculate that parallel lines, which cannot meet on earth, may yet meet somewhere in infinity. He cautions Alyosha never to think about that, and least of all to think about whether God exists, because such questions are unsuitable for a mind which conceives of only three dimensions. Bely underscores his substitution of aesthetic for ethical values when, in reference to Ivan's discussion with Alyosha, he identifies the fourth dimension not with the city of God, but with the city of art, which, for him, is the city of the devil. "Petersburg does not have three dimensions," Shishnarfne tells Dudkin, "it has four. The fourth is subject to uncertainty and on maps it is not indicated unless perhaps by a point, for the point is where the plane of this existence intersects the curve of an enormous astral cosmos." Here the word "point" alludes to the novel's prologue, where the narrator informed us that Petersburg is not merely "apparent" to us in the three dimensions of experience. It also really "appears," not, as we would expect, because it houses the imperial bureaucracy but because it is signified by a point on the map. This point is a sign without a referent unless its referent be the novel *Petersburg*, a city of signs for which the real city need not exist. In accord with Dostoevsky, for whom Petersburg was "the most abstract and intentional city on the whole globe," Bely populates this city of signs with the mythical figures of nineteenth-century Russian literature. The fourth dimension in which it exists is a verbal dimension, the point of entry to which Shishnarfne finally situates in Dudkin's throat. "Thus any point of the Petersburg spaces is able, in the twinkling of an eye, to eject the inhabitant of this dimension, from which not even a wall can save us; and thus a minute ago I was there, in those spots located on the window sill, but now I have appeared . . ." "Where?" "I've appeared . . . from the point of your throat. . . ."[12]

When Shishnarfne explains to Dudkin that in the fourth dimension everything is spaced in reverse order, Dudkin suddenly grasps that the name Shishnarfne is a reversal of *enfranshish*, the force which has now come for his soul. The notion that, in the fourth dimension, everything is spaced in reverse order, is open to various interpretations, but if the fourth dimension corresponds to the terrible reality of art, then, like art, it holds the mirror up to nature and thus reverses its image as it doubles it. Once Dudkin grasps that the name Shishnarfne is a reversal of *enfranshish*, he is able to subdue the devil he has conjured and thus finds himself liberated (Bely would say "enfranchised") from the fear of evil. Shishnarfne informed Dudkin that his immigration to the fourth dimension would take place in two stages, residence permit and passport, for which Dudkin would qualify by two consecutive crimes. Both crimes, the initial "act" (the word used for terrorist crimes), with which Dudkin associates *enfranshish*, and the "extravagant measure," are acts both of repression and of liberation. Dudkin at first repressed the knowledge that Lippanchenko had betrayed the party, and then repressed the knowledge that he himself had betrayed Nikolai Apollonovich to Lippanchenko (just before Shishnarfne appeared). Now, with the word magic by which he conjured Shishnarfne, Dudkin's previously repressed guilt becomes conscious and we know that, infused with the molten bronze of the Promethean horseman, he will murder Lippanchenko and thus resolve the central conflict of the plot.

We have already seen that, after his conversation with the devil, the protagonist of *Petersburg*, like that of *The Brothers Karamazov*, goes mad; and that, whereas Ivan, once mad, is unable to act morally, Dudkin murders the double agent Lippanchenko. But the reason why Dudkin's conversation with Shishnarfne marks the dramatic and thematic climax of *Petersburg* is not that it renders his guilt conscious and thereby enables him to act (although it does both those things). The reason is that Shishnarfne, as Dudkin's alter ego, incarnates the word as music and, although the word as music be designated with a sign on the pages of a novel, it sounds with Dionysian force. Thus, in substituting for the "written" word of the realist novel the spoken word of his own, Bely fulfills his stated obligation "to clean out, with free and cadent music, the Augeian stables of psychology."

The imagery of *Petersburg*, like that of Russian literature as a whole, is overwhelmingly Christian, but Bely, unlike Dostoevsky, is not a Christian writer, and the Petersburg metapolitics in which Bely indulges are distinctly anti-Christian. In his hands the eschatological vision of Christianity—not, however, its ethic—produces what might be called the eternal return of the poetic rather than the divine word. Nietzsche calls himself the Antichrist: Bely calls him the Christ of a new (but thoroughly un-Evangelical) gospel, by which we shall all be transfigured into supermen, first in the spirit, like Nietzsche himself in the Dionysian abyss of his insanity, and then, at Nietzsche's second advent, in the body. So it is that, in *Petersburg*, we ultimately perceive the mirror image of the apocalyptic city of God, which is the city of the devil. Nietzsche wrote in *Ecce Homo* of Zarathustra as though he were identical with Nietzsche the writer, and of *Thus Spake Zarathustra* as though it were the medium through which his concept of Dionysus became a "supreme deed."[13] Dudkin is the only character in Petersburg capable of heroic action, but the ultimate act or (as Nietzsche would put it) the "supreme deed" in *Petersburg* is the terroristic act by which Bely destroys the nineteenth-century novel and creates his own city, his new Jerusalem, of words.

NOTES

1. Andrei Bely, "Ibsen i Dostoevsky," *Arabeski* (Moscow: Musaget, 1911; repr. Munich: Wilhelm Fink Verlag, 1969), p. 93.

2. There are two major published redactions of *Petersburg*, the "Sirin" edition of 1916 (which first appeared serially in 1913–14) and the Berlin edition of 1922, which shortens the Sirin edition by roughly a quarter of its length. The stylistic economy of the Berlin redaction and its bibliographic value as the final authorized text have contributed to make it the basis of two recent annotated editions of *Petersburg*, the Soviet edition of 1978, by L. K. Dolgopolov et al., and the English translation of the same year, by Robert A. Maguire and John E. Malmstad. However, the stylistic economy of the Berlin redaction deprives the interpreter of sometimes invaluable clues to the riddles it poses, and for that reason this essay will refer to the earlier, untranslated Sirin redaction on the assumption that the system of analogies fundamental to it should be fundamental to the Berlin redaction as well. All quotations from *Petersburg* and other Russian or German texts will be translated by the author of this essay.

3. Pushkin is a poet known better for his narrative than for his lyric poetry; his poem *Eugene Onegin*, which subordinates the lyric to the epic genre, is subtitled "A Novel in Verse." Gogol was a poet *manqué*, who destroyed all available copies of his only published poem, *Ganz [sic] Küchelgarten*. Thereafter he devoted himself to highly lyrical prose, of which the supreme example, his novel *Dead Souls*, is subtitled, "A Poem." It will become clear from what follows that Bely regarded the mode of Pushkin and Gogol as profoundly musical and hence tragic in contradistinction to that of Tolstoy and Dostoevsky.

4. Andrei Bely, "Fridrikh Nitshe," *Arabeski*, pp. 60–90.

5. "Sportsman of the revolution" was one of the two sobriquets given to the Social Revolutionary terrorist Boris Savinkov; the other sobriquet was "horse-guardsman of the revolution" (Z. Zenzinov, *Perezhitoe* [New York: Chekhov Publishing House, 1953], p. 301; cited in Manfred Hildermeier, *Die Sozialrevolutionäre Partei Russlands* [Cologne: Bohlau Verlag, 1978], p. 392). Both these sobriquets convey a certain patrician elegance and detached virtuosity, which is why I have chosen to translate *sportsmen* (a Russian word borrowed from English) as "sportsman" rather than "athlete." This seems doubly justified because professional sports, with which the Russian word is now associated, were not highly developed in prerevolutionary Russia. Critics have argued that Savinkov must have been the model for Dudkin because Savinkov, like Dudkin, was ideologically unreliable (see *Peterburg* [Petrograd: Sirin, 1916; repr. no pl.: Bradda, 1967], p. 97, where Dudkin calls himself a provocateur for that reason). I would contend that, if Savinkov was indeed the model for Dudkin, it is because Savinkov, as a terrorist who was also a novelist, conforms perfectly to Bely's concept of art as terror. Bely's fourth and last memoir, *Mezhdu dvukh revolyutsy*, records that Dudkin is a portrait of Savinkov as described to him by the wife of the novelist Aleksei Remizov in 1905; the most vivid description of Savinkov belongs, however, to the British novelist Somerset Maugham, whose *Writer's Notebook* records how they rubbed elbows in the civil war which followed the revolution in 1917.

6. The narrator of "The Portrait," who is one of the painter's two sons, is in fact the only member of the family who does not succumb to destruction by art. "Hardly had he pronounced the first word when my mother *suddenly* cried out with a smothered voice and fell unconscious on the floor." In the case of the narrator's brother, as in that of his mother, this destruction by art is punctuated by the use of the adverb *suddenly*. "'At last I shall reveal the whole secret to you. . . .' *Suddenly* an abrupt cry forced me to turn around: my brother was not there."

7. Andrei Bely, "Gogol," *Lug zelyony* (Moscow: Altsion, 1910), p. 121.

8. Bely lays out these assumptions most systematically in his essay of 1909, "Magia slov," *Simvolizm* (Moscow: Musaget, 1911). There are similarities between the ideas expressed in "Magia slov" and those expressed in Nietzsche's essay of 1873, "Über Lüge und Wahrheit im aussermoralischen Sinn," which Bely could have read in the *Grossoktavausgabe* (Leipzig: C. G. Naumann, 1894–1904), volume 10 (1903). Bely compares Potebnya with Nietzsche in "Mysl i yazyk (Filosofia yazyka A. A. Potebni)," *Logos* 2 (1910): 240–58.

9. "Magia slov," p. 424.

10. Ibid., p. 431.

11. Ibid., pp. 437–38.

12. Bely read *The Brothers Karamazov* with the eyes of a reader of *The Fourth Dimension* (Moscow: Trud, 1910), in which the author, Pyotr Demyanovich Uspensky, drew on Charles Howard Hinton's book of the same title. Here Uspensky maintains that, if there be a fourth dimension, two and only two possibilities arise: either we are able to perceive it, or we are unable to do so. If we are unable to perceive it, then we are just three-dimensional figments of someone's four-dimensional imagination. Uspensky affirms that he is able to perceive a fourth dimension which stands in the same relation to the third dimension as poetry does to prose. This analogy between the fourth and third dimensions we see borne out in the relation between Bely's novel, which generates the metaphorical discourse of poetry, and the imperial bureaucracy, which generates the official, conceptual discourse of prose. The artistic fourth dimension most clearly mirrors the bureaucratic third dimension where, in the Sirin text of Dudkin's nightmare, Dudkin takes his interlocutor Shishnarfne for the passport officer of the world beyond. As a terrorist resident of three-dimensional Petersburg, and therefore an illegal one, Dudkin bears a passport with the fictitious name Alexander Ivanovich Dudkin. But Shishnarfne hints that, as an artist in terror and therefore a legal resident of Bely's four-dimensional city, he bears the quite different name Aleksei Alek-

seyevich Pogorelsky. This real name is also, however, fictitious because, in a pun which Vladimir Nabokov might have envied, it substitutes the pen name of the nineteenth-century romantic Pogorelsky for Pogorelsky's real name, Perovsky ("of the pen")!

13. *Ecce Homo* was written in 1888, after the onset of Nietzsche's insanity, but until 1910 it was available only in the limited and expensive "bank director's" edition of 1908; as of 1910, the year before he began work on *Petersburg*, Bely could have (and probably did) read it in the *Grossoktavausgabe*, 2d ed. (Leipzig: Alfred Kröner, 1901–13), volume 15.

VICTOR ERLICH

The Novel in Crisis: Boris Pilnyak and Konstantin Fedin

One of the salient facets of the Russian literary situation in the early 1920s is the reemergence of narrative fiction, most notably of the novel, as a dominant literary mode. Once again, as some ninety years earlier, when the golden age of Russian poetry was nearing its end, the pendulum began to swing. In reviewing a 1922 "Serapion Brotherhood" miscellany,[1] Yuri Tynyanov observed: "Prose will soon occupy the place which until recently belonged exclusively to poetry." Elsewhere he noted, without endorsing the trend, a widespread demand for the novel: "the novel appears to be essential and necessary (*nuzhnym i dolzhnym*)."[2] As the turmoil of the War Communism years was subsiding into the relative stability of the NEP, the novel inevitably emerged as the ample, capacious, and socially responsive genre that alone could attempt to encompass the sweep of the events which changed the face of Russia.

No less prevalent than the felt need for the novel was the conviction, shared by writers and critics alike, that Russian artistic prose was in the throes of an acute crisis, a sense of the inadequacy of the extant models and traditions in the face of the new situation. "I am getting away from *belles lettres* for good," averred Pilnyak in 1924. "One has got to write differently."[3] The need for a new departure in narrative fiction was urged on widely disparate, if not necessarily incompatible grounds. There were those—and not all of them were card-carrying Marxist-Leninists—who simply assumed that the "New Man," allegedly emerging from the revolutionary upheaval, could only be done justice by a "new" novel, or that the sheer magnitude and violence of social dislocation made the old literary ground rules irrelevant and obsolete. A protagonist in Konstantin Fedin's *Cities and Years* (*Goroda i gody*) put it thus: "I used to think that one wrote novels the way one knocked together a box—that is, by carefully aligning the boards. That was the way the novels were written before the war. . . . Now . . . the glue doesn't work, it no longer holds."[4]

At the same time the spokesmen for modernistic aesthetics, especially the Formalists and quasi-Formalist critics, for example, Boris Eikhenbaum, Viktor Gofman, Viktor Shklovsky, and Tynyanov, insisted on the obsolescence of traditional literary strategies, on the importance of restoring to the reader of prose the "sense of genre," the perception of the "large form" as a distinctive and aesthetically efficacious mode. As a group the Formalists were most visibly committed to the principle of "decisive novelty" in artistic prose than to any particular set of innovations. In 1921 Shklovsky lent a sympathetic ear to his brilliant disciple Lev Lunts's article "Westward!," which urged the need to scrap the earnest, slow-moving, social problem- and milieu-oriented Russian novel for the sake of the intricate plot structure, the color and pace of the Western *roman d'aventures*. Only a couple of years later Shklovsky, along with his neo-Futurist associates, was to champion a quite different solution, the revitalization of Russian narrative fiction by crossbreeding it with non-literary documentary modes, for example, reportage and feuilleton.

To some observers the crisis of the novel seemed so deep-seated as to call into question the viability of the genre, its potential for survival. "The novel," argued Osip Mandelshtam in a provocative essay, "was suddenly deprived both of the plot—that is, the personality that acts in time belonging to it—and of psychology, because psychology no longer motivates action of any sort. The modern prose writer becomes perforce a chronicler and the novel returns to its sources, to the *Igor Tale* (*Slovo o polku Igoreve*), the chronicle, hagiography." Large impersonal forces— "powerful social movements"—said Mandelshtam, have reduced the "personality" to relative insignificance.[5] The individual protagonist—the traditional concern of the novelist—can no longer command the reader's interest. In a shrewd estimate of the "successes and failures of Maksim Gorky" (1926) Shklovsky made a similar point: "Many authors are no longer satisfied with old plots centering around the hero's plight."[6]

One of the factors contributing to the problematic status of the Russian novel in the early twenties was the state of the art throughout the Silver Age. Not only was the "large form" largely overshadowed by lyric verse and, to a lesser extent, by short fiction. No less importantly, the most stunning novel of the Symbolist era, A. Bely's *Petersburg* (*Peterburg*), was in a sense an antinovel, a phantasmagoria, saturated by characteristically "poetic" devices and dazzlingly subversive of the standard plots of nineteenth-century Russian fiction. A parodistic tour de force and a masterpiece of verbal orchestration, it was a difficult act to follow and a precarious model to emulate. So was the fiction of another turn-of-the-century master of stylization, Aleksei Remizov. For a budding prose writer lacking Bely's poetic virtuosity and Remizov's prodigious literary and philological culture, "ornamental prose," with its centrifugal tendencies, with its built-in bias in favor of the "independence of the smaller unit" (D. S. Mirsky), could become a perilous path.

I

In a sophisticated essay published in 1927 Viktor Gofman characterized the thoroughgoing crisis of Russian artistic prose as the

> disintegration of the essential elements of narrative fiction and of their traditional interrelationships. . . . Plot, narration, style broke up into their constituent parts and acquired independent existence as elements of a potential construction, as illustrative (and approximate) samples of plot, narration and style—a *sui generis* literary inventory.[7]

Not inappropriately, this cheerless diagnosis was offered in conjunction with an astute and harshly critical assessment of Boris Pilnyak, a prolific and resourceful writer, dubbed by D. S. Mirsky in 1925 "a sort of epitome of modern Russian fiction."[8] In his unselective responsiveness to virtually all the styles, techniques, and quests available to an early-twentieth-century Russian prose writer and his near-obsession with the ultimate meaning of the Russian revolution, he is indeed one of the most representative literary figures of his era.

Pilnyak began his career on the eve of the revolution. His early stories, couched in the vein of somber poetic realism, owed more to Bunin than to either Bely or Remizov. By comparison with the novels that followed, "Over the Ravine" ("Nad ovragom"), "The Lure of Death" ("Smertelnoe manit"), "Mother Earth" ("Mat syra zemlia"), were relatively subdued and succinct performances. Yet the themes which were to become Pilnyak's trademark—nature versus civilization, the call of the wild, the indomitable power of the instinct—were unmistakably present in those tales as well as in his first small-scale attempts to portray post-October realities. Such narratives as "At Nikola's" ("U Nikoly"), "Wormwood" ("Polyn"), "Arina," "The Belokonsky Estate" ("Imenie Belokonskoe") (1919) offer suggestive glimpses of the Russian countryside gripped by revolutionary fever.

It is a tribute to Pilnyak's hankering after the "large form" as a necessary vehicle for rendering the rhythms and textures of "Russia's terrible
years" that, in spite of his demonstrable affinity for the shorter narrative,
he should have promptly embarked on what became his most characteristic and most influential work, *The Bare Year* (*Goly god*, 1922), a vivid,
fragmentary, disheveled pageant of the year 1919, the year of famine and
hope, of savagery and euphoria. By the same token, it is a symptom of the
relative fluidity of genre boundaries in Russian narrative fiction of the
early twenties that this, Pilnyak's first novel, should have been made up in
large part of several of the post-1917 stories cited above. (Previously fea-
tured episodes and characters—the dreamy anarchist Andrei, the free
and sensuous Arina, the idealistic young noblewoman Natalia, the arche-
ologist Budek—surface again in *The Bare Year*.) This proclivity for self-
quotation, for drawing heavily upon one's previous works, is still more
apparent in Pilnyak's second novel, *Machines and Wolves* (*Mashiny i
volki*), (1924) which, in addition to multiple echoes from *The Bare Year*,
incorporates several short narratives Pilnyak had produced in the intervening two years. "A Pilnyak novel," quipped Shklovsky, "is a cohabitation
of several short stories. One can take apart two novels and paste together
out of them a third one."[9]

This potential of the early Pilnyak novel for absorbing what Robert
Maguire has called "ready-made materials" is inseparable from its loose-
jointed, permissive, not to say inchoate structure, its tendency to draw
into its orbit in a seemingly unselective, random fashion elements of various literary as well as nonliterary modes. In his excellent study *Red Virgin Soil* Maguire speaks aptly of an "assemblage of pages from a diary,
letters, historical tracts, ethnographical sketches, anecdotes, dramatic
monologues, political slogans, high rhetoric and obscene expletives."[10]
No wonder the champion of the well-constructed Western novel, Lev
Lunts, was moved by Pilnyak's novelistic debut to concern and dismay.
Writing to Maksim Gorky, he dubbed *The Bare Year* "a characteristic and
outrageous phenomenon. . . ." "This is not a novel," he insisted, "but a
collection of materials."[11]

Interestingly enough, Lunts's scornful reference anticipated by some
two years Pilnyak's own designation. About one-third of his *Machines and
Wolves* was a slightly reshuffled version of a fragmentary sequence fea-
tured in 1922 in the journal *Red Virgin Soil* (*Krasnaya nov*) and entitled
"Materials for a Novel." The collagelike quality of *Machines and Wolves*
was further signaled by a facetiously long-winded subtitle: "About the
Kolomna province, about the Wolves and Machines, about black bread

and Ryazan apples, about Russia, Rasseya [a folksy, substandard variant], Rus, about Moscow and the Revolution, about people, Communists and quacks, about the statistician Ivan Aleksandrovich Nepomnyashchy [literally "nonremembering"] and many others. . . ." Elsewhere, incidentally, Ivan Nepomnyashchy, whose dry facts and figures bearing on matters such as demography and industrial production keep obtruding themselves on the narrator's lyrical meanderings, is described, somewhat misleadingly, as the chief hero of the novel, even though he makes his first appearance on page 148!

The generic implications of this modus operandi are not easily pinned down. The proliferation of the folkloric and journalistic materials, the grafting upon the narrative of excerpts from old legal codes, newspaper clippings, or statistical tables represent an "orientation toward the document" (V. Gofman), or, in Pilnyak's own words, a "getting away for good from traditional belles lettres." At the same time, the blatant manipulation of recognizable literary models (Pilnyak's short novel The Third Metropolis [Tretia stolitsa] [1923] includes a lengthy excerpt from Bunin's "The Gentleman from San Francisco" ["Gospodin iz San-Frantsisko"]), elaborately Sternian chapter headings in Machines and Wolves (for example, "A section of the book which lies outside of the narrative frame"), authorial leanings out of that frame ("This is not Robert Smith, this is I. B. Pilnyak speaking")—all these appear to be designed to point up the "literariness" of the proceedings. In either case the distinction between fact and fiction is called into question and the fluidity of the boundaries of the novelistic enterprise "laid bare," in Shklovsky's famous phrase.

One of the inevitable consequences of subverting the novel's traditional structure is the relative weakness of its two essential components: plot and characterization. The frantic shuttling between different locales, the interweaving of disparate episodes, makes a sustained narrative impossible and saps the reader's interest in the crisscrossing subplots. Perhaps more importantly the multiple characters, which emerge from and dissolve back into the "stylistic blizzard" (Tynyanov) and migrate, under identical or different names, from one Pilnyak narrative to another, remain underdeveloped if not shadowy. Shklovsky notes shrewdly that Pilnyak's heroes are actually not so much heroes as vehicles for, or signals of, the quasi-autonomous fragments with which they are associated. One might add that their function is thematic as well as compositional. They are also epitomes of social settings or groupings, of recognizable sociohistorical roles or plights. The cast of each Pilnyak novel, be it The Bare Year, Machines and Wolves, or The Third Metropolis, is apt to include a guilt-stricken, idealistic scion of a decaying aristocratic family reaching toward the new (Gleb Ordynin in *The Bare Year*, D. Roshchislavsky in *Machines and Wolves*), a crusty peasant wizard full of "saws and modern instances," an iron-willed Bolshevik, a lusty young woman in search of sexual fulfillment, as well as a pure maiden who seems to have stepped out of the pages of a Turgenev novel (Natalia Ordynina in *The Bare Year* or Liza Kalitina in *The Third Metropolis*), and finally, a passive observer-chronicler steeped in the old Russian lore.[12] In addition to embodying some of the standard predicaments of the revolutionary era, many of Pilnyak's protagonists serve to illustrate the author's pat generalizations, to help articulate his obtrusive, not to say obsessive, historiosophic concerns. For one of the characteristics of the early Pilnyak novel is the proclivity for what Boris Eikhenbaum in his *The Young Tolstoy* calls "*generalizatsia*," that is, for arguing—and emoting—in the large.

The tendency to subsume destinies of individuals under unwieldy cultural-historical entities looms especially large in *The Third Metropolis*, an avowedly "nonrealistic" narrative, pointedly dedicated to Aleksei Remizov: "I dedicate this thoroughly nonrealistic novel [actually Pilnyak uses the noncommittal term *povest*] to Aleksei Remizov in whose workshop I was an apprentice."

In its opening passage, a wedged-in bit of "reality," an advertisement for the "people's baths" is followed by a staccato statement of the time and place of the *agon*, and a cast of characters:

> Time: the Lent of the eighth year of the First World War and of the downfall of the European civilization and the sixth Lent of the Great Russian Revolution. Place: there is no place of action. Russia, Europe, the world. *Dramatis personae*: there are none. Russia, Europe, the world, faith, disbelief, civilization, blizzards, thunderstorms, the images of the Holy Virgin. People—men in overcoats with collars turned up. Women—but women are my sadness, to me, a romantic, the only thing, the most beautiful, the greatest joy . . .

The passage is doubly characteristic of Pilnyak. Quite apart from the self-indulgent "romantic" effusion triggered by the mention of women, it highlights, indeed overstates, the nearly anonymous or illustrative quality of Pilnyak's protagonists, overshadowed as they are by the large cultural complexes, "Russia, Europe, the world." In fact, it is the pervasiveness in Pilnyak's fiction of historiosophic, or, if you will, historio-publicistic concerns—the authorial addiction to dichotomies such as Russia / Europe, East / West, Moscow / Petersburg, city / village, nature / civilization— which serves here as a sui generis organizing principle and prevents the

seemingly anarchic mass of styles, genres, time levels, episodes that constitutes the Pilnyak novel from actually disintegrating. These antinomies
provide discernible, if at times tenuous, links between the disparate elements of a gaudy mosaic whose only common denominator otherwise
would have been carefully contrived incoherence.

Pilnyak's ideational leitmotifs have a counterpart in insistent verbal
refrains. In a careful analysis of Pilnyak's early fiction, A. Schramm dis-
cerns in its tissue a high incidence of rhythmical-syntactical parallelism
and alliteration as well as a strong predisposition for repeating opening
words, "Here there are no roads. Here wild ducks cry. Here it smells of
slime, peat, marsh gas" (*Zdes netu dorog. Zdes krichat dikie utki. Zdes
pakhnet tinom, torfom, bolotnym gazom*), and indeed, entire passages.[13]

No less pervasive are Pilnyak's favorite images, most notably the
snowstorm (*metel*), which lends the title and the ambience to one of Pilnyak's best short stories and which sweeps or howls its way through
many pages of *The Bare Year*. In a rather telling effect which proved too
"Futurist" for the taste of Lvov-Rogachevsky, an aesthetically conservative
critic, the all-Russian blizzard becomes an auditory correlative of social
innovation as it is made to sing out bizarre-sounding early Soviet institutional abbreviations: "And today's song in the snowstorm. Snowstorm.
Pines. Clearings. Terrors. Shooyaya, shooyaya, shooyaya . . . Gviuu, gaauu,
giviiiuum, giviiiiiuuuu. And - Gla-vboom! Gla-bvooomm!! . . ." One hundred and thirty pages later the snowstorm sings again, and the persona
clearly delights in the Tyutchevian "chaos of sounds": "Ah! What a storm
when the wind eats the snow! Shoyaa, Shoy-oyaa! Shoooyaaa! . . . Giviiu,
gaaum! Glav-bum! Glav-bum! Guvuzz! Ahh! What a snowstorm! How
snowstormy! [*Kak metelno!*] How g-o-o-d!" As the novel closes, the snowstorm surfaces again as "it hurls itself like furies" against the indestructi-
ble, primeval Russian forest, which "stands firm like a stockade. . . ."

The symbolic import of the image which dominates *The Bare Year* is
as obvious as it is derivative. Pilnyak's *metel* comes in a straight line from
the *vyuga* which blows snow in the faces of Alexander Blok's bloodstained
apostles. (Pilnyak's indebtedness to the author of *The Twelve* [*Dvenadtsat*]
is pointed up by the epigraph drawn from Blok's famous 1914 lyric,
whose operative line is "We, children of Russia's terrible years.") In Pilnyak as in Blok the blizzard stands for the October Revolution, viewed by
both as an elemental force, a purifying storm. In *The Bare Year* this notion is given a primitivist and nativist slant. The upheaval turns out to be
an indigenous peasant rebellion which owes much more to Pugachov
than to Karl Marx and which threatens to shatter the painstakingly erected

edifice of alien, post-Petrine bureaucracy, a resurgence of eternal, unreconstructed, rural, grass roots Russia. The theme is repeatedly sounded and variously orchestrated as it weaves its way from the impassioned monologues of upper-class intellectuals to the more pungent mutterings of canny rustic old-timers. The gentle dreamy Gleb Ordynin provides one of the most explicit statements:

> The Revolution set Russia against Europe. . . . Russia, in its way of life, customs and towns . . . returned to the seventeenth century. . . . Popular rebellion is a seizure of power and creation of their own genuine Russian truth by genuine Russians. . . . Who will win this struggle—mechanized Europe or sectarian, orthodox spiritual Russia? . . .

To the old peasant wizard Yegorka, the revolution is a throwback to Stenka Razin:

> There is no International, but there is a popular Russian revolution, rebellion after the image of Stepan Timofeyevich [Razin]. . . . How about Karl Marx? He is a German, I say, so he must be a fool. As for the Communists, to hell with them! The Bolsheviks will manage without them!

Are we justified, one might inquire at this point, in reducing the polyphony, indeed cacophony, of the Pilnyak universe to a common ideological denominator? Can his disheveled literary chronicle, which passes in review the entire spectrum of contemporary attitudes toward the revolution from "decadent" aristocratic escapism through the neo-Slavophile and anarchist modes of acceptance to Bolshevism, be said to yield an unambiguous message? At least one recent student of the early Pilnyak, the already mentioned A. Schramm, thinks not. Calling attention to such structural characteristics of *The Bare Year* as mediating some sections of the novel through the consciousness of the individual protagonists (for example, the relevant chapter headings are "Through Andrei's Eyes," "Through Natalia's Eyes," "Through Irina's Eyes"), she posits the underlying pluralism and open-endedness of *The Bare Year* and *Machines and Wolves*. The choice of the optimal stance or perspective is allegedly left to the reader: "Der Leser is auf seinen eigenen Ehrfahrungshorizont angewiesen, um die sich aus der Montage der einzelnen Bruchstucke, bzw., Kapitel ergebende Bedeutung zu erschliessen, die hier noch nicht durch eine durchgangige 'geschichtsphilosophische' Konzeption vorgegeben wird." (p. 102)

Schramm has a point, but she fails to make important distinctions. To be sure, ideological consistency was not Pilnyak's forte. It is a matter of record that through the 1920s, often to the dismay of the orthodox Soviet critics, he shunned doctrinal commitment and kept his sensibility wide open to the ambiguities and contradictions of the revolutionary process. Yet, the montagelike accumulation of heterogeneous detail, often resulting in a virtual orgy of enumeration, apparently designed to produce the impression of the bewildering multifariousness of the new reality, should not be mistaken for a pluralistic vision or a genuine sense of complexity. By the same token, toying with multiple points of view is not tantamount here to nondirective, let alone self-effacing, authorial stance. One of the reasons why Pilnyak's dramatis personae often fail to emerge as memorable or distinctive presences is the imperiousness or near-ubiquitousness of the author's preoccupations, the frequent obtrusion of the "monological" upon the seeming polyphony. ("The hero of these books," Pilnyak wrote in 1923, "is my life, my thought, and my actions.") The "pervasive historiosophic concept" that haunts his novels may not represent their unequivocal conclusion, but it does have the force of the privileged frame of reference. It seems to serve as a salient rationalization for the underlying gut reaction to the upheaval, a sense of exhilaration over the sheer sweep of events, a reveling in the chaos which plays havoc with normal inhibitions and constraints: "Ah! What a snowstorm! How snowstormy! How good!" In spite of his somewhat helpless attraction to ideas or rather to generalities, Pilnyak is not an intellectual novelist.

If this celebration of untrammeled and often destructive spontaneity (*stikhiinost*) is not always as full-throated as it might have been, that has, to my mind, less to do with Pilnyak's novelistic evenhandedness than with his deep-seated ambivalence toward the regime which emerged from the October Revolution and the mentality which presided over it. The section of *The Bare Year* dealing with the Bolshevik activists has drawn much comment. Robert Maguire is quite justified in calling attention to Pilnyak's sarcasm:[14] "This is what we know, this is what we want, this is what we have stated—that's all there is to it." Yes, the "men in leather jackets" are single-minded, self-assured, know-it-all simplifiers. Moreover, they insist on using foreign words and on mangling them, to boot (*enegichno fuktsirovat*). But if Pilnyak's influential protector, A. Voronsky, missed the sarcastic note in this portrayal of the "new men," the American critic seems oblivious to Pilnyak's grudging admiration for the Bolsheviks' vigor, energy, and sense of purpose: "Of the Russian crumbly, rough nation, a topnotch selection." Nor do they merely "fuction enegetically." Some of them are clearly capable of love and tenderness, of delicacy of feeling. The nearly chaste encounter between the dedicated

Communist Arkhipov and Natalia Ordynina is an oasis of "purity and in-
telligence" in the violence-ridden and brutally carnal universe of *The
Bare Year*.

If ambivalence is one of the undercurrents in *The Bare Year*, it seems
to lie at the core of Pilnyak's second full-length novel, *Machines and
Wolves*, whose very title announces its central dichotomy. In the early
portion of *Machines and Wolves* the wolf prowling in the Russian countryside, an all too obvious symbol of untamed, savage nature, cuts a glam-
orous, nearly heroic figure. This romanticization is promptly undercut by
the luridly naturalistic portrayal of a savage struggle for survival between
wolves and peasants, a struggle in which the moral boundary between
the hunters and the hunted often appears fluid. As the disjointed narrative
presses on, the myth of the proud, beautiful wolf—"terrible like Stenka
Razin's rebellion"—is increasingly challenged by another brand of romanticism, that of the "machine revolution":

> Along with the peasant rebellion, hostile, like Pugachov's, to cities and facto-
> ries, there marched on the romanticism of the proletarian revolution. . . .
> Communists, men of the machine, heretics . . . reached toward the truth of
> the machine . . . and toward a world stern like the diesel. . . . Russia is the
> first country to dare replace man by machine and in so doing to build
> justice. . . .

The paths of the Roshchislavsky brothers recall those of the Or-
dynins in *The Bare Year*, heirs to a decaying aristocratic family. They part
tragically. The pure-of-heart but unhinged Yuri, who threw in his lot with
the "wolves," perishes, overcome by madness. Dmitri espouses the gospel
of the machine revolution: "Emancipated labor will dig canals, dry out
seas . . . bring the good news to Man. This will be accomplished by genius, culture and the proletariat. Russia was the first to call out to the
workers of the world. This is the metaphysics of the proletariat and I am
with the machine-minded Communists." Dmitri could proclaim the vision but it was not given to him to implement it. The gentle apostle of
industrialization is vanquished by native backwardness and savagery; he
is killed by village hoodlums. It falls to a dedicated foreign specialist, the
English engineer Frost, to pick up the banner of liberation through the
machine and wave it in the faces of the backsliders and neophilistines:
"Only labor, only accumulation of values can save Russia."

Throughout the novel the status of the "metaphysics of the proletariat" remains precarious. The triumph of technology may liberate
man, but it is no less likely to displace or supersede him. The finale of

Machines and Wolves offers neither a denouement nor a resolution of the dilemma. The conflict between the two myths is smothered by the booming rhetoric of momentary nationwide consensus as the peasant and the proletarian join in the mourning of "the man who was an era," "a man who died in order to become a legend"—Vladimir Lenin. As the sirens of new Russia proclaim the ascendancy of the machine ("The human revolutions of machines and the world march on"), somewhere in the heart of rural Russia the tame, innocuous chronicler, the statistician Ivan Alexandrovich Nepomnyashchy, collapses in an epileptic fit and two ultra-Russian earth mothers hasten to his rescue.

It is symptomatic of Pilnyak's much advertised romanticism that his apparent inner conflict should have assumed the form of an uneasy shuttling between two rival utopias, those of the Noble Savage and of liberation through technology, rather than of a more common stalemate between nostalgia and a grudging recognition of new realities. Apparently, Pilnyak found it difficult to resist the lure of any ideology that could be construed as a myth.

This proclivity, indeed gluttony, for mythmaking, coupled incongruously with a measure of creative intransigence and a keen eye for stark realia, may well underlie what appears to me a still deeper, and more fundamental, Pilnyakian polarity. At times he seems to have been of two minds not only about the relative virtues of spontaneity and organization, of nature and technology, but also about the relative merits of truth and illusion. *The Third Metropolis* contains an astounding passage. Robert Smith, an affluent and smug yet perceptive English businessman visiting Russia in the early twenties, notes in his diary a striking discrepancy between what is being said and what is actually happening, a ubiquitous affinity for denial: "The lie is everywhere, in work, in social activity, in family relations. Everybody's lying—the Communists, the bourgeois, the workers, even the enemies of the Revolution, the entire Russian nation is lying. What is this?—a mass psychosis, an illness, a blindness?" Quite unexpectedly, the profoundly disturbing syndrome turns out to be a positive phenomenon. "I have thought much," continues Mr. Smith, "of the will to see and related it to the will to dare [literally, "to want"—*khotet*]; apparently, there is another will—the will not to see whenever the will to see clashes with the will to dare. Russia lives today by the will to dare and the will not to see. . . ."

It would be much too hasty to assume that Mr. Smith speaks here for Boris Pilnyak, the more so since in his nearly concurrent literary credo, "Excerpts from a Diary," "the will not to see" is invoked in a pejorative context: "I do not acknowledge that a writer ought to live with the 'will not to see' or, to put it bluntly, the will to lie. I know very well that I am not able to write otherwise than I write now. . . . I do not know how, I will not. . . . There is a law of literature which prohibits, makes impossible, the violation of a literary gift."[15] As a chronicler of the birth pains of the new Russia, Pilnyak neither ignored nor soft-pedaled the appallingly high human cost of social change, the "hunger, death and terror." (The justly acclaimed description, in *The Bare Year*, of freight train #57 "crammed with people, flour and filth," is a telling spectacle of human degradation, as well as human resilience.) Because of his habit of blurting out unauthorized, inconvenient truths, he repeatedly ran afoul of the powers-that-be, whether by hinting at the ruthlessness of the incipient Stalin rule in the poignant "Tale about the Unextinguished Moon" ("Povest nepoga-shennoi luny") (1926)[16] or by a sympathetic portrayal, in "Mahogany" ("Krasnoe derevo") (1929), of the last Mohicans of revolutionary fundamentalism, including—horribile dictu!—a Trotskyite.

But this, it seems to me, is only part of the story. While *The Third Metropolis* is no more conclusive or ideologically coherent than *Machines and Wolves*, its central theme is the contrast between moribund, decadent, "Spenglerian" Europe and Russia, "destitute, hungry lice-ridden," but vital, throbbing, "on the march." May not the "blindness" observed by Mr. Smith, the "will not to see," be one of the essential sources of this dynamism, of this headlong thrust toward the future, a thrust which could well have been paralyzed or slowed down by undue awareness of the price exacted by it? As usual, one cannot be sure, but there is little in *The Third Metropolis* to offset this implication.

At times Pilnyak's frenzied rhetoric tends to blur the boundary between truth and untruth as it insists strenuously on the "greatness" of the mystiques which move men and women to heroic action. The above-quoted passage from *Machines and Wolves* where the narrator emotes about the "machine and truth about to be embodied in the world" is preceded by the statement that "a great lie, like a great truth, was being created in Russia." A critic such as Robert Maguire, who sees Pilnyak as a more or less consistent *Maschinensturmer*, might well interpret this bizarre phrase as "a great lie posing as a great truth." But to me the tenor of the sequence does not appear as straightforward as that. The issue here, one suspects, is not a willful distortion of reality by self-deceived or dishonest propagandists, but the fluidity of the boundary between truth and illusion in a realm where the scope, the "grandeur," of a social vision matters more than its validity.

It is no reflection, finally, on the integrity of Pilnyak's quest for the

ultimate meaning of his profoundly bewildering era to say that his re-
sidual commitment to one of the Russian novelist's time-honored traditions, that of truth-telling, was jeopardized by his peculiar susceptibility
to eschatological bombast, to the intoxicating fumes of utopian mystique.
One can only speculate that his apparent moral confusion did little to
prevent his hasty "reorientation" (*perestroika*) in the face of a vicious official campaign, as the pointed candor of "Mahogany" gave way to the essentially meretricious and hyperbolically celebratory tenor of *The Volga
Flows into the Caspian Sea* (*Volga vpadaet v Kaspiiskoe more*) (1930).

But this, as Dostoevsky might say, is the beginning of a new story. My
concern here is with the place of Pilnyak in early Soviet fiction, with
his role as one of the pioneers of the postrevolutionary Russian novel.
Whether one sees his early large-scale narrative as a possible solution to
the much-touted crisis of the novel, or one of its most acute symptoms, it
was designed to serve as a fictional correlative of a profoundly traumatiz-
ing historical experience.[17] The manner and the matter, the medium and
message, were made to cohere in their very incoherence, with the actual
chaos rendered, or approximated, by seeming compositional anarchy.
Even as the novel's structure contrived to emulate its subject, its imagery—a whirl of antinomies—embodied the underlying stance of a writer
impaled on the horns of a dilemma he was unable to resolve.

II

Another significant attempt to come to terms with the onslaught of
history through the medium of the novel, somewhat refurbished for the
occasion, was Konstantin Fedin's *Cities and Years* (1924).

An active member of the "Serapion Brotherhood," Fedin was more
visibly indebted to the Russian realistic tradition and more mindful of the
social relevance of literature than was the fiery spokesman for that tightly
knit but heterogeneous literary fraternity, Lev Lunts. In fact, if one is to
believe Fedin's vivid but not always reliable memoir, *Gorky Among Us*
(*Gorky sredi nas*), the two young writers stood at the opposite ends of the
Serapion spectrum. And yet, there is much in Fedin's novelistic debut
that could be seen as a response to Lunts's impassioned injunctions in
his essay "Westward!" *Cities and Years*, which spans a period from 1914 to
1922 and shuttles between Germany, seized by chauvinistic fever, and
revolutionary Russia, is a fictional chronicle of a turbulent era, cast in the
form of an elaborately contrived novel of suspense, of a romantic thriller.

It is a measure of the imperiousness of the literary zeitgeist that so essentially traditional a writer as Fedin, whose first narratives, "Anna Timofeyevna" and "The Garden" ("Sad"), were couched, to quote Lunts, in the vein of "old-fashioned lyrical realism," [18] was impelled when embarking on his first novel to give the medium a new twist. In his survey "Literature Today" the ever-perceptive Yuri Tynyanov noted briefly that *Cities and Years* was a sui generis literary experiment, a stratagem of constructing a plot-oriented (*syuzhetny*) novel out of topical material.[19] Fedin himself, in writing to his mentor Maksim Gorky about his emerging novel, lapses into quasi-Formalist terminology: "I'm trying to mediate layers of social reality [*sdvinut plasty obshchestvennogo materiala*] through the plot structure of a romantic novel of adventure." [20] Elsewhere, he confesses to a deliberate attempt to enliven his narrative: "Out of a fear of making my book monotonous, dull, unreadable, I became carried away by the device of contrast." [21] It is fair to assume that Fedin is referring here to the device, noted by some critics, of juxtaposing contrasting or disparate styles—"old-fashioned," leisurely narration, occasional authorial effusions, especially, lyrical apostrophes, and unmediated bits of non-literary discourse, for example, newspaper clippings, military orders, advertisements, grafted upon the narrator's prose. Yet the most blatantly experimental aspect of the novel is lodged in the composition rather than in the style, notably, in the bewildering and suspense-enhancing temporal shifts, in an elaborate dislocation of the normal chronological sequence.

In the best detective story tradition, *Cities and Years* begins with the denouement. The first chapter about the year which concludes the novel (apparently 1922) features an incoherent monologue of one Andrei, who is clearly losing his mind, his love letter to Marie, full of references to Kurt, and a grimly businesslike report of the latter before a Committee of Seven on having murdered his erstwhile friend who "out of personal motives" saved the life of an archenemy of the revolution and betrayed "the cause we all serve." In the next chapter, set in 1919, in civil war–battered Petrograd, we are vouchsafed a glimpse of the encounter between Andrei Startsov and a canny German officer-aristocrat, von Schönau, whose illegal departure from Russia under somebody else's name appears to have been facilitated by Andrei's previous act. Chapter 3 takes the reader all the way back to 1914. The scene, set in a cozy German town on the eve of the First World War, is dominated by the warm friendship of the two protagonists, a gentle, sensitive Russian university student, Andrei Startsov, and a fierce young German painter, Kurt Wahn, a friendship that will be temporarily shattered by Kurt's patriotic intolerance. (The symbolism of the two names is almost too obvious. Startsov, as we will see, cannot shake off the influence of the old [in Russian, *stary*] prerevolutionary code. Wahn is fanatical almost to the point of madness [in German, *Wahnsinn*].) From then on the narrative progresses normally with the exception of chapter 4—"one of digressions," which consists in large part of a flashback focusing on the childhood and youth of the female lead, Marie Urbakh. The chapter on the year 1919 shifts to Russia as it features Andrei's return to his native land and his reunion with a long-lost friend, who in the meantime had changed from an ardent German chauvinist into an implacable Bolshevik.

Gradually, the antecedents and the implications of the fatal confrontation between the friends–antipodes are unraveled. In the penultimate chapter of the novel, entitled "The Second Chapter on 1919 which Precedes the First," Andrei tragically undercuts his finest hour of revolutionary activism by a fatal moment of weakness: he permits the devious counterrevolutionary von Schönau to slip out of the trap. The last chapter—by now it is 1920!—brings us to the edge of the final disaster. A gleeful letter which Andrei receives from the aristocratic villain, now safely ensconced in his ancestral castle, reveals to him the disastrous political and personal consequences of his misguided charity and plunges him into the depths of despair and self-loathing:

> And at night . . . he roamed the boundless wastelands like a madman . . . looking for a road. But around him there were only wastelands, over him hung a black sky. There were no human settlements, no roads. . . . Thus, he remained stranded until the year which was fated to complete our novel. With the advent of that year, Kurt did for Andrei all that a comrade, a friend, an artist could do.

The intricate, indeed baffling plot, which helped make *Cities and Years* one of the few truly gripping novels of the period corresponds to only one dimension of Lev Lunts's program. Its other facet, which Fedin unwittingly implements here, is the novel's unmistakably Western flavor. Not only is the setting predominantly Western; about two-thirds of *Cities and Years* takes place in Germany. More important, perhaps, the literary models which preside over the novel are drawn from Western Romantic fiction. Fedin calls attention to this fact in his two epigraphs, which derive respectively from Dickens's *A Tale of Two Cities* ("We had everything before us, we had nothing before us") and Victor Hugo's *Les Misérables* ("Quant au vin, il buvait de l'eau"). Both epigraphs, incidentally, share the novel's predilection for the "device of contrast."

At first glance, Dickens seems to be more relevant here than Hugo. Outside of the partial convergence of titles, *A Tale of Two Cities* shares with Fedin's novel the theme of the revolution as an ordeal which tries men's souls and presents them with poignant moral dilemmas, and the motif of shuttling between two cities, or more broadly, between two cultures. Yet at closer range, the Hugo connection turns out to be the more crucial one. To say this is not to press the claims of *Les Misérables* as an operative model of *Cities and Years* but rather to suggest that the clues offered by the epigraphs are partly misleading. To put it more positively, the actual subtext of *Cities and Years* is hinted at rather than identified here. It is my contention that Fedin took his cue neither from Victor Hugo's famed epic nor from Dickens's saga of the French Revolution, but from Hugo's relatively little known novel about the French Revolution, *Quatre-vingt-treize*.

If *A Tale of Two Cities* is Dickens at his most romantic, *Quatre-vingt-treize* is Victor Hugo at his most theatrical. I must confess that the scene in which Danton, Robespierre, and Marat confront each other across the table of a Paris cafe made a profound impression on me when I first read *Quatre-vingt-treize* and, for better or worse, shaped for years to come my image of the formidable triumvirate. Revisited many years later, at a less impressionable age, the staccato dialogue, replete with deadly repartees and epigrammatic growls, struck me as totally, if brilliantly, implausible. But the melodramatic staginess of the novel's manner should not blind us to the tragic resonance of its central theme—that of a conflict between the initial humanitarian impulse of the revolution and the implacable exigencies of revolutionary action. This, arguably, brings us fairly close to the moral universe of Fedin's first novel. Yet my hypothesis about his profound indebtedness to *Quatre-vingt-treize* rests not on thematic affinities but on a near-convergence of the two story lines.[22]

Let us reconstruct briefly the last movement of *Quatre-vingt-treize*. At the peak of the civil war in the Vendée, the committee of public safety delegates to an expeditionary corps battling the royalist insurgents a somber priest, an epitome of republican integrity and Jacobin implacability, Simourdain. The unit in which he is to serve as a prototype of the political commissar is headed by a charismatic leader, a brilliant young aristocrat turned revolutionary, intrepid but gentle Gauvain who, as it happens, is Simourdain's only close friend and an erstwhile disciple. Their joint mission is to track down and capture the archenemy of the republic, the ruthless and cunning leader of the rebellion, the Marquis Lantenac. As the republicans lay siege to the fortress held by the rebels, the old fox manages to steal out of the trap. Yet he returns to the fortress, moved by an unpredictably generous impulse, in order to rescue from certain death by fire joyously babbling children trapped in the tower. Lantenac is now at the mercy of his enemy, and mercy is what prevails in Gauvain's heart. If an archreactionary, a defender of the corrupt and wicked ancien régime, proves capable of selflessness and generosity, are not these values binding on one dedicated to a quest for a better world? After hours of inner struggle, Gauvain lets the prisoner go and remains in his cell, only to face the inevitable. At the court martial he asks for the supreme penalty. It falls to Simourdain to break the tie between the other two judges and cast his vote for death. Over the vehement protests of the troops Gauvain is executed. At the same moment Simourdain shoots himself in the mouth. "Et les deux âmes, soeurs tragiques" concludes the novel in true Hugo fashion, "s'envolèrent ensemble, l'ombre de l'une mêlée à la lumière de l'autre."

An ardent friendship between a gentle humanitarian and an austere fanatic, the figure of an aristocratic "enemy of the people," pursued by the revolutionary authorities, his fateful rescue by the more charitable of the two protagonists, and finally, the latter's death at the hands of his antipode—all these parallels seem too striking and too numerous to be merely coincidental.

And yet the similarities may well be less significant than the differences. The Hugo model, if it is indeed one, is given in *Cities and Years* a revealing twist. The overall direction of the shift could be described as downgrading (*snizhenie*) or deglamorization. In Fedin, the "enemy" has few redeeming features. The Margrave von Schönau is a more consistently repellent character than is Hugo's Marquis Lantenac. He is all cunning, deviousness, power lust. His relatively charitable handling in 1916 of Andrei Startsov's futile attempt at escape from Germany was an act of courtesy toward his artist protégé's friend, but scarcely a momentary change of heart, a morally transcendent act such as the one which generates Gauvain's inner conflict and triggers the tragedy. Nor is Kurt Wahn, whose only motivating force is hate and who espouses the revolution with the same single-mindedness which made him shun his Russian friend back in 1914, as admirable a figure as is Hugo's republican ascetic. Yet the most revealing disparity in moral stature is the one between Gauvain and Andrei Startsov. For one thing, Gauvain is not a vacillating would-be intellectual who for only one brief moment, having stumbled into the firing line, merges with the "masses." He is at once a man of action and a dreamer, a revolutionary whose political-military *engagement* is ennobled by poetic vision and tempered by charity. His transgression against the implacable civil war code—a transgression for which he is ready to pay the ultimate price—comes from an exquisite sense of honor and a firm conviction that universal human values are at least as germane to his project as they are to the enemy's. As for Startsov, it is true that in facilitating von Schönau's escape he is motivated in no small measure by gratitude for a favor received a few years earlier. Yet his "betrayal of the cause we all serve" is seen as due mainly to an understandable but a "purely personal" reason, notably his eagerness to send through the fugitive prisoner of war a message to his beloved. More important, Andrei's fatal move is presented not only by his executioner but apparently also by the narrator as a sign of an ineradicable weakness, and is made to lead inexorably to his utter downfall. Outwitted by a resourceful and unscrupulous adversary, Andrei is reduced to the level of a howling animal. Under the circumstances his summary execution, undergirded, by his killer's own admission, by a mounting revulsion, could be construed ironically as an act of mercy, as putting the half-insane, desperate man out of his misery.

To be sure, until his dismal demise Andrei Startsov is the one protagonist in *Cities and Years* with whom the reader is apt to identify and for whom the author clearly has considerable affinity. This fact, as well as the relentlessly grim quality of the Bolshevik activist, drew comment from both the orthodox Soviet critics and the Western students of Soviet literature. Most of the former deplored Fedin's excessive concern, in a novel that attempted to do imaginative justice to the realities of the war and the revolution, with a flabby, spineless intellectual (*intelligent*). The latter noted with interest a relatively sympathetic treatment in *Cities and Years* of a character who had considerable difficulty embracing wholeheartedly any political cause, and who clearly had more use for love than for class struggle.

Yet sympathy is one thing, respect or, if you will, self-respect, quite another. There is no question but that Goncharov feels closer to Ilya Oblomov than he does to the priggish "positive hero" Andrei Shtolts. But this does not prevent him from presenting the lovable Ilia Ilich as incurably sick and historically doomed.

The analogy may not be altogether fanciful or spurious. Arguably, Fedin's topical thriller, heavily indebted as it is to Western Romantic fiction, orchestrates in a postrevolutionary setting one of the salient themes of the nineteenth-century Russian novel, that of a "superfluous man." Yet it does so in an era that takes a grim view of indecision, that has scant tolerance for social misfits:

Thus, we are ending a novel about the man who yearned to be accepted by life. We look back on the road which he trod in the wake of cruelty and love, a road decked in flowers and sprinkled with blood. And not a drop of blood fell upon him; he did not crush a single flower. Oh, if only he had let himself be stained by one drop of blood! If only he had crushed en route at least one flower! Maybe then our pity for him would turn into love, and we would not have allowed him to perish so painfully and so pathetically.

"So painfully and so pathetically." Need one insist on the difference between this way of going and the exalted merger in death of Hugo's two noble souls, "tragic sisters"?

When in his *Soviet Russian Literature* Gleb Struve defines the theme of *Cities and Years* as "the tragedy of a typical member of the intelligentsia caught in the Revolution and swept aside,"[23] he uses the word "tragedy" in the sense of an imminent doom. "Tragedy" as a fateful clash of two values, of two truths, equally compelling and unassailable within their respective realms, is conspicuously absent from Fedin's novel, where sensitivity, however appealing, stands revealed as disability, gentleness as weakness. In a heart-to-heart talk, in 1918, with the new Kurt Wahn, Andrei is unable to challenge his friend's contention that there is "only one way"; all he can say is that personally he finds this way "terrible and humiliating." Where history is so clearly on the side of the Wahns, the only choice faced by the Startsovs of this world is to get in step or be "swept aside."

This is not to say that in the mid-twenties Fedin was ready to accept without question the grim implications of that dilemma. In his second novel, *The Brothers* (*Bratia*) (1927), much more traditional in form than *Cities and Years*, another way, that of a dedicated composer whose primary loyalty is to his art, is given sympathetic if inconclusive hearing. In retrospect, this may be adjudged to be no more than a delaying tactic, moral foot-dragging: the rest of Konstantin Fedin's career has been a gradual and highly literate adaptation to the pieties of Socialist Realism. By 1956 he was ready to explain to Boris Pasternak in temperate but unflinchingly orthodox prose why *Dr. Zhivago* (*Doktor Zhivago*) could not be published in the Soviet Union. The former "Serapion Brother" had become a literary dignitary.

But once again I am getting ahead of my story and courting the perils of hindsight. For it is one thing to suggest that Fedin's modification of his apparent Western subtext within an ostensibly heterodox novel might well contain the seeds of his subsequent adjustments and worldly successes. It is quite another thing to fail to appreciate the qualities that make *Cities and Years*, in spite of its flaws and immaturities, one of the more arresting early Soviet novels. However self-conscious and willed was Fedin's experimentation with his medium, however derivative his plot and problematical his stance, the vitality of his novelistic debut remains a characteristic manifestation of the creative ferment in Russian fiction of the early twenties.

The same is true, a fortiori, of Boris Pilnyak. To some of his most astute contemporaries, Pilnyak's brand of modernism appeared facile and a bit mechanical, his allegedly mimetic use of incoherence an alibi for a congenital lack of artistic discipline, his insistent philosophizing portentous and muddled. But the muddle, in its very exuberant eclecticism, was unmistakably his own. In its underlying resolve to marshal the resources of Russian artistic prose in order to fashion a vehicle for a personal vision of Russia in travail, Pilnyak's early fiction can serve as a vivid reminder of a significant moment in the history of the modern Russian novel, a moment of crisis and disarray, of quest and hope.

NOTES

1. "*Serapionovy bratia* Almanakh I," *Poetika, Istoria literatury. Kino* (Moscow, 1977), p. 132.

2. "Literaturnoe segodnya" ("Literature Today"), *op. cit.*, p. 150.

3. Quoted in G. A. Belaya, *Zakonomernosti stilevogo razvitia sovetskoi prozy* (*Patterns in the Stylistic Evolution of Soviet Prose*), (Moscow, 1977), p. 116.

4. *Goroda i gody* (Moscow, 1969), p. 308.

5. Osip Mandelshtam, "Konets romana" ("The End of the Novel"), in *Sobranie sochineny* (Washington, 1969), vol. 2, p. 310.

6. V. Shklovsky, *Udachi i porazhenia Maksima Gorkogo* (Moscow, 1926), p. 3.

7. "Mesto Pilnyaka" ("Pilnyak's Place"), *Pilnyak, statii i materialy* (Leningrad, 1928), pp. 9–10.

8. *Tales of the Wilderness* by Boris Pilnyak (New York: Alfred A. Knopf, 1925), p. xxviii.

9. V. Shklovsky, "O Pilnyake," *Lef*, no. 3 (7) (1925): 127.

10. *Red Virgin Soil, Soviet Literature in the 1920's* (Princeton: Princeton University Press, 1968), p. 118.

11. Quoted in Tynyanov, *Poetika, Istoria literatury. Kino*, pp. 467–68.

12. A partial exception is provided by *The Third Metropolis* variant of the type: E. Razin breaks out of a hitherto passive stance to commit what strikes me as one of the least motivated murders in Russian fiction.

13. *Die frühen Romanen B. A. Pilnyak's* (Munich: Fink Verlag, 1976), p. 102.

14. Maguire, *Red Virgin Soil*, p. 110.

15. Quoted in Vera T. Reck, *Boris Pilnyak. A Soviet Writer in Conflict with the State* (Montreal, 1975), p. 103.

16. The plot of this uncharacteristically firm and straightforward story, one of Pilnyak's best, is based on the persistent rumor that the popular civil war hero Frunze was virtually forced by Stalin to undergo an unnecessary and lethal operation.

17. "Only against the background of a total disintegration and a total imperceptibility

of genre could there emerge this prose writer who keeps dissolving into fragments (literally "lumps"—*glyby*), with each fragment striving for autonomy," as Tynyanov argued in "Literaturnoe segodnya."

18. "Pochemu my Serapionovy bratia?" ("Why are we Serapion Brothers?"), *Literaturnye zapiski*, vol. 3 (1922).

19. "Literaturnoe segodnya," p. 161.

20. Quoted in G. A. Belaya, *Zakonomernosti sovetskoi prozy*, p. 129.

21. Ibid., pp. 130–31.

22. It could be argued that the title of Fedin's novel as well as its chronology oriented chapter headings were additional signals pointing toward *Quatre-vingt-treize*. In fact, *Cities and Years* might be viewed as a cross between *A Tale of Two Cities* and *(The Year) 1793*.

23. *Soviet Russian Literature* (Norman: University of Oklahoma Press, 1951), p. 91.

JURIJ STRIEDTER

Three Postrevolutionary
Russian Utopian Novels[1]

In Konstantin Fedin's novel *Cities and Years* (*Goroda i gody*) (1924) Kurt Wahn, once a German artist, now a Communist and partisan of the Russian revolution, applies his recent experiences to his new concept of the novel.

> If I had sat out this time somewhere in a workshop, perhaps the world would seem something whole to me, as it did before, as we said and understood before—humanity, the world, looking from above. But I sat below, under the floor, I saw how everything was arranged. . . . Before everything was complete, like a company on the march. Man was fitted to man like board to board in a door. Now everything has disintegrated. . . . I thought once, that novels are written the way boxes are made. Every board must fit the other boards on all sides. That, at least, is how novels were written before the war. Now, it's probably impossible. . . . Those boards which still hold must be separated, perhaps smashed, because they are glued together artificially and because people can't be glued together into humanity with that kind of glue. But that, after all, is our aim.[2]

In Marietta Shaginyan's novel *Mess-Mend* (published in the same year, 1924) a Soviet worker shows the American agent Vasilov, alias Arthur Rockefeller, the new Petrograd, a symmetrically and hierarchically organized futuristic city. "Looking from above" at the city and its happy crowd, the guide comments:

> "Look at them; they are happy. We have achieved the greatest revolution in the world, but we would be stupid not to go further, my friend. Having conquered the means of production we wanted to make man happy."
>
> "Utopia!" sighed Vasilov.
>
> "Yes, precisely," Enno vividly replied. "We made the realization of utopia our task."[3]

177]

These two quotations, taken together, give the historical context and the set of problems, in the framework of which the Russian postrevolutionary utopian novel appeared. Many of the protagonists, novelists, and critics of Kurt Wahn's generation could have echoed his argument about writing novels before and after the world war. In this framework the novel is still supposed to mirror reality and its experience. The emphasis, however, is on the point of view and on the *structural* analogy between the novel and the world it represents. Hence, the ideal of formal "wholeness" unmasked by war and revolution as a mere "fiction" has to be rejected, and the fragmentation of the world has to be reflected in the construction of the novel itself. What many contemporaries proclaim or deplore as the crisis of the novel can be regarded as a reflection of a general political, social, and cultural crisis. And only such a novel in crisis can adequately express the contemporaneous situation of the individual and the society.

If, however, the typical protagonist of the lost generation contents himself with disillusionment and the unmasking of "fictions," a *Soviet* novelist is supposed to present the crisis as a transition from a disintegrating past to a better, reintegrated future. Is not, "after all," the "aim" of the revolution a happy humanity, "glued together" in "the realization of utopia"? If so, should not the most efficient traditional device for anticipating a happy humanity in an ideal social order—the utopian novel— be a particularly adequate aesthetic tool for realizing this task? Indeed, experiments with the utopian novel, and attempts to combine the utopian task with the demands of the novel, form one of the most productive and intriguing topics in early postrevolutionary Russian literature.

To conceive of the novel as a reflected image of a disintegrated society in search of reintegration, and to conceive of revolution as a kind of concrete utopianism—such concepts recur not only in revolutionary Russia, and not only in novels. They are also articulated in contemporary theories of the novel. Georg Lukács's *Theory of the Novel* (*Die Theorie des Romans*) (1920) represents one of the most cosmopolitan, topical, and influential approaches of this kind. For Lukács, as for Fedin's Kurt Wahn, the experience of the world war led to the conviction that the novel was the adequate expression of a world which had lost its "wholeness." The individual had been left "shelterless" (*transzendentale Obdachlosigkeit*) and alone in the search for meaning. For Lukács, this was not only a requirement for the new postwar novel, it was the general constructive principle of the novel as the new epic form, contrasted to the old epic poem as the reflected image of an archaic, complete society. As the author himself later observed (in the foreword to the new edition of 1963), his early concept strove for "a radical revolution" and was based on "primitive utopianism, expressing a spiritual movement which really existed at this time."[4]

The examples of Lukács and the authors he mentions indicate the extent to which, during this period, European Marxist or post-Hegelian literary criticism and philosophy were involved in revolutionary utopianism. But they also stand for the controversial relationship between Marxism and utopianism. Friedrich Engels made a strict discrimination between his own new Marxist approach and the preceding French Utopian Socialists—a school which had a strong impact on Russian socialism and revolutionary utopianism. Engels also significantly entitled his criticism: *The Development of Socialism from Utopia to Science (Die Entwicklung des Sozialismus von der Utopie zur Wissenschaft* [London, 1882]). This suggests Engels's conviction that Marxism, as the only genuinely "scientific" approach, had definitely left behind, and therefore disqualified, all kinds of utopianism. Hence, a genuinely Marxist literature should also avoid utopian speculations in favor of scientific (Marxist) analyses and conclusions.

This equation—utopianism = antiscientific : scientific = Marxist— had a crucial impact on Soviet criticism of utopian literature, including science fiction. Such a criticism, however, did not exclude the development of a productive Soviet Russian science fiction, as long as this "scientific fantasy" (*nauchnaya fantastika*) did not contradict the only genuinely scientific approach, that is, the dialectical and historical materialism of Marxism-Leninism.[5]

I am not arguing for a causal connection between Engels's publication of 1882 and the current canonization of Soviet science fiction. The purpose here is only to illustrate that the tension between "utopia" and "science," a tension of general importance for modern literature and science fiction, has long-lasting importance and a particular meaning in a context ideologically and politically dominated by Marxism.

The debate about the validity of revolutionary utopianism for Marxism, the Communist revolution and its result, the Soviet Union, was most fervent during the revolutionary period itself. In this respect, Lenin's pragmatism is well known. In 1918, when Bukharin asked him to draw an outline of future socialism, Lenin replied: "What socialism will be like when it reaches its final form, we do not know: we cannot predict it."[6] In literature, too, Lenin did not like speculations about future, ideal societies, especially when these were combined with poetic experiments (as in the utopian poetry of the Futurists). We know, for example, how angry he became when he learned that Lunacharsky had supported the publication of Mayakovsky's utopian-futuristic poem *150,000,000*. The fact, however, that Bukharin asked such a question, that Lunacharsky favored Mayakovsky and Futurism—not to speak of Trotsky and his concept of revolution and revolutionary literature—proves that even the leading representatives of the young Soviet Union had very differing views on this topic. The Communist revolution itself favored the reactivation and adaptation of old utopian traditions as well as the creation of new utopian visions—from chiliastic hopes including the resurrection of the dead to projects of political economists disguised or popularized as utopian novels; from the renewed myths and programs of rural Russia to the urban and proletarian pamphlets and poems of the Futurists and the Proletkult; from strictly Russian messianism to internationalism and "cosmism"; from anarchist dreams to constructivist models.

At the very moment, however, when authors with such intentions began their "Search for a Genre," a crucial question arose. Was the utopian novel an adequate form in which to express the dynamics of revolution and the modern "Spirit of Utopia"?[7] As we have seen, the postwar generation expected the novel to reflect, in its own structure, the *crisis* in the world itself. The novel was supposed to abandon complete, whole forms and to simultaneously unmask these forms as misleading fictions about an ostensibly complete and whole world. Such a completeness seemed to be precisely what the traditional utopian novel had suggested and how it was constructed: the description of a static, closed system, a self-contained ideal, separated from the real world.

However, both assumptions just mentioned are questionable—the notion that the novel must mirror the current situation of the society or epoch in its own structure and the view that the utopian novel is a closed and isolated system which excludes a dynamic relationship with contemporary society.

The first premise was challenged by contemporary Russian theorists of the novel even from a Marxist point of view. Mikhail Bakhtin and his group on the one hand criticized the Formalists for neglecting the interaction between literature as verbal art and society, for not taking into account the "ideological" quality of the word.[8] On the other hand, they proved that the relationship between text and context, between the novel and the surrounding society, is far more complex than the relationship implied in the idea of mirroring (even conceived of as a "structural mirroring"). In his own Theory of the Novel, his "The Word in the Novel" ("Slovo v romane"),[9] Bakhtin requires a reformulation of the claim that "the novel has to be a complete and all around mirroring of the epoch. In the novel all socio-ideological voices of the epoch must be represented— i.e., all essential languages of the epoch. The novel has to be a microcosm of different voices [*raznorechie*]" (p. 222).

The Russian word *raznorechie* indicates both "different voices," and "contradictions" or "conflicts." What he calls the "dialogical" or "polyphonic" character of the "novelistic word" can, as Bakhtin demonstrates in his outline of the genre's history, be realized in two different ways, in two basically different types of novel. The "polyphonic" type reflects, in its own structure, the polyphony of the cultural and social context. It organizes its own controversial voices and views into an intrinsic dialogue which is also a dialogue with the respective voices and views articulated in the ongoing discourse of the given society (including its tradition). The "monophonic" or "univocal" type intends, or pretends, to represent one world in one voice. But even this type enters, explicitly or implicitly, into a dialogue with the context, with other controversial voices in the cultural discourse, referring to the same topics from other points of view and in other verbal patterns. Both types, while challenging and testing the ideological context, are themselves challenged and tested by the context, by the reality which they refer to through the medium of language. The novel, Bakhtin concludes, is first of all a genre of "trials": the trial of the hero on his search, the trial of the given society, reflected in the novel, and, last but not least, "the trial of the literary word of the novel by life and reality." The latter means not only that the particular "views" of the novel (its characters, its narrators, its author) are questioned; it means, in addition, that the novel and the novelistic word are self-critical, challenging the pretension of language and literature "to mirror correctly reality." This pretension is, for Bakhtin, "the utopian pretension of the word."

One can and should apply Bakhtin's concept of the novel, including his distinction between the two basic types, to the utopian novel, its general typology and history, and to the representation of this particular subgenre in early postrevolutionary Russia.

From this point of view the classical utopian novel appears in a new light, and its usual classification has to be reformulated. Despite the wide range of variety in the history of the utopian novel and despite the controversial definitions and approaches in the extensive criticism of utopian literature, there is widely shared agreement about some features characteristic of the genre. These features result, apparently, from the intention which lies behind it. In order to present an ideal society, the author has to abstract his utopia from reality (to place the *U-topos*, "nowhere," or radically "elsewhere," in a different world, in a distant future). To demonstrate the perfect functioning of this ideal society he has to construct it as a closed, isolated system (a "Polis" surrounded by insurmountable mountains or walls, an island, a distant planet). This system, being perfect and closed, excludes change. Therefore, it is static. "Abstract idealism," "isolation," and "stasis" are the labels most often applied to the classification of utopian novels.

But one should not confuse (as many critics of the utopian tradition do) the constitutive features of the utopian state (or status) represented *in* a novel with the manner of its representation, with the construction and function of the utopian novel itself. Thomas More's *Utopia*, as a novel, is not an isolated island located "nowhere"; it is a text written and read in a concrete, controversial, social and historical context. Its intention is precisely to be compared and contrasted with this context, this very real social order, or disorder, which surrounds it. Its function is to lay bare the shortcomings of the existing social and political system by confronting them with an ideal model. This model should inspire improvement. The purpose of the novel can be moral, political, satirical, but in any case the explicit or implicit reference to the external context or, to use Bakhtin's terminology, the "dialogue" with this "polyphonic" reality, counteracts the isolation and the abstract idealism of the utopian polis itself. The distance—presented as a spatial or temporal distance (or as both)—is perceived as a tension between the utopian vision and the reader's real world. It is this distance which makes the perception of the static model in fact dynamic.

This is already true for the "univocal" type in which one voice reports about one (the utopian) world. This report, however, can itself become dialogical and polyphonic. The author can frame the narration and use the frame (at the beginning and the ending, or as a given speech-situation during the report) as a chance for the narrator and his auditor(s) to ask and answer questions. They can interrupt the report with comments, comparisons, objections, or conclusions. Or the whole presentation can be dramatized as a dialogue between a visitor in utopia and a native guide who leads the visitor through utopia, explaining the utopian way of life. Already Thomas More's *Utopia*, the prototype of the European utopian novel, presents its utopian construct as such an interaction of frame and report and different voices (with the dramatized author Morus as a special voice besides the dominant voice of the narrator, Raphael Hythlodeus). Later in the general development of the novel, when the polyphonic type became dominant, some authors of utopian novels tried to make their works genuinely polyphonic by multiplying the variety of voices from each of the represented or reported worlds, thus avoiding a mere black-and-white contrast. In this way they tried to create a more complex pattern of references.

A relevant example among the Russian utopian novels of the first postrevolutionary years is Aleksei Tolstoy's *Aelita* (1923).[10] Two Soviet astronauts journey to Mars and are introduced to a Martian utopia, whereupon we follow their various adventures of love, revolt, combat, and escape. The Martian state and its history (which includes "the Fall of Atlantis") are conceived as an analogy to the concept of the "declining West." Masses of workers are enslaved in the City which, at the same time, is regarded as "the breeding ground for the anarchic individual." This exploitation, which is the condition for the happiness of the few who are "blessed," is justified by a philosophy which combines—besides many motifs from myth, religion, and history—a criticism of transcendental Idealism with ideas from Nietzsche, Schopenhauer, and Spengler. (Spengler's *Decline of the West* was published in 1918–23; Aleksei Tolstoy lived, at this time, as an emigrant in Germany; he wrote and published *Aelita* in Berlin in 1923, returning to the Soviet Union in the same year.)

What interests us in regard to the polyphony of utopian novels is Tolstoy's method of presenting each of the two worlds (Mars and the Soviet Union) through different, interrelated voices. He sheds a threefold light on Martian society by representing it through Tuskub, the ruler and defender of the system, through Gor, the proletarian leader of the unsuccessful revolt, and through Aelita, Tuskub's daughter, whom the father has secluded away in a special, idyllic Arcadia. Aelita functions as a mediator between the two worlds. On the one hand she introduces the men from Earth to the Martian language, to the Martian way of, and view on, life, and to Martian history (narrated by her in special chapters). On the other hand, she falls in love (mutual and Platonic love) with the human visitor from Earth. But she, as well as Gor and Tuskub, notwithstanding their differences, are genuine Martians, conscious of being doomed to decline and death.

Tolstoy also complicates the function of the visitor in utopia in its relationship to the Soviet Russian point of view. The spacecraft brings not one, but two Soviet citizens to Mars, both heroes and both positive representatives of their country (that is, not a master–servant or a hero–confidant combination). But Gusev, the former Red Army soldier, is a spontaneous, pragmatic, optimistic fighter, while Los, the engineer and

inventor of the spacecraft, is a mourning widower, devoted to a romantic
love and haunted by loneliness and melancholy. Due to these differences
in character, each protagonist becomes the center of a different system of
motifs, views, moods, stylistic devices, and values—a specific "voice" in a
"dialogue" with his cotraveler. This distinction allows the author to associate one Soviet protagonist with the doomed Martian woman and the
other with the Martian rebel. This helps the author demonstrate that
both love and revolt are doomed to failure in a Martian society. It is true,
however, that the romantic and romanesque love overcomes separation
and death in the form of a transcosmic voice. After the two astronauts
escape and return to the Soviet Union, and after Aelita is left behind and
sentenced for her betrayal, her voice reaches the lonely lover in the last
chapter, entitled "The *Voice* of Love" (my italics). But love, too, remains an
open search and a question. The last words of this chapter, and of the
novel, are: "Where are you, where are you, love . . ."

The political moral of this utopian novel is clearly indicated immediately before this romantic ending. The pursuit of happiness and revolutionary dynamics should not be sought in other worlds or planets—at
least not for the moment. Revolutionary fighters and inventors must return to "the homeland of the revolution and of socialism," where the shift
from revolutionary destruction to revolutionary construction has just begun. The novel began in Petrograd, in August 1921, with a picture of a city
devastated by revolution, civil war, and hunger. It ends in the same place,
in June of 1925, with an image of construction and collective happiness
achieved through collective work. The novelist also adds a remark that
this became the genuine topic for literature:

> Time has now changed: the poets are carried away neither by blizzards nor
> by stars, nor by countries beyond the clouds, but by the sound of hammers
> throughout the country, the sizzling of saws, the rustle of sickles, the whis-
> tling of scythes—enjoyment, earthly songs. In the country in this year
> started the construction of unprecedented (*nebyvalye*) so-called "blue cities."
>
> [p. 228]

The attentive reader will notice that the date "3 June 1925" marks an
anticipation of two years (1923 was the date of publication and of the author's return to the Soviet Union). This touches on the general problem of
utopia as anticipation. For centuries, utopias were either abstract ideals
placed "nowhere" or anticipations of a better future (even in cases where
this future was conceived of as a reinstitution of a happier past). Tolstoy's
utopia on Mars, however, is a utopia oriented toward a negative past. It

regards its own history and political organization as the results of an un-avoidable "decline and fall." Since, however, this utopia is conceived of as an analogy to the "declining West," and since this West is, in fact, the pres-ent (and future) opposition to the revolutionary Soviet Union, the un-masking and negation of the Martian utopia serves as an affirmation of the revolutionary Soviet Union's hopes for a successful, happy future. This can be achieved *per negationem*, without the novelist being forced to present his own, contemporaneous system in its "extensive totality" (Lukács). Nor is the novelist required to anticipate the final state of his own social and political system in the form of an elaborated utopian vi-sion. In accordance with Lenin's reply to Bukharin's question, the long-range or final anticipation can be replaced by a short-range anticipation of a few years. This will indicate the most urgent current task (now "re-construction"). The early Soviet Russian utopian novel *Aelita* (alluding symbolically to the emblems of the new state, the hammer and the sickle) ends with an implied criticism of utopian dreams "beyond the clouds," and with an anticipation of the novel of production which was soon to come.

The last paragraph may seem to digress from the issue of polyphony to the issue of the concrete political situation. But polyphony, in Bakhtin's understanding, is never just a stylistic device or a principle of intrinsic construction. Since it is both, it is first of all the way in which a polyphonic artifact, or verbal construction, organizes a view of the surrounding world in all its polyphonic, controversial reality. As we have seen, the utopian novel is, to a particularly high degree, dependent on such a dialogue. It can, of course, begin as a univocal construction, challenging, as an ideal, an unsatisfactory reality. But Aleksei Tolstoy, as a novelist rooted in the tradition of the polyphonic, sociopsychological realistic novel, con-structed his Martian work in a polyphonic way, thereby creating a pat-tern of different voices and views complex enough to represent the controversial political and cultural context and not merely a utopian "country beyond the clouds."

The polyphonic and the univocal are, however, only the two poles of the scale. Both types can merge, and the transition from a univocal pre-sentation of the world to a controversial polyphonic presentation can it-self become an expression of the "self-criticism of the novelistic word." As we have seen, Bakhtin describes this self-criticism as a criticism of the "utopian pretension," particularly the pretension that one univocal voice, or language, can represent reality as a univocal, noncontroversial world. Hence, the unmasking of such pretensions of the novelistic word can shift into the unmasking of those corresponding utopian pretensions in the surrounding social and political reality which claim to represent the only valid, univocal world.

No type of novel could be so suited to this task and at the same time so endangered by this kind of self-criticism, as the utopian novel. This is so because the process of self-criticism is reciprocal. Unmasking political utopian pretensions by laying bare the utopian pretensions of the novel-istic word destroys the utopian pretensions of the utopian novel itself. The history of the utopian novel leads to the antiutopian novel. Revolutionary Russia, where the debate about utopianism, socialism, and Marxism was particularly intensive and concrete, was the home of the first great, internationally effective experiment and achievement of this kind: Zamyatin's novel *We* (*My*) (written in 1920, published abroad in 1924, and as yet never published in the Soviet Union).[11]

I cannot discuss, in these general remarks, the matter of the particular style and structure of Zamyatin's novel, including its complex polemical dialogue with the contemporary context and the anticipated future. These issues have been discussed in the extensive Western criticism about Zamyatin and his novel. Here I can only try to indicate that in this work the connection between novel and utopia is particularly stringent. Furthermore, this relationship fits particularly well with Bakhtin's general conception of the novel as a self-critical discovery and rejection of the utopian pretension.

As Bakhtin observes, any kind of absolutism and centralism tends to establish a "unified and unique language." It excludes individual voices which can be worked out only gradually and slowly by "acknowledging and acquiring the words of others." Therefore, "all forms introducing a narrator or stylized author document to a certain degree the freedom of the author from the unified and unique word." The novel as a polyphonic genre rejects the "unique" as well as the "authoritarian" word which can only be "quoted":

> The novel is an expression of a Galilean linguistic consciousness, rejecting the absolutism of the unified and unique language. . . . The novel presupposes a decentralization of language and meaning in the ideological world, a certain linguistic shelterlessness of the literary consciousness which has lost the unquestioned and unified milieu of ideological thought.[12] [p. 178]

Zamyatin's utopia is a (or better: *the*) "Unique State" (*Yedinoe Gosudarstvo*). It is presented in the report of a narrator (D-503) who is also the builder of the "Integral," a spacecraft which is about to begin a cosmic journey. In order to bring the message about this state and its collective happiness to other planets, the government has asked everybody to "compose pamphlets, poems, manifestoes, odes or other works about the beauty and greatness of the Unique State." The "notes" of D-503 are intended as a fulfillment of the state's request. A *Unique* State, however, can accept only a "unique and unified language." A narrator who starts to write under such conditions cannot yet have his own voice. He explicitly understands his contribution as an expression of the collective "We." He starts, loyal to the "authoritarian word," with a long quotation from the *State Gazette*, the official voice of the "unquestioned and unified milieu of ideological thought" (Bakhtin). With regard to Bakhtin's statement about the narrator, one should remember that Bakhtin spoke about the "freedom from the unique and unified word" to which the author testifies by using a narrator. This purpose can also be documented by noting the dependence of the narrator himself on a stereotyped language, particularly when this dependence is underscored for the reader by the ironic hyperbolism of the quotation and its praise.

But D-503 has to communicate his message to other worlds, which have other experiences, expressed in other languages. For this purpose he has to imagine their "linguistic consciousness." Thus, discovering the possibility of the "words of others," he discovers, gradually and slowly, his own "word." At first, he does this in a quite literal sense and with some resistance. He becomes self-critical about his repeating the word "clear." However, words used as utterances imply ideological judgments and values. Hence, the questioning of this previously unquestioned word becomes a criticism of an entire notion. Integrity and security under the collective linguistic "shelter" begin to disintegrate. Linguistic consciousness, becoming aware of the possibility of different words and voices, begins to discover the polyphony of the surrounding society. Behind the official unique language of the Unique State, other voices, even other languages appear—the language of love (personified in I-330), the language of the past (the "Old House"), the language of poetry (R-13, the Poet). This polyphony challenges and erodes the authoritarian political language, as well as the absolute language of algebra or mathematics so familiar to the mathematician D-503 (and the engineer Zamyatin) and canonized by the absolute state out of its commitment to "clear" rationalism. This language must also fail precisely because, as an absolute and unified language, it is unable to express irrationality, individuality, and the polyphony of real life.

Thus, linguistic consciousness unmasks the "utopian pretension" of the authoritarian, unique, and absolute word to mirror correctly the reality. But, this utopian pretension is also the pretension of the surrounding political, social, scientific reality, and the basic premise of its ideology. Therefore, such a consciousness, in becoming self-critical, also becomes critically involved in a polemical dialogue with a society claiming to be univocal. The individual has to start his own adventurous search for his own meaning and his own individual expression. And his writing as a discovery of his own voice in a polyphonic discourse lays bare the "shelterlessness" of the "linguistic and literary consciousness." Only at this moment do the "notes" of Zamyatin's D-503 become a self-conscious, self-critical novel:

> "I see with regret that, instead of a harmonious and strict mathematical poem in honour of the Unique State, my work is turning out to be some kind of fantastic, adventure novel" (p. 89).

This is not the place to show how Zamyatin unfolds the fantastic adventures of the narrator and protagonist D-503 as adventures of love and revolt. Nor is this the place in which to discuss how both motifs, and their development, represent the contrast and conflict between, in Zamyatin's terminology, "Energy" and "Entropy." This conflict is crucial for the whole novel, as well as for Zamyatin's general view of literature, life, and revolution.[13]

It should, however, be evident from these few introductory remarks, that the dynamics of Zamyatin's *We* work on three different levels, or in three different dimensions.

The first level, constitutive for all kinds of utopian novels, is the dynamic dialogue between the text and its context, meaning both the contemporary cultural and political context of the author in the Soviet Union of 1920, and the context of later readers who, with their concrete experience of different totalitarian systems, read the text by acknowledging how strikingly the author anticipated characteristic features and tendencies of historical development.

The second kind of dynamics, neither obligatory nor unusual for utopian novels, is the dynamic construction of the story line as a chain of adventures. This level is intended to make the story suspenseful and, at the same time, reflective of the uncertainties of human life. "Man is like a novel: until the very last page you do not know how it will end. Otherwise it would not be worth reading" (p. 139).

The third kind of dynamics is the way the word in the novel works itself out, following Bakhtin's formula, by "acknowledging and acquiring the words of others," and by discovering and rejecting the "utopian pretension" of the unique, the authoritarian, the absolute language. In doing this, the novel becomes genuinely polyphonic and dialogical (in the sense of Bakhtin's *raznorechie*).

In regard to aesthetic tasks and standards, this third kind of dynamics is the most significant and original achievement of Zamyatin's novel (even when compared with his great successors in the field of modern antiutopian novels—Huxley's *Brave New World* and Orwell's *1984*). Its aesthetic value includes, in this case, more than artistic style and composition. It also includes the cognitive and social function of verbal art, demonstrates how, in an established totalitarian Unique State, the individual can rediscover himself through his linguistic consciousness and how the plurality or polyphony of reality can be rediscovered and become manifest through literature, through the creation of a novel.

For Zamyatin (in *We* as well as in his essays on H. G. Wells and on other related topics) the novel represents "dynamics" and revolutionary "energy"; utopia, on the contrary, presents a completed, final state which as such excludes dynamic change. It leads therefore to "entropy"; it is "always static, always descriptive" and lacks the "dynamics of *sujet*."[14] This classification or disqualification is valid for many descriptions of utopian societies. But it neglects the interaction between the utopian work and its cultural context. And it neglects also the fact that the utopian novel as a genre in its variety and tradition always combined the description of strictly organized, more or less static societies in isolated "cities" (Polis, Metropolis, Cosmopolis) with more or less fantastic and adventurous, dynamic "journeys." What changed historically was the growing emphasis on the second, more dynamic aspect. The description of utopia became a journey to and through utopia. But at the same time the conception of utopia itself and the perception of the distance to utopia (ontologically and temporally) changed.

More's Utopia was, by definition (and name), a *No*-where. Bacon's New Atlantis was no less irreal, but it was already conceived as an ideal model which should be striven for. Such an intention is highlighted by replacing spatial distance with temporal distance, as already in Mercier's *L'an deux mille quatre cent quarante* (1770) and later in many romantic utopias (in Russian literature, for example, in V. F. Odoevsky's *The Year 4338*). After romanticism French Utopian Socialism developed utopias as models for better societies in the real future or as concrete political programs, presented often not in the form of utopian novels but as utopias *in* novels (in Russian literature, for example, in Chernyshevsky's novel

What Is to Be Done?). In opposition to such socialist concepts, the Russian so-called antinihilistic novel of the same period testifies to the fact that the same device could also be used to attack socialist activities and utopias. Dostoevsky's great novels synthesize both possibilities—the presentation of different, controversial utopian visions, and the rejection of their one-sided utopian pretension through the dialogical polyphony of the novel.

Despite such polemics, the prevailing tendency during this period was to believe increasingly in social and particularly in scientific and technological progress. It is sufficient just to mention Jules Verne, the most popular foreign novelist in pre- and postrevolutionary Russia (who combines this tendency with the motif of the journey to and through utopia). It is this belief in (and experience of) technological progress, which favored the appearance and rapid development of science fiction, and with it a development of utopian fiction which can be understood in terms of the title of M. Schwonke's monograph *Vom Staatsroman zur Science Fiction* (1957).

The other line of development can be labeled: From Utopia to Anti-Utopia. It is also bound up with the belief that utopias can and will be realized because of the general historical tendencies implicit in modern technology, used or abused by modern social and political technology and leading to negative, frightening results.

> Utopias are realizable. Life marches towards utopias. And perhaps a new century is beginning, a century in which the intellectuals and the cultivated class will dream of the means of avoiding utopias and of returning to a non-utopian society, less "perfect" and more free.[15]

This statement from the turn of the century was made by Nikolai Berdyaev, the Russian philosopher of the revolutionary period who was an expert on both Russian Marxism and the Russian utopian tradition. Furthermore, this statement by a *Russian* intellectual later became (in *French!*) the motto of an *English* antiutopian novel directed against a technologically regulated and unified life—Huxley's *Brave New World*. The anticipation of fatal utopias, and the representation of fatal experiences with such utopian pretensions became, due to World War I, revolution, Stalin, and Hitler, an international theme elaborated in "antiutopian" novels.

But as Irving Howe puts it in his essay "The Fiction of Anti-Utopia" even these great antiutopian novels of our century are "based on the vision of the Golden Age." They can realize their own values only in the image of its distortion. They show us how the "wish-dream" is perverted into a "nightmare," thus asserting "the continuous urgency of the wish-dream." [16] Hence, besides antiutopian novels which wage war against completed and therefore static utopias, there remained the possibility and the urgent task of using the form of the novel for creating self-critical and polyphonic images of dynamic revolutionary utopias. Such utopianism had to be presented as the moving force, as the "Principle of Hope" (Ernst Bloch) behind the revolution, the individual and the collective pursuit of happiness. The Soviet Russian author Andrei Platonov carried out such an experiment in the 1920s in his novel *Chevengur*.[17]

Both Lukács and Bakhtin defined the novel as an expression of human "shelterlessness." Platonov's novel is, in a literal sense, a novel about the shelterless in search of their utopias. This search requires neither travel to other planets nor a journey into the far future. It takes place in the Russian steppe, during the period of war and revolution. The work starts with a condition of almost subhuman shelterlessness, in the withered steppe, near a village which has been deserted by its starving population. For these people, survival itself seems to be a utopian task. In these conditions, those who do not possess the "principle of hope" die. Others, capable of "inventing" their own dream life, start their journey in search of a utopian ideal. One of them is Dvanov, the son of a fisherman who had drowned himself in the lake to discover the silent secret of death. His son starts and remains in a condition of radical "shelterlessness"—an orphan, expelled from his foster father's hut, a homeless lifelong traveler. He and his cotravelers are all topical versions of the Russian "pilgrims" and "seekers," including Gorky's version of tramps. But the October Revolution transforms individual or social shelterlessness into collective, general experience. It creates a socially universal tabula rasa, a situation in which the utopian invention of a new and better life becomes not only possible but indispensable. The network of different journeys of the shelterless through different utopias becomes the dynamic *sujet* and the polyphonic message of Platonov's novel.

Dvanov's main companion on his travel is Kopyonkin, who is obviously a revolutionary, proletarian version of Don Quixote—the most famous idealistic traveler, fighter, searcher, and dreamer in all of world literature (and, at the same time, the initiator of the modern novel). Kopyonkin, however, the revolutionary-idealist who fights on behalf of the insulted and humiliated, has the commissar's revolver rather than a sword and a lance. His horse is named not Rosinante, but instead The Power of the Proletariat ("Proletarskaya sila"). His Dulcinea is Rosa Luxemburg, the feminine symbol and martyr of world revolution. It is to her distant grave that Kopyonkin makes his adventurous pilgrimage.

Whereas in this case the literary allusion refers to the protagonist of a novel, in other cases the reference can be to the novelist himself. Thus, in their first encounter with a personified utopia, Kopyonkin and Dvanov meet a man who has changed his name to Fyodor Dostoevsky. He has done this because the utopian dream he started to realize takes "self-perfection" and the spontaneous "socialism as a society of good men" as its goal.

These few examples, part of a long chain of literary allusions and of utopian "stations" passed through during the "pilgrimage," show how the text works as a dialogue with a cultural, literary context in its own poly-phony of utopian traditions, visions, and voices. To use another notion of Bakhtin's, the text generates its own "intertextuality." It must be read as a system of allusions, quotations, montages, etc. This makes the novel a complex aesthetic object inseparable from a literary tradition. But this also makes it open to the ideological, social, and political implications of its contemporary context.

The same is true for Chevengur, the utopian city, in which the dif-ferent journeys converge (approximately halfway through the novel). This city becomes the protagonists' goal because it is there, so the report goes, that Communism has been realized. But Chevengur has a problem. It claims to have achieved the utopian ideal of a freely shared happiness, and, at the same time, to have embodied revolutionary communism. How, then, is the city going to integrate dynamics and openness into a system which, due to its completeness, must tend toward the static and the isolated? This, indeed, is the problem which confronts completed utopias in general.

Regarded in spatial terms, this problem involves both the city's exter-nal situation and its internal organization. Chevengur is a small town, lost in the steppe. This means that it is, on the one hand, almost as re-mote and as isolated as a utopian island, and that, on the other hand, it is totally open to the infinity of the surrounding steppe, the sky, and the wind—the "purging" wind of the steppe and the revolution. Thus Che-vengur is open to all shelterless travelers. But the problem is how to sus-tain spatial dynamics inside such a utopian island. The communal mem-bers of Chevengur are sufficiently wise or naive or utopian to understand that the solution to this problem cannot consist solely in sharing their shelters. Banning private property is not a sufficient answer; collective ownership tends to be at least as static as private ownership. Hence, after having made all private property collective, the communists cf Cheven-gur organize their "Saturdays" (the Soviet *subbotniki*) not as days of collective production but as days of collective movement. Each Saturday they move their houses or huts from one street to another, thereby reminding themselves that their commune should reflect the dynamics of revolutionary communism.

Of course, for the people of Chevengur, problems cannot be solved by mere spatial dynamics. They also need food, warmth, and shelter. In other words, they need productivity. They try to find answers to these problems through Nature and Love. Food and warmth are provided by that inexhaustible natural producer—the sun. For the remaining material and psychological requirements, an answer is provided through an interpretation of communism as brotherhood and charity. As experience shows, however, both premises are questionable. Innocent children continue to die, and "there isn't any kind of communism in Chevengur when a child dies." Furthermore, to take care of others, by organizing the limited needs and the happiness of other, less clever people (an attitude personified in Sasha Dvanov's foster brother Prokofi) may in the end deprive them of the most basic human quality—personal freedom. Read intertextually, both examples allude, once more, to Dostoevsky (Ivan Karamazov's Grand Inquisitor and Ivan's "return of God's entrance ticket"). And this fact does not preclude but rather intensifies their reference to the economical and political Russian reality of these first postrevolutionary years.

It is not hunger, however, which brings about the failure of the Chevengur experiment. The end grows directly out of the city's two initial aims—dynamics and openness. On the one hand, as Dvanov realizes, the limited space of the utopian city becomes too narrow for the dynamics of time, but even time itself, including "history," proves in the end to be too narrow for the limitless longing of the human soul. On the other hand, the same openness that made Chevengur a shelter for travelers through the open steppe makes it a defenseless target for enemies. The Cossacks destroy the commune and its utopian dream. In the battle the revolutionary Don Quixote is killed, joining in the death for communism and revolution his beloved Rosa Luxemburg. On Kopyonkin's horse, Dvanov returns to his native village, where the novel started, and rides into the lake in order to join his father in death and in the search for the secret meaning of life. The horse, The Power of the Proletariat, continues his journey through the limitless steppe, returning to Chevengur, where once the utopian pretension of an already completed communism made the lives of shelterless people worth living.

Thus, the journey into the utopian future returns to its beginning and meets the remembered, resurrected past. This memory can be individual (the father) or historical (Rosa Luxemburg). In any case, it must be a past which was itself striving for the future, willing even to die for it. Hence, the return to this past is at the same time the beginning of a new, shared journey into a new, shared future, a future even beyond personal death. This movement can be represented by the symbol for infinity, the figure of the lying eight, which starts from the central point, returns to it, and merges there with a line which is the mirror image of the first, thus endlessly continuing the movement.

European romanticism had already pointed out that this "figure" could symbolize the merging of the anticipated future and the remembered past in the present, as well as the journey of the romantic wanderer who goes out into the world and returns for a journey into his own soul, imagination, and memory. And as such a symbol for romantic life and poetry it had to be reflected in the structure of romantic works, including romantic novels composed as such "figures" and "prefigurations."[18]

Platonov's novel is not romantic poetry. It is, however, a very characteristic product of what—by Gorky and since Gorky—is called "revolutionary romanticism." When Platonov's revolutionary wanderer Dvanov is asked to invent a "Monument of the Revolution," he draws a "figure" which consists of a "horizontal figure eight" and a "vertical arrow with two heads," symbolizing together the temporal and spatial "eternity and endlessness" of the revolution.[19] The addition of the arrow is significant for the revolutionary aspect of this kind of romanticism. The figure eight in itself symbolized an eternal movement, but this movement remained self-reflected and closed in itself; it could, therefore, indicate both completeness and autonomy, as well as closeness and isolation. The same is true with regard to its symbolizing or structuring of romantic poetry (or of completed utopias). The arrow indicates the revolutionary movement away from self-reflection as well as the straightness of the revolution. But in addition to this the arrow, with two heads which point in two different directions, indicates a concept of revolutionary dynamics, which stands for more than a pointing toward a fixed goal. And both symbols together indicate a problem, crucial for revolutionary utopias as well as for romantic poetry.

How can one express infinity in a limited, closed form? Inevitably, each individual life and each individual work of art is a limited form with a beginning and an ending. Hence, the striving for openness and infinity can be integrated only as the awareness of this paradox, as a process of self-reflection and self-elevation by self-negation (*Selbstaufhebung*), embodied in the meaning and structure of the work. For the romantics this

was the notion and task of *irony*. And irony was for them the basic principle of the novel. In this respect, too, Platonov's novel represents revolutionary romanticism. Whereas many works of Soviet Russian revolutionary romanticism share with the romantics primarily the emphasis on
emotional dynamics, but clearly lack irony, *Chevengur* is a genuinely
ironic novel.

Its ending is ironic as a return to the beginning in the sense of a
Selbstaufhebung. Ironic also is the narrator's view of the characters, their
actions, their utopias, and the general cultural and political context. To
name a half-crazy peasant Fyodor Dostoevsky (and at the same time "the
Lenin of our district") or to make Rosa Luxemburg the Dulcinea of an un-
educated Don Quixote both generalizes and deepens their respective
utopias and puts the protagonists and their ideals in an ironic light. The
combining of the serious with the ridiculous, the primitive with the wise,
the brutal with the humane has the effect of calling into question each
motive, each character, and each topic. To demonstrate this in regard to
the novel's general view of the world or in regard to its style of presentation would call for a thorough analysis. Regarding the work's obvious
irony and its effect on the context, it may suffice to quote Gorky, the initiator of revolutionary romanticism.

Platonov had sent Gorky the manuscript after Soviet editors had refused to publish it on the grounds of its "wrong" representation of the
revolution. Gorky replied that he found the novel "extremely interesting,"
but added:

> Whether you meant to or not, you gave your illumination of reality a lyrico-
> satirical quality. Despite all the tenderness in your relation to people, they
> are colored ironically and appear to the reader less as revolutionaries than
> as "eccentrics" and "half-witted." . . . This is of course unacceptable for our
> censorship.[20]

It has remained so, evidently, to this very day.

If we look back from *Chevengur* to the two other utopian novels we
have discussed, *Aelita* and *We*, it is possible to discern in all three works
certain common tendencies and constructive principles which connect
them with general tendencies in the recent development of the utopian
novel.

For example, all three Russian novels close with a kind of return to
the beginning, to the point of departure. Such a device is, however, quite
common in the tradition of the utopian novel. Most stories about utopian
dreams and journeys, from the Hellenistic beginnings of the genre until

today, finish in the same bed, the same circle of listeners, the same port or aerodrome where they started. One may argue that these traditional dreams and fantastic journeys simply used this device as a narrative motivation for the description of a utopia. But even where this is the case, the device has the additional, intended effect of bringing the novel back to the reader's own reality. This leaves to the reader the task of transforming the closing of the "completed" utopia (and utopian novel) into the "dynamics" of his own mind in his own world.

The difference, however, lies rather in the journey itself, its function, and its relation to the reader's experience of reality. The traditional motivation, as we discussed before, was often to provide a frame. It always had the function of stressing the radical ontological difference between the reality of the reader's world and the utopian dream, tale, invention. In the recent development of the utopian novel, the journey through space or time becomes a constitutive part of the utopian concept. It has, in addition, the function of making the utopian anticipation seem more real or realizable. Because the modern reader conceives of his own real world as a historical process and a technological progress, the utopian journey itself must be seen as technologically and (or) historically possible, or even probable.

This first, or technological, aspect of the utopian journey is evident in *Aelita*, *We*, and in many other modern utopian novels. It is symbolized by the spacecraft. The second, historical dimension of the journey explains why, in these two novels (and in many other modern utopias), the prehistory of the respective utopias plays an important part, quantitatively and qualitatively. Again, one may object on the grounds that this is true not only for these examples, and that flying machines and prehistories may also be found in older utopian novels. But it is only now, after the invention of airplanes and the actual realization of historicism as a living mode of thought, that these factors can make the reader perceive utopias as, in fact, realizable. Furthermore, the historical experience of the October Revolution makes it possible to dispense with the journey to other worlds. Instead, the journey to and through different utopias becomes located in present reality (*Chevengur*).

Such an integration of the journey into the heart of a utopian work contributes to what Zamyatin called the "dynamics of the *sujet*." We have seen, however, that the dynamics of these three novels are also a result of polyphonic construction and of the dialogue between their controversial voices and the given cultural and political context. Such an integration of the polyphonic and dialogical principles into the utopian world itself is a tendency that modern utopia (including these three novels) shares with the general tendency of the modern novel. This tendency is the shift from the univocal to the polyphonic type of novel. And *We* demonstrates that the shift from the seemingly univocal report to the discovery of polyphony, and back again to the unified word and world, can itself become the constructive principle of a modern utopian novel which aims at unmasking utopian pretensions.

The more polyphonic the utopian novel became, the more capable it became of combining the "lyrical" and the "satirical." In this way the utopian novel could present the same world, whether it was a utopian one or a real one, in different, controversial voices, placing it in both a lyrical and a satirical light. This is also true for all three novels under consideration. The utopian woman Aelita, as well as the Soviet astronaut Los, are lyrical. So too are both endings—the cosmic "voice of love" and the "earthly songs" of collective work and "enjoyment" in the Soviet Union. The target for satire is, first of all, the Martian utopia, and through it the West as the real opponent of Soviet Russia. The utopia described by Zamyatin's D-503 is both satirical and lyrical (the discovery of love and poetry is part of this utopian world), and so is its effect, its coloring on the view of reality. That all utopias and realities represented in *Chevengur* are lyrico-satirical was obvious not only to Gorky.

A combination of modes, however, makes a utopian work more ambiguous. This ambiguity favors irony. In general, the modern utopian novel is clearly more ironic than those older works which praised utopian ideals (such as Campanella's *City of the Sun*). Most postrevolutionary Russian utopian novels are, indeed, more or less ironic, but such irony can be realized in different ways and to different degrees. On one end of the scale there is the slight ironic hint, and on the other end the construction of a whole novel as a playful parody of an already existing ironic model (for example, Kataev's utopian novel *The Island Erendorf* (*Ostrov Erendorf*), conceived of as a parody of Erenburg's ironic novels). Our three novels also testify to the possibilities for variety. *Aelita* is certainly the least ironical. Many of the characters, events, and topics are totally untouched by irony. If Gusev, the fighter, sometimes appears in a slightly ironic light, the irony actually comes more out of the heroic-comic tradition. Nevertheless, the representation of a utopia pretending to be the best possible state in a bad, doomed world, and the unmasking of this utopian pretension, puts Tuskub's rhetoric, the whole Martian utopia, and the allusions to the West in an ironic light.

We and *Chevengur* are both profoundly ironic works. They are ironic, however, in different ways. If one understands irony in a strict, rhetorical sense and construes the notion in terms of Zamyatin's "mathematical language," one can say that irony is the device which enables one to speak explicitly of the "sign +" so that it is actually understood as the "sign −". This is precisely what happens in *We*. Put in the same mathematical language, the irony of *Chevengur* consists not in the substitution of a verbally articulated "+" for an implied "−", but in the radical synthesis of "+" and "−". In other words, each position (+) is followed by its negation (−), but not with the purpose of proving the negativity of each position. The purpose is instead to indicate the limits, and hence the inadequacy, of each position in relation to the intended ideal—that is, a *Selbstaufhebung* in the sense of romantic irony.

Seen in this way, all three novels negate their own utopias, and this calls into question the "mathematical" classification of a novel as "*anti*-utopian" when, in fact, its own utopia receives "the sign −". Nobody would seriously classify *Chevengur* or *Aelita* as antiutopian novels in spite of the fact that Tolstoy's Martian utopia moves as clearly under "the sign −" as does Zamyatin's Unique State. And, if one objects that in *Aelita* the negative utopia on Mars is counterbalanced by the positive utopia of the revolutionary Soviet Union (two years in advance), then one is forced to agree that in *We*, too, the negative utopia of the Unique State is counterbalanced by the positive revolt of I-300, R-13, and D-503. Evidently, then, the decision to classify a novel as utopian, or as *anti*utopian, does not depend solely on its having, or not having, "the sign −". It depends primarily on the relationship to the context, to the cultural and political reality. This does not make a discrimination between utopian and antiutopian novels, between positive and negative utopias, worthless, but it does force the critic to remember that any kind of utopia has a negating aspect. This means that, in each case, an author's negating of his own utopia has to be understood as a function of this utopia inside the novel's text and in regard to the context (both the author's and the reader's context).

All this must also be understood in regard to the specific kind of irony implied by a work. The romantics pointed to irony as a constructive principle of the novel. This point was stressed again, and modified, during the period of crisis which followed World War I and the October Revolution. The Russian Formalists, as well as Bakhtin, stress it. And for Lukács irony is explicitly the essence of the novel.[21] But in Lukács's later view, the historical situation and with it the conditions and tasks for the novel as a genre, changed radically with the October Revolution and the establishment of the Soviet Union. With these developments, "disillusioned romanticism" was replaced by "revolutionary romanticism" and "critical realism" was replaced by "socialist realism." The possibility that an "Éducation sentimentale révolutionnaire" could lead to a new critical realism as a disillusioned revolutionary romanticism was excluded. Hence, the new task of the novel became not the expression of shelter-lessness, but the finding and building of a new, collective shelter. Bakhtin's view, propounded during the same years, was far less one-sided, and it emphasized both possibilities and tasks of the novel—the search for a shelter in a shelterless world and the putting on trial of every given, established shelter.

The utopian novel is a particular, and particularly stimulating, answer to this general challenge. It can also be an answer in both directions, depending on the given historical context and the intention of the author. In well-established cultural and political systems the utopian novel can challenge the arrogance of the status quo by confronting it with a utopian ideal. Or the novel can unmask a system's utopian pretensions by creating antiutopias. In a situation of general shelterlessness the utopian novel can reflect and stimulate the utopian search for an individual and collective shelter.

The concrete historical event of the October Revolution stimulated both tendencies. On the one hand, the world war and the revolution created a kind of tabula rasa, a situation in which human survival and meaningful life became, in themselves, a utopian task. This task had to be imagined through the medium of journeys to and through utopia. On the other hand, the October Revolution, and its result, the Soviet Union, claimed to be the Marxist-Leninist representation of the only genuinely scientific and valid approach to human life. This approach also implied the realization of collective human happiness in the future. Such a claim could challenge the novel, and could be challenged by the novel, as a genre which reflects the polyphony of human life and unmasks the utopian pretensions implied or manifest in Unique States and their unique and unified languages.

The Russian postrevolutionary utopian novel reflects both possibilities and tasks, covering the full range of variety between the two poles. As a result, neither a predominance of positive utopian novels nor a predominance of antiutopian novels is the most characteristic feature of the period. Not even the coexistence of both types of novels constitutes our main critical point. The most characteristic feature is the reflectedness found in all utopian works—an awareness of an ongoing crisis in the surrounding reality, in the contemporary novel, and in the discussion about utopianism. In this context, then, the utopian novel becomes a self-reflected and self-critical novel, and only in this capacity does it gain a new critical power. We may see this power as a function of irony. The

Russian postrevolutionary utopian novel is, then, an *ironic* utopian novel. The best representatives of the genre are the most ironic, in the sense we have indicated. This is so because it is the search for a utopian ideal which makes irony human, and it is, in turn, irony which renders more human the search for utopia.

NOTES

1. This essay is an abbreviated and revised version of my original contribution to the Symposium on the Russian Novel at Bellagio, 1979. The complete text was published in *Poetics Today* 3, no. 1 (Winter 1982): 33–60. I am grateful to the editors of this journal for the arrangement which made possible the publication of both versions.

2. Konstantin Fedin, *Goroda i gody* (Leningrad, 1924); Engl. trans.: *Cities and Years*, by Michael Scammell (Westport, Ct., 1962), p. 284.

3. Marietta Shaginyan, *Mess-Mend*, in *Sobranie sochineny 1905–1933* (Moscow, 1935), vol. 3, pp. 105–374 (quote: p. 253).

4. Georg Lukács, *Die Theorie des Romans* (Berlin, 1920); 2d ed. with an additional foreword (Neuwied and Berlin, 1963). The following quotations from the text, including the foreword, are my own translations from this second edition. Engl. trans. György Lukács, *The Theory of the Novel* (Cambridge, Mass., 1971).

5. Cf. as one example the *History of the Soviet Russian Novel* (*Istoria russkogo sovetskogo romana*), published by the Academy of Sciences (Moscow-Leningrad, 1965), in which each of the two volumes includes special chapters on the utopian novel, especially on science fiction (vol. 1, pp. 367–92 and 638–94; vol. 2, pp. 352–415, both written by A. F. Britikov).

6. V. I. Lenin, *Works* (Moscow, 1941–57), vol. 27, p. 1922.

7. "The Search for a Genre" ("V poiskakh zhanra") was the significant title of an essay, published also in 1924 by the Russian formalist Boris Eikhenbaum (cf. the reprint in the volume: B. Eikhenbaum, *Literatura: Teoria, kritika, polemika* (Moscow, 1927). *The Spirit of Utopia* (*Geist der Utopie*) was the title of Ernst Bloch's book, published in 1918, which became one of the initiators and main representatives of the new concern with utopian thought after World War I and the revolution.

8. Cf. P. N. Medvedev and M. M. Bakhtin, *The Formal Method in Literary Scholarship*, trans. A. J. Wehrle (Baltimore, 1978) (Russian publ.: Leningrad, 1928).

9. Mikhail Bakhtin, "Slovo v romane," written in 1934–35, published (posthum.) in M. Bakhtin, *Voprosy literatury i estetiki* (Moscow, 1975), pp. 72–233. All quotations of Bakhtin are my own translations from this edition because my essay was completed before the recent publication of: *The Dialogical Imagination: Four Essays by M. M. Bakhtin*, ed. Michael Holquist, trans. Caryl Emerson and Michael Holquist (Austin and London, 1981). See the essay "Discourse in the Novel," pp. 259–422.

10. Aleksei Tolstoy, *Aelita* (Berlin, 1923). All quotations are my own translations from this original edition.

11. Yevgeni Zamyatin, *My* (New York, 1952). All quotations are my own translations from this edition. Engl. trans. *We*, by Gregory Zilboorg (New York, 1924; 2d ed., 1959).

12. Bakhtin specifies the sociohistorical condition for the novel with the same word "shelterlessness" (Russ. "bespriyutnost") which Lukács in his *Theory of the Novel* used for the same purpose (Germ. "Obdachlosigkeit").

13. Cf. the collection of his essays in Ye. Zamyatin, *Litsa* (New York, 1955). Engl. ed.:

The Essays of Yevgeny Zamyatin, trans. and ed. Mirra Ginsburg (Chicago, 1970), which includes the essay "On Literature, Revolution, Entropy, and Other Matters."

14. The essays on H. G. Wells are reprinted (in Russian) in the collection *Litsa* (cf. note 13), pp. 101–38 and 139–46 (quoted from this edition).

15. Cf. the epigraph of Aldous Huxley, *Brave New World* (Garden City, N.Y., 1932). The Engl. translation quoted from George Woodcock, "Utopia in Negative," *The Sewanee Review*, 64 (1956): 81.

16. Irving Howe, "The Fiction of Anti-Utopia," in *Orwell's "Nineteen Eighty-Four": Text, Sources, Criticism*, ed. I. Howe (New York, 1963), pp. 176–80.

17. Andrei Platonov, *Chevengur* (Paris, 1972); and *Proiskhozhdenie mastera*, in A. Platonov, *Potomki solntsa: Povesti i rasskazy* (Moscow, 1974). The quotations are my own translations from those editions.

18. For this concept of Novalis, cf. Jurij Striedter, *Die Fragmente des Novalis als 'Präfigurationen' seiner Dichtung* (Diss. Heidelberg, 1953).

19. *Chevengur*, p. 88.

20. For the correspondence between Platonov and Gorky, cf. *Gorky i sovetskie pisateli. "Neizdannaya perepiska,"* in *Literaturnoe Nasledstvo*, vol. 70 (Moscow, 1963), p. 313.

21. Cf. *Theorie des Romans*, particularly the parts "Die Ironie als Formprinzip" and "Die Ironie als Mystik." For Lukács's concept of "disillusioned romanticism," exemplified in Flaubert's *Education sentimentale*, cf. pt. II, chap. 2 of his *Theory*.

GEORGE GIBIAN

Doctor Zhivago, Russia, and Leonid Pasternak's Rembrandt

Writing *Doctor Zhivago* was an unusually important undertaking for Boris Pasternak. He said on several occasions that in this work he hoped to communicate with a wider audience than his poetry had reached, and that what he wanted to convey was extraordinarily significant to him.

It was in order to be read and understood by a mass readership that he turned to prose fiction, believing that lyrical and reflective poetry and complex, symbolist-modernist prose, such as he had written earlier, were not suitable vehicles for accomplishing the goal which he had chosen for himself toward the end of his life. He was convinced that in the middle of this century the public was prepared to receive such content as he wanted to convey only in a work of clear prose fiction. Pasternak wanted to express a summation of his most cherished views, a conclusion to all his work—his thoughts about life in Russia, in this historical era, as well as about the human condition in general. He called it his "chief, important work,"[1] "a book about the most important matters for which our century has paid such a price in blood and madness," which "had to be written absolutely clearly and simply."[2]

The thesis of this essay is that the central themes of *Doctor Zhivago* (*Doktor Zhivago*), embodying the ideas which animated Pasternak, represent a double journey backward in time—leading him to confrontations (with reversals and transmutations), first, with his father's views on the special character of Judaism (set down in a booklet on Rembrandt); and second, with traditional Russophile conceptions of the historic mission and special qualities of the Russian nation and Russian literature.

Leonid Pasternak (1862–1945) was born in a Jewish family in Odessa. His father was an innkeeper who leased an eight-room guesthouse and

203]

attached yard, which he rented to farmers and cattle drovers.[3] Leonid studied medicine in Moscow, then switched to law, and finally, in 1882, turned to painting as his life's work. He became a widely known portrait-ist and illustrator and was commissioned to paint portraits of members of the highest Russian aristocratic society, as well as of the artistic and intellectual elite. He was adroit at pointing up his own assimilated Rus-sianness, at the same time that he avoided being baptized an Orthodox Christian in order to continue to enjoy the worldly advantages of tsarist Russia. For example, when in 1894 he was offered a professorship at the Moscow School of Painting, Sculpture, and Architecture, a position pre-supposing that its holder would be at least nominally a convert to Rus-sian Orthodoxy, Leonid Pasternak behaved with consummate tact, stress-ing his Russianness and safeguarding his appointment, while remaining Jewish in religion. In his own words:

> I thanked Prince Lvov for his kind offer which I was delighted to accept. At the same time, however, I pointed out that I doubted the realization of this proposal, as it still had to be formally confirmed by the trustee of the school, the Grand Duke Serge Alexandrovitch, and I feared that my being of Jewish origin would stand in the way of the latter's approval. I added that although I had been brought up in a Jewish family, admittedly religious but free from adherence to ritual, whose members, including myself, felt completely as-similated to our Russian surroundings, and although I believed in God but did not in practice belong to any religious denomination, I would never con-sider baptism as a means of facilitating my progress in life or raising my so-cial status. The very humane and tolerant Prince Lvov understood me very well, and promised to inform Serge Alexandrovitch of my standpoint. Con-trary to my expectations, the Grand Duke sanctioned my appointment, a thing unusual in those days, when civil servants had to belong to the Rus-sian Orthodox Church, or at least to profess another Christian creed.[4]

Leonid Pasternak left the Soviet Union in the fall of 1921 and settled in Berlin. In 1924 he visited Palestine, commissioned by a publisher to illustrate a book about the country.[5] In the 1930s, because of the rise of Nazism, he considered returning to live in the Soviet Union (he is said to have maintained his Soviet citizenship and passport), but a serious ill-ness of his wife necessitated medical treatment in England. In 1938 the Pasternaks moved to England instead of to the USSR, and he died there in 1945.

The question of Leonid Pasternak's Zionism has been obscured by his daughter's denial, in 1961,[6] that anyone in the Pasternak family had been a Zionist and by the understandable absence from the 1975 Moscow publication[7] of Leonid Pasternak's notebooks of anything suggesting Zionist sympathies. However, the evidence of Pasternak's book on Rembrandt is clear, whatever changes of outlook he may have undergone later.

Since the booklet is little known and not easily accessible, it may be useful to summarize those of its main ideas which are relevant to our understanding of the relation between its views and the themes of *Doctor Zhivago*. A notation at the end of Leonid Pasternak's text states that it was written in "Moscow, 1918–20." It was published in Russian in Berlin in 1923.[8] A Hebrew translation also exists.

Leonid Pasternak begins by describing a visit to the Bavarian spa Kissingen a few years before World War I. Kissingen was a favorite watering place for European and Russian Jews; Pasternak reacted with strong dislike to those he saw there, dressed up in their fashionable finery. He fled from Kissingen to Kassel, where he went to the gallery—and saw a painting by Rembrandt representing a Jewish God and a Jewish subject, which, in contrast to the Jewish visitors in Kissingen, aroused his admiration. He was impelled to study the theme of Jews in Rembrandt, and eventually was led to the conclusion that Rembrandt was an *anima naturaliter Judaica*. Leonid Pasternak goes so far as to assert that Rembrandt, in his understanding and sharing of Jewish values, was the most Jewish of all artists of any age and country.

In the process of commenting on Rembrandt's models (Jews from the ghetto and harbor of Amsterdam), his Old Testament subjects, and the artistic and human values of his paintings, Pasternak makes clear his conception of what constitutes typically Jewish characteristics. According to Pasternak, the Jewish God—as presented by Rembrandt—is a stern judge, who punishes his people severely when they disobey him, but who at the least sign of repentance turns into an all-forgiving, loving father. This process is repeated: the Jewish people stray off the path of obedience to God again and again; each time they are smitten by the avenging God-the-Judge; they again ask for mercy, are reaccepted, and so forth, in a spiral of sin-punishment-contrition-forgiveness.

Jewish values, according to Leonid Pasternak's interpretation of Rembrandt, affirm humility, spiritual concerns, and contempt for outward splendor and pretentiousness. The Jewish people are long-suffering and enduring. Jewish boys in Rembrandt's paintings display in their expressions a taste for learning; Jewish mothers are imbued with strong family feeling. Old Jews are sad; their faces reflect the grief they have suffered in their lives, as well as the spiritual wisdom they have learned through it.

Judaic Old Testament values tend toward the primeval simplicity and naturalness of a shepherd nation; closeness to the earth; a majestic, patriarchal way of life. They incline toward poetic moods and the principles of religion. Their bible covers all humanity and glorifies the perennial vitality (*zhiznennost*) of the Jews. It transforms humble details, through its art, into significant universal statements. Rembrandt, too, changed everyday reality into something ideal and mystical. As an illustrator of the Bible, he elevated trivia with his mysterious, spiritual touch from the world of banality to a realm of higher significance.

Moreover, Leonid Pasternak notes the Jewish (and Rembrandtian) predilection for tracing startling, fateful continuities—in historical coincidences. He reports that Rembrandt was a friend of a learned rabbi, Menasseh Ben Israel, the author of *La Piedra Gloriosa o, de la estatua de Nebuchadnesar* (1655), a treatise on biblical strands of recurrences. For instance, Menasseh Ben Israel's book argues that Nebuchadnezzar's dream foretold the coming of Messiah, as confirmed in Daniel's vision, and that the stone which broke the statue of the Assyrian emperors was the same stone on which Jacob fell asleep and also the same which David used to kill Goliath. Rembrandt even made four etchings as illustrations for Menasseh Ben Israel's book.

Outwardly, according to Pasternak, the Jews may be careless in dress, clumsy, naive, seemingly helpless—characteristics common to people who live mainly for spiritual values. The Jews' efforts are directed to inner self-perfecting, to feelings.

In his conclusion, Leonid Pasternak eulogizes Rembrandt and Judaism, referring to the Zionist Theodor Herzl, Palestine, and the downtrodden Jewish artisans of Odessa—tailors and shoemakers who revere the picture of Montefiore (the Zionist philanthropist) hanging on the walls of their humble quarters.

Boris Pasternak, we know from his friends' reports, did not share his father's pro-Zionist interpretations of the Jewish national character and his celebrations of Jewish spirituality. In fact, his attitudes toward his father were complex. A letter written in 1934 reveals a mixture of self-abasement and flattery bordering on adulation:

> I am now as old as you were in 1906 in Berlin. It is enough for me to remember you at that period to shrink back from the comparison. You were a real man . . . a Colossus, and before this image, large and wide as the world, I am a complete nonentity and in every respect still a boy. . . .
>
> I have been looking through your monograph again, after a long period

of time and was suddenly struck by the impact of your personality. . . . In your place, with such a life behind you, I should feel in the seventh heaven. Such a life, such a hand, such encounters and recollections.[9]

(The "monograph" referred to was probably a German book published on Leonid Pasternak's work in Warsaw in 1932.)

Yet, in direct reversal of his father's views, an important element in *Doctor Zhivago* is an attack on the central tenet of Zionism—the high valuation of the survival of Jewish identity and separateness as a nation. In addition, the novel performs other transformations on Leonid Pasternak's views, amounting to a wholesale invasion of his assertions about Jewish qualities and a reattribution of these qualities to the Russians instead, and to Christianity and the New Testament instead of the Old Testament.

The memoirs of Isaiah Berlin (and many other sources) aver that Boris Pasternak was "a Russian patriot—his sense of his own historical connection with his country was very deep," and that

> This passionate, almost obsessive, desire to be thought a Russian writer with roots deep in Russian soil was particularly evident in his negative feelings towards his Jewish origins. He was unwilling to discuss the subject—he was not embarrassed by it, but he disliked it; he wished the Jews to assimilate, to disappear as a people. . . . He spoke to me as a believing, if idiosyncratic, Christian. . . . If I mentioned Jews or Palestine, this, I observed, caused him visible distress.[10]

Boris Pasternak himself wrote in a letter in 1959:

> I was baptized as a child by my nanny, but because of the restrictions imposed on Jews particularly in the case of a family which was exempt from them and enjoyed a certain reputation in view of my father's standing as an artist, there was something a little complicated about this, and it was always felt to be half secret and intimate, an object of rare and exceptional inspiration rather than being calmly taken for granted. I believe this is at the root of my distinctiveness (*originalité*). I lived my life the most intensely occupied by Christian thought in the years 1910–12, when the main roots, foundations of this distinctiveness (*originalité*)—my way of seeing things, the world, life—were taking shape.[11]

A forceful statement of his faith in Russian cultural traditions is recorded in Alexander Gladkov's memoir of Pasternak:

> The grand traditions of the great Russian novel, of Russian poetry and drama, express the living features of the Russian spirit as it took shape historically in the course of the last century. To rebel against them is to con-

demn yourself to something forced, artificial and unorganized. *War and Peace*, *A Dreary Story* and *The Idiot* are just as much features of Russia as the birchtrees and the quietly-flowing river.

There is no point in trying to cultivate palm trees in Peredelkino. . . . Our literature is the concentrated spiritual experience of the nation, and to ignore it means to start all over again from nothing.[12]

The direct attack in *Doctor Zhivago* on Leonid Pasternak's 1920 Zionist sympathies begins after Yuri Zhivago first comments on the horrors suffered by Jews in Galician villages in World War I. Zhivago deplores the atrocities and then embarks on a discussion of nationhood: "I can understand that nations like that existed under Caesar—Gauls or Swabians or Illyrians. But since those days, this is only an invention, existing so that Tsars, politicians, and kings could make speeches about it—'Nation, my nation'" (p. 123).[13] Zhivago's friend Misha Gordon carries the argument one step further:

What are nations now, in the Christian era? They aren't just nations, but converted, transformed nations, and what matters is this transformation, not loyalty to ancient principles. . . . The Gospel holds out the idea of a completely new way of life, of spiritual happiness. . . . In that new way of living invented by the heart and the new kind of associating, which is called the Kingdom of God, there are no nations, there are only individuals. [p. 125]

It is the "mystery of the individual" which has become the central concern since the arrival of the Christian epoch. Then the argument is applied specifically to the Jews. Gordon continues:

The idea of nationhood placed on them [the Jews] the demeaning necessity of being and remaining a nation and nothing but a nation for ever and ever, during a time when a force which came out of their own midst delivered the whole world from that humiliating task. How extraordinary! How could that have happened? This holiday, this liberation from cursed mediocrity, this flight above the dreariness of everyday existence, all this was born in their land, spoken in their language, and belonged to their tribe. And they saw it, heard it, and let it go. How could they allow a soul of such absorbing beauty and force to leave them, how could they think that along with its triumph and assumption of power, they will remain like an empty envelope of that miracle cast down to them once upon a time? What use is it to anyone, this voluntary martyrdom? To what purpose have completely innocent old men, women, and children, so subtle and capable of goodness and of community of the heart, been for ages covered with ridicule and bloodshed? Why are the nation-loving writers of all nationalities so lazily lacking in talent? Why did their intellectual leaders not move beyond the facile forms of Weltschmerz and ironizing wisdom? Risking that they would burst from holding on to their duty, like kettles from too much pressure of steam, battling and being killed God knows for what. Why did they not dissolve their ranks? Why did they not say, "Come to your senses, enough, no more. Do not hold on to the same name. Don't go on sticking together in one lump. Dissolve. Join everybody else. You are the first and best Christians in the world. You are precisely that against which the worst and weakest among you have been pitting you."   [pp. 125–26]

This frontal attack on that which Zionists as well as many non-Zionist Jews and non-Jews admire as an astonishing achievement—the preservation of Jewish national identity through millennia of diaspora and persecution—Pasternak's characters view as the clinging to a principle antithetical to highest human individuality, to which Pasternak attributes an esoteric value.

Can we resolve the contradiction between Pasternak's disapproval of nationhood and his intense Russianness? I believe we can reconcile the two attitudes only in part. He opposes a collective sense of identity as part of a nation, but approves and embodies bearing national qualities as an individual. But some of the contradiction in Pasternak's thinking and feeling remains, unresolved and unacknowledged.

The view expressed by Pasternak's character credits Christianity with the elevation of the life of human individuals to the state of history. He considers the demise of nationhood a necessary precondition for the birth of life in a state of history instead of life in the state of nature. Pasternak links this concept with the struggle to triumph over death without significance (like that of "a dog by the side of the road"). The Jews, by dint of their clinging to survival as a group, as a nation, in Pasternak's view, have excluded themselves from this higher stage of existence.

The Jews' passing by—their nonrecognition of what Gordon terms the "holiday," their not sharing of "flight," "liberation"—is the price they have to pay. By clinging to their nationhood, the Jews have, in this view, forfeited participation in those highest states of consciousness.

We may find it difficult to accept this argument; the philosophical, idealistic aspects of this thesis may not suffice to dissuade us from some tremor of shock at such inveighing against Jewish national survival.[14] Nevertheless, to understand the novel and its relation to his father's thought, it is necessary to see clearly what philosophy of human history lies behind Pasternak's characters' stance.

Pasternak curiously twists his father's views on Jews and the Old Testament. He reassigns to the New Testament and to Christianity some of those qualities which his father praised in the Old Testament and in Rembrandt as quasi- (and super-) Jewish artist. Humble incidents and members of low social classes turned into significant objects are regarded in *Doctor Zhivago* as characteristic of the New Testament and as manifestations of Christian attitudes. For instance, the Old Testament parting of the sea, the salvation of the Jewish columns, and the destruction of enemy armies—elevated, historical, majestic events—are contrasted in *Doctor Zhivago* with seemingly petty, everyday New Testament incidents, which nevertheless are endowed with a significance which the Old Testament would impart only to impressive, huge events. The principle is the same in *Doctor Zhivago* as in Leonid Pasternak's book on Rembrandt, but the son attributes the ability to imbue trivia with significance to Christianity, whereas the father had done so to the Judaic Old Testament.

There is an interesting parallel in the two relationships we have been examining. In both there is a son versus father struggle: first, Boris Pasternak overturns his father's opinions on the subject of identity (individual versus national); second, he substitutes the New Testament for the Old Testament. In both cases, the new overcomes the old, the "son" principle conquers the "father" one.

Boris Pasternak also stresses suffering and endurance as characteristic of Russia. In *Doctor Zhivago* it is Russia which has borne a plethora of exceptional afflictions. Leonid Pasternak believed this trait to be a special mark of the Jewish people and history. Boris Pasternak, then, takes away from the Jews what his father had attributed to them and reassigns it to Russians. However, it must be pointed out that Leonid Pasternak, in his turn, was attributing to Jews and Jewish history that which nineteenth-century Slavophiles had stressed as particularly Russian. Dostoevsky, Nekrasov, and many other writers had praised the supposed exceptionality of Russian acceptance of suffering and the Russian ability to turn it, through spiritual alchemy, into an uplifting asset. The son, then, could be said to be merely returning characteristics purloined by his father to their former owners.

Other traits, Jewish according to Leonid Pasternak's treatise, are turned into Russian ones in *Doctor Zhivago*. Simplicity, aversion to outer show, modesty, reappear as very Russian qualities. Again, the content is similar, the virtues identical, but the bearers incarnating them have been turned from Jews in Rembrandt and in history into Russians in the twentieth century.

We are facing another aspect of the historical competition of Russians and Jews for the same sacred slot—the Promised People in a Promised Land, exemplified in the view of Moscow, as the Third Rome, occupying the position of the New Jerusalem.

Leonid Pasternak, in keeping with the traditional view of the Jews as the chosen people, describes their special relationship to their God, as His sometimes mutinous and disobeying, and at other times, repentant and submissive children. To Boris Pasternak in *Zhivago*, it is the Russians who exist in a special relation, not to God, but to history. They have the role of serving as exemplars to the rest of mankind—as the nation which has suffered the most and surpassed all others "in blood and madness," thereby serving as the bellwether and spiritual model. The historical and spiritual message was imprinted on them the most clearly. By dint of primacy—as the first socialist country, and having gone to the furthest extremes of suffering, violence, and devastation—Russia demonstrated through the convulsions of her body politic what happens when those who believe above all in abstract principles and in the remaking (recutting, retailoring: *perekroika*) of society win power and set about to remold a country with disregard for (and disbelief in) the opposite attitude: the contemplation of and marveling at life as mystery, as sacrifice, and as eternal rebirth and renewal.

Still other qualities praised by Leonid Pasternak in the Jews and reattributed to Russians in *Doctor Zhivago* are primeval naturalness, closeness to earth, and a majestically patriarchal way of life. These are presented as strong and laudable attributes in Zhivago, in Lara, and in Tonya.

The relationship of Boris Pasternak's Slavophile ideas to his father's Judaic ones is complicated by the fact that many of the Russian intelligentsia's values resembled the supposedly traditionally Jewish ones. One such Jewish self-view was that "In contrast to their neighbors, the Jews did not entertain a belief in the divinity or sacredness of the rules. . . . The version of the past which generation transmitted to generation included many episodes the lesson of which inculcated skepticism, not to say mistrust, of political power and the life of politics."[15] Again, in the Jewish outlook, there often was a duality of authority, divided between what we might call temporal and spiritual authority-king and prophet. The prophetic values emerge invariably as the superior, enduring ones.[16]

Similarly, in Russian history of the last two hundred years, the views and the authority of the intelligentsia—critical of the status quo, protesting against serfdom, criticizing the state and the legal structure of tsarist

Russia—were held to be morally superior to and much more admirable than the official governmental views. The distrust shown by various characters and the narrator of *Doctor Zhivago* in tsarist and Bolshevik authority, and in political and social action altogether, is very similar to the ancient Judaic view, but it may also draw, for the same attitudes, on Russian antecedents.

A passage about historical Jewish attitudes could be applied without changing a word to *Doctor Zhivago*: "Political skepticism, mistrust of power and of its exercise, an awareness of the narrow limits of what politics can really achieve are recognizable features of the traditional Jewish ethos, which the lessons of this transmitted past inculcated."[17] The coincidences which Menasseh Ben Israel claimed pervaded Old Testament Judaic history, such as the same stone reappearing in a series of cardinal historical events, are echoed in *Zhivago*, on a far more humble level, not in the lives of rulers and leaders but in the everyday life of Pasternak's characters. Individuals who later become important to each other gather in one place, without yet knowing who the others are. The same room, window, advertising billboard, house, and other places and things will be witnesses, or locations, of repeated crossings and recrossings of the life courses of various characters.

In the world of *Doctor Zhivago*, randomness does not entirely rule the distribution of people and events. There is design and destiny, beyond any individual character's will or awareness. The signs in which significance may be detected are scattered all around the characters; the raw materials for a possible reading of what fate or some other Designer-Planner is laying out, myriads of little incidents, are present in a pattern discernible to those who have eyes to see.

An especially insistent claim to significance is suggested for the two quasi-angels in the book—the protective Good Angel, Yevgraf, and the destructive Evil Angel, the predator Komarovsky. The two characters reappear at crucial moments of the action, one extending a protecting hand, the other tempting, exploiting, wreaking havoc. Their roles stand out as peaks above the already high level of significance constituted by the web of coincidences and by the semiallegorical characters and events. Yevgraf and Komarovsky constitute two poles of a basic axis, between nurturing and destroying, as a fundamental duality of the structure of the novel's world.

Boris Pasternak not only redistributes his father's values, he also deepens them. In contradicting and metamorphosing his father's views, he goes creatively beyond him and his sources.

II

Pasternak's second ideological return in *Doctor Zhivago* is to confrontation with the views of the Slavophiles concerning the nature of Russia, as well as with traditional Russian views of the role of the writer.

Doctor Zhivago is a very Russian work in its various features and in the concepts which it expresses, through characters, events, and the narrator, of the national Russian character and the Russian historical mission.

Pasternak's sense of himself as Russian is evident in many of his works and has been attested to by many of his friends and correspondents. Isaiah Berlin writes:

> Pasternak loved everything Russian, and was prepared to forgive his country all her shortcomings, all save the barbarism of Stalin's reign. . . . He believed himself to be in communion with the inner life of the Russian people, to share its hopes and fears and dreams, to be its voice, as, in their different fashions Tyutchev, Tolstoy, Dostoevsky, Chekhov and Blok had been.[18]

Pasternak repeatedly told Berlin, in Moscow, when they were alone, that

> he lived close to the heart of his country, and sternly and repeatedly denied this role to Gorky and Mayakovsky, especially to the former, and felt that he had something to say to the rulers of Russia, something of immense importance, which only he could say, although what this was—he spoke of it often—seemed dark and incoherent to me.[19]

Anna Akhmatova said of herself and Pasternak that their "deep patriotism was not tinged by nationalism; the thought of emigration was hateful to both."[20] She said also that Pasternak had a mythological sense of history in which quite worthless people played mysterious, significant roles.[21] We may partly discount the sentences which Pasternak sent under duress (and which were possibly even written for him by others, for his signature) when he was threatened with expulsion from the Soviet Union, after being awarded the Nobel Prize. He was warned by Vladimir Semichastny, the head of the Komsomol, that the government "would not put obstacles in the way of his departure from the USSR."[22] Pasternak then wrote to Nikita Khrushchov, begging not to be made to leave the country:

> For me this is impossible. I am tied to Russia by birth, by my life and work. I cannot conceive of my destiny separately from Russia, or outside it. . . . Departure beyond the borders of my country would be for me tantamount to death and I therefore request you not to take this extreme measure against me.[23]

Olga Ivinskaya, the companion of his last years, says that the friends who drafted his reply used the term "Soviet Union" in their text; Pasternak insisted on replacing it with "Russia."[24]

We may accept at its full face value the pride he expressed, in a poem, in his love for Russia—as the inspirer of his poetry. He referred to himself as one

> Who made the whole world weep
> At the beauty of my native land.
>
> [*Ya ves mir zastavil plakat*
> *Nad krasoi zemli moei.*]

To Olga Carlisle he claimed that

> I wanted to record the past and in *Doctor Zhivago*, specifically, Russia was the inspiration and the goal. I wanted to record the past and to honor in *Doctor Zhivago* the beautiful and sensitive aspects of Russia of those years. . . . There will be no return of those days or of those of our fathers and forefathers, but in the great blossoming of the future, I foresee their values will revive.[25]

Naturally, in drawing conclusions about Pasternak's attitudes toward "Russianness" from his novel, we must proceed tentatively and undogmatically, remembering his own warning (to a correspondent in Germany in 1958):

> I am not so arrogant, categorical, and bold as to speak about nations, and to say, "We, we the Russians." You must read *Doctor Zhivago*. It is all deeper, more limited, more modest, more definite [*bestimmter*]. Everything hinges on the center of the personality.[26]

Pasternak made it clear on numerous occasions that he thought of *Doctor Zhivago* as a Russian work about Russian destiny. The action of the entire novel takes place in Russia. The Russian earth is the ubiquitous stage, the chief actor, and also the chief sufferer of the action. We cannot ponder the role of Russia in the novel without realizing that Pasternak's conception of the significance of the history of Russia in the twentieth century is its central subject. It is not some abstracted Russia, outside of time, about which he writes, but events in the country, happening to its people, in the first fifty years of our century.

The novel, first of all, presents images of Russia in explicit references. It is rural Russia which forms a backdrop to the earliest portions of the novel when the eleven-year-old boy Misha Gordon accompanies his father, a lawyer who has been transferred to Moscow. They travel by train for three days, while "Russia, her fields, steppes, towns, and villages bleached white like lime by the sun, flew past them wrapped in clouds of hot dust. Lines of carts stretched along the highways, occasionally lumbering off the road to cross the tracks . . ." (p. 12).

This is the first of many references to the vastness of the Russian countryside, presented here factually, without interpretation, coloring, or any philosophical-historical-religious charge. Only two paragraphs later, however, the narrative modulates into a philosophical argument about motion and relativity, and rises swiftly to one of Pasternak's most sweeping assertions of his fundamental and most esoteric belief: human interrelatedness and the existence of two different worlds in which things exist, an idea to which we shall return later in more detail.

Among the rather conventional, received ideas concerning Russia is Zhivago's assumption that naturalness is a basic Russian national trait. When the tsar visits the troops in Galicia, Zhivago reflects, "He was natural, in the Russian way," superior to the banalities and theatricalities of the German kaiser, and, "That kind of theatricalism is unthinkable in Russia" (p. 123), although the naturalness here praised in Russians, we have seen, had been attributed by Leonid Pasternak to the Jews.

Later, when speaking to his father-in-law, Zhivago also attributes to the Russian national tradition the uncompromisingness and resoluteness of the initial stages of the revolution. Furthermore, the "uncompromising lucidity" of Pushkin, the "unwavering faithfulness to the facts" of Tolstoy, and "this way of seeing the thing fearlessly through to the end seemed to have a familiar, national look" (p. 198) to Zhivago. At that time, he still felt them to be admirable, connected with and based on Russian national habits and ways of reacting.

A little later, though, the view that ancient dreams were coming true in the revolution was shattered. "Is there any reality in Russia today?" Zhivago asks. Reality "has been so frightened that it is hiding" (p. 228).

The ability to transform the everyday, petty detail into something significant that would speak to later generations is, according to Zhivago, shared by the Gospels and by the greatest Russian writers. It is the "Russian, childlike" quality of Pushkin which Zhivago also invokes as a model of transforming "the ordinary into the fairy tale-like, at the touch of the hand of a genius" (p. 294). While being reticent about such high-sounding matters as the ultimate purpose of mankind or his own salvation, Pushkin (and Chekhov), in Zhivago's view, wrote of the private, modest concerns of everyday life. The Gospels too had spoken of modest matters, of simple people (in contrast to the Old Testament).

Zhivago even believes, moreover, in a connection between Russia and such a technical feature of literature as meter.

> Pushkin's tetrameter, later so famous, was some kind of measuring unit of Russian life, a yardstick, as it were, a gauge patterned after the measure taken from the whole of Russia's existence, as you draw the outline of a foot to cut a shoe or give the size of a glove so it will fit the hand. Later in much the same way the rhythms of spoken Russian, the intonations of conversational speech were expressed in the quantitative lengths of Nekrasov's trimeters and dactylic meters.   [p. 293]

"The whole of Russia's existence" is absorbed into, becomes the shaping source of, the matrix and the pattern of its favorite poet's metric foot. One of the highest means for human beings to overcome individual mortality and achieve communion with the immortal part of themselves across the vault of the ages, poetry, is in its turn based on Russia, like the tailor's pattern of a coat.

A view which Pasternak shares with Slavophiles is his high valuation of simplicity, just as the lack of that quality is to him a serious defect. He prizes spontaneity and immediacy in human behavior. Lara too shares values expressed in Russian proverbs and in Slavophile writings from the nineteenth century. She disapproves of holding rigidly to principles and discipline and deplores timidity of imagination (p. 311). The novel repeatedly eulogizes the intuitive.

Very Russian to Pasternak also is contempt for outward formalities such as ceremony, pomp, the external. (This reminds us of the nineteenth-century Slavophiles' teaching about differences between Russians and West Europeans.) Equally hostile is the attitude toward the will: living by will power, asserting primacy of will, is opposed as un-Russian in *Doctor Zhivago* (pp. 256–57).

The Westernized Russians cling to dogma, to "words and appearances" (p. 7). Nikolai seeks an idea which would be simple, yet intense, and one which would speak directly to the emotional and intuitive side of man, especially to a child, to illiterate, simple people—something graspable, sensuous, speaking through concrete particulars (pp. 7–8).

Kubarikha, a cattle healer, a sorceress to whom Doctor Zhivago refers laughingly as his "rival," (p. 372) sings a very old Russian song of which the narrator says, "A Russian song is like water held back by a dam," expressing a "sorrowing, yearning force"—"an insane attempt to stop time with words." Pasternak spoke of the overcoming of time through art, again, by reference to that ancient, traditional, very national theme, a Russian song. In Gogol's *Dead Souls* (*Myortvye dushi*), in eighteenth-century literature, and ever since the nineteenth-century Slavophiles, Russian song has been felt to be the quintessence of Russianness, and its particular features—mournfulness and the association with suffering—to be expressive of Russian sensibility.

The references in *Doctor Zhivago* to Russia which we have been looking at so far, and the attitudes toward Russianness, have been for the most part rather conventionally Russian. They have consisted of Slavophile attitudes toward Russia and of reversals or redirections of Pasternak's father's interpretations of Jewishness.

In other regards, also, such as the literary characteristics of his own novel, Pasternak's *Doctor Zhivago* is typical of the mainstream of Russian prose fiction in the nineteenth century. Pasternak plunges right into huge questions of philosophy and history, in keeping with Russian tradition. Erich Auerbach, for example, in his vast survey of Western realism, characterizes the Russian realistic novel as prone to leap into improvisations of "immense theoretical countersystems"[27] and to tackle "ultimate ethical, religious, and social questions." Moreover, according to Auerbach, "It seems that the Russians were naturally endowed with the possibility of conceiving of everyday things in a serious vein; that a classicist aesthetic which excludes a literary category of 'the low' from serious treatment could never gain a firm foothold in Russia." This describes accurately Pasternak's practice in *Doctor Zhivago*, and also the theory advanced in the novel (echoing what his father had said in his booklet about Judaic tradition and the Old Testament): seeing vast significance in the apparently trivial.

Russian realism, moreover, Auerbach observed, "is based on a Christian and traditionally patriarchal concept of the creatural dignity of every human individual regardless of social rank and position, and hence it is fundamentally related rather to old-Christian than to modern occidental realism."

The introduction of a multitude of characters at the outset of the novel is reminiscent of the beginnings of *War and Peace* (*Voina i mir*). Upon a first reading, the reader has difficulty sorting out who is minor, who will be important. There are many very brief scenes, as in *War and Peace*. Only after a hundred pages or so does the novel clarify who the chief characters will be; but the interconnections of human lives will reappear and be reemphasized. The vastness of the canvas, the oscillation from private to historical events and characters, the close involvement of the personal lives of fictional characters with historical events are also in the Tolstoyan tradition.[28]

As the novel progresses, the explicit mentions of Russia become more and more significant. The early ones refer to Russian land—to natural features—rather traditionally, with some emotion but no special depth. After the first half, however—in the postrevolutionary civil war sections of the book—Russia assumes a deep, tragic meaning: it is the land of exceptional suffering; a representative country.

Pasternak presents events happening in Russia in those years as messages, as parts of Revelation. It is a central assumption of Russians that the writer is the bearer of an important message. He speaks the "word." He is not a mere entertainer or artist but the bringer of exhortations and interpretations concerning the main moral and public issues of the day. In the West, it is the traditional view that the epic is the genre in which a bard sums up the chief values of his age. The Russian writer is expected to do exactly this, in all genres, especially in poetry and in the novel. More often than not, he expresses values animating the opposition, rather than the establishment. He is the hero of the resistance, the seeker of martyrdom. Pasternak's conception and practice in *Doctor Zhivago* are fully in line with this tradition.

"The Last Judgment is now taking place on earth. This is a time for angels with swords from the Apocalypse and winged beasts" (p. 258), Strelnikov says to Zhivago; and Zhivago accepts this part of the statement, but not the conclusions drawn by Strelnikov from his description of his period and its exceptional demands. He rejects Strelnikov's remark that it is not a time for merely "wholeheartedly sympathizing doctors" (p. 258). Zhivago considers the proper human activity to be contemplation, meditation, and the perception and communication of beauty and love, which Zhivago carries on through his poetry, whereas eager participation in action, in the world of deeds and political remoulding of "life," are erroneous and lead to dehumanization and self-abstraction. This is what he designates, to Strelnikov, as the issue which he has "been arguing with an imaginary accuser all my life" (p. 258). Pasternak applies his father's description of Jewish exceptionality, raised to a mystical, esoteric level, to the Russians. Their history, not the Jews', is in *Doctor Zhivago* the paragon of going the farthest, and the soonest, and communicates the most clearly the essence of the universal predicament—the *condition humaine* in our century.

It is by way of Zhivago's thoughts of Lara that we reach these views of

Russia. When Zhivago escapes from captivity among Liberius' partisans and reaches Lara's room in Yuriatin, his pondering of what Lara meant to him, of what she was, leads him to brooding on Russia and back to Lara:

> A spring evening in the yard. The air punctuated with sounds. The voices of children playing, coming from varying distances as if to show that space is alive through and through. And this vast expanse is Russia, his incomparable mother, famed beyond the seas, parent, martyr, stubborn, crazy, irresponsible, created by God, naughty, with externally splendid, disastrous, unpredictable escapades. Oh, how sweet to exist. How sweet to be alive and to love life! Oh how one is always drawn to thank life itself, thank existence itself, to thank them directly, face to face.
>
> This was exactly what Lara was. You could not talk with them, but she was their representative, their expression, the gift of hearing and speaking, bestowed upon the mute principles of existence.   [pp. 401–02]

Expression, communication, a means of contact between one human being and the death-defying element of another's being with whom it is possible to speak, all these are sensed in and through contradictory Russia and described in the nine attributes—which here form one complex for Pasternak (space, Russia, mother, godfearing, splendor, martyr, disastrous, unpredictable, adventures).

Earlier in the book, Pasternak had already associated Russia with "destiny." She was fated "to become the first socialist state since the beginning of the world" (p. 185). This tremendous event would bring about a "new order of things, as familiar as the woods on the horizon or the clouds over our heads." All the rest shall be gone. Nothing else will be left, and, we shall see, Lara and Zhivago will be like Adam and Eve in a newly devastated world. Russia has primacy, in its fate to be the first socialist country. She is the model, the leader, in this apocalyptic stage of the world community, with a mission, powerful, elemental.

Lara is the incarnation and expression of what is essential in Russia and the revolutionary twentieth century, not only for Zhivago, but also for Antipov-Strelnikov. In their last talk (frenzied and desperate "as only Russians can talk,") the narrator says, "All the themes of the time, all its tears and insults, all its motives, all its piled up resentments and pride were written in her face and bearing. From her, out of her mouth, the indictment of the age could be spoken. Its predestination" (p. 472).

In this expressive role, Lara is closely associated with Russia. In the context of the present passage, in the interpretation of Strelnikov, not the narrator, Lenin joins Lara and Russia to form a threesome. Strelnikov is the former follower of an extreme and abstract social cause, but by this point in the novel, doomed as he is, his words carry the convincingness of a man speaking the truth shortly before his death. Strelnikov begins by claiming that the "whole of this nineteenth century" was "absorbed and expressed, in a generalized way, in Lenin, who fell upon the old world as the personified retribution for all that had been done. Side by side with him the unforgettable, vast figure of Russia, Russia bursting into flames, a light of redemption for all the idleness and adversity of mankind, arose before the eyes of the world" (p. 473).

Again starting with Lara as the human form expressing suffering, the progression of ideas moves through Lenin (the reaction against, and the answer to, the preceding century's wrongs) to the "vast figure" of Russia, associated again with sorrows but in the role of the redeemer.

Komarovsky, Lara's seducer and exploiter, whose vision of her was that of the object of a sensual passion, is gone. The two other chief men who love her, the husband Antipov and the lover Zhivago, between them have a vision of her as a human individual incarnating the time-hallowed redeemer: sorrowing, suffering Russia.

It is Lara who explains to Zhivago that

> Everything settled and conventional, everything related to the everyday, to home and to order, all this has turned into dust along with the upheaval of all of society and its reorganization. All the details of everyday existence have been cast aside and destroyed. Only the force—the force apart from every-day actual life—of the soul stripped to the last thread remained, for which nothing has changed, because it felt cold in all times, it shivered and was drawn to its nearest neighbor soul, equally naked and alone. We two are like the first two human beings, Adam and Eve, who at the beginning of the world had nothing to cover themselves with, and now we are equally naked and homeless at the world's end. And you and I are the last recollection of that immeasurably great treasure which has been created in the world in the many millennia between them and us, and in memory of those vanished miracles we breathe and love, and weep, and hold each other, and cling to each other.   [p. 413]

Lara speaks as if there had been two moments in human history (biblical times and the twentieth century in Russia) which achieved peaks of clarity and self-expressiveness.

In their memory Lara and Zhivago preserve the awareness of the two times of nakedness and deprivation. One point was the time of the beginning, of Adam and Eve; the other, the end, in the revolution and the early 1920s in the Soviet Union. They share this understanding and offer their love and closeness "in memory," sacramentally, as a gift and monument to the greatness of past human achievements between the two limits of time.

Zhivago himself had expressed related thoughts earlier in the book, speaking in the military hospital during World War I:

> Just think what times these are! And you and I are living at such a time. Such things happen only once in an eternity. Just think of it, the whole of Russia has had its roof torn off and you and I and the whole nation are out under the open sky. And there's nobody to spy on us! Freedom! Real freedom. . . .
> [p. 147]

The temporary delight over the throwing off of oppression; the expansiveness of newly received freedom; the feeling of exceptionality of Russian destiny—all add up to the great rarity of the events: the special privilege, the extraordinariness of living in such an epoch, and these are associated with Russia and the revolution.

Zhivago went on to underscore the exceptionality of it by linking it with another special period—that of Jesus Christ and the Gospels—and with his basic belief in unity and communication between all creatures:

> Last night I was watching the meeting in the square. An extraordinary sight. Mother Russia is on the move. She can't stand still. She's walking and can't stop walking, she's talking and she can't stop talking. And it isn't as if only people were talking. Stars and trees meet and converse, flowers talk philosophy at night, stone houses hold meetings. Something like the Gospels, isn't it? The times of the Apostles. Remember St. Paul? "You will speak in tongues and you will prophesy. Pray for the gift of understanding."   [p. 148]

Russia, then, under the liberating impetus of the revolution, is the scene of an activity reminiscent of a greater earlier period, that of the Gospels: a liberation which brings about a transcendent understanding. There is contact: there is ability to speak and to understand. Zhivago speaks of the stage on which all these happenings occur in the proverbial idiom, "Mother Russia." Communication leads to communion, to a sense of the unity of all creatures, men and nature, "stars and trees." [29]

III

When Pasternak heard that friends and relatives of his, worried about the harm which the religious ideology of *Doctor Zhivago* might do to his reputation, were trying to buy up and put out of circulation copies of his book in the West, he wrote to Jacqueline de Proyart, on August 4, 1958,

> What are these relatives of mine, people close to me, "friends" of mine, doing for me? Are we to love one another simply, or are we to love in us that which is immortal, the only thing which matters? That is the only thing *qui se pose* between myself and the masters of my age and the critics and the friends, the only thing which I bear and hold within myself, so physically, in such a passionate impassioned and earthly way. It is a handful of Russian earth. And that is what Christ was asking of us, I think.[30]

This "immortal" element, vague, undefined, is the kernel of something that survives us. It was not simple, ordinary love but love for the immortal, basic element, of superpersonal existence, in other human beings—an esoteric (not simple, earthly) love for the rare portion in the other, not the conventional, ordinary Christian soul, but something else. To express this belief in *Doctor Zhivago* was more important to him than his supposed poetic reputation and is the essential, primary thing in the novel to Pasternak. It is significant that he equates his expression of the love for the immortal part of human beings—when he is at his most transcendental—with a "handful of Russian earth."[31]

NOTES

1. Boris Pasternak, *I Remember: Sketch for an Autobiography* (New York: Pantheon, 1959), p. 121.

2. Letter of May 7, 1958, Renate Schweitzer, *Freundschaft mit Boris Pasternak* (Vienna: Kurt Desch, 1964), p. 47. Pasternak's handwritten letter is reproduced in facsimile on pp. 44–45.

3. David Buckman, *Leonid Pasternak: A Russian Impressionist, 1862–1945* (London: Maltzahn Gallery, 1974), p. 9.

4. Guy de Mallac, "A Russian Impressionist: Leonid Osipovich Pasternak, 1862–1945," *California Slavic Studies* 10 (1977): 95.

5. Buckman, *Leonid Pasternak*, p. 75.

6. Quoted by Rannit, in the *Bulletin of the New York Public Library* (August 1960), pp. 437–51, from a letter by Pasternak's sister Lydia Slater: "My parents had a Jewish Orthodox background, but we grew up without any religion. Our circle was mostly Russian, but we had some Jewish friends. . . . We never have been Zionists." In a "Letter to the Editor" of the *New York Times Book Review*, October 29, 1961, p. 50, disagreeing with Robert Payne's book on Pasternak, which had been reviewed earlier, Lydia Slater formulated her views somewhat differently. She says there that the Pasternaks were "a Jewish family," "admittedly religious but free from adherence to ritual," and that "my father was not baptized; but neither was he a Zionist." She stresses that he spent only about a month in Palestine, as a member of an artistic expedition (i.e., he did not visit for Zionist motives).

7. *Zapisi raznykh let* (Moscow: Sovetsky khudozhnik, 1975), ed. Josephine Leonidovna Pasternak and Alexander Leonidovich Pasternak.

8. L. O. Pasternak, *Rembrandt i yevreistvo v yego tvorchestve* (*Rembrandt and Jewry in his work*) (Berlin: D. Saltzmann Verlag, 1923). Leonid Pasternak's interpretation of Rembrandt may be viewed as a reaction against that presented in Julius Langbehn, *Rembrandt als Erzieher* (1890). Langbehn's book described Rembrandt as an artist in the Teutonic spirit, who stressed the strength of irrationalism (associated by Langbehn with the Germans) as against pernicious rationalism (typified by the Jews). Langbehn's book was widely known in Europe for decades and repopularized by the Nazis.

Judith Stora, in her article "Pasternak et le Judaïsme," *Cahiers du monde russe et soviétique* 9, no. 3–4 (1968): 353–64, discusses why Pasternak abandoned his Jewish inheritance and turned toward Orthodox Christianity. She attributes his shift to the failure of Judaism to satisfy his thirst for mysticism, but does not refer to his father's book on the "Jewishness" of Rembrandt.

9. Quoted from a letter in possession of the Pasternak family, by Lydia Pasternak, in her introduction to Boris Pasternak, *Fifty Poems* (London: George Allen and Unwin, 1963), pp. 15–16. The "monograph" referred to in Boris Pasternak's letter was most probably a German work on Leonid Pasternak's paintings and illustrations, Max Osborn, *Leonid Pasternak* (Warsaw: Stybel, 1932). A sumptuous book published to celebrate Leonid Pasternak's seventieth birthday. The painter himself participated in the preparation of the volume.

10. Isaiah Berlin, "Meetings with Russian Writers in 1945 and 1956," in *Personal Impressions* (New York: The Viking Press, 1980), pp. 179–80.

11. The French text of Pasternak's letter to Jacqueline de Proyart of May 2, 1959, is given in a footnote to p. xi in the University of Michigan (Ann Arbor, 1961) edition of Pasternak's *Stikhi i Poemy, 1912–1932*. The English translation in the text of this essay is my revision of Max Hayward's translation in Olga Ivinskaya, *A Captive of Time*, p. 137.

12. Alexander Gladkov, *Meetings with Pasternak* (New York: Harcourt Brace Jovanovich, 1977), p. 137.

13. All page references to *Doctor Zhivago* are to the Russian text published by the University of Michigan Press (Ann Arbor, n.d.). The translations are mine, but I checked them against the Max Hayward and Manya Harari translation and in many places benefited from their version. My aim was to be as close as possible to the literal meaning of Pasternak's Russian text, even at the cost of smoothness and idiomatic English.

14. Jacob Glatstein, "*Doctor Zhivago*: A Jewish Dissent," *Congress Weekly*, Dec. 9, 1958, pp. 3–5, gives the arguments which can be made against Pasternak on this score. Gladkov reports that Pasternak once remarked, "I am not in the least worried by this talk of anti-Semitism which sometimes seems to start up quite suddenly—probably because I regard complete assimilation as the best possible thing for the Jews. The theory of race is quite specious and is needed only to justify odious practice. Try to explain the mulatto Pushkin from a racist or extreme nationalist viewpoint!" Gladkov, *Meetings with Pasternak*, p. 134.

15. Elie Kedouri (editor of *The Jewish World*), "Reflections on Jewish History," *American Scholar* 50 (Spring 1981): 234.

16. Ibid.

17. Ibid.

18. Berlin, "Meetings with Russian Writers," p. 180.

19. Ibid., p. 181.

20. Ibid., p. 197.

21. Ibid., p. 204.

22. Ivinskaya, *A Captive of Time*, pp. 237, 240.

23. Quoted by Ivinskaya, *A Captive of Time*, pp. 240–41.

24. Ibid., p. 240.

25. Olga Carlisle, "Three Visits with Boris Pasternak," *The Paris Review* 24 (Summer–Fall 1960): 58.

26. Schweitzer, *Freundschaft mit Pasternak*, p. 11.

27. Erich Auerbach, *Mimesis* (Garden City, N.Y.: Doubleday, 1957), p. 462.

28. Similarities have also been pointed out between Pasternak's novel and Dostoevsky, especially *The Brothers Karamazov*—in their emphasis on rebirth and religious regeneration, in contrast to political-social attitudes toward life, which are rejected in both works. Dmitri Grigoriev, "*Pasternak i Dostoevsky*" ("Pasternak and Dostoevsky"), *Vestnik russkogo studencheskogo khristianskogo dvizhenia* 2, no. 57 (1960): 44–51, Paris. Nikita Struve has argued in a very interesting note that the religious poems in *Doctor Zhivago* belong to a third class of religious Russian poetry, which they carry to an extreme. Struve's first two categories of Russian religious poems are, first, those expressing religious moods, and second, metaphysical works. N. Struve, comments on Pasternak's poem "Garden of Gethsemane," *Vestnik russkogo studencheskogo khristianskogo dvizhenia* 1, no. 48 (1958): 41–42.

29. A sweepingly negative judgment on Pasternak's presentation of Russia in *Doctor Zhivago*, antithetical to that offered in this chapter, is that of Alexander Gladkov, *Meetings with Pasternak*, pp. 162–63.

30. Jacqueline de Proyart, *Pasternak* (Paris: Gallimard, 1964), p. 233.

31. I am indebted in this chapter to Caryl Emerson, who read the draft and generously offered many comments and valuable suggestions on it. Since this chapter was completed, an excellent biography of Pasternak has appeared: Guy de Mallac, *Boris Pasternak: His Life and Art* (Norman: University of Oklahoma Press, 1981), deals expertly with Pasternak's religious, philosophical, and aesthetic views, particularly those embodied in *Doctor Zhivago*.

IV

Critics and Criticism

MICHEL AUCOUTURIER

The Theory of the Novel in Russia in the 1930s: Lukács and Bakhtin

I

The title of this paper immediately suggests two paradoxes. The first is that the novel, which found its classic forms in Russia, had to wait until the fourth decade of the twentieth century to find its theoreticians there. B. A. Griftsov's essay, *Theory of the Novel* (*Teoria romana*) (1927),[1] hardly justifies its title: it rather provides a sketchy overview of the *history* of the novel, in the course of which, to be sure, certain theoretical problems (of definition, origins, and typology) are raised. On occasion the author takes a position on these, but he never ventures to offer an original solution of his own. As for the short bibliography at the end, it contains not a single Russian title! When Griftsov mentions in his preface "the theoretical and formal studies that have developed in Russia over the past fifteen years" (a clear allusion to the work of the Formalists), he is moved to note how Russian thinking has followed "traditional theories of literature which construed the verbal arts as consisting primarily of works in verse," with the result that

> attention has gone chiefly to prosody. . . . And a great deal has been accomplished in this area. [But] the phenomena of prose have been studied infrequently, individually and unsystematically, with no attempt to establish such boundaries between genres, as for example, have long been drawn between the ode, the ballad and the elegy, and with no attempt to identify any fundamental constructive principle analogous to rhythm in the field of verse.[2]

These remarks help explain the first paradox. The theory of the novel in Russia suffered precisely from what made its practice so successful there: the crushing domination of a realist aesthetic that was, by its very

227]

nature, unconcerned with matters of form and so disposed to regard the novel not as a separate "form" but as something coextensive with litera-ture itself—and, in extreme cases, with life itself. One finds this attitude exemplified in the "sociological poetics" of the Pereverzev school, and es-pecially in G. N. Pospelov's contribution to a volume entitled *The Study of Literature (Literaturovedenie)* in 1928.[3] The principles Pospelov sets forth for analyzing any work of literature are in fact an extrapolation of the cat-egories commonly used in speaking of fiction (thus behind his central notion of "image" one clearly recognizes that of "character").

By contrast and by way of reaction, the rebirth of theoretical concern with literature found itself tied to an avant-garde aesthetic that centered on poetry. To be sure, the Formalists did construct a theory of prose; it is in that area that Viktor Shklovsky in particular achieved renown. But their theory leads to either an elementary grammar of narration more applica-ble to the short or long story than to the elaborate forms of the novel, or else to a theory of "laying bare the device" which suits only the more ec-centric forms of the "anti-novel."

The second paradox is that, although the two most important theo-ries of the novel did develop in Russia over the course of the 1930s, they appear to have done so in total isolation from each other, as if they were on two different planets. (The isolation, incidentally, continues to this day.) Born a decade apart, their authors, Lukács and Bakhtin, were none-theless contemporaries (the former being forty-five years old in 1930, the latter thirty-five). Both are philosophers of culture, strongly influenced by contemporary German thought (albeit by different branches: Lukács draws on the idealist tradition, Bakhtin on phenomenology). For both, the novel is less one genre among others than it is a point of departure for wide-ranging philosophical and methodological reflections.

The Theory of the Novel, written in 1914–15 and published in 1920, is one of the first essays where, under the influence of Hegel, Lukács elabo-rated his philosophy of history and his aesthetic. A convert to Marxism at the time of the revolution, he emigrated to Russia in 1932, quickly became one of the leading figures of the "current" (*techenie*) that formed around the journal *Literary Critic (Literaturny kritik)* and undertook, against the positivist-inspired sociologism that prevailed up to 1930, to put Marxist literary criticism back on a philosophic base by returning to Marx and Hegel. The core of this philosophic conception is set forth precisely in the entry "Novel" (*Roman*) which Lukács drafted for the *Literary Encyclo-pedia (Literaturnaya entsiklopedia)* and which, in December 1934 and Jan-uary 1935, became the object of a three-day discussion before the literary section of the Communist Academy.[4] The majority of the articles he published in Russian in *Literaturny kritik* and in German in *Das Wort* and *Internationale Literatur*, as well as his books on French and Russian realism and on the historical novel, develop the themes presented in summary form in this encyclopedia article.

As for Bakhtin, the initial orientation of his thought is that of an epistemological reflection on what are called in France *les sciences humaines* —linguistics and psychology in particular—most probably influenced by Husserl and in any case closely akin to phenomenology. Formalism was to make its contribution by centering his concerns on aesthetic and literary problems. But if Bakhtin unreservedly endorsed the Formalists' respect for specification and "positivity," he nonetheless rejected the kind of "positivism" that reduced literary data to material "objects," since in his view they could be identified only by reference to a specific *intention*. It is from such a phenomenological standpoint that he attempts in one of his first studies[5] to define the central problem for an aesthetics of the novel, that of the relations between author and protagonist. His study of Dostoevsky's poetics (1929) exemplifies this perspective.[6] The reflections it contains on the genesis of fiction as a genre were to eventuate in the monograph on Rabelais (1941; published in 1965), as well as in the more general studies, "The Word in the Novel" ("Slovo v romane," 1934–35) and "Forms of Time and Chronotopos in the Novel" ("Formy vremeni i khronotopa v romane," 1937–38), whose theses were summed up in a lecture given in October 1940 at the Institute of World Literature in Moscow. A second lecture, devoted to the interrelations between the novel and the epic, was delivered there in March 1941.[7]

II

That these two theories of the novel could take form so independently, so entirely without reference (at least without explicit reference) to each other, is doubtless to be explained by the particular conditions of literary and intellectual life in the USSR. Throughout the period when Lukács's theories represented Marxist orthodoxy, Bakhtin was under a ban, forbidden to visit Moscow. It may not be entirely coincidental that his first lectures on the novel, at the Institute of World Literature in October 1940 and March 1941, came soon after the official condemnation of *Literaturny kritik* (in March 1940), which marked the liquidation of the *techenie* and the fall from grace of Lukács. Conversely, when at the beginning of the 1960s Bakhtin's work begins to emerge little by little from the silence to which it had been condemned—and even becomes, after his death (and without his being responsible), one of the ideological supports for the antistructuralist current that forms around the annual publication *Kontekst*—it is the name of Lukács, compromised by the Hungarian revolution of 1956 and by his "revisionist" positions, that is no longer pronounced save in the most discreet way in the USSR.

The fluctuations of orthodoxy, however, do not by themselves account for the absence of any real contact between these two theories. In fact, the question concerns not so much two different (and indeed, opposite) answers to the same problem as it does two different ways of posing the problem—of the novel, and, more generally, of genre. The way of Lukács is the classical way. It is connected with German idealist aesthetics and especially with Hegel, who provides the basic inspiration for *The Theory of the Novel*. Art being conceived as one of the stages (the first, according to Hegel, the other two being religion and philosophy) by which the World Spirit assumes consciousness, literary genres are defined as the only three possible modalities of this assumption of consciousness: epic (through narration), lyric, and dramatic. In this conceptual framework the novel can find a place only as a modern variant of the epic genre; it appears thus as the heir of the classical epopee—not via a genetic line but according to a functional typology. For Hegel the differences between the novel and the epopee are what separate the "bourgeois" world of the former, individualist and prosaic, from the heroic and collective world of the latter. The novel is defined accordingly as a prose narration centered on an individual in his relations with society, the latter seen at once as formative framework and opaque environment, with which subjective aspirations constantly collide.

Lukács in his *Theory of the Novel* adopts this fundamental opposition, though in apocalyptic or utopian accents which he was later to attribute to the historical situation in which the essay was written (the First World War as experienced by the progressive intelligentsia of Central Europe). He regards the novel as an index of the degradation of the human (and of the desperate struggle of great writers against that degradation) in a world where the soul of man is no longer at home as it had been in the world of the epic, so permeated with significance. Lukács's conversion to Marxism was to "historicize" this conception and remove its pessimistic overtones. "The era of utter sinfulness," as Fichte termed it,[8] was now to be depicted in Marxist terms as the era of capitalism; that is, of alienation, when the institutions and relations created by man become detached from him and turn oppressive. And yet, in the Marxist perspective assumed by Lukács after 1920, the capitalist world stands not only for degradation: it represents as well the liberation of the forces of the individual and the increasing dominion of man over nature—clearly signs of progress by comparison with the world of feudalism. It is, in short, only the prelude to a return of the golden age, whose preconditions the bourgeoisie has created by liberating the individual and the productive forces of humanity at large (though the bourgeoisie cannot complete the process, since its existence is tied to that of a society split into antagonistic classes and generating alienation). The proletariat, in bringing about a classless society, will be able to restore to mankind that feeling of totality which characterized the epic age. So the epopee is no longer simply the inaccessible archetype of great epic narrative (for which the novel could never do more than foster a nostalgia in us): it is also the future that awaits the novel in socialist realism, the art of the triumphant proletariat.

One can see that in this scheme the form of the novel is defined very broadly and generally in terms of epic *narration*, opposed to that *description* of a world of inert objects (be it simple or symbolic) which Lukács takes to mark the decline of great fictional art. The latter appears as a mysterious ability to achieve through imagination a fusing of the individual and the general, of a concerted action, vividly depicted, and a deep historical sense. Lukács's theory, in other words, defines the *genre* quite apart from *style* in the narrow sense, treating style as a purely technical accessory, unrelated to the features that give fiction and the art of the novelist their specificity.

What Lukács neglects is precisely what Bakhtin takes as his point of departure: "Considering genre apart from questions of style and language," he writes, "has fostered a situation in which one studies chiefly the overtones of style (individual or collective), while ignoring that fundamental social tonality from which they derive."[9] Bakhtin, for his part, wishes to define the genre in terms of style; that is, to discover the novel's distinctive characteristic on the most immediate and concrete level, that of language. Here the kinship of his approach with that of the Formalists is most apparent, for they too tried to seize "literariness" at the level of language. For them, however, literariness—"the literary function"—is in fact reduced to the poetic function; that is, to the organization of discourse based on its sound patterns. Thus they renounced at the outset any approach to prose from this angle. For them (and particularly for Shklovsky) prose fiction was rather to be defined by its deployment of narrative motifs and devices. So two parallel but heterogeneous poetics arose: a poetics of language in the area of poetry, and a poetics of narrative in the area of prose.

The principle on which Bakhtin insisted held that the novel, like poetry, must be seen first of all as a phenomenon of language. But this insistence rests on another: language must be seen as more than merely an object. Here Bakhtin's theory of the novel rests on his critique of the "abstract objectivism" of Saussurean linguistics. The latter, in his view, defines language by a system of abstract norms and loses sight of the living reality. For Bakhtin, language is nothing apart from the *parole* which brings it to life by investing it with intentionality (one detects here a fundamental notion of phenomenology). And the *parole*, in turn, is nothing apart from dialogue, which alone brings it to life (for in monologue, it becomes fixed and dies).[10]

The word, that is, in its living reality is always the ground where two or more interlocutors meet—where two or more intentions, concurrent or opposed, complementary or in confrontation, jointly determine the semantic structure of the utterance. Conscious and systematic exploitation of the "dialogic" structures of language, of the "multivoicedness" of the word, of the simultaneous presence in any given speech act of "my voice" and "another's"—this, for Bakhtin, constitutes the fundamental characteristic of fictional discourse, which is thereby opposed to poetic discourse proper, since the latter is "monologic" and "authoritative," the only kind recognized by traditional poetics and rhetoric. Hence traditional poetics ignores the novel while rhetoric reduces it to a stylistic rhapsody—both alike in being unable to approach its essential character, which lies in its exploitation and increasingly complex orchestration of "the discourse of another." As Bakhtin conceives and develops it, the poetics of the novel is first of all a stylistics of the relations which can obtain in a text, a statement, or (at the extreme) a single word between the discourse of a speaker (or author) and a variable number of independent discourses.

So the history of the novel is connected, for Bakhtin, with the history of linguistic consciousness. The novel is born, he contends, of a new attitude toward language, reflexive and critical, which appears when language ceases to be simply experienced "from within," as an absolute, and is perceived instead "from without," as language, and thus made relative. Historically speaking, the novel appears in eras when the absolute authority of a single language—consubstantial with a society and a civilization—is put into question by the emergence on the cultural horizon of one or more alien languages. Examples are the Hellenistic age and the dawn of the Renaissance, when West European vernaculars replace Latin.

This calling into question of the single and "absolute" language of the great traditional literary genres can be seen for the first time in the parodic genres that reflected "great" literature in the distorting mirror of laughter—from classical times through the Middle Ages to the Renaissance. Parody is the simplest example of a "bivocal" language, superimposing a comic intention on the serious intention of the material parodied. And parody in its turn is connected to carnival—to that popular counterculture of laughter whose structures Bakhtin analyzes in his book on Rabelais. "It is precisely in folk laughter," he writes, "that the authentic popular roots of the novel must be sought. . . . It is there that a fundamentally new attitude toward language, toward the word, can be seen taking form."[11] Carnival laughter, like plurilingualism, helps make plain the essential "multivoicedness" of the word, whose literary exploitation is the novel.

III

At first glance it might appear that the theories of Bakhtin and Lukács differ not only in their point of view but in their very object. The typology of the novelistic genre as Lukács elaborates it in his 1920 study rests on the analysis of three works—*Don Quixote*, *L'Éducation sentimentale*, and *Wilhelm Meister* (to which he connects the Tolstoyan novel as well). In the article on the novel for the *Literary Encyclopedia* he extends this typology into periodization. Cervantes's work serves to define the novel "*in statu nascendi*," characterized by a "fantastic realism." The eighteenth-century novel, especially the English, illustrates the "conquest of everyday reality," whereby "the broad historical horizons of the early novel constrict," but the optimism of the triumphant bourgeoisie is expressed by the creation of relatively "positive" heroes. The "poetry of the spiritual realm of animals," incorporating a full depiction of "the contradictions of bourgeois society," marks the apogee of the genre, as exemplified in the works of Goethe, Scott, Balzac, Stendhal, and the Russian novelists from Pushkin to Tolstoy. (The latter, owing to the historical backwardness of Russia, "signal a stage in the development of the novel analogous to that of Goethe, Balzac and Stendhal.") A decline sets in with naturalism, when writers "consciously or unconsciously avoid the fundamental question of their age"—that is, socialism—and slip from narration into description or symbolic representation. The coming to power of the proletariat at length opens a new era in which the objective historical conditions associated with the epic are once more brought together, so that one may consider it either as marking the end of the novel proper or its blossoming into epic.[12]

Clearly, what is a starting point for Lukács—the European novel of the Renaissance—is for Bakhtin a point of arrival. Bakhtin, of course, does speak of the English comic novel of the eighteenth century, and his two principal studies are devoted to Rabelais and Dostoevsky. But his strictly theoretical studies are essentially concerned with the prehistory of the novel, and it is in classical and medieval fiction above all that he seeks evidence of the role played by bilingualism and carnivalesque laughter in the structure of the genre. Rabelais and Dostoevsky are, from this point of view, a fulfillment.

This division of the historical material, however, opens the way to a possible reconciliation between the two points of view. Bakhtin is interested in the *genesis* of the genre, in the sources which he finds for a new attitude toward language; Lukács, for his part, studies the genre in its flowering, at the moment when the degree of elaboration achieved permits it to take up the work of the epic, to equal it in ambition, to achieve a universal range, expressing the essence of the historical moment better than the other literary genres or philosophy can do. Lukács's point of view would certainly appear to be more teleological and normative than Bakhtin's. But are they in fact mutually exclusive?

In fact, Bakhtin and Lukács can indeed be found to emphasize certain analogous features of the novel as a genre. Thus Lukács underscores the importance assumed by plebeian elements in the modern novel's "alteration of the feudal culture of narrative" (that is, the chivalric novel). "The new material which had to be artistically mastered in order to lay the foundation for the new novelistic form," he writes, consists notably in "this material regeneration and remodelling of the chivalric novel in a plebeian direction which brought it closer to life."[13] Bakhtin, too, constantly insists on the plebeian nature of "carnival laughter," from which the novelistic word takes its source.

Another striking convergence between Lukács and Bakhtin can be seen in the role which the former attributes to irony "as a formal constituent of the novel form."[14] "The situation of the writer with respect to the universe he has created," as one of his commentators observes, "is, in the novel, different from his situation with respect to the universe of all the other literary forms. Lukács calls this situation irony. . . . The novelist must go beyond the consciousness of his characters and . . . this going beyond is esthetically constitutive of fictional form."[15] The same feature appears, on the level of discourse, as that distance which "plurilingualism" (in Bakhtin's theory) allows the author to assume with respect to his own language. It is striking that Bakhtin should illustrate it by referring to the English humorists of the eighteenth and nineteenth centuries.

One may, conversely, find in Bakhtin's analysis of fictional discourse a confirmation of the sociohistoric conceptions of Lukács. "Plurilingualism" is related to the opening-up of a closed collectivity, whether tribal or feudal, by the development of trade and the birth of a market economy; thus it is related to the coming of an urban or bourgeois society. By the same token, the culture of "folk laughter," an essentially unofficial and subversive phenomenon, arises among the urban "*demos*." So the novel—even when it is approached from the point of view of discourse—appears as what Lukács, following Hegel, sees it as being: the characteristic genre of the bourgeois world.

"Bourgeois world" is used here as the opposite of "ancient world" or "feudal world"; so, in fact, it becomes the equivalent of "modern world." And here one finds the most important convergence of all between Lukács and Bakhtin. For both, the novel is not simply a genre to be ranged alongside others in any hierarchy or coherent system. It is, rather, the very expression of modernity. In this respect, Lukács parts company with Hegel, who saw the novel as replacing the epic in an age which could no longer find its adequate expression in art but only in philosophy. For Lukács it is precisely the novel which, by virtue of its problematic or "ironic" character, expresses most deeply the essence of an age "in which the immanence of meaning in life has become a problem, yet which still thinks in terms of totality."[16] For Lukács the novel, far from being one art form among others, becomes the quintessential expression of modern man.

Bakhtin even more expressly opposes the novel not to one or another literary genre but to all genres as defined from classical antiquity on and as systematized by the classical *artes poeticae*. The novel arose, developed, and continues to develop on the periphery of this system and against it. Thus the "canonization" of the novel signals the downfall of the old system of genres. Bakhtin explains:

> The novel is made out of different stuff from the start. Its nature is different from that of the fixed genres. With and in its birth one might claim that the future of literature as a whole was born. Therefore, once it came into being,

it could not simply take its place as one genre among others, and it could
not build its interrelations with them on the level of a peaceful and harmonious co-existence. For alongside the novel, all other genres take on a new
and different resonance. So there began a long struggle for the "novelization"
of other genres, for drawing them into the zone of contact with an uncompleted reality. . . . [But] the novelization of other genres is not a matter of
subordinating them to canons which are not theirs; on the contrary, it is a
matter of liberating them from everything conventional, paralyzed, stilted,
and lifeless that inhibits their own development—from everything that
makes them appear, alongside the novel, as stylizations of outmoded forms.[17]

One sees here that for Bakhtin no less than for Lukács the notion of the
novel covers virtually the whole of modern literature.

IV

This convergence, surprising as it may seem given the distance between the starting positions of the two theoreticians, nevertheless has its
legitimate logic. It only confirms that the novel as a genre does possess
certain objective characteristics and a certain significance, irrespective of
the angle of one's approach. And yet, to the extent that both men view the
novel as a sort of key to the modern world, it is inevitable that a comparison of their interpretations should ultimately make plain the essential divergence of two aesthetic systems and, at a still deeper level, two visions
of the world.

The divergence in question appears most clearly in the opposition of
the novel and the epic, which plays such an important role in the theories of both. For Lukács, this opposition serves above all to point up the
continuity that exists between the two forms. What separates them, as we
have seen, is the historical distance between the "concrete totality" of the
epic universe and the alienation of its modern counterpart. Still, this distance is fated to disappear: with the end of capitalism and the advent of
the classless society, the novel will reincorporate the epic. The mission
they share—the expression of totality—is thus much more substantial. It
is this aspiration toward totality that makes the novel the heir of the epic,
even if its very form testifies to the failure of that aspiration. Now, it is
through *narration*—that is, the representation of a concrete action (or
"praxis")—that this aspiration to totality is expressed or realized. For
Lukács it is thus the problem of action that constitutes the central point
in the theory of novelistic form:

Any knowledge of social relations will remain abstract and uninteresting from the narrative point of view unless it has been made a basic and unifying aspect of the action; every description of things and situations remains dead and hollow if it is merely the description of an uninvolved observer, rather than a component that actively furthers or retards the action. This centrality of action is not a purely formal invention of esthetics; on the contrary, it arises out of the necessity to reflect reality as completely as possible. If it is a matter of representing the real relation of man to society and nature (that is, not only a man's notion of these relations but the actual existence underlying his consciousness), then the representation of action is the only appropriate means to that end. For only when a man acts—i.e., only in the sphere of his social existence—does his true essence, the true form and content of his consciousness, find expression.[18]

The epic and the novel alike share "the necessity of laying bare the distinctive peculiarities of a particular society through the depiction of individual fates, through the actions and sufferings of individual people."[19] It is in terms of *narration*, as opposed to the *description* of inert objects (whether naturalist or symbolic), that Lukács defines realism in a famous article where he compares the role of the evocation of a horse race in *Anna Karenina* and *Nana*.[20]

The essence of the epic as of the novel—narration, tied to the idea of totality—is the central category of Lukács's aesthetic.[21] The fact that narration is always in the past tense totalizes the time of the action, encloses it in limits that fix it by separating it from the present in which the narrator lives. This means that the author places himself (and us) outside the time of the action, in a position from which we dominate it, and thus deny it its temporal reality. The novel as Lukács conceives it is, accordingly, like the epic, the totalization of a completed time, hence a denial and a negation of real time as we live it, uncompleted and unforeseeable.

Now it is this notion of time as closed, dead, distanced, denied, which for Bakhtin characterizes the epic in contrast to the novel. His opposition of the novel to the epic is much more radical: it rests on the juxtaposition of two absolutely heterogeneous and irreconcilable *times*: the "absolute past" of the epic, closed in on itself and separated from the present by an unbreachable boundary, and, on the other hand, novelistic time, which is always an uncompleted time (even when presented as being past), set up on the same coordinates as the present and, through the mediation of the present, opening out on a future. In this respect the epic is only the most accomplished and typical form of "the great literature of the classical age," which projects its world into the past, onto a distant level of memory—not into the real and relative past that is connected with the present by an uninterrupted series of temporal transitions, but into a valorised past of beginnings and pinnacles. This past is distanced, completed and closed, like a circle—which does not mean, of course, that there is no movement in it. . . . But all the points of this completed and circle-like time are equidistant from the real time-in-motion of the present.[22]

For ancient or classical literature, fixed in a hierarchy of defined genres with the epic at the top, present time "is deprived of any true completion, hence of any essential reality."[23] If the novel stands in so radical an opposition to the hierarchy of these genres it is because in the novel the immediate present becomes, if not the only true reality, at least the standpoint from which all reality to be is articulated and understood.

So for Bakhtin the constitutive "mode" of the novel is not epic narration but dialogue; that is, the relation that is established, thanks to the essentially "dialogical" nature of the novelistic word, among several autonomous discourses in respect to which the author himself takes the position of an interlocutor and not of a sovereign master. For dialogue, in its nature and by definition, is always in the present: it is the creative encounter with the "Other" in and through which thought escapes sclerosis, coagulation into a system, by being actualized in contact with another's thought, another's freedom. It is in authentic dialogue, in the polyphony that inheres in the very structure of novelistic discourse (which Dostoevsky was the first to actualize fully, according to Bakhtin), that literature opens out onto life, onto the basic uncompletedness of the present, and the epic becomes a novel. One can understand why Lukács, for whom the novel is always historical, sees Tolstoy as the novelist par excellence, and why Bakhtin takes as his "hero" a figure whom Lukács in his *Theory of the Novel* had refused to consider a novelist at all—Dostoevsky, whose engagement as a writer was always with a problematic time in process of becoming, and whom one can scarcely imagine writing a historical novel.

One might add by way of conclusion that this opposition between Lukács and Bakhtin over the relations of the novel and time is highly revealing. Lukács's unshakable attachment to the literary models of traditional "realism," his violent and sometimes fanatical hostility to the avant-garde, make him one of the most conscious and convinced defenders of the aesthetic of socialist realism (even though he remains a demanding and difficult critic of the works so labeled). There is no question that Lukács's aesthetics is conservative; it might even be called reactionary in the etymological sense, for its models are all in the past. But it is such by virtue of being utopian: does not utopia always enclose the future in an image of a golden age drawn from the past? The notion of narration that dominates the aesthetics of Lukács expresses the same need to dominate time—that is, to purify it of openness, uncertainty, and risk. In this sense Bakhtin's conception is more authentically "progressive," to the extent that it is based not on a dream of a perfect world (completed, closed, immobilized once and for all) but on an attentive openness to the Other, whether the free interlocutor of any authentic dialogue or the essential otherness of a present opening on to a future (and not one already contained in the past).

To this opposition may be added another, perhaps no less fundamental. In making narration the supreme form of consciousness, Lukács seems to be setting art over knowledge, and so turning back from Hegel to Nietzsche, under whose influence (direct or indirect) his philosophic formation took place. But this return may be only apparent, for when narration becomes an instrument of knowledge does it not risk losing its aesthetic specificity? When the novel fulfills the functions of history and philosophy, does it not risk leaving those of art unfulfilled? Bakhtin, by contrast, roots the novel in laughter, which is to say in the gratuitousness of play. That may be to assign it a less ambitious function, but it is clearly one more consistent with its nature as a work of art.

NOTES

1. B. A. Griftsov, *Teoria romana* (Moscow, 1927).

2. Ibid., p. 6.

3. G. N. Pospelov, "K metodike istoriko-literaturnogo issledovania," in *Literaturove-denie* (Moscow, 1928), pp. 39–104.

4. Lukács's paper and an account of the discussion were published in the journal *Literaturny kritik* 2 (1935): 214–50; and 3, 231–54.

5. M. Bakhtin, "Avtor i geroi v esteticheskoi deyatelnosti," *Voprosy literatury* 12 (1978): 269–310.

6. *Problemy tvorchestva Dostoevskogo* (1929); a second edition appeared in 1963 under a different title: *Problemy poetiki Dostoevskogo* (3d ed., 1972). English translation of second edition: *Problems of Dostoevsky's Poetics*, trans. R. W. Rostel (Ann Arbor, Michigan: Ardis, 1973).

7. These two lectures, under the titles "Iz predystorii romannogo zhanra" and "Epos i roman," are included with the two studies mentioned above in M. Bakhtin, *Voprosy literatury i estetiki* (Moscow, 1975).

8. Fichte's phrase is "das Zeitalter der vollendeten Sundhaftigkeit."

9. M. Bakhtin, "Slovo v romane," in his *Voprosy literatury i estetiki*, p. 72.

10. On this subject see V. N. Voloshinov, *Marksizm i filosofia yazyka* (Leningrad, 1928)

(English ed.: *Marxism and the Philosophy of Language*, trans. Ladislav Matejka and I. R. Titu-nik [New York: Seminar Press, 1973]). This work, attributed by some to Bakhtin himself, is in any case written under his influence.

11. Bakhtin, "Epos i roman," in *Voprosy literatury i estetiki*, p. 464.

12. Lukács, "Roman," in *Literaturnaya entsiklopedia* (Moscow, 1929–39), vol. 9, pp. 795–831.

13. Ibid.

14. Georg Lukács, *The Theory of the Novel*, trans. Anna Bostock (Cambridge, Mass.: The M.I.T. Press, 1971), p. 74.

15. Lucien Goldmann, *Pour une sociologie du roman* (Paris, 1964), p. 30. The word "irony" should be taken here in a very broad sense which is not opposed to humor but rather subsumes it.

16. Lukács, *The Theory of the Novel*, p. 56.

17. Bakhtin, "Epos i roman," p. 482.

18. Lukács, "Roman," *Literaturnaya entsiklopedia*, vol. 9, p. 804.

19. Ibid.

20. Cf. G. Lukács, "Rasskaz ili opisanie," *Literaturny kritik* 8 (1936): 44–67.

21. On this subject see Fredric Jameson, *Marxism and Form* (Princeton: Princeton University Press, 1971), pp. 201–05.

22. Bakhtin, "Epos i roman," pp. 462–63.

23. Ibid., p. 463.

RENÉ WELLEK

The Nineteenth-Century Russian Novel in English and American Criticism

"Russian fiction is like German music—the best in the world," stated William Lyon Phelps, a Yale professor of English, in the preface to his *Essays on Russian Novelists*.[1] How and when did such a view come about? I shall try to describe and judge the strictly literary criticism in English about the nineteenth-century Russian novel, reflecting on the main affiliations, motivations, and implications of the interpretations and evaluations voiced. My survey will conclude with the decisive novelty of the last decades: the rise of professional Slavic scholarship. Those who write on the Russian novel today know the language, draw on Russian sources and research. They are a different breed from the critics who did not know Russian or knew only a little, read the books in translation, were practicing novelists or critics and journalists concerned with gaining a general reading public for the Russians. Nobody will dispute the merits of the new Slavic scholarship: its breadth of information, its sense of the setting, its new techniques of analysis, but we may also reflect on the losses: the contraction of the audience, which reflects the widening gulf between the Academy and the ongoing life of literature.

I shall pass over some problems of the reception of the Russian novelists. What, for instance, was known of Russian literary criticism in the West and how far did it influence critical opinion? What was the role of French and German reactions to the Russian novel and the political events of the last 130 years? It is surely no chance that Turgenev's *A Sportsman's Sketches* (*Zapiski okhotnika*) appeared first in 1854 in English translation, in the year of the Crimean War, and that in the same year a Polish refugee, Lach Szmyrna, published an adaptation of Gogol's *Dead Souls* (*Myortvye dushi*) as *Home Life in Russia* ascribing it to a "Russian

241]

Noble," concealing the name of the author and assuring the reader that
the story is literally true.[2] I need only allude to the Russian revolutions
and the two world wars. Finally there are the questions of traditional
comparative literature: the role of intermediaries, translators, and travelers. Turgenev was the earliest important figure. He had visited England
since 1847, at first to see Alexander Gertsen in exile in London and later to
meet English writers and public figures. *A Sportsman's Sketches* was at
first interpreted mainly as an attack on Russian serfdom. The early translations of his stories are called "Photographs from Russian Life" and "Children of the Tsar."[3] Though Turgenev accomplished the breakthrough for
Russian literature, the role of translators was indispensable. W. R. S.
Ralston, who translated *A Nest of Gentlefolk* (*Dvoryanskoe gnezdo*) and
Liza in 1869, and C. E. Turner, who lectured at the Royal Institution on
Tolstoy as Novelist and Thinker (1888), were among the first. But Constance Garnett (1862–1946), who translated all of Turgenev, most of Tolstoy, almost all of Chekhov, Dostoevsky, and Gogol, stands out supreme.[4]
Her translations have been criticized, revised, modernized, and sometimes replaced, but regardless of some deficiencies, particularly the imposition of a certain uniformity of style, they represent an unparalleled
achievement of loving care and general accuracy.

All the political motivations, curiosity about Russia, the zeal of intermediaries, the personal contacts of Turgenev, do not explain the enthusiastic reception of Turgenev's novels in the United States. The art historian
C. E. Norton, the critic Thomas Sargeant Perry, the reviewer for *The Atlantic Monthly* who in 1877 translated *Virgin Soil* (*Nov*) from the French, and
later William Dean Howells and the young Henry James, make up the first
wave of a genuinely critical reception of the Russian novel. Turgenev's
novels and stories lent support for these Americans' own concern, which
in the 1870s crystalized around the concept of realism in the specific
sense of "the author hiding himself."[5] Turgenev was—somewhat mis-
takenly—invoked for what has been called "the disappearance of the author," *exit author*, or *impassibilité*, the doctrine formulated by Flaubert
and Maupassant which was devised to reject the confessional novel in
the style of George Sand, the overt didacticism of most nineteenth-
century novels, and the author's indulgence in commentary. Howells, in
1873, praised Turgenev as "the most self-forgetful of the story-telling
tribe": "he is more enamored of his creations than of himself; he pets
none of them; he upbraids none; you like them or hate them for what
they are; it does not seem to be his affair." Turgenev's method is opposed
to the "deliberate and impertinent moralizing of Thackeray" and the
"clumsy exegesis of George Eliot."[6] Both Howells and James admired

what seems to follow from objectivity, the minimizing of plot, and what they called the dramatic or pictorial method.

The interest in the Russian novel assumed new proportions with the advent of Tolstoy. How much Tolstoy's reputation abroad owes to Turgenev's contacts in France is a moot question. Turgenev did arrange for Tolstoy's Sebastopol stories to be published in *Le Temps* (1876), and he elicited a lukewarm letter from Flaubert, to whom he had sent the French translation of *War and Peace* (*Voina i mir*) (1880). But Turgenev certainly made the breakthrough for a literature hardly known before in England and America. As late as 1887 Matthew Arnold could say that "the Russians have not yet had a great poet."

There was some knowledge of Tolstoy before Arnold. The German diarist Malvida von Meisenbug translated *Childhood* (*Detstvo*) and *Youth* (*Yunost*) into clumsy English as early as 1862, and Eugene Schuyler, who had been American consul in Moscow, translated *The Cossacks* (*Kazaki*) in 1878. W. R. S. Ralston wrote an article on "Count Tolstoy's Novels"[7] which gives a careful synopsis of *War and Peace*. But Tolstoy's fame in England and America was due at first mainly to his sensational conversion. The renunciation of his title and the pamphlet *What I Believe* (*V chom moya vera*) (translated by C. Popoff in 1885) excited wide interest. Matthew Arnold read the pamphlets and *Anna Karenina* in French in 1887, the English translation by Nathan Haskell Dole published in New York having "come into his hand late."[8] Arnold's essay on Tolstoy[9] contained the most influential account and judgment of *Anna Karenina*, though Arnold said it was written "because of Tolstoy's religious ideas."[10] Arnold set the tone of much subsequent criticism by saying: "But the truth is we are not to take *Anna Karénine* as a work of art; we are to take it as a piece of life." "As a work of art it is defective. There are many characters in *Anna Karénine*—too many if we look in it for a work of art in which the action shall be vigorously one, and to that one action everything shall converge." But, Arnold admits, "what his novel loses in art it gains in reality," and he lists examples of Tolstoy's "extraordinary fineness of perception." Arnold anticipates much subsequent criticism when he finds the "English mind startled by Anna's suffering herself to be so overwhelmed and irretrievably carried away by her passion . . . showing not a hope, hardly a thought, of conquering her passion," though Arnold acknowledges "the impression of her large, fresh, rich, generous, delightful nature" which "keeps our sympathy, keeps even, I had almost said, our respect."[11] Arnold sees that the conversion of Tolstoy is adumbrated in Lyovin's ruminations toward the end of the book.

Most importantly for later criticism, Arnold draws a contrast between *Anna Karenina* and *Madame Bovary*, between the Russian and the French novel. "The Russian novel though dealing abundantly with criminal passion and adultery is free from anything which could trouble the senses, while the French owes service to the goddess Lubricity." There seems to be no evidence that Arnold knew Melchior de Vogüé's *Roman russe*, published the year before. There the Russian novel is also presented as an antidote against the immorality and scientific indifference of the French naturalistic novel, though Vogüé's fire is rather directed at *Bouvard et Pécuchet*. In England Arnold's essay confirmed the sudden ascendancy of Tolstoy. It set the pattern: Tolstoy is lifelike, vivid, moral, but his novel is shapeless and even unartistic in its strict adherence to reality. The Russian novel has become a stick to beat the French with.

In America the praise for Tolstoy was even louder. William Dean Howells became a fervent admirer. Tolstoy, he wrote, had become his "final consciousness." "The supreme art in literature had its highest effect in making me set art forever below humanity."[12] Howells lost interest in the technique of the novel, which had attracted him to Turgenev. Tolstoy seems to him the only writer who has "no manner" at all, whose fictions "seem the very truth always," whose "frank and simple kindliness is what style is in the merely literary author." Tolstoy's art seems to him so simple, so "unassuming," so "real," that it "ceases to be literature in the artistic sense at all" and becomes life itself.[13] The echo of Arnold is obvious and like Arnold and Vogüé he pits the Russian novel against the French: "the ugly French fetish which has possessed itself of the good name of Realism."[14]

Though *War and Peace* had been carelessly translated from the French in 1879, it made hardly any impression compared with *Anna Karenina* at that time. Havelock Ellis's long essay on Tolstoy mainly concerns his religious ideas, considers *War and Peace* "of comparatively slight interest."[15]

A more perceptive early essay is that by Edmund Gosse. It comments on Tolstoy's "conjectural analysis" (what Chernyshevsky had observed and called "interior monologue" as early as 1856), and Gosse draws, like Chernyshevsky, whom he could not have known, a parallel to impressionism in painting, mentioning Bastien-Lepage. Like Arnold he complains of the hiatus "in the progress of Anna's mind from after the first meeting with Vronsky to the original formation of her infatuated feeling for him," and he rejects the view of Tolstoy's nihilism, expressed even by Vogüé. "His radical optimism, his belief in the beauty and nobility of the human race, preserves him from the Scylla and Charybdis of naturalism, from squalor and insipidity."[16]

But Tolstoy's reputation as a novelist slumped with his later writings, though they kept him in the limelight. *The Kreutzer Sonata* (*Kreitserova sonata*) shocked most readers. Gosse considered it a "relapse toward barbarism," and G. K. Chesterton complained that Tolstoy would forbid the "divine act of procreation" as well as harmless tobacco and dangerous drink to the poor; "A small and noisy moralist inhabits one corner of a great and good man," is Chesterton's verdict.[17] *What Is Art?* (*Chto takoe iskusstvo?*) excited mostly resentment, though George Bernard Shaw tried to defend Tolstoy's views in 1898.[18] *Resurrection* (*Voskresenie*) was generally considered a disappointment, a decline from *Anna Karenina*.

There were even a few dissenting voices about his early fiction. George Saintsbury in his *The Later Nineteenth Century* (1907) not only preferred Turgenev but with the exception of *The Death of Ivan Ilich* (*Smert Ivana Ilicha*) found nothing to praise in Tolstoy.[19] But in general Tolstoy remained a great public figure and a patriarch of letters on the basis of his past novels. Howells's view that Tolstoy was "the greatest imaginative writer that ever lived"[20] was not a rare hyperbole. There was an excellent *Life* of Tolstoy by Aylmer Maude (2 volumes, 1910), an English socialist, but little literary criticism. Two other biographies[21] are decidedly inferior.

Soon after Tolstoy's death Dostoevsky began to overshadow his great rival. Dostoevsky was not of course unknown before. *Crime and Punishment* (*Prestuplenie i nakazanie*) had been translated in 1886, published by Vizetelly, the London publisher who suffered imprisonment for publishing Zola. Even before, *Memoirs from the House of the Dead* (*Zapiski iz myortvogo doma*) appeared as *Buried Alive* in 1881 and there was a translation of *The Insulted and the Injured* in 1882, which was reviewed by Oscar Wilde as not inferior to *Crime and Punishment*. Robert Louis Stevenson read *Crime and Punishment* in French in 1886 and wrote a letter to John Addington Symonds saying that "Raskolnikov is easily the greatest book I have read in ten years. . . . Many find it dull; Henry James could not finish it: all I can say, it nearly finished me."[22] But in general Dostoevsky was simply classed with the sensational naturalists: George Moore called him a "Gaboriau [a French crime-story writer] with a psychological sauce,"[23] and Saintsbury thought Dostoevsky "unattractive and 'such as one could have done without.'"[24] In 1910 a literary weekly called Dostoevsky "a mere feuilletonist, a concocter of melodrama, to be ranked with Eugène Sue and Xavier de Montepin."[25] Lyon Phelps complained about Dostoevsky's morbidity and lack of form. *Crime and Punishment* is "abominably diffuse, filled with extraneous matter, and totally lacking in the principles of good construction."[26]

The change is heralded in *Landmarks in Russian Literature* (1908) by Maurice Baring (1874–1945), who had been a newspaper correspondent with the Russian armies in Manchuria during the Russian-Japanese War and had stayed on in Russia during the 1905 revolution. He pronounced Dostoevsky "equal to Tolstoy and immeasurably above Turgenev." He retold the *Memoirs from the House of the Dead*, thinking it "one of the most important books ever written," and he recognized the relevance of *The Possessed* (*Besy*) in the light of the 1905 revolution. Baring gave an enthusiastic account of the later novels, declaring that if the Gospel according to St. John were lost Dostoevsky's work "would be nearer to replacing it than any other book written by any other man." His books are a "cry of triumph, a clarion peal, a hosanna to the idea of goodness and to the glory of God." Baring grants that Dostoevsky's work is "often shapeless" and "the incidents in his books are sometimes fantastic and extravagant to the verge of insanity," but the religious message touched him deeply.[27] In 1909 Baring was received into the Roman Catholic church.

Baring's book was reviewed by Arnold Bennett. He had read *The Brothers Karamazov* (*Bratia Karamazovy*) in French translation and thought it contained "some of the greatest scenes" he had "ever encountered in fiction."[28] In 1912, at last, the Garnett translation of *The Brothers Karamazov* appeared, followed by the other hitherto untranslated novels and stories. Then came the war, which shook the optimism of the English and brought them into alliance with Russia. A veritable wave of enthusiasm for Dostoevsky hit England during the war, whereas in America the prominent critics were still shocked by the world he conjured up. Paul Elmer More complained of "filth, disease, morbid dreams, bestiality, insanity, sodden crime" as "pathways to the emancipation of the spirit" in Dostoevsky.[29] James Huneker, in *Ivory Apes and Peacocks* (1915), still considered Turgenev "infinitely the superior artist," even above Tolstoy, and described Dostoevsky in lurid terms. With him "life itself fades into a dream compounded of febrile melancholy and blood lust."[30]

The first full-length English book is Middleton Murry's *Fyodor Dostoevsky* (1916). It is an attempt to describe the evolution of Dostoevsky toward salvation (meaning reconciliation, acceptance), a salvation proposed to humanity and implicitly to Murry himself. Murry ignores Dostoevsky as an artist, declaring that "Dostoevsky was not a novelist, and cannot be judged as a novelist." "He could not represent life as he was obsessed by a vision of eternity." His characters are "disembodied spirits. They have the likeness of men, we are told, but we know we shall never look upon them." "Their bodies are but symbols." Stavrogin, for instance, "is not a man but a presence."[31] Murry reflects: "It may be there really was no Smerdyakov as there really was no Devil, and that both had their abode in Ivan's soul. But then who did the murder? Then of course it may have been Ivan himself, or, on the other hand, there may have been no murder at all"—and, we may add, no book. The sense of phantasmagoria with total disregard for what may be called Dostoevsky's realism leads to the allegorizing of almost every character. "Rogozhin is Body, Myshkin is Soul" is obvious. But saying that "Nastasya is not a woman but the embodiment of Pain" vaporizes a distinct person. Every novel is supposed to be a stage on Dostoevsky's spiritual pilgrimage which also charts the epochs of human consciousness culminating in a faith in humanity which Dostoevsky claimed to be peculiarly Russian. Only in Russia has "mankind taken a great stride to its inevitable goal. In Russian literature alone can be heard the trumpetnote of a new word." In Tolstoy and Dostoevsky "humanity stood on the brink of the revelation of a great secret," but we are never told what this secret may be.[32] D. S. Mirsky called Murry's book "Pecksniffian sobstuff."[33] Still, Murry's book was the first in English which broke with the tradition of realism, made possible by the changed literary atmosphere in England.

For Murry, Dostoevsky becomes the incarnation of the spirit of Russian literature. "Russian literature," Murry tells us elsewhere, "has done more than any other single influence to diminish the prestige of the French conception of literature,"[34] "French" meaning here *l'art pour l'art*, aestheticism, as well as the well-made novel in the wake of *Madame Bovary*. Russian literature is exalted for its concern with conduct, with the harmony of the human faculties, for its tolerance for the failings of men. Russian literature, he concludes, is "more Christian than any literature has ever been." It is "historically the fulfillment of our own," answering the striving of Wordsworth, Shelley, and Keats for "an apprehension of harmony which includes, and by including, justifies all evil and pain."[35] The Russian novel thus appears, surprisingly, as a continuation of the English Romantic movement. Dostoevsky is grouped with Keats and Shakespeare, to whom Murry devoted his most impressive critical books. In November 1916 he could say: "In Russia things of the spirit are held in honour above all others."[36] He always lived in a dream world.

Murry, at that time, was married to Katherine Mansfield and lived in close proximity with D. H. Lawrence and Frieda. They violently disagreed on Dostoevsky. Lawrence had only contempt for Dostoevsky's religion. Dostoevsky, he writes in a letter, was "a pure introvert, a purely disintegrating will—there was not a grain of the passion of love within him

—all the passion of hate, of evil. It has become, I think, now a supreme wickedness to set up a Christ worship as Dostoevsky did; it is the outcome of an evil will, disguising itself in terms of love." Dostoevsky "mixing God and Sadism is foul." Drastically he is called "a rotten little stinker," and Dostoevsky, Lawrence writes, "can nicely stick his head between the feet of Christ, and waggle his behind in the air." [37] A poem sums it up:

> Dostoevsky, the Judas,
> with sham christianity
> epileptically ruined
> the last bit of sanity
> left in the hefty bodies
> of the Russian nobility. [38]

The outbursts of hatred acerbated by the quarrel with Murry would not be worth recording if Lawrence had not been induced in the last year of his life to write a preface to the *Grand Inquisitor* (1930) which, in a calm tone, retells the legend but misreads its point completely. Dostoevsky, Lawrence tells us, says there, "Jesus, you are inadequate. Men must correct you. And Jesus at the end gives the kiss of acquiescence to the Inquisitor." "Jesus kisses the Inquisitor: Thank you, thank you, you are right, old man." [39] Oddly enough this interpretation has been widely accepted and repeated even by knowledgeable scholars like Helen Muchnic.

Lawrence's view of Tolstoy rather meshes with his view of Thomas Hardy. "Tolstoi had a marvelous sensuous understanding but very little clarity of mind." "Tolstoi had a perverse pleasure in making the later Vronsky abject and pitiable; because Tolstoi so meanly envied the healthy passionate male in the young Vronsky." Lawrence grossly simplifies the issue when he states that "all the tragedy comes from Vronsky's and Anna's fear of society. . . . They couldn't live in the pride of their sincere passion, and spit in Mother Grundy's eye." "Imagine any great artist making the vulgar social condemnation of Anna and Vronsky figure as divine punishment." [40] Lawrence's own obsession is crassly obvious when he calls *War and Peace* "downright dishonourable, with that fat, diluted Pierre for a hero, stuck up as preferable and desirable, when everybody knows that he wasn't attractive, even to Tolstoi." [41] Lawrence simply repudiates the "nauseating Christian-brotherhood idea." One could rather agree with Lawrence that Prince Nekhlyudov in *Resurrection* is a "muff," as "dead as lumber." [42]

Lawrence came to detest the whole of Russian literature with the possible exception of Vasili Rozanov. "Russian writers had a certain crudity and thick uncivilized stupidity about them."[43] "That is almost the whole of Russian literature: the phenomenal coruscations of the soul of quite commonplace people. That's why the Russians are so popular. Every character in Dostoevsky or Chekhov thinks himself *inwardly* a nonesuch, absolutely unique."[44] One wonders whether F. R. Leavis was right in calling Lawrence "the finest literary critic of our time—a great literary critic if ever there was one."[45]

The enthusiasm for the Russian novel reached fever pitch in the writings of Virginia Woolf. She is given to easy generalizations about the "entirely new conception of the novel," "larger, saner and more profound than ours." "Could any English novel survive," she asks, "in the furnace of that overpowering sincerity," "their undeviating reverence for truth?"[46] "The Russian Point of View" puts it more strongly. "The simplicity, the absence of effort, the assumption that in a world bursting with misery the chief call upon us is to understand fellow-sufferers, and not with the mind—for it is easy with the mind—but with the heart—this is the cloud which broods above the whole of Russian literature." The soul is "chief character in Russian fiction." She exaggerates, saying that in Russian fiction "there is none of that precise division between good and bad to which we are used."[47]

Virginia Woolf prefers Tolstoy, Turgenev, and Chekhov to Dostoevsky. Tolstoy is the "greatest of all novelists." "Life dominates Tolstoi as the soul dominates Dostoevsky" seems a variation or correction of Merezhkovsky's contrast between the Seer of the Flesh and the Seer of the Soul.[48] A late entry in her diary calls Tolstoy "genius in the raw. Thus more disturbing, more 'shocking,' more of a thunderclap, even on art, even on literature, than any other writer."[49] Dostoevsky rather bewildered her. After Turgenev, with his "rare gift of symmetry, of balance," she cannot read Dostoevsky.[50] She reviewed two volumes of the Garnett translation of the minor Dostoevsky, praising *The Eternal Husband* (*Vechny muzh*) but puzzled by *The Double* (*Dvoinik*). "The whole of its amazing machinery seems to spin fruitlessly in the air." "It is an elaborate failure with all its brilliance and astonishing ingenuity," and *The Gambler* (*Igrok*) seems to her "a second rate work of a great writer."[51] Virginia Woolf thus rather harks back to the time when Turgenev and the early Tolstoy loomed over the horizon. Dostoevsky had not yet won out.

Surprisingly, her close friend Lytton Strachey, who disliked mysticism and Victorian sages, was carried away by the enthusiasm for *The Brothers Karamazov*. He compared Dostoevsky to Jacobean dramatists for the feverish atmosphere and melodramatic events, but he had the good sense, rare at that time, to see that Dostoevsky was also a humorist. He singled out Madame Yepanchin and Stepan Trofimovich.[52]

Howells was converted to Tolstoy, but Henry James remained of the party of Turgenev or the French party which believed in form. Four pronouncements hardly noticed in their time turned out to become influential. In an essay on Turgenev (1897) James speaks of Tolstoy as "a wonderful mass of life," "a reflector as vast as a natural lake; a monster harnessed to his great subject—all human life!—as an elephant might be harnessed, for purposes of traction, not to a carriage, but to a coachhouse. His own case is prodigious, but his example for others is dire: Disciples not elephantine he can only mislead and betray."[53] In the preface to the New York edition of *The Tragic Muse* (1907) James spoke of Thackeray's *Newcomes*, Dumas's *Three Musketeers*, and *War and Peace* (oddly enough calling it *Peace and War*) as "such large loose baggy monsters." "We have heard it maintained . . . that such things are 'superior to art;' but we understand least of all what *that* may mean." James rather delights "in a deep-breathing economy and an organic form."[54] In James's last essay, "The New Novel" (1914), Tolstoy is called "the great illustrative master-hand on all this ground of the disconnection of method from matter," an epic genius, but "execrably, pestilentially, as a model."[55] And finally there is a letter to Hugh Walpole (19 May 1912) calling Tolstoy and Dostoevsky "fluid pudding, though not tasteless, because the amount of their own minds and souls in solution in the broth gives it savour and flavour, thanks to the strong, rank quality of their genius and their experience." But their vice is "lack of composition, their defiance of economy and architecture": James believes that "Form alone *takes* and holds and preserves substance."[56]

Percy Lubbock edited James's letters (including the letter to Walpole) in 1920 and wrote the very Jamesian *Craft of Fiction* (1921). There he criticizes *War and Peace* as lacking in proportion and design. "The total effect is inconclusive." "The war and the peace are episodic, not of the centre." "Youth and age, the flow and ebb of the recurrent tide—this is the theme of Tolstoy's book. [Or] so it seems." Actually Tolstoy was writing "two novels at once." "I can discover no angle at which the two stories will appear to unite and merge in a single impression. . . . Nor are they placed together to illustrate a contrast; nothing *results* from their juxtaposition." The book is "a confusion of two designs." "It has no centre"— and so it goes, perversely to my mind. The "impression of swarming life," the sense of its continuity, is all that Lubbock will allow. He refuses to see the carefully planned interaction of war and peace and is wrong about the epilogue. It is not true that "nothing will ever happen" to Tolstoy's heroes, that Pierre will do nothing though he is full of schemes, and that Nikolenka in the corner is merely "the last word [of] the new generation." Actually, a conflict between Pierre and Nikolai Rostov is being prepared. The concluding words of the epilogue, "Oh Father, Father. Yes, I will do something with which even you will be satisfied," spoken by Nikolenka, suggest a fusion of Pierre and Andrei, the identification in the boy's and the author's mind. The boy's decision for greatness at the side of Pierre, against his uncle Nikolai, is in the spirit of the dead father. The epilogue functions as a bridge to a new book on the Decembrists that Tolstoy planned. But the body of the novel is finished before in Pierre's love for Natasha and all humanity. He has found the meaning of life "to be perfectly good so he [cannot] be afraid of death," and he has found this meaning not by thinking but in the experience of the war. There are not two stories: war influences and shapes decisively the fate of every character of importance. The book is not "named carelessly," as Lubbock suggests.[57]

Nor is his similar criticism of *Anna Karenina* convincing. Again we are told that the book has no unity. The stories of Anna and Vronsky on the one hand and of Lyovin and Kitty on the other are merely contrasted. But the contrast "leads to no clash between the two, no opposition, no drama." Besides, Tolstoy "damaged a magnificent book by his refusal to linger over any kind of pictorial introduction." Like Arnold and Gosse before him, Lubbock complains that Anna's falling in love with Vronsky is not properly motivated. "For the reader it is all too abrupt, the step by which she abandons her past and flings herself upon her tragic adventure."[58] Tolstoy refuses to shape his story as a pictorial impression: he wants to keep it all in immediate action. But Lubbock does not succeed in justifying his dogma: one may properly ask why a book of such scope cannot have two centers and why a sexual attraction needs to be motivated in detail. Actually in *Anna Karenina* the two stories are not only juxtaposed and contrasted. They are dovetailed and even fused at crucial moments, as in the final meeting of Lyovin with Anna, and Anna's motivation, her boredom with her jointcracking bureaucrat, is sufficiently clear.

Lubbock's discussion of Tolstoy, in a book that is still the best exposition of the Jamesian view, excited some dissent and modification in two rival books, E. M. Forster's *Aspects of the Novel* (1927) and Edwin Muir's *The Structure of the Novel* (1928). Forster argues against Lubbock's stress on the flow of time in *War and Peace*: "Space is lord in *War and Peace*, not time." If it were youth and age, and aging, it would be depressing, but the expanse in space rather exhilarates and "leaves behind it an effect like music." Lubbock's insistence on a single point of view is not convincing. A shifting point of view succeeds in Dickens and Tolstoy. "This power to expand and contract perception [of which the shifting point of view is a symptom], this right to intermittent knowledge," seems to Forster an advantage of the novel form.[59] Forster feels the power of what may be called "open form." *War and Peace* may be an untidy book, not "rounding off but opening out." Forster is too good a novelist to be ignored.

Edwin Muir is also dissatisfied with the Jamesian "point of view." But he agrees with Lubbock that the action of *War and Peace* "takes place in time and time alone." *War and Peace* is a novel in which time is not so much articulated as generalized and averaged. *War and Peace* as a chronicle is then contrasted with a dramatic novel such as *The Idiot* (*Idiot*). There "the sense of the urgency of time is given by a particular fear, by the knowledge, sometimes hidden but always revealed again, of a definite event that will happen." The premonition that Rogozhin will kill Nastasia speeds up time. This sense is announced at the very beginning of the novel when Myshkin says that a man condemned to the guillotine has an accelerated feeling for time as fate.[60] It is a well-observed contrast. In all of these three books on the novel Tolstoy and Dostoevsky (Turgenev is ignored) serve, we should realize, only as examples in a general theory.

The interest of the British critics in the Russian novel seems to have declined since the twenties. The main critics—I. A. Richards, William Empson, Ezra Pound, T. E. Hulme, T. S. Eliot, G. Wilson Knight, Herbert Read—concentrated on poetry and rarely discussed the novel and even more rarely the Russian. I do not suggest that they did not know it or even that they did not care for it, although Ezra Pound in *How to Read* (1929) dismissed "The Rooshuns." "Let a man judge them after he has encountered Charles Bovary; he will read them with better balance." Actually Pound could not have had a low opinion of them when he praised Wyndham Lewis as "the only English writer who can be compared with Dostoevsky," and *Tarr* as "the most vigorous and volcanic English novel of our time."[61]

T. S. Eliot also compared *Tarr* with Dostoevsky. "The direct contact with the senses, perception of the world of immediate experience with its own scale of values, is like Dostoevsky, but there is always a suggestion of a purely intellectual curiosity in the senses which will disconcert many readers of the Russian novelist."[62] Here the unity of feeling and thinking, the "unified sensibility," is anticipated. Just the year before, Eliot in a review of Edward Garnett's book on *Turgenev* speculated about the advantages of the expatriate: both Turgenev and Henry James came "from a large flat country which no one wants to visit." "This grasp on the uniformity of human nature and this interest in its variations made Turgenev cosmopolitan and made him a critic. He did not acquire those two quali- ties in Paris, he brought them with him." Eliot must have thought of him- self bringing those qualities with him to England. In the same essay, never reprinted, Eliot states the new approach to criticism. He dissents from Garnett's decision not to discuss "technical beauties," which "tend to defeat its own object. It is better," Garnett asserts, "to seek to appreci- ate the spirit of the matter, and to dwell on [Turgenev's] human value rather than on his aesthetic originality." "But a patient examination," Eliot protests, "of an artist's method and form (not by haphazard detection of 'technical beauties') is exactly the surest way to his 'human value;' is ex- actly the business of the critic."[63]

I. A. Richards, the other originator of the New Criticism, wrote an early essay on "Dostoevsky's God" which argues, mainly using Shatov's saying "I will believe in God," that "Dostoevsky considered belief in God inessential,"[64] surely a perverse conclusion whatever the difficulties of Dostoevsky's creed may be.

The archprovincial, the dictator of the English critical scene, F. R. Leavis, who avoided writing on any non-English writer, came late in his career to pay his homage to *Anna Karenina* (1967). The essay is marred by an insidious parallel drawn to a real-life situation, the relationship of D. H. Lawrence and Frieda, but gives a sensitive reading of the moral is- sue of the book. Leavis sees that the Lyovin–Kitty marriage is a foil to the Anna–Vronsky relationship but that the apparent norm of Lyovin's mar- riage is disturbed by Lyovin's later development. Anna's conflict is not simply with society or due to fear of society: she suffers from a sense of guilt growing from a "delicate inner pride."[65] The essay is an outgrowth of Leavis's moral preoccupation: there is nothing Eliotic or Richardsian about it.

Nor is there in the earlier essay on Dostoevsky by one of Leavis's fol- lowers, Derek Traversi, written from a frankly Roman Catholic point of view. Traversi disapproves of Berdyaev's attempt to exalt Dostoevsky to "a spiritual guide for modern man." Dostoevsky's mysticism is a "frightening concentration of the self," "an inconceivable flame burning in a vacuum" which is base and false, leading as it does to anarchism. Dostoevsky's hatred of the Roman church, his "refusal to see any reason for a visible Church," is a consequence of his "unbounded metaphysical egoism." Oddly enough, Dostoevsky's advocacy of the Russian Orthodox church is simply ignored. Among the novels *The Idiot* is singled out as the best, while the figure of Alyosha seems to Traversi "pasted on the main body of the work." "A definite artistic flaw." Dostoevsky for Traversi was "the master of all explorers of physical and spiritual disorder," but no moral teacher.[66]

Wyndham Lewis, in a retrospective broadcast in 1947, stated: "In England there has been decline in sympathy with the Nineteenth Century Russian novelists, which is partly in fashion, and in part to do with the long infatuation of British intellectuals for everything Russian of a much more recent date. This raised an ideologic barrier to enjoyment."[67] There may be some truth in this, but one reason must not be ignored, and that is the rise of professional Slavic studies, which, I think, more and more warned off the critics without a knowledge of Russian. D. S. Mirsky's *History of Russian Literature* (1924) and his *Contemporary Russian Literature* (1926) are not stuffy handbooks like the learned Brückner (available in English translation) but enormously wide-ranging books, full of information and dogmatic opinions. Here Gogol and Lermontov were exalted, Dostoevsky and Chekhov downgraded, and a host of writers described who could have been known only to specialists before. Historians and literary scholars took over: E. H. Carr's sober, too sober *Dostoevsky* (1931) is the first English scholarly biography of Dostoevsky based on Russian sources, and Isaiah Berlin's *The Hedgehog and the Fox* (1953) shows a mastery of Russian intellectual history. I can only allude to the new generation of professional students of the nineteenth-century Russian novel in England: John Bayley, R. F. Christian, Richard Freeborn, Henry Gifford, David Magarshack, Richard Peace, Gilbert Phelps, Leonard Shapiro, G. W. Spence, to name only those who have written books on the three major novelists I have discussed. Dilettantes are still around, but they lack the freshness of earlier critics: V. S. Pritchett's book on Turgenev, *The Gentle Barbarian* (1977), has nothing new to say, and C. P. Snow's *The Realists* (1978) has chapters on Dostoevsky and Tolstoy that emphasize their sexual lives and are trivial as criticism. A quiet revolution has been accomplished.

The situation in America is somewhat different. There in the twenties the New Criticism arose, which was preoccupied with poetry and language and at first neglected the novel and non-English literature. In the thirties there was a brief flurry of Marxism which was turned inward, concerned with a revaluation of American literature. The most prominent critic, Edmund Wilson, spent some months in Russia in 1935, learned some Russian, and read *War and Peace* in the original. He cultivated the language and collected his writings on Russian topics in *A Window on Russia* (1972) in the year of his death. The most substantial piece is devoted to Turge-

nev (1957), largely a retelling of Turgenev's biography, relying heavily on
Magarshack's, and of some of Turgenev's novels and stories. Like everything else Wilson wrote it is skillful, readable, well written but basically
conventional. Wilson's view that "Turgenev got a good deal farther with
the challenging social problems of Russia than either Tolstoy or Dostoevsky" shows his predilection for sensible liberal solutions. The "Notes on
Tolstoy" are informal jottings. *War and Peace*, he agrees with Mirsky, is
"something of an idealized idyll of the life of the old nobility,"[68] which
makes *War and Peace* "not quite one of the very summits of literature."[69]
According to Wilson Anna is damned by the "biblical epigraph,"[70] a common misreading. *Resurrection*, he feels, is an "underrated book," though
it "ends in the air."[71] Ivan Ilich is an "impossible character."[72] Wilson had
Marxist and psychoanalytical leanings but none of this shows in his comments on the nineteenth-century Russian novel.

The chief editor of the *Partisan Review*, a professed Marxist all his
life, Philip Rahv (1908–72, born in Odessa as Ivan Greenberg) wrote five
articles on Dostoevsky and two on Tolstoy. He is a borderline case: he
knew Russian from childhood and read Russian scholarship. But he first
and foremost was a critic and journalist. An early essay, "The Death of
Ivan Ilyich and Joseph K." (1940), draws a strained parallel between Tolstoy's story and Kafka's *Trial*. Tolstoy's story is allegorized in Marxist
terms: "as to the mysterious catastrophe which destroys Ilyich, what is it
in historical reality if not the ghost of the old idealism of status returning
to avenge itself on its murderer? Through Ilyich's death the expropriators
are expropriated."[73] Fortunately Rahv soon outgrew this kind of Marxism.
A later essay on Tolstoy, "Tolstoy: The Green Twig and the Black Trunk"
(1946), preserves the Marxist slant: Tolstoy's "attack on civilization is essentially an attack on the conditions that make for alienation." His doctrine of Christian anarchism has little religious content but is rather a
"formulation of a social ideal and a utopian program."[74]

The essays on Dostoevsky are much more perceptive. The one on
The Possessed (1938) analyzes the ideological issues well and formulates
what has been said before: "Reactionary in his abstract content . . . Dostoevsky's art is radical in sensibility and subversive in performance." Rahv
suggests interestingly that "Dostoevsky had a prodigious appetite for people, but is insensitive to texture and objects. . . . It is this quality which
permits his narrations their breakneck pace—there is no need to stop,
when there is nothing to look at."[75]

The article on "The Legend of the Grand Inquisitor" (1954) formulates the debate most clearly. "Dostoevsky so represents the truth of his-

tory . . . that we see it as patently belonging to the Inquisitor, not to Christ. Dostoevsky nonetheless takes his stand with Christ." "If Dostoevsky rejects the wisdom of the Inquisitor, it is solely in the terms of the desperate paradox of his faith in Christ."[76]

The discussion of *Crime and Punishment* (1960) rejects any simple motivation of the crime, singling out Dostoevsky as the first novelist who "fully accepted and dramatized the principle of uncertainty or indeterminacy in the presentation of character." Rahv rejects all allegorizing which would make Svidrigailov a double of Raskolnikov instead of a character in his own right with "no affinity of the mystical order" with the protagonist. The epilogue is disparaged as "implausible and out of key with the work as a whole." Rahv puts his finger on the weakness of the antiradical polemics of the book. "The novel depends on the sleight-of-hand of substituting a meaningless crime for a meaningful one."[77]

The article "Dostoevsky: The Descent into the Underground" (1972) makes a paradoxical defense for the suppression, by the censors, of the passage in chapter 10 of *Notes from Underground* (*Zapiski iz podpolia*) about "faith and Christ." "They were acting like genuine literary critics," and Dostoevsky acknowledged it implicitly: he never restored the cut passage. Dostoevsky "denounced the quite concrete social and political freedoms demanded by his radical contemporaries in the name of an 'absolute freedom' devoid of any experiential basis in the real life of man—a freedom whose absolute character is metaphysically contrived, purely imaginary, abysmally utopian, and historically inconceivable."[78]

Actually Rahv's last paper, "The Other Dostoevsky" (1972), makes much of the utopian Dostoevsky dreaming the dream of the golden age which, in its secularism and implied atheism, contradicts the Christian vision. Rahv insists on the conflict between "the extreme sceptic and the extreme believer" which embodies the contradictions of the historical moment in which Dostoevsky lived. In the discussion of "The Dream of a Ridiculous Man" ("Son smeshnogo cheloveka") Rahv dismisses the ending as "factitious" and tries to show that Dostoevsky accomplished a double aim. "He exhibits the splendor of the longed-for golden age while simultaneously exhibiting the innate evil of our nature which brings about its disintegration. This procedure fully expresses his own basic duality." Dostoevsky because of his pessimism about human nature cannot fully commit himself to his utopian vision. Rahv uses images from Wallace Stevens's poem "Sunday Morning" to conclude that "Dostoevsky never put out of his mind the 'dominion of the blood and sepulchre,' but at times, however equivocally, he came close to discovering his paradise in the 'balm and beauty of the earth.'"[79] Rahv here puts strongly the case for a Dostoevsky seen as an almost erotic poet, celebrating the earth and human brotherhood, as the foremost Czech critic, F. X. Salda, argued in 1929.[80]

Another unorthodox Marxist, Irving Howe, wrote a book entitled *Politics and the Novel* (1957) which contains two substantial chapters on *The Possessed* and *Fathers and Sons* (*Ottsy i deti*). Howe, who admires Lenin and Trotsky (on whom he wrote a little book), thinks that Dostoevsky's knowledge of the Russian radicals is limited: he knew next to nothing about the popularist-terrorists of the *Narodnaya Volya* ("People's Will") or of the incipient Marxists. The whole circle of plotters seems to Howe "malicious, slanderous, unjust" caricatures, and Dostoevsky's politics appear to him as "a web of confusion." Still, Dostoevsky, Howe concludes, is "the greatest of all ideological novelists because he always distributes his feelings among all his characters. . . . Dostoevsky looks at the world through the eyes of all his people. . . . None escapes humiliation and shame . . . none is spared, but there is a great consolation: no one is excluded." Something like Bakhtin's polyphonic novel seems suggested.[81]

The politics of Turgenev's novels, Howe argues, "may be described as a politics of hesitation." Bazarov is described as a "revolutionary personality, but without revolutionary ideas or commitments." Howe defends the arbitrariness of Bazarov's death. "The accident of fate that kills him comes only after he has been defeated in every possible social and personal encounter." Turgenev "speaks for us for the right of indecision, for a politics of hesitation, a politics that will never save the world but without which the world will never be worth saving."[82]

The dominant figure among the New York intellectuals was Lionel Trilling (1905–75), who contributed to Rahv's *Partisan Review* and greatly sympathized with its combination of social concern, "liberal" ideas, and Modernist taste. He wrote one essay on a Russian novel, *Anna Karenina*, rather late in his career (in *The Opposing Self*, 1955). It is disappointing as it is conventional in rehearsing the traits of lifelikeness, objectivity, moral quality, and affection displayed by Tolstoy. The praise for *Anna Karenina* is generous but the limits of Trilling's interest in Tolstoy are obvious when he states that Tolstoy is "not the greatest of novelists" because he does not have "the imagination of disaster" like Dickens, Dostoevsky, and Henry James (who invented the term).[83]

George Steiner can be grouped with Wilson, Trilling, and Leavis. Steiner's book *Tolstoy or Dostoevsky* (1959) is a tour de force. It does what had been done before: compare the two by using Merezhkovsky's con-

trast between the "seer of the flesh" and the "seer of the spirit," Thomas
Mann's confrontation of Goethe and Tolstoy, and the distinction between
epic and drama drawn in Georg Lukács's *Theorie des Romans*. The subtitle of the book: "An Essay in the Old Criticism" is curiously misleading.
It gives Steiner the clue for a ringing affirmation of the view that literature
exists "not in isolation but as central to the play of historical and political
energies." The old criticism looks for moral purpose. It is philosophic in
range and temper but, in practice, Steiner more than most other critics
insists on the inseparability of form and content and uses, insistently, the
main methods of the New Criticism: close attention to the text, to meta-
phors, ironies, and paradoxes, frankly avowing Kenneth Burke's ideal of
criticism: "to use all that there is to use." [84]

Steiner refutes the "baggy monsters" charge, demonstrating Tolstoy's
careful plotting and the role of improbable chance encounters both in
War and Peace and *Anna Karenina*. He makes much of Tolstoy's affinity
with Homer: they are "both rooted in the veracity of our senses." The parallel seems to be pushed too far in spite of Tolstoy's own claims. In Homer
there is nothing of Tolstoy's struggle between spirit and flesh nor of his
antiheroic view of life as Steiner himself recognizes. The contrast between
the epic Tolstoy and the dramatic Dostoevsky is prepared by a discussion
of Tolstoy's suspicion of the theatre, his view of Shakespeare and opera,
which Steiner has to modify by acknowledging the greatness of at least
two or three of Tolstoy's own plays. The dramatic nature of Dostoevsky's
art is skillfully elaborated, also in a close commentary on the use of time
in *The Idiot*. There are good observations on the background of Dostoevsky's fiction in the Gothic and sensational novels of the early nineteenth
century. Steiner comments sensibly: "To read into [his plots] matters of
private obsession may be illuminating; but such a reading should follow,
not precede, awareness of the public material at hand." I would also sub-
scribe to his remark on Ivan's indignation at the torture of children. "We
debase the great terror and compassion of his challenge by ascribing it to
some unconscious rite of expiation." Steiner thinks melodrama "anti-
tragic, its formula calls for four acts of apparent tragedy followed by a
fifth act of rescue and redemption" and sees Dostoevsky using this formula. Steiner speaks of "the compulsion of the genre" in *Crime and Punishment* and *The Brothers Karamazov* as "action terminates on the 'up-
ward swing'" characteristic of the "happy endings of melodrama," while
The Idiot and *The Possessed* are "generically tragic." [85] This gross formalism ignores Dostoevsky's deepest convictions and hopes.

The opposition of the metaphysics of Tolstoy and Dostoevsky is then sharply formulated. Tolstoy is seen as a pagan who envisages God as a metaphoric equivalent for a social and rational utopia or as a being rather similar to himself, while Dostoevsky's God is the Other. Man's freedom is his vulnerability to God. Steiner quotes Berdyaev that for Dostoevsky "the existence of evil is a proof of the existence of God." The contrast between Tolstoy and Dostoevsky is so crassly drawn that it allows Steiner to read "The Legend of the Grand Inquisitor" as an allegory of the confrontation between Dostoevsky and Tolstoy. Steiner realizes that this is an "artifice," that Dostoevsky could not have had Tolstoy in mind and that the Inquisitor cannot represent Tolstoy as he differs completely in his advocacy of authority and violence.[86] One can only wonder why Steiner still engaged in this irresponsible fancy.

An anonymous reviewer of Steiner's book said that in "the field of Russian literature there is no other criticism than the old."[87] But this is not strictly true or rather assumes a narrow concept of what the New Criticism stood for: a criticism concerned only with the close reading of poetic texts, indifferent to biography, literary history, and the novel. It is true that the New Criticism started with poetry and had its greatest initial successes in the interpretation of poetry but the critics soon saw that its theories and techniques need to be tested also in the drama and the novel.

Attention to fiction proliferated and could not ignore the Russian novel. John Crowe Ransom, who had baptized the New Criticism in 1941, asks expressly, "To what extent can the understanding of poetry be applied to the understanding of fiction?" He answers that this can be done by isolating specific passages, examples, indications of fixed images, which "will not be poetry but will be like fictional analogues of lyrical moments." Ransom selected three passages: one from Jane Austen, one from Henry James, and one from *War and Peace*, the scene with Napoleon riding through the battlefield of Austerlitz, looking at the fallen Bolkonsky and saying: "That's a fine death." Ransom thinks the passage obviously greatly inferior to the quotations from Jane Austen's *Mansfield Park* and James's *Daisy Miller*. "Its author does not fully possess the technical advantages of a style. For concentration he substitutes repetition; the episode of the sky is given four times in the short chapter, this being the second time; in order that we may be sure to experience it profoundly." Prose style seems to him a first requisite for distinction though he is baffled by the example from Tolstoy. "I should not quite know what to do

about Tolstoy, who is a giant but not a mature stylist. Without doubt
Tolstoy manages to present his characters and scenes in the round, and
he loves them and makes us love them. But as the range of our reading
widens I think we resist him increasingly because he does this artlessly
and wastefully." But style (and one wonders how Ransom can ignore the
fact that he read Tolstoy in translation) is only a prerequisite for building
an "imaginary world of spontaneous and natural affections," a new version of Ransom's old idea that poetry is there to restore the "world's
body" to us.[88]

Ransom's oldest pupil, Allen Tate (1899–1979), has actually used
Ransom's attention to detail in Russian fiction before. An essay, "The
Hovering Fly" (1943), takes the fly which in the last scene of *The Idiot*
hovers over the corpse of Nastasia Filippovna as an example of an artist's
reach into the actual world. "We may *look* at the hovering fly; we can to a
degree *know* the actual world. But we shall not know the actual world by
looking at it; we know it by looking at the hovering fly." Tate grants that
the power of the scene might not be diminished by the absence of the fly
but "by means of the fly the human order is compromised. But it is also
extended, until through a series of similar conversions and correspondences of image the buzz of the fly distends, both visually and metaphorically, the body of the girl into the world. Her degradation and nobility are in that image. Shall we call it the actual world?" Tate then uses
the very same passage Ransom was to quote about Prince Andrei fallen in
the battle of Austerlitz contemplating the empty sky as another example
of how an image or a symbol may create reality or bridge the gulf between language and reality.[89]

In a panel discussion of *War and Peace*, Tate argues cogently against
Lubbock's view that "the war and the peace don't go together" and makes
a personal remark when he says that "the old Russian society very closely
resembled the society of the old South," something Tate knew intimately
as a student of southern history and as the author of a fine historical
novel, *The Fathers*. I am puzzled why Tate could agree that the characters in *War and Peace* are "first of all types" and could not be sure whether
the book conveys a sense of sadness, "not very different from the classical
melancholy, the *lacrimae rerum*, the tears of things, the melancholy of
human life."[90]

Among the critics of the wider group usually called New, only R. P.
Blackmur wrote extensively on the Russian novel. But these essays collected in *Eleven Essays in the European Novel* (1964) belong to a late stage
of his writing when he had repudiated the New Criticism in the strongest

terms. Blackmur had become frankly a moralist and possibly even a somewhat shamefaced theologian. "The novel is ethics in action" and "literature is our theoretic struggle with behavior."[91] The early concern with language completely disappeared from Blackmur's novel criticism possibly because he had to read the continental novels in translation. Not that interest in the novel as such was absent from Blackmur's early writings. An essay "The Loose and Baggy Monsters of Henry James" (1951) turns the table on James on this point. "*War and Peace*," Blackmur argues, "does have every quality James prescribes: composition, premeditation, deep-breathing economy and organic form." Rather *The Ambassadors*, *The Wings of the Dove*, and *The Golden Bowl* are "large baggy monsters."[92]

Blackmur's paper on *Anna Karenina* (1950) is not, however, particularly concerned with the question of form. Its subtitle is "The Dialectic of Incarnation" and it opens with a quotation from Carl Gustav Jung's *Psychology and Religion* about the "terrible ambiguity of an immediate experience" and asserts that Tolstoy "exposes his created men and women [to it] and expresses their reactions and responses to that experience." This allows Blackmur to speak of a "dialectic of incarnation . . . the bodying forth in aesthetic form by contrasted human spirits of 'the terrible ambiguity of an immediate experience' through their reactions and responses to it."

For two pages Blackmur has not said anything that would not be true of any novelist and has arrived only at the trivial distinction between passive (reacting) and active (responding) characters. In the body of the essay we can find acute observations such as the remark that the new compassionate judgment Lyovin makes of his brother Nikolai is due to "the pressure of his own brooked love." Picking up the parallel between the mare Frou-frou and Anna, first, I believe, suggested by Merezhkovsky, Blackmur elaborates that Vronsky's "unpardonable act was no accident; neither was it done by intention." Rather "something like fate broke the rhythm." "It is the fault that inheres in Kitty and Levin, Dolly and Stiva, Anna and Vronsky alike: the fault of not keeping pace." Blackmur admires Tolstoy's honesty and genius "that he could have broken the back of the mare in the midst of the crisis in the passion of Anna and Vronsky without either adding or diminishing *human* significance but rather deepening the reality."

But most of the paper indulges in abstruse speculations about the "great business of the novel, to create out of manners and action motive, and out of the conflict of created motive with the momentum to find significance: an image of the theoretic form of the soul" or in defining the tragedy of Anna. "Her own strength cannot be equal to her cause," the cause of independence, I presume.[93] There is much more obscure verbiage unrelated to Tolstoy's novel where I cease to understand the workings of Blackmur's mind and begin to suspect him of deliberate obfuscation.

The essay on *Anna Karenina* is the only one on Tolstoy. There are six essays on Dostoevsky. The essay on *Crime and Punishment* (1949) is mainly a meditation on Raskolnikov's motive and on the main characters of the novel, often formulated tortuously but generally true and often even trite. But when Blackmur says that "the crime of Raskolnikov and its punishment in created suffering, could have been as great if he had never stirred from his room" I cease again to follow him. There would not be a novel at all. But elsewhere Blackmur makes arguable points when he defends the use of coincidence "as it heightens the sense of inevitability" or when he speaks of Raskolnikov's love for Sonya which is "also and simultaneously hate, and there is no difference between the emotions as he feels them, only as he intellectually knows what they are. And this is an example of the profound psychological rightness of Dostoevsky's judgment to see that as hate or pride is the burden Raskolnikov carries so love or humility is the *burden* of Sonia's life." This seems finespun and possibly strained but saying that Svidrigailov is "incredible as an example of sexual behavior" or that Porfiri is "unreal, except as an agency of the plot" seems definitely mistaken. Still, the essay is a normal inquiry into motivation and characterization. Only at the end Blackmur makes the claim that "all of us without exception are deeply implicated in the nature of the Crime." Dostoevsky, Blackmur asserts, believed "that the individual man has in him an innocent part which must take on the suffering caused by the guilty part," a new interpretation of the double, the *raskol* (schism). Blackmur emphasizes that Dostoevsky envisaged the transformation, and not the reformation of the criminal. "Reformation would have dealt with the mere guilty act against society. Transformation, through suffering, is alone able to purge the guilt of being." Obscurely, in a final flourish, this lesson is applied to the Sacco and Vanzetti case. Vanzetti assumed "the whole devastating guilt of the industrial society which killed him."[94] How this follows from a consideration of *Crime and Punishment* remains obscure. It is not anymore literary criticism and has nothing to do with Dostoevsky.

The essay on "The Idiot: A Rage for Goodness" (1942) contains some pointless maundering such as a long passage illustrating mounting humiliation by a story from Jean-Marie Fabre, the French entomologist, about the Pine Processional Caterpillar. But, on the whole, the essay makes a real effort at sustained literary criticism. The criticism of the figure of Myshkin as having "no being, no existence apart from the vision of those who believe in him" is arguable. Blackmur well formulates the theme of the book as the "drama of the good man who, in submitting to evil is doomed not only to become evil but to enact evil without losing a jot of his goodness." Also the attempt to line up Myshkin with primitive Christianity contrasted with Pauline is striking. "Dostoevsky's dualism . . . is only the dramatic collapse into an undifferentiated groveling humiliation": humiliation, in Dostoevsky, being the condition of humility. Blackmur makes then distinctions which seem to me persuasive. The first part of the novel up to the burning of the roubles is superb, then the middle areas of the book "lose sight of the image of the Idiot in a maze of undramatized notions about the Russian soul, the east, the west, atheism, socialism, drunkenness, and so on." These passages seem to Blackmur examples "of a great sensibility violated by an idea," while chapters 3, 4, and 5 of part II leading up to Myshkin's saving epileptic fit are the climax of the novel. It seems to him unfortunate that Dostoevsky conceived the drama in terms of Myshkin's further relationship with Nastasia and Aglaya. The two women "are not so much incredible as inadequate. Both women rage too much." "Actually the inadequacy turns out to be Myshkin's, not the women's." "He has nothing within him capable of satisfying the passionate desires which dominate both Nastasya and Aglaya in their feeling for him." "There is always, in the great creations of Dostoevsky, someone else screaming from within the man. In *The Idiot* it is the rage of goodness."[95] This is a good paradoxical formula for what Blackmur would consider the deepest motive force in Dostoevsky's work.

The essay on *The Possessed*, with the subtitle "In the Birdcage" (1948), is again an exasperating mixture of mere cobwebbing and good characterization. The stimulus of the Nechaev affair, the danger that the novel would become a bloated pamphlet, was overcome by Dostoevsky's passion as a novelist. This simple idea is phrased and rephrased tortuously in order to assert Dostoevsky's success in assimilating ideas, suggested by the Nechaev affair, to a fictional context. One theme is the double—the other self of the other: whether the god-man (Stavrogin) and man-god (Pyotr Verkhovensky), Dostoevsky asks, "are in actual experience the same." This genuine critical question, though phrased in Blackmur's worst manner from which one can extricate a rational meaning only with some effort, leads to much more conventional and more lucid reflections on the characters and the action. Some of these comments are dubious. To say that Stepan Trofimovich is "the eternal possibility of the man clothed and in his right mind," that he is "the man who *knows* that he sits on his own bottom, no matter what pomp or servility he may pass through," is a misreading. The most striking passage is an attempt to make Dostoevsky something of a Rousseauist. "Dostoevsky was more Western than he thought, and a child of the French revolution and brother to the Commune." "He saw," like Rousseau, "that all that is evil in man's life comes from the institutions he has created to prevent—or to forestall—a continuing revelation." Rousseau's "temptation was to assert panacea in popular sentiment and popular will, which, since none can conform to them, leaves every state illegitimate. Dostoevsky's temptation is to assert panacea in popular sentiment guided by absolute authority reached by conversion and faith; which leaves every government not a theocracy illegitimate." Blackmur ignores Dostoevsky's approval of the tsarist state but is right in stating that Dostoevsky thought that the only "true politics is in religion" and that "it would almost seem that the whole of Dostoevsky's thoughts and tendencies can be summarized in the single idea that, whether for the individual or for all mankind, the cost of the real vision of Christ was the previous, actual experience of anti-christ." Blackmur admires the image of Stavrogin which "makes it possible for the reader to tolerate the breakdown of form and uncertainty of intention in the middle of the book, where what seem riddles are tensions, where blows in the face become holy burdens, and where also there is a vast deal of high jinks, Dickensian, Quixotic, and perfectly hellish at the same time."[96]

The three lectures on *The Brothers Karamazov* (1963)—one wonders how an audience could have followed them—have subtitles: "The Galloping Troika and the Momentum of the Underground," "The Grand Inquisitor and the Wine of Gladness," and "The Peasants Stand Firm and the Tragedy of the Saint," which indicate that Blackmur discusses the novel roughly in the order of its main divisions. Again fairly straightforward commentary on characters and events is introduced and interrupted by dense meditations suggested rather obliquely by the book, and more insistently than in the earlier essays, its issues and concerns are referred to us, readers, human beings, and presumably Blackmur himself. The first essay starts with the striking declaration that "Dostoevsky is the great master of the unmotivated and nowhere more so than in *The Brothers Karamazov*." Motivation, if I understand Blackmur rightly, seems to mean an ethical direction as he explains that "in him [Dostoevsky] you see how hard it is to achieve lasting or adequate motive, how almost impossible to escape from evil into good and yet live, but also how deep is the affliction of hope within us that we may do so. You see action, whether of the Psyche or of the hand, that springs from random hope." The force of hope, says Blackmur, shifting disconcertingly from the author to the novel, is transformed, through suffering and the conscience of sin, into motive. "This is why in so many of his books Dostoevsky wanted to write The Life of a Great Sinner—as if only the Great Sinner could achieve ultimate motive." This intention got lost in the rush and momentum of life which Blackmur allegorizes by picking up the image of Gogol's troika and the underground man. "The man from underground . . . is the driver of the galloping troika which is, I take it, a name for the vehicle of our behavior." This pompous introduction is followed by a characterization of Fyodor Karamazov, the four brothers and an explanation of the blessings of Father Zosima. Some of this is well put, some is formulated paradoxically, and some seems to me farfetched or definitely wrong. How can one say that "stinking Lizaveta is a debased Alyosha"? The murder is labeled "anonymous and communal" though Blackmur knows of course that Smerdyakov did it. "He is the one person who cannot take on himself the guilt of it; the guilt merely demolishes him." In describing the action and the movements of Dmitri up to the would-be murder Blackmur feels the communal involvement strongly, almost personally. "Dmitri grasps us so warmly by the hand and pulls us after him into his guilt. There are heroic moments in us when actions such as his flood our dearest thoughts."[97]

The second lecture or rather essay discusses the "Legend of the Grand Inquisitor," stating at the outset that Dostoevsky is "so far the only writer of the first class who has attempted to dramatize the religious experience in this world and within the frame of the human psyche." In interpreting the "Legend," Blackmur makes much of the ambiguity of Ivan's own attitude. "Ivan is between the Grand Inquisitor and the Prisoner Christ" and three times Blackmur speaks of Ivan's swaying walk and stooped right shoulder as a symbol of his indecision. Ivan cannot accept the answer of the Grand Inquisitor. But Blackmur seems undecided himself about Ivan's attitude when he tells us that "as Ivan sees it, the people will reject the temptation of the Second Coming until it is accompanied by the end of the world. Though it is what they might desire, they are not strong enough to accept it as the loss of miracle, mystery, and authority—bread, worship, absolute authority—for with that loss the world would become immitigably intolerable." Ivan here is presumed to endorse the Grand Inquisitor "out of the baseness of the Karamazovs" in flagrant contradiction to the following emphasis on Ivan's hesitation. Ivan's poem is contrasted with Alyosha's, which is the story of Zosima and Alyosha's conversion when he falls down and kisses the earth. Blackmur gives it a hyperingenious allegorical interpretation: "It is something like an instinc-

tive resurrection of the medieval fourfold structure for the creation or interpretation of meaning. Here the sense would be Alyosha himself and
the scene; the morals would be Grushenka; the allegory Zosima; and the
anagoge, the Gospel of Cana." Zosima is seen as an analogue or parallel to
the Grand Inquisitor. "Both believe man incapable of sustaining his own
notions of freedom. For both, miracle, mystery, and authority are the primary needs of man," a good point elaborated by the contrast between the
Inquisitor, who would impose them by human reason, while Zosima "in
terms of the peasants' miserable suffering." Both put the redemption in
an impossible future and see "the path to it through a tyranny which is
an affront to human nature: the one through the tyranny of total irre-
sponsibility, the other through the tyranny of total guilt." But Blackmur
objects "to say that no man is guilty and all things are lawful is not much
different from saying that all men are guilty of every man and all things
are law. In either case the individual disappears." But here and elsewhere
Blackmur loses sight of the book and Dostoevsky and pontificates on religion and art. "Art does not tell you what to do but what you have to do
with" and apparently the brothers are what Blackmur wants us to do
with: "The brothers in baseness, in energy, in buoyant forward vitality,
love of life, which makes them our brothers. That is why they are there
for: and that is what novels are for, to show them there." Blackmur thinks
that "the poetic or novelistic conception is a greater source of its [the
book's] strength than any 'merely' religious consideration," though he admits that he does not "know any logic suitable to argue the matter." It
amounts to a belief in an original identity of poetry and religion, "which
rise through us from a deeper and earlier source than any theology or
any church—any prosody or any rule of genre."[98] Blackmur seems to
have found religion through the novels (not the theology) of Dostoevsky.

The third essay is straightforward comment on the judicial error, on
the story of the boys and on the final chapters. One is struck by Blackmur
saying that "Dmitri's dream of the peasants and the weeping babe is a
lower version—perhaps a more fundamental version—of Alyosha's dream
of his Elder," and the remark that Dmitri's rebirth after it "is not permanent, but only a deeper form of New Year's resolution." But I don't understand what it means to say that the "dreams of Alyosha and the Elder, and
of Ivan, are fierce theoretic creations of the ideal which the flesh abuses
and which abuse the flesh." It is good to know that the usually solemn
Blackmur recognizes that there is "a great deal of comedy in the ordeals
and examinations of Dmitri" and that he can characterize Kolya as "a
kind of buffoon *manqué*" who is "not so very different from Ivan," "a primi-

tive and ferocious form of Ivan." But it is difficult to agree with the view that Lise Khokhlakov "was the pure expressive form of that which Ivan was only the critical form" or with the strange reflection that "the guilt of Ivan, or Smerdyakov, or of the others, is not adult guilt but childish guilt." Blackmur defends Dmitri's hesitation between the plan to escape to America and the acceptance of guilt represented by the hymn from underground. That the peasants stood firm and condemned Dmitri seems to Blackmur "a reaction by caprice, by a goatish act of their own inner natures" which Blackmur recognizes Dostoevsky "would not have admitted." This odd misreading takes up the reflection about the peasantry as being there only to "strike down and after an indecent interval in hell, to raise up" which, in turn, leads to an irrelevant pairing of peasant and proletarian who need not judge those who presume to understand him. Blackmur asks, "Does the proletariat represent the extremity of that 'mighty movement against nature' (Bergson's phrase) which we call democracy?" Has Blackmur become an enemy of democracy? He certainly takes the greatest art out of history: Sophocles, Dante, the later Shakespeare, and *The Brothers Karamazov*. "Such imaginative acts are so rare as to escape particular moments of history." But in the last page Blackmur returns to his sense of awe. The story of the murder "is lifted into the condition of miracle, mystery, and authority. Hurrah for all the Karamazovs! for here is the condition where all are guilty and none are guilty. To live in that condition, and to love life, is to endure the tragedy of the saint. In this novel the saint is migratory among the three brothers, nowhere at home." [99] These are the last puzzling words of the series which I have tried to describe and to comment on, as it has, I believe, never been examined in any detail and always been accepted on trust. But I paid so much attention to a text which is often opaque and rebarbative, pretentious and obfuscating because I believe that a writer who has written (as Blackmur has) many lucid, perceptive, and even profound pages must be given the benefit of the doubt. [100]

Among the younger defenders of the New Criticism Murray Krieger stands out. But he also moved away in the direction of a version of existentialism. His book, *The Tragic Vision* (1960), contains an excellent analysis of the figure of Myshkin. Krieger uses the pronouncements of Radomsky, whom he considers a raisonneur-mouthpiece of the author, to show that Myshkin is not simply a "truly beautiful soul," a Christlike figure. "Myshkin moves from saintly to human attitudes; and then, after Aglaia has been partly persuaded to trust his human emotions, he reverts to saintliness that must desert her for a wider obligation of love." Myshkin is guilty of the tragedy as "his irrational Christ-like transcendence of mere ethical judgment turns deadly." "What is so destructive in him is the sense others must get from his infinite meekness that they are being judged." Thus *The Idiot* is "a novel of the desperate struggle for personal human dignity in a world that finds endless ways of depriving man of it."[101] Myshkin, though the perfectly good man, is assimilated to Krieger's modern tragic hero (or rather "visionary"), the man of the "sickness unto death," the modern nihilist.

Krieger was a pupil of the philosopher Eliseo Vivas, who in his collection of essays, *Creation and Discovery* (1955), gave a lucid exposition of the issues in *The Brothers Karamazov*. He was a dramatist rather than a philosopher. Vivas sets Dostoevsky's religious dimension against what he calls "liberalism." One cannot dismiss, Vivas argues, Dostoevsky's philosophy for its denial of progress or its reactionary opinions such as his anti-Semitism. The truth of his insight into the disaster of unbelief seems to Vivas demonstrated by the later course of history leading to the horrors of totalitarianism. Vivas interprets the "Legend of the Grand Inquisitor" well. Both socialism and Catholicism have the same end: "to relieve men of the burden of freedom." "Dostoevsky sees the horror of the choice: either happiness without freedom or freedom *and* hell." The answer to Ivan is found in the love of Zosima. To call it "failure of nerve" may be comprehensible but what is "difficult to understand is how any serious reader can accept his [Dostoevsky's] psychological insights and simply ignore the matrix whence they rise and the theoretical and practical implications to which they lead."[102] Vivas wants us to accept Dostoevsky *in toto*. He became an ideologist of conservatism.

What strikes one, in general, about recent American criticism is the preoccupation with Dostoevsky. One can argue that the New Criticism or versions and derivatives of it was forced by the presence of the Russian novel (primarily Dostoevsky and Tolstoy) either to abandon its formalism or to widen it to include more and more traditional problems of ideology, lifelikeness, characterization or to make attempts to look for symbols, allegories, and myths to which Dostoevsky obviously lent himself much more readily than Tolstoy.

More and more, as in England, professional Slavists have taken over the task of commentary, interpretation, and criticism. Readers still discover Dostoevsky or Tolstoy for themselves but critics who have no Russian shy increasingly away from the topic, realizing that there is a wealth of information and scholarship inaccessible to them or accessible only at second hand. Slavic studies were practically nonexistent in the United

States before the Second World War, though early in the century Leo
Wiener (1862–1939) at Harvard translated Tolstoy and later George Rapall
Noyes at Berkeley wrote a life of Tolstoy (1914). Among the early Slavic
scholars Avrahm Yarmolinsky (1890–1981) stands out as a biographer of
Turgenev (1926) and Dostoevsky (1934), although we should note that he
wrote an early Columbia dissertation on Dostoevsky's ideology (1921).

But the actual founder of a professional study of the Russian nineteenth-century novel was, without doubt, Ernest J. Simmons (1903–72).
His *Dostoevsky, The Making of a Novelist* (1940) seems to me his best book,
a reliable digest of the Russian scholarship focused on the evolution of
Dostoevsky as an artist and thinker fully using the notebooks and letters.
Also his bulky book on *Tolstoy* (1946) is a valuable digest of all that is
known about his life, although the critical interest of the book is feeble
and marred by Simmons's propensity to reproduce other people's opinions and even phrases without acknowledgement.[103] He has to retell even
Anna Karenina translating Gusev though he must have known the novel
intimately. As a critic he can go completely astray, for example, in an introduction to Turgenev's *Fathers and Sons*. But Simmons's merits should
be acknowledged.

Since the war American scholars have discovered the other great
novelists ignored by earlier criticism. Gogol was not entirely unknown—
particularly the *Inspector General (Revizor)* was appreciated and per-
formed, for the first time at Yale in 1908—but his revival is due mainly
to Nabokov's witty though often perverse little book (1944). Since then,
Vsevolod Setchkarev's German book has appeared in English (1965), Victor Erlich has written an instructive monograph (1969), and recently two
brilliant students, Simon Karlinsky (in 1976) and Donald Fanger (1979),
have reinterpreted Gogol very differently. Goncharov has had his specialist, Milton Ehre (1973), Pisemsky his, Charles Moser (1969), and Leskov
was the subject of a large volume by Hugh MacLean (1977). Oddly enough
there is only one American book on Tolstoy, Edward Wasiolek's (1978),
since Simmons's time. I need only allude to the growing number of substantial American contributions to Dostoevsky scholarship. Two books by
Robert Louis Jackson (1958, 1966), Wasiolek's (1964), Fanger's (1965), Victor
Terras's (1969), Joseph Frank's (1976), and Michael Holquist's (1977) stand
out, not to speak of numerous smaller monographs and articles.

I hope that this survey has sketched, as if in miniature, a history of
English and American criticism of the last 125 years: in America we
found the early preoccupation with realism in the specific sense of the
disappearance of the author in James and Howells, and from James came

the criticism of the supposed formlessness of the Russian novel. Around 1912 with the translation of *The Brothers Karamazov* the generally realist atmosphere in criticism and literature had changed. In Middleton Murry's book on Dostoevsky (1916) a new almost mystical romanticism becomes vocal. The exaltation of the religious and ideological message of Dostoevsky and Tolstoy answered the mood of the First World War and its aftermath. In America the New Criticism had to cope with the challenge of the Russian novel (and the novel in general). Marxist or semi-Marxist interpretations tried to come to terms with writers quite contrary in outlook to their assumptions. Tolstoy and Turgenev receded in the past as great figures of little immediate relevance while Dostoevsky in spite of all criticisms of his ideology survives for his great imaginative achievement, which is felt to be representative not only of old Russia but of modern man and his predicament.

BIBLIOGRAPHICAL NOTE

The following books proved most useful in assembling the materials for this paper.

Royal A. Gettman, *Turgenev in England and America*. Urbana, Illinois, 1941.

Helen Muchnic, *Dostoevsky's English Reputation (1881–1936)*. Northampton, Massachusetts, 1939.

J. Allen Smith, *Tolstoy's Fiction in England and America*. Dissertation, University of Illinois. Available in abstract.

Dorothy Brewster, *East-West Passage*. London, 1954.

Gilbert Phelps, *The Russian Novel in English Fiction*. London, 1956.

NOTES

1. William Lyon Phelps, *Essays on Russian Novelists* (New York, 1911), preface.
2. See C. Lefevre in *American Slavic and East European Review* 8 (1949): 106–25.
3. See Royal A. Gettman, *Turgenev in England and America* (Urbana, Ill., 1941). See my review in *The Russian Review* 1 (1941): 118–19.
4. For biography and list of translations see Carolyn G. Heilbrun, *The Garnett Family* (London, 1961).
5. Thomas S. Perry, *Atlantic Monthly* 33 (1874): 569.
6. *Atlantic Monthly* 31 (February 1873): 239.
7. W. R. S. Ralston, "Count Tolstoy's Novels," London, *Nineteenth Century* 5 (1879): 650–69.

8. *Essays in Criticism* (2d series, 1888), p. 259.

9. In *The Fortnightly Review* (December 1887), repr. in *Essays in Criticism* (2d series).

10. G. W. E. Russell, ed., *Letters* (London, 1895). Letter to Florence Earle Coates (24 February 1888).

11. *Essays in Criticism* (2d series), p. 271.

12. *My Literary Passions* (New York, 1895), pp. 254, 258.

13. *Prefaces to Contemporaries*, ed. G. Arms, W. M. Gibson, and F. C. Marston, Jr. (Gainesville, Florida, 1957), pp. 4, 42.

14. *Harper's* 72 (1886): 812.

15. In *The New Spirit* (1890), pp. 190, 193.

16. In *The Spectator* 62 (1889), repr. in *Critical Kit-Kats* (London, 1896), pp. 123–31.

17. Gosse in *Critic* 16 (17 May 1890): 252; Chesterton, "Tolstoy and the Cult of Simplicity," *Varied Types* (London, 1903), pp. 125–44.

18. Repr. in *Pen Portraits and Reviews* (London, 1932), pp. 256–60.

19. *The Later Nineteenth Century* (Edinburgh, 1907), p. 347.

20. *Criticism and Fiction*, ed. C. M. Kirk and R. Kirk (New York, 1959), p. 174; dates from 1897.

21. C. H. Perris (London, 1898) and Nathan Haskell (New York, 1911).

22. *Letters to his Family and Friends*, ed. Sidney Colvin (New York, 1899), vol. 2, p. 23.

23. *Fortnightly Review*, n.s., 43 (1888), p. 239.

24. *The Later Nineteenth Century* (Edinburgh, 1907), p. 340.

25. Quoted in Maurice Baring, *Landmarks in Russian Literature* (London, 1960 repr.), p. 81.

26. W. L. Phelps, *Essays on Russian Novelists* (New York, 1911), p. 152.

27. *Landmarks in Russian Literature*, pp. 38, 119, 157, 161.

28. *The New Age* 6, n.s.: 518.

29. Quoted in Helen Muchnic, *Dostoevsky's English Reputation (1881–1936)* (Northampton, Mass., 1939), p. 103.

30. *Ivory Apes and Peacocks* (New York, 1915), pp. 65, 66.

31. *Fyodor Dostoevsky* (London, 1916), pp. 48, 37, 47, 161.

32. Ibid., pp. 228, 152, 263.

33. Preface to E. H. Carr, *Dostoevsky* (London, 1931).

34. *Discoveries* (London, 1924), p. 47.

35. Ibid., pp. 63, 69, 72.

36. *The Evolution of an Intellectual* (London, 1920), p. 26.

37. *Collected Letters*, ed. Harry T. Moore (1962), pp. 332, 420, 492, 470.

38. *Complete Poems* (New York, 1971), p. 537. "Now It's Happened," in *Pansies*.

39. *Phoenix*, ed. Edward A. McDonald (New York, 1972), pp. 283, 290.

40. Ibid., pp. 246–47, 479.

41. *Phoenix II*, ed. Warren Roberts and Harry T. Moore (New York, 1970), pp. 417, 423.

42. Ibid., pp. 416, 420, 421.

43. *Collected Letters*, pp. 387–88.

44. *Phoenix*, pp. 227–28.

45. *Scrutiny* 6 (1937): 352.

46. *Granite and Rainbow* (New York, 1958), pp. 49–50.

47. Repr. in *The Common Reader* (London, 1925), pp. 173, 177–78, 179.

48. Ibid., p. 181.

49. *A Writer's Diary* (London, 1953), 21 March 1940, p. 317.

50. *The Captain's Death Bed* (New York, 1950), p. 54.

51. *Times Literary Supplement*, 7 June 1919 and 11 October 1917.

52. *Spectatorial Essays* (1964), p. 174, originally 18 September 1912, and *Characters and Commentaries* (New York, 1933), p. 168, dating from 1914.

53. In *A Library of the World's Best Literature*, ed. Dudley Warner (New York, 1891–97), 45 vols. James's essay on Turgenev in vol. 37, p. 15059.

54. *The Art of the Novel*, ed. R. P. Blackmur (New York, 1934), p. 84.

55. Repr. in *Notes on Novelists* (London, 1916), p. 328, originally 1914.

56. *Selected Letters*, ed. Leon Edel (London, 1956), p. 171.

57. *Craft of Fiction* (London, 1921), pp. 28, 30, 31, 32, 33, 45, 54.

58. Ibid., pp. 236, 237, 243.

59. *Aspects of the Novel* (London, 1927), pp. 40, 39, 78.

60. *The Structure of the Novel* (1928), pp. 74, 78, 95, 98, 99, 103.

61. *Literary Essays*, ed. T. S. Eliot (London, 1958), pp. 40, 424.

62. *The Egoist* 5 (September 1918): 105.

63. *The Egoist* 4 (December 1917): 167. Eliot quotes Edward Garnett's *Turgenev* (London, 1917), p. 23.

64. *Forum* 78 (1927), repr. in *Complementaries* (Cambridge, 1976), pp. 148–55.

65. *Anna Karenina and Other Essays* (London, 1967), pp. 14, 22, 26, 27, 31, 30.

66. *The Criterion* 16 (1937): 585–602; repr. in R. Wellek, ed., *Dostoevsky* (Englewood Cliffs, N.J., 1962), pp. 159–71. Quotations on pp. 170, 159, 161, 164, 169, 171.

67. *Enemy Salvos*, ed. C. G. Fox (London, 1975), pp. 78–79.

68. *A Window on Russia* (New York, 1972), pp. 102, 168.

69. *Classics and Commercials* (New York, 1950), p. 448.

70. *A Window on Russia*, p. 169.

71. Ibid., p. 180; and *Classics and Commercials*, p. 451.

72. *A Window on Russia*, p. 178.

73. *Literature and the Sixth Sense* (Boston, 1969), pp. 46, 50.

74. *Essays on Literature and Politics* (Boston, 1978), pp. 212, 221.

75. Ibid., pp. 128, 126.

76. Ibid., pp. 147, 148.

77. Ibid., pp. 155, 160, 172, 173.

78. Ibid., pp. 177, 180, 182.

79. Ibid., pp. 189, 190, 202.

80. *Šaldův zápisník* 3 (1929): 337ff.

81. *Politics and the Novel* (New York, 1957), pp. 54, 58, 60, 68, 71, 75.

82. Ibid., pp. 120, 130, 135, 137–38.

83. *The Opposing Self* (New York, 1955), p. 68.

84. *Tolstoy or Dostoevsky* (New York, 1959), pp. 6, 141.

85. Ibid., pp. 80, 201, 204, 209.

86. Ibid., pp. 267, 269, 328, 340.

87. *The Times Literary Supplement*, March 11, 1960.

88. "The Understanding of Fiction" in *Kenyon Review* 12 (1950): 193, 196–97, 200–01, 218.

89. *Essays of Four Decades* (Chicago, 1968), pp. 117, 119.

90. *Invitation to Learning*, ed. Huntington Cairns (New York, 1941), pp. 156, 158.

91. *The Lion and the Honeycomb* (New York, 1955), pp. 289, 305.

92. Ibid., pp. 268, 272.

93. *Eleven Essays in the European Novel* (New York, 1964), pp. 3–4, 7, 15, 10, 18.

94. Ibid., pp. 123, 126, 134, 136, 138, 140.

95. Ibid., pp. 150, 142, 148, 162.

96. Ibid., pp. 167, 168, 171, 172, 170, 179.

97. Ibid., pp. 185, 186, 190, 198, 199, 203.

98. Ibid., pp. 205, 209, 210, 212, 209, 221, 216, 215, 213, 217.

99. Ibid., pp. 223, 224, 226, 229, 224, 241, 234, 235, 242, 243.

100. See my paper "R. P. Blackmur Re-examined" in *The Southern Review* 7, n.s. (Summer 1971): 825–45.

101. *The Tragic Vision* (New York, 1960), pp. 216, 222, 223, 226.

102. *Creation and Discovery* (New York, 1955), pp. 47, 66, 69.

103. Waclaw Lednicki, "Tolstoy through American Eyes" in the *Slavonic Review* 25 (1946–47): 455–77.

Appendix 1. Chronology of Russian Novels and Novelists

Where it seemed useful to provide a context, some Russian works other than novels have been included. Dates given are publication dates.

EIGHTEENTH CENTURY

1763	Fyodor Aleksandrovich Emin (1735–1770), *Nepostoyannaya fortuna, ili Pokhozhdenie Miramonda* (*Inconstant Fortune, or The Adventures of Miramond*)
	Emin, *Priklyucheniya Femistokla* (*The Adventures of Themistocles*)
1764	Emin, *Nagrazhdyonnaya postoyannost, ili Priklyuchenia Lizarka i Sarmandy* (*Constancy Rewarded, or The Adventures of Lizark and Sarmanda*)
1766–1789	Mikhail Dmitrievich Chulkov (1744–1792), *Peresmeshnik, ili Slavenskie skazki* (*The Mocker, or Slavic Stories*). Parts 1–4, 1766–68; Part 5, 1789.
1766	Emin, *Pisma Ernesta i Doravry* (*The Letters of Ernest and Doravra*)
1770	Chulkov, *Prigozhaya povarikha, ili Pokhozhdenie razvratnoi zhenshchiny* (*The Comely Cook, or The Adventures of a Debauched Woman*)
1775	Matvei Komarov (1730?–1812?), *Neschastny Nikanor* (*The Hapless Nikanor*)
1782	Komarov, *Istoria Vanki Kaina* (*The Story of Vanka Kain*)
	Komarov, *Povest o priklyuchenii aglinskogo milorda Georga . . .* (*The Story of the Adventures of the English Lord George . . .*)
1790	Alexander Nikolaevich Radishchev (1749–1802), *Puteshestvie iz Peterburga v Moskvu* (*Journey from Petersburg to Moscow*)
1791–1801	Nikolai Mikhailovich Karamzin (1766–1826), *Pisma russkogo puteshestvennika* (*Letters of a Russian Traveller*). Sep. ed. 1797.
1792	Karamzin, *Bednaya Liza* (*Poor Liza*)

275]

NINETEENTH CENTURY

1802–1803   Karamzin, *Rytsar nashego vremeni* (*A Knight of Our Time*)

1814   Vasili Trofimovich Narezhny (1780–1825), *Rossiisky Zhilblaz, ili Po-khozhdenia knyazya Gavrily Simonovicha Chistyakova* (*A Russian Gil Blas, or The Adventures of Prince Gavrila Simonovich Chistyakov*). Complete ed. 1938.

1825–1832   Alexander Sergeyevich Pushkin (1799–1837), *Yevgeni Onegin* (*Eugene Onegin*). Sep. ed. 1833.

1829   Faddei Venediktovich Bulgarin (1789–1859), *Ivan Vyzhigin*
Mikhail Nikolaevich Zagoskin (1789–1852), *Yuri Miloslavsky, ili Russkie v 1612 godu* (*Yuri Miloslavsky, or The Russians in 1612*)

1830   Pushkin, *Povesti Belkina* (*The Tales of Belkin*)

1831–1832   Nikolai Vasilievich Gogol (1809–1852), *Vechera na khutore bliz Dikanki* (*Evenings on a Farm near Dikanka*)

1832   Alexander Aleksandrovich Bestuzhev-Marlinsky (1797–1837), *Ammalat-Bek*

1832–1833   Pushkin, *Dubrovsky*

1833–1836   Pushkin, *Kapitanskaya dochka* (*The Captain's Daughter*)

1833   Pushkin, *Pikovaya dama* (*The Queen of Spades*)

1833   Zagoskin, *Askoldova mogila* (*The Tomb of Askold*)

1835   Gogol, *Arabeski* (*Arabesques*)

1835   Gogol, *Mirgorod*
Ivan Ivanovich Lazhechnikov (1792–1869), *Ledyanoi dom* (*The House of Ice*)

1839–1840   Mikhail Yurievich Lermontov (1814–1841), *Geroi nashego vremeni* (*A Hero of Our Time*)

1841–1846   Alexander Ivanovich Gertsen (1812–1870), *Kto vinovat?* (*Who is Guilty?*). Sep. ed. 1847.

1842   Gogol, *Myortvye dushi* (*Dead Souls*)

1844   Vladimir Fyodorovich Odoevsky (1803 or 1804–1869), *Russkie nochi* (*Russian Nights*)

1846   Fyodor Mikhailovich Dostoevsky (1821–1881), *Bednye lyudi* (*Poor Folk*)
Dostoevsky, *Dvoinik* (*The Double*)
Dmitri Vasilievich Grigorovich (1822–1899), *Derevnya* (*The Village*)
Alexander Fomich Veltman (1800–1870), *Salomeya: Priklyuchenia pocherpnutye iz zhiteiskogo morya* (*Salomeya: Adventures Taken from the Sea of Life*)

1847   Alexander Vasilievich Druzhinin (1824–1864), *Polinka Saks*
Ivan Aleksandrovich Goncharov (1812–1891), *Obyknovennaya istoria* (*A Common Story*)
Grigorovich, *Anton-Goremyka* (*Anton the Hapless*)

1847–1852   Ivan Sergeyevich Turgenev (1818–1883), *Zapiski okhotnika* (*A Sportsman's Sketches*). Sep. ed. 1852.
1850   Turgenev, *Dnevnik lishnego cheloveka* (*Diary of a Superfluous Man*)
1851–1852   Leo Nikolaevich Tolstoy (1828–1910), *Detstvo* (*Childhood*)
1852–1868   Gertsen, *Byloe i dumy* (*My Past and Thoughts*)
1853–1863   Tolstoy, *Kazaki* (*The Cossacks*)
1854   Tolstoy, *Otrochestvo* (*Boyhood*)
1855–1856   Tolstoy, *Yunost* (*Youth*)
1856   Sergei Timofeyevich Aksakov (1791–1859), *Semeinaya khronika* (*A Family Chronicle*)
   Turgenev, *Rudin*
1858   Aksakov, *Detskie gody Bagrova-vnuka* (*The Childhood of Bagrov's Grandson*)
   Aleksei Feofilaktovich Pisemsky (1821–1881), *Tysyacha dush* (*A Thousand Souls*)
1858–1859   Tolstoy, *Semeinoe schastie* (*Family Happiness*)
1858   Turgenev, *Asya*
1859   Dostoevsky, *Dyadyushkin son* (*The Uncle's Dream*)
   Dostoevsky, *Selo Stepanchikovo i yego obitateli* (*A Friend of the Family*)
   Goncharov; *Oblomov*
   Turgenev, *Dvoryanskoe gnezdo* (*A Nest of Gentlefolk*)
1860   Turgenev, *Nakanune* (*On the Eve*)
   Turgenev, *Pervaya lyubov* (*First Love*)
1861   Dostoevsky, *Unizhonnye i oskorblyonnye* (*The Insulted and Injured*)
1861–1862   Dostoevsky, *Zapiski iz myortvogo doma* (*Notes from the House of the Dead*)
1862   Turgenev, *Ottsy i deti* (*Fathers and Sons*)
   Nikolai Gerasimovich Pomyalovsky (1835–1863), *Ocherki bursy* (*Seminary Sketches*)
1863   Nikolai Gavrilovich Chernyshevsky (1828–1889), *Chto delat?* (*What Is to Be Done?*)
   Aleksei Konstantinovich Tolstoy (1817–1875), *Knyaz Serebryany* (*The Silver Prince*)
1864   Dostoevsky, *Zapiski iz podpolia* (*Notes from Underground*)
   Nikolai Semyonovich Leskov (1831–1895), *Nekuda* (*No Way Out*)
1865   Leskov, *Ledi Makbet Mtsenskogo uyezda* (*Lady Macbeth of the Mtsensk District*)
1865–1869   Tolstoy, *Voina i mir* (*War and Peace*)
1866   Dostoevsky, *Igrok* (*The Gambler*)
   Dostoevsky, *Prestuplenie i nakazanie* (*Crime and Punishment*)
   Leskov, *Ostrovityane* (*The Islanders*)
1867   Turgenev, *Dym* (*Smoke*)
1868   Dostoevsky, *Idiot* (*The Idiot*)

1869   Goncharov, *Obryv* (*The Precipice*)

1869–1870   Mikhail Evgrafovich Saltykov-Shchedrin (1826–1889), *Istoria odnogo goroda* (*History of a Town*)

1870–1871   Leskov, *Na nozhakh* (*At Daggers Drawn*)

1871–1872   Dostoevsky, *Besy* (*The Possessed*)

1872   Leskov, *Soboryane* (*Cathedral Folk*)

1873   Leskov, *Ocharovanny strannik* (*The Enchanted Wanderer*)
            Leskov, *Zapechatlyonny angel* (*The Sealed Angel*)

1875   Dostoevsky, *Podrostok* (*The Adolescent*)

1875–1880   Saltykov-Shchedrin, *Gospoda Golovlyovy* (*The Golovlyov Family*)

1876–1877   Tolstoy, *Anna Karenina*

1877   Turgenev, *Nov* (*Virgin Soil*)

1879   Nina Aleksandrovna Arnoldi (1843?–1921?), *Vasilisa*

1879–1880   Dostoevsky, *Bratia Karamazovy* (*The Brothers Karamazov*)

1882   Pyotr Dmitrievich Boborykin (1836–1921), *Kitai-gorod* (*China Town*)

1883   Vladimir Galaktionovich Korolenko (1853–1921), *Son Makara* (*Makar's Dream*)

1884   Tolstoy, *Ispoved* (*Confession*)

1887   Anton Pavlovich Chekhov (1860–1904), *Step* (*The Steppe*)

1889–1899   Tolstoy, *Voskresenie* (*Resurrection*)

1892   Chekhov, *Palata nomer shest* (*Ward No. 6*)
            N. Garin-Mikhailovsky (Nikolai Georgievich Mikhailovsky) (1852–1906), *Detstvo Tyomy* (*Tyoma's Childhood*)

1893   Garin-Mikhailovsky, *Gimnazisty* (*High School Boys*)

1895   Garin-Mikhailovsky, *Studenty* (*Students*)

1896   Dmitri Sergeyevich Merezhkovsky (1866–1941), *Khristos i Antikhrist*, Part One: *Smert bogov (Yulian Otstupnik)* (*Christ and Antichrist*, Part One: *Julian the Apostate or The Death of the Gods*)

1899   Maksim Gorky (Aleksei Maksimovich Peshkov) (1868–1936), *Foma Gordeyev*
            Gorky, *Dvadtsat shest i odna* (*Twenty Six Men and a Girl*)

TWENTIETH CENTURY

1900   Chekhov, *V ovrage* (*In the Ravine*)

1901   Merezhkovsky, *Khristos i Antikhrist*, Part Two: *Voskresshie bogi (Leonardo da Vinchi)* (*Christ and Antichrist*, Part Two: *Leonardo da Vinci or The Gods Resurrected*)

1905   Leonid Nikolaevich Andreyev (1871–1919), *Khristiane* (*The Christians*)
            Valeri Yakovlevich Bryusov (1873–1924), *Respublika yuzhnogo kresta* (*The Republic of the Southern Cross*)

Merezhkovsky, *Khristos i Antikhrist*, Part Three: *Antikhrist (Pyotr i Aleksei)* (*Christ and Antichrist*, Part Three: *Peter and Alexis*)

1906   Mikhail Alekseyevich Kuzmin (1875–1936), *Krylia* (*Wings*)

1907   Mikhail Petrovich Artsybashev (1878–1927), *Sanin*

1907–1908   Bryusov, *Ognenny angel* (*The Fiery Angel*)

1907   Garin-Mikhailovsky, *Inzhenery* (*Engineers*)
Gorky, *Mat* (*The Mother*)
Sergeyev-Tsensky (Sergei Nikolaevich Sergeyev) (1875–1958), *Babaev*
Fyodor Sologub (Fyodor Kuzmich Teternikov) (1863–1927), *Melky bes* (*The Petty Demon*)

1908   Andreyev, *Rasskaz o semi poveshennykh* (*Seven That Were Hanged*)

1908–1912   Artsybashev, *U poslednei cherty* (*At the Brink*)

1908   Gorky, *Ispoved* (*Confession*)
Aleksei Mikhailovich Remizov (1877–1957), *Prud* (*The Pond*)

1909   Andrei Bely (Boris Nikolaevich Bugaev) (1880–1934), *Serebryany golub* (*The Silver Dove*)
Alexander Ivanovich Kuprin (1870–1938), *Yama*, Part One (*The Pit, Part One*)

1910   Ivan Alekseyevich Bunin (1870–1953), *Derevnya* (*The Village*)

1911   Bunin, *Sukhodol* (*Dry Valley*)
Remizov, *Krestovye syostry* (*Sisters of the Cross*)

1912   Tolstoy, *Khadzhi Murat*

1913–1914   Bely, *Peterburg* (*Petersburg*). Rev. ed. 1922.

1913   Bryusov, *Altar pobedy* (*The Altar of Victory*)

1914–1915   Kuprin, *Yama*, Part Two (*The Pit*, Part Two)

1914   Sologub, *Tvorimaya legenda* (*The Legend in the Process of Creation*)

1915   Bunin, *Gospodin iz San-Frantsisko* (*The Gentleman from San Francisco*)

1917   Bely, *Kotik Letaev*

1918   Yevgeni Ivanovich Zamyatin (1884–1937), *Ostrovityane* (*The Islanders*)

1921   Vsevolod Vyacheslavovich Ivanov (1895–1963), *Partizany* (*The Partisans*)
Remizov, *Shumy goroda* (*Noises of the City*)

1922   Ilia Grigorievich Erenburg (1891–1961), *Neobychainye pokhozhdenia Khulio Khurenito i yego uchenikov . . .* (*The Extraordinary Adventures of Julio Jurenito and His Disciples . . .*)
Ivanov, *Bronepoezd 14-69* (*Armored Train No. 14-69*)
Boris Leonidovich Pasternak (1890–1960), *Detstvo Lyuvers* (*The Childhood of Luvers*)
Boris Pilnyak (Boris Andreyevich Vogau) (1894–1937), *Goly God* (*The Bare Year*)

1922–1923   Aleksei Nikolaevich Tolstoy (1882–1945), *Aelita*

1922	A. N. Tolstoy, *Khozhdenia po mukam*, Part One: *Syostry* (*The Road to Calvary*, Part One: *The Sisters*)
	Vikenti Veresaev (Vikenti Vikentievich Smidovich) (1867–1946), *V tupike* (*Dead End*)
	Mikhail Mikhailovich Zoshchenko (1895–1958), *Rasskazy Nazara Ilicha, gospodina Sinebryukhova* (*The Tales of Nazar Iliich, Mr. Sinebryukhov*)
1923	Mark Aldanov (Mark Aleksandrovich Landau) (1889–1957), *Devyatoe Termidora* (*The Ninth of Thermidor*)
	Erenburg, *Trinadtsat trubok* (*Thirteen Pipes*)
	Dmitri Andreyevich Furmanov (1891–1926), *Chapaev*
	Ivanov, *Golubye peski* (*Azure Sands*)
	Alexander Georgievich Malyshkin (1892–1938), *Padenie Daira* (*The Fall of Dair*)
	Alexander Neverov (Alexander Sergeyevich Skobelyov) (1886–1923), *Gusi-lebedi* (*The Swan-Geese*)
	Neverov, *Tashkent—gorod khlebny* (*Tashkent, the City of Plenty*)
1923–1929	Mikhail Mikhailovich Prishvin (1873–1954), *Kashcheyeva tsep* (*The Chain of Kashchei*). Sep. ed. 1930.
1923	Remizov, *Skazki russkogo naroda, skazannye Alekseyem Remizovym* (*Tales of the Russian People, told by Aleksei Remizov*)
1924	Mikhail Afanasievich Bulgakov (1891–1940), *Dni Turbinykh (Belaya Gvardia)* (*The White Guard, or The Days of the Turbins*)
	Konstantin Aleksandrovich Fedin (1892–), *Goroda i gody* (*Cities and Years*)
1924–1925	Olga Dmitrievna Forsh (1873–1961), *Odety kamnem* (*Clad in Stone*)
1924	Leonid Maksimovich Leonov (1899–), *Barsuki* (*The Badgers*)
	Alexander Serafimovich (Alexander Serafimovich Popov) (1863–1949), *Zhelezny potok* (*The Iron Flood*)
	Marietta Sergeyevna Shaginyan (1888–), *Mess-mend, ili yanki v Petrograde* (*Mess-Mend, or a Yankee in Petrograd*) (pseudonym, Jim Dollar)
	Zamyatin, *My* (*We*)
1925	Bulgakov, *Rokovye yaitsa* (*The Fatal Eggs*)
	Zinaida Nikolaevna Gippius (1869–1945), *Zhivye litsa* (*Living Faces*)
	Fyodor Vasilievich Gladkov (1883–1958), *Tsement* (*Cement*)
	Gorky, *Delo Artamonovykh* (*The Artamonov Affair*)
	Yuri Nikolaevich Tynyanov (1894–1943), *Kyukhlya*
1926	Isaak Emmanuilovich Babel (1894–1941), *Konarmia* (*Red Cavalry*)
	Bely, *Moskva*, Part One: *Moskovsky chudak*; Part Two: *Moskva pod udarom* (*Moscow*, Part One: *The Moscow Eccentric*; Part Two: *Moscow Under the Blow*)
	Forsh, *Sovremenniki* (*The Contemporaries*)

Valentin Petrovich Kataev (1897–   ), *Rastratchiki (The Embezzlers)*

Veniamin Aleksandrovich Kaverin (Zilberg) (1902–   ), *Devyat desyatikh sudby (Nine Tenths of Fate)*

Kaverin, *Konets khazy (The End of a Gang of Thieves)*

Yuri Nikolaevich Libedinsky (1898–1959), *Kommisary (The Commissars)*

Sergei Ivanovich Malashkin (1888–   ), *Luna s pravoi storony, ili neobyknovennaya lyubov (The Moon from the Right-Hand Side, or Unusual Love)*

Vladimir Vladimirovich Nabokov (1899–1977), *Mashenka*

Pilnyak, *Povest nepogashennoi luny (Tale about the Unextinguished Moon)*

Mikhail Leonidovich Slonimsky (1897–   ), *Lavrovy (The Lavrovs)*

Artyom Vesyoly (Nikolai Ivanovich Kochkurov) (1899–1939), *Strana rodnaya (Native Land)*

1927   Alexander Aleksandrovich Fadeyev (1901–1956) *Razgrom (The Nineteen)*

Fedin, *Bratia (The Brothers)*

1927–1936   Gorky, *Zhizn Klima Samgina (The Life of Klim Samgin)*

1927   Leonov, *Vor (The Thief)*

Yuri Karlovich Olesha (1899–1960), *Zavist (Envy)*

Slonimsky, *Sredny prospekt (The Middle Way)*

A. N. Tolstoy, *Khozhdenia po mukam*, Part Two: *Vosemnadtsaty god (The Road to Calvary*, Part Two: *The Eighteenth Year)*

1927–1928   Tynyanov, *Smert Vazir-Mukhtara (The Death of Vazir-Mukhtar)*

1928   Ilia Ilf (Ilia Arnoldovich Fainzilberg) (1897–1937) and Yevgeni Petrov (Yevgeni Petrovich Kataev) (1903–1942), *Dvenadtsat stuliev (Twelve Chairs)*

Nabokov, *Otchayanie (Despair)*

Olesha, *Tri tolstyaka (Three Fat Men)*

1928–1940   Mikhail Aleksandrovich Sholokhov (1905–   ), *Tikhy Don (And Quiet Flows the Don)*

1928   Vladimir Sirin (Vladimir Vladimirovich Nabokov) (1899–1977), *Korol. Dama. Valet. (King. Queen. Knave.)*

Tynyanov, *Podporuchik Kizhe (Second Lieutenant Kizhe)*

1929   Kaverin, *Skandalist, ili vechera na Vasilievskom ostrove (The Scandal-monger, or Evenings on the Vasily Island)*

Leonov, *Sot (Soviet River)*

Pilnyak, *Krasnoe derevo (Mahogany)*

Andrei Platonovich Platonov (Klimentov) (1899–1951), *Proiskho-zhdenie mastera (Origin of the Master)*. Later reworked and published as *Kotlovan (The Foundation Pit)*.

1929–1930   Sirin (V. Nabokov), *Zashchita Luzhina* (*The Luzhin Defence*)
1929–1930   A. N. Tolstoy, *Pyotr I* (*Peter the First*), Part One.
1930   Bunin, *Zhizn Arsenieva* (*The Well of Days*)
                  Alexander Grin (Alexander Stepanovich Grinevsky) (1880–1932),
                  Doroga v nikuda (*The Road to Nowhere*)
                  Libedinsky, *Rozhdenie geroya* (*Birth of a Hero*)
                  Malashkin, *Pokhod kolonn* (*The Columns March*)
                  Pilnyak, *Volga vpadaet v Kaspiiskoe more* (*The Volga Flows into the
                  Caspian Sea*)
1931   Babel, *Odesskie rasskazy* (*Odessa Stories*)
                  Forsh, *Sumasshedshy korabl* (*The Mad Ship*)
                  Ilf and Petrov, *Zolotoi telyonok* (*The Golden Calf*)
                  Kaverin, *Khudozhnik neizvesten* (*Artist Unknown*)
1932   Kataev, *Vremya, vperyod!* (*Time, Forward!*)
                  Nabokov, *Podvig* (*The Heroic Deed*)
1932–1935   Novikov-Priboi (Aleksei Silych Novikov) (1877–1944), *Tsushima*
1932–1934   Nikolai Alekseyevich Ostrovsky (1904–1936), *Kak zakalyalas stal*
                  (*How the Steel was Tempered*). Sep. ed. 1935.
1932   Sholokhov, *Podnyataya tselina* (*Virgin Soil Upturned*), Part One.
1933–1934   A. N. Tolstoy, *Pyotr I* (*Peter the First*), Part Two
1933   Zoshchenko, *Vozvrashchonnaya molodost* (*Restored Youth*)
1934–1936   Kaverin, *Ispolnenie zhelany* (*The Fulfilment of Wishes*)
1934   Zoshchenko, *Istoria odnoi zhizni* (*Story of a Life*)
1935–1936   Nabokov, *Dar* (*The Gift*)
1935   Konstantin Georgievich Paustovsky (1892–1968), *Chornoe more*
                  (*The Black Sea*)
1936   Kataev, *Beleyet parus odinoky* (*The Lone White Sail*)
                  Leonov, *Doroga na okean* (*Road to the Ocean*)
1938–1944   Kaverin, *Dva kapitana* (*The Two Captains*)
1938–1940   Yuri Krymov (Yuri Solomonovich Beklemishev) (1908–1941), *Tanker
                  "Derbent"* (*The Tanker Derbent*)
1938   Nabokov, *Priglashenie na kazn* (*Invitation to a Beheading*)
1940–1941   A. N. Tolstoy, *Khozhdenia po mukam*, Part Three: *Khmuroe utro*
                  (*The Road to Calvary*, Part Three: *A Gloomy Morning*)
1942   Erenburg, *Padenie Parizha* (*The Fall of Paris*)
                  Vasili Semyonovich Grossman (1905–1964), *Narod bessmerten* (*The
                  People are Immortal*)
1943–1944   Alexander Alfredovich Bek (1902–   ), *Volokolamskoe shosse* (*The
                  Volokolamsk Highway*)
1943–1944   Konstantin (Kirill) Mikhailovich Simonov (1915–   ), *Dni i nochi*
                  (*Days and Nights*)
1943   Zoshchenko, *Pered voskhodom solntsa* (*Before the Sun Rises*)
1944   Leonov, *Vzyatie Velikoshumska* (*Chariot of Wrath*)
1944–1945   A. N. Tolstoy, *Pyotr I* (*Peter the First*), Part Three.

1945	Fadeyev, *Molodaya gvardia* (*The Young Guard*). Rev. ed. 1951.
	Fedin, *Pervye radosti* (*First Joys*)
1946	Viktor Platonovich Nekrasov (1911–), *V okopakh Stalingrada* (*In the Trenches of Stalingrad*)
	Vera Fyodorovna Panova (1905–), *Sputniki* (*The Traveling Companions*)
1947–1948	Fedin, *Neobyknovennoe leto* (*Unusual Summer*)
1947	Emmanuil Genrikhovich Kazakevich (1913–1962), *Zvezda* (*The Star*)
	Panova, *Kruzhilikha*
1948	Kazakevich, *Dvoe v stepi* (*Two in the Steppe*)
1949	Kazakevich, *Vesna na Odere* (*Spring on the Oder*)
1950	Yuri Valentinovich Trifonov (1925–1981), *Studenty* (*The Students*)
1952	Grossman, *Za pravoe delo* (*For a Just Cause*)
	Valentin Vladimirovich Ovechkin (1904–1968), *Raionnye budni* (*District Weekdays*)
1953	Panova, *Vremena goda* (*Seasons*)
	Leonov, *Russky les* (*Russian Forest*)
1954–1956	Erenburg, *Ottepel* (*The Thaw*)
1954	Daniil Granin (Daniil Aleksandrovich German) (1919–), *Iskateli* (*Those Who Seek*)
	Nekrasov, *V rodnom gorode* (*Home Town*)
1955	Panova, *Seryozha*
	Paustovsky, *Zolotaya roza* (*The Golden Rose*)
1956	Vladimir Dmitrievich Dudintsev (1918–), *Ne khlebom yedinym* (*Not By Bread Alone*)
	Kazakevich, *Dom na ploshchadi* (*House on the Square*)
1957	Anatoli Vasilievich Kuznetsov (1929–), *Prodolzhenie legendy* (*Continuation of a Legend*)
	Pasternak, *Doktor Zhivago*
	Sholokhov, *Sudba cheloveka* (*The Fate of a Man*)
1958	Fyodor Aleksandrovich Abramov (1920–), *Bratia i syostry* (*Brothers and Sisters*)
	Pavel Filippovich Nilin (1908–), *Zhestokost* (*Comrade Venka*)
	Panova, *Sentimentalny roman* (*Sentimental Novel*)
1958–1959	Sholokhov, *Podnyataya tselina* (*Virgin Soil Unturned*), Part Two. Sep. ed. 1960.
1960	Abram Tertz (Andrei Donatievich Sinyavsky) (1925–), *Sud idyot* (*The Trail Begins*)
1961	Vasili Petrovich Aksyonov (1932–), *Zvyozdny bilet* (*Ticket to the Stars*)
	Nekrasov, *Kira Georgievna*
	Bulat Shalovich Okudzhava (1924–), *Bud zdorov, shkolyar!* (*Good Luck, Schoolboy!*)
1962	Abramov, *Vokrug da okolo* (*The Dodger*)

Yuri Vasilievich Bondarev (1924–   ), *Tishina* (*Silence*)

Granin, *Idu na grozu* (*I Enter the Storm*)

Kaverin, *Kosoi dozhd* (*Slanting Rain*)

1962–1963 Sinyavsky (Tertz), *Lyubimov*

1962   Alexander Isaevich Solzhenitsyn (1918–   ), *Odin den Ivana De-nisovicha* (*One Day in the Life of Ivan Denisovich*)

1963   Aksyonov, *Apelsiny iz Morokko* (*Oranges from Morocco*)

Boris Balter (–   ), *Do svindania, malchiki* (*Goodbye, Boys*)

1964   Yuri Osipovich Dombrovsky (–   ), *Khranitel drevnostei* (*The Keeper of Antiquities*)

Vladimir Fyodorovich Tendryakov (1923–   ), *Svidanie s Nefertiti* (*A Rendezvous with Nefertiti*)

Sergei Pavlovich Zalygin (1913–   ), *Na Irtyshe* (*On the Irtysh River*)

1965   Vitali Nikolaevich Syomin (1927–   ), *Semero v odnom dome* (*Seven in One House*)

Vasili Makarovich Shukshin (1929–1974), *Lyubaviny* (*The Lyubavins*)

1966   Chingiz Aitmatov (1928–   ), *Proshchai, Gulsary* (*Farewell, Gulsary*)

Vasili Ivanovich Belov (1933–   ), *Privychnoe delo* (*The Usual Thing*)

1966–1967 Bulgakov, *Master i Margarita* (*The Master and Margarita*)

1966   Lidia Korneyevna Chukovskaya (1907–   ), *Opustely dom* (*The Deserted House*). Written in 1939–40.

Fazil Abdulovich Iskander (1929–   ), *Sozvezdie kozlatura* (*The Goatibex Constellation*)

Kaverin, *Dvoinoi portret* (*Double Portrait*)

Kuznetsov, *Baby Yar*

Vladimir Alekseyevich Soloukhin (1924–   ), *Mat-machekha* (*Coltsfoot*)

1967   Yevgenia Semyonovna Ginzburg (–   ), *Krutoi marshrut* (*Journey into the Whirlwind*)

1968   Abramov, *Dve zimy i tri leta* (*Two Winters and Three Summers*)

Bulgakov, *Sobachie serdtse* (*Heart of a Dog*)

Solzhenitsyn, *Rakovy korpus* (*Cancer Ward*)

Solzhenitsyn, *V kruge pervom* (*The First Circle*)

Tendryakov, *Konchina* (*The Death of the Boss*)

Zalygin, *Solyonnaya pad* (*Salt Valley*)

1969   Okudzhava, *Bedny Avrosimov* (*Poor Avrosimov*)

Tendryakov, *Apostolskaya komandirovka* (*On Apostolic Business*)

Trifonov, *Obmen* (*The Exchange*)

1970   Abramov, *Derevyannye koni* (*The Wooden Horses*)

Aitmatov, *Bely parokhod* (*The White Steamer*)

Grossman, *Vsyo techot* (*Forever Flowing*)

Valentin Grigorievich Rasputin (1937–   ), *Posledny srok* (*The Final Stage*)

Trifonov, *Predvaritelnye itogi* (*Preliminary Stocktaking*)

1971   Vladimir Yemilianovich Maksimov (1932–   ), *Sem dnei tvorenia* (*The Seven Days of Creation*)

Shukshin, *Ya prishol dat vam volyu* (*I Have Come to Give You Freedom*)

Solzhenitsyn, *Avgust chetyrnadtsatogo goda* (*August of 1914*)

1972   Chukovskaya, *Spusk pod vodu* (*Going Under*). Written in 1949–1957.

Arkadi Natanovich Strugatsky (–   ) and Boris Natanovich Strugatsky (–   ), *Gadkie lebedi* (*Nasty Swans*)

1973   Shukshin, *Kalina krasnaya* (*Snowball-Berry Red*)

1973–1976   Solzhenitsyn, *Arkhipelag Gulag* (*The Gulag Archipelago*)

1973–1979   Iskander, *Sandro iz Chegema* (*Sandro of Chegem*)

1974   Rasputin, *Zhivi i pomni* (*Live and Remember*)

1975   Georgi Nikolaevich Vladimov (1931–   ), *Verny Ruslan* (*Faithful Ruslan*)

Vladimir Nikolaevich Voinovich (1932–   ), *Zhizn i neobychainye priklyuchenia soldata Ivana Chonkina* (*The Life and Extraordinary Adventures of Private Ivan Chonkin*)

1976   Rasputin, *Proshchanie s Matyoroi* (*Farewell to Matyora*)

Trifonov, *Dom na naberezhnoi* (*House on the Embankment*)

Alexander Aleksandrovich Zinoviev (–   ), *Ziyayushchie vysoty* (*The Yawning Heights*)

1977   Venedikt Yerofeyev (1933–   ), *Moskva-Petushki* (*Moscow to the End of the Line*)

1978   Andrei Georgievich Bitov (1937–   ), *Pushkinsky dom* (*The Pushkin House*)

1979   Voinovich, *Pretendent na prestol: novye priklyuchenia soldata Ivan Chonkina* (*Pretender to the Throne: The Further Adventures of Private Ivan Chonkin*)

1980   Aksyonov, *Ozhog* (*The Burn*)

Granin, *Kartina* (*The Painting*)

Trifonov, *Starik* (*The Old Man*)

1981   Aitmatov, *I dolshe veka dlitsya den* (*The Day Lasts Longer Than the Age*)

Bondarev, *Vybor* (*The Choice*)

Appendix 2.
Recommended Translations

Bely, Andrei. *Petersburg*. Translated by Robert A. Maguire and John E. Malmstad. Bloomington: Indiana University Press, 1978.

Bulgakov, Mikhail. *Master and Margarita*. Translated by Michael Glenny. New York: Harper and Row, 1967.

Chernyshevsky, Nikolai. *What Is to Be Done?* Translated by Nathan Haskell Dole and S. D. Skidledsky. New York: Crowell, 1886.

Chulkov, Mikhail. *The Comely Cook, or The Adventures of a Debauched Woman*. In *The Literature of Eighteenth Century Russia*, Harold B. Segal, vol. 2. New York: E. P. Dutton and Co., 1962.

Dostoevsky, Fyodor. *The Brothers Karamazov*. Translated by Constance Garnett. Norton Critical Edition, ed. Ralph E. Matlaw. New York: W. W. Norton Co., 1976.

———. *Crime and Punishment*. Translated by Jessie Coulson. Norton Critical Edition, ed. George Gibian. 2d ed. New York: W. W. Norton Co., 1975.

———. *The Idiot*. Translated by Henry and Olga Carlisle. New York: New American Library, 1978.

———. *The Insulted and the Injured*. Translated by Constance Garnett. Westport, Conn.: Greenwood Press, 1975.

———. *Notes from Underground and the Grand Inquisitor*. Translated by Ralph E. Matlaw. New York: E. P. Dutton, 1960.

———. *The Possessed*. Translated by Andrew R. MacAndrew. New York: New American Library, 1962.

———. *A Raw Youth*. Translated by Constance Garnett. New York: Macmillan Co., 1923.

Emin, Fyodor. *The Letters of Ernest and Doravra*. In *The Literature of Eighteenth Century Russia*, Harold B. Segal, vol. 2. New York: E. P. Dutton and Co., 1967.

Fedin, Konstantin. *Cities and Years*. Translated by Michael Scammell. Westport, Conn.: Greenwood Press, 1975.

Gogol, Nikolai. *Dead Souls*. Translated by David Magarshack. Baltimore: Penguin Books, 1961.

Goncharov, Ivan. *Oblomov.* Translated by Ann Dunnigan. New York: New American Library, 1963.

Gorky, Maksim. *The Mother.* Translated by Margaret Wettlin. Moscow: Progress Publishers, 1980.

Karamzin, Nikolai. *Letters of a Russian Traveller, 1789–1790: An Account of a Young Russian Gentleman's Tour Through Germany, Switzerland, France and England.* Translated by Florence Jones. New York: Columbia University Press, 1957.

Kataev, Valentin. *Time, Forward!* Translated by Charles Malamuth. Bloomington: Indiana University Press, 1976.

Lermontov, Mikhail. *A Hero of Our Time.* Translated by Vladimir Nabokov. New York: Doubleday, 1958.

Leskov, Nikolai. *The Cathedral Folk.* Translated by Isabel F. Hapgood. Westport, Conn.: Greenwood Press, 1977.

Pasternak, Boris. *Doctor Zhivago.* Translated by Max Hayward and Manya Harari. New York: Pantheon, 1959.

Pilnyak, Boris. *The Naked Year.* Translated by Alexander R. Tulloch. Ann Arbor, Mich.: Ardis, 1975.

Platonov, Andrei. *Chevengur.* Translated by Anthony Olcott. Ann Arbor, Mich.: Ardis, 1978.

Pushkin, Alexander. *The Captain's Daughter and Other Stories.* Translated by Natalie Duddington. New York: E. P. Dutton and Co., 1961.

———. *Eugene Onegin.* Translated by Charles Johnston. New York: Viking Press, 1977.

Saltykov-Shchedrin, Mikhail. *The Golovlyov Family.* Westport, Conn.: Hyperion, 1977.

Sholokhov, Mikhail. *And Quiet Flows the Don* and *The Don Flows Home to the Sea.* Translated by Stephen Garry. New York: A. A. Knopf, 1941.

Solzhenitsyn, Alexander. *The Cancer Ward.* Translated by Rebecca Frank. New York: Dial Press, 1968.

———. *The First Circle.* Translated by Thomas P. Whitney. New York: Harper and Row, 1968.

———. *The Gulag Archipelago, 1918–1956.* Translated by Thomas P. Whitney. New York: Harper and Row, 1974–78.

———. *One Day in the Life of Ivan Denisovich.* Translated by Max Hayward and Ronald Hingley. New York: Praeger, 1963.

Tolstoy, Aleksei. *Aelita.* Translated by Lucy Flaxman. Moscow: Foreign Languages Publishing House, 196-?

Tolstoy, Leo. *Anna Karenina.* Translated by Louise and Aylmer Maude. Norton Critical Edition, ed. George Gibian. New York: W. W. Norton Co., 1970.

———. *Childhood, Boyhood, Youth.* Translated by Louise and Aylmer Maude. London: Oxford University Press, 1961.

————. *Resurrection*. Translated by Louise Maude. London: Oxford University Press, 1935.

————. *War and Peace*. Translated by Louise and Aylmer Maude. Norton Critical Edition, ed. George Gibian. New York: W. W. Norton Co., 1966.

Turgenev, Ivan. *Fathers and Sons*. Translated by Constance Garnett. Norton Critical Edition, ed. and rev. Ralph E. Matlaw. New York: W. W. Norton Co., 1966.

————. *On the Eve*. Translated by Constance Garnett. New York: A. M. S. Press, 1970.

————. *Rudin*. Translated by Constance Garnett. New York: A. M. S. Press, 1970.

Voinovich, Vladimir. *The Life and Extraordinary Adventures of Private Ivan Chonkin*. Translated by Richard Lourie. New York: Farrar, Straus and Giroux, 1977.

————. *Pretender to the Throne: The Further Adventures of Private Ivan Chonkin*. Translated by Richard Lourie. New York: Farrar, Straus and Giroux, 1981.

Zamyatin, Yevgeni. *We*. Translated by Mirra Ginzburg. New York: Bantam, 1972.

Index

A "C" preceding a page number indicates the page in the Chronology of Russian Novels and Novelists which contains the full name and the birth and death dates of the author indexed.

291]